CULTURES OF LEGALITY

Ideas about law are undergoing dramatic change in Latin America. The consolidation of democracy as the predominant form of government and the proliferation of transnational legal instruments have ushered in an era of new legal conceptions and practices. Law has become a core focus of political movements and policy-making.

This volume explores the changing legal ideas and practices that accompany, cause, and are a consequence of the judicialization of politics in Latin America. It is the product of a three-year international research effort sponsored by the Law and Society Association, the Latin American Studies Association, and the Ford Foundation, which gathered leading and emerging scholars of Latin American courts from across disciplines and across continents.

Javier A. Couso is a Professor of Law at Universidad Diego Portales, Santiago, Chile. In 2006–7, Couso was the Tinker Distinguished Visiting Professor of Law at the University of Wisconsin–Madison. His work focuses on the study of Chilean and Latin American constitutional law and processes of judicialization of politics in the region. He has published extensively on such matters, in journals such as *Democratization*, *Verfassung und Recht in Übersee* (VRÜ), *Griffith Law Review*, and the *Revista de Ciencia Política*. He has also contributed chapters to a number of edited volumes.

Alexandra Huneeus is Assistant Professor of Law at the University of Wisconsin–Madison, where she is also a faculty member of the Legal Studies Program. Huneeus has been a postdoctoral Fellow at the Center on Democracy, Development, and the Rule of Law at Stanford University; a Visiting Scholar at Universidad Diego Portales, Chile; and a Fellow of the International Human Rights Clinic at the Berkeley Law School. Her research focuses on judicial politics and human rights in Latin America.

Rachel Sieder is Research Professor at the Centro de Investigaciones y Estudios Superiores en Antropología Social (CIESAS), Mexico City. She is also Affiliated Senior Researcher at the Chr. Michelsen Institute, University of Bergen, Norway. She was previously a Senior Lecturer in Politics at the Institute for the Study of the Americas, University of London, where she remains a research Fellow. She has published widely on indigenous rights, human rights, and sociolegal studies, with a particular geographical focus on Guatemala.

CAMBRIDGE STUDIES IN LAW AND SOCIETY

Cambridge Studies in Law and Society aims to publish the best scholarly work on legal discourse and practice in its social and institutional contexts, combining theoretical insights and empirical research.

The fields that it covers are studies of law in action; the sociology of law; the anthropology of law; cultural studies of law, including the role of legal discourses in social formations; law and economics; law and politics; and studies of governance. The books consider all forms of legal discourse across societies, rather than being limited to lawyers' discourses alone.

The series editors come from a range of disciplines: academic law, sociolegal studies, sociology, and anthropology. All have been actively involved in teaching and writing about law in context.

Books in the Series

The World Trade Organization Knowledge Agreements
2nd Edition
Christopher Arup

Law and Nature
David Delaney

Constitutionalizing Economic Globalization: Investment Rules and Democracy's Promise
David Schneiderman

Law, Anthropology, and the Constitution of the Social: Making Persons and Things
Edited by Alain Pottage and Martha Mundy

Law and Globalization from Below: Towards a Cosmopolitan Legality
Edited by Boaventura de Sousa Santos and César A. Rodríguez-Garavito

Series list continues following the Index.

Cultures of Legality

JUDICIALIZATION AND POLITICAL ACTIVISM IN LATIN AMERICA

Edited by

JAVIER A. COUSO

Universidad Diego Portales

ALEXANDRA HUNEEUS

University of Wisconsin–Madison Law School

RACHEL SIEDER

Centro de Investigaciones y Estudios Superiores en Antropología Social (CIESAS)

CAMBRIDGE
UNIVERSITY PRESS

CAMBRIDGE UNIVERSITY PRESS
Cambridge, New York, Melbourne, Madrid, Cape Town, Singapore,
São Paulo, Delhi, Dubai, Tokyo

Cambridge University Press
32 Avenue of the Americas, New York, NY 10013-2473, USA

www.cambridge.org
Information on this title: www.cambridge.org/9780521767231

First published 2010

Printed in the United States of America

A catalog record for this publication is available from the British Library.

Library of Congress Cataloging in Publication data

Cultures of legality : judicialization and political activism in Latin America / edited by
Javier Couso, Alexandra Huneeus, Rachel Sieder.
p. cm. – (Cambridge studies in law and society)
Includes bibliographical references and index.
ISBN 978-0-521-76723-1 (hardback)
1. Law – Latin America – Philosophy. 2. Justice, Administration of – Latin America.
3. Courts – Latin America. I. Couso, Javier, 1964– II. Huneeus, Alexandra, 1967–
III. Sieder, Rachel.
KG83.C85 2010
349.8 – dc22 2009042022

ISBN 978-0-521-76723-1 Hardback

Contents

Contributors *page* ix

PART I INTRODUCTION

1 **Cultures of Legality: Judicialization and Political Activism in Contemporary Latin America** 3
Alexandra Huneeus, Javier Couso, and Rachel Sieder

PART II COURTS AND JUDICIALIZATION THROUGH A CULTURAL LENS

2 **Legal Language and Social Change during Colombia's Economic Crisis** 25
Pablo Rueda

3 **How Courts Work: Institutions, Culture, and the Brazilian *Supremo Tribunal Federal*** 51
Diana Kapiszewski

4 **More Power, More Rights? The Supreme Court and Society in Mexico** 78
Karina Ansolabehere

5 **Rejecting the Inter-American Court: Judicialization, National Courts, and Regional Human Rights** 112
Alexandra Huneeus

PART III JUDICIALIZATION BEYOND THE COURTS

6 **The Transformation of Constitutional Discourse and the Judicialization of Politics in Latin America** 141
Javier Couso

7 **Legal Cultures in the (Un)Rule of Law: Indigenous Rights and Juridification in Guatemala** 161
Rachel Sieder

8 **Political Activism and the Practice of Law in Venezuela** 182
Manuel A. Gomez

9 **The Mapuche People's Battle for Indigenous Land: Litigation as a Strategy to Defend Indigenous Land Rights** 207
Anne Skjævestad

10 **Judicialization in Argentina: Legal Culture or Opportunities and Support Structures?** 234
Catalina Smulovitz

11 **Novel Appropriations of the Law in the Pursuit of Political and Social Change in Latin America** 254
Pilar Domingo

Index 279

Contributors

Karina Ansolabehere is Research Professor at the Latin American Faculty of Social Sciences in Mexico (FLACSO, Mexico). She has a sociology degree from the University of Buenos Aires and a doctorate in political science from FLACSO–Mexico. She specializes in judicial politics, human rights, and legal cultures in Latin America. Her recent publications include *La política desde la justicia: Cortes Supremas, gobierno y democracia en Argentina y México* (México: Fontamara-FLACSO, 2007); "Legalistas, legalistas moderados y garantistas moderados: ideología legal de maestros, jueces, abogados, ministerios públicos y diputados" (*Revista Mexicana de Sociología*, No. 2, 2008); "Una reflexión en torno de la caracterización de las cortes constitucionales" (*Iberoamericana*, Vol VIII, No. 31, 2008); "Poder Judicial, entre el protagonismo y la desorientación. Un poder en busca de su papel," in Antonella Atilli (coord.), *30 años de cambio político en México* (UAM–Ixtapalapa/Miguel Ángel Porrúa, 2006); "Inercias, intereses y miedo a la ciudadanía: Suprema Corte de Justicia, Libertades y Derechos" in Gustavo Fondevila, *Instituciones, legalidad y estado de derecho* (México: Fontamara, 2006); "Jueces, política y derecho: alcances de la politización de la justicia en Argentina y México," in *Isonomía: Revista de Teoría y Filosofía del Derecho*, ITAM, No. 22, 2005.

Javier A. Couso is Associate Professor in the Law Faculty at the Diego Portales University in Santiago, Chile. He is also an Affiliate Professor of the University of Chile. He has a law degree from the Catholic University of Chile and a doctorate in jurisprudence and social policy from the University of California, Berkeley. Couso specializes in sociolegal studies, comparative public law, and judicial politics. His recent publications include "La Judicatura como organización" (Santiago, Chile: Instituto de Estudios Judiciales y Expansiva, 2007), coedited with Fernando Atria; "The Seduction of Judicially Triggered Social Transformation: The Impact of the 'Warren Court' in Latin America," in Harry Scheiber (ed.), *Earl Warren and the Warren Court: The Legacy in American and Foreign Law* (Plymouth, UK: Lexington

Books, 2007), and "When the 'Political Complex' Takes the Lead: The Configuration of a Moderate State in Chile," in Halliday, Karpik, and Feeley (eds.), *Fighting for Political Freedom: Comparative Studies of the Legal Complex and Political Liberalism* (Oxford, UK: Hart Publishing, 2007).

Pilar Domingo is Research Fellow in the Politics and Governance team at the Overseas Development Institute (ODI) in London. Previously she was a researcher at the Institute for Iberoamerican Studies at the University of Salamanca, Spain and Senior Lecturer at the Institute for the Study of the Americas, University of London. Her research interests include the rule of law, judicial politics, and human rights in Latin America. Her recent publications include "Judicialization of Politics or Politicization of the Judiciary? Recent Trends in Latin America," in *Democratization* (2004); *Courts and Social Transformation in New Democracies: An Institutional Voice for the Poor?*, co-edited with Roberto Gargarella and Theunis Roux (Aldershot: Ashgate, 2006); *Proclaiming Revolution: Bolivia in Comparative Perspective*, co-edited with Merilee Grindle (London/Harvard: ILAS/Harvard University Press, 2003); *Democracia, participación y gobernabilidad en Bolivia 1993–2003: fin de un ciclo y nuevas perspectivas*, edited volume (Barcelona: Bellaterra, 2006); *Rule of Law in Latin America: The International Promotion of Judicial Reform*, co-edited with Rachel Sieder (London: Institute of Latin American Studies, 2001); and "Las relaciones de poder y la justicia" in Luis Pásara (ed.), *Los actores de la justicia en América Latina* (México: UNAM, 2007).

Manuel A. Gomez is an Assistant Professor at Florida International University College of Law, where he currently teaches international and comparative law, international commercial arbitration, collective litigation, and legal institutions in Latin America. Before joining FIU, Professor Gomez was a Lecturer in Law and a Teaching Fellow at Stanford Law School (2005–7), where he previously completed his doctoral (JSD) and master's degrees (JSM) in law. Since 1995, he has also been a member of the faculty at the Universidad Central de Venezuela Law School (Caracas, Venezuela), and on different occasions, a Visiting Professor at the Universidad Católica del Táchira (1996), Universidad Católica Andrés Bello (2000–1), and Universidad Metropolitana Law School (2005). Professor Gomez obtained his first law degree with cum laude from the Universidad Católica Andrés Bello in Caracas, Venezuela (1993), where he also completed a specialization in civil procedure (1995) and practiced law for several years. Professor Gomez has conducted research and has written academic papers in a variety of areas including dispute resolution, comparative civil procedure, complex litigation, legal and institutional reform, legal education, and the legal profession. In 2007, Gomez received the Richard S. Goldsmith Award for the most outstanding paper in dispute resolution at Stanford University as well as a prize awarded by the Venezuelan Studies Section of the Latin American Studies Association (LASA). His doctoral dissertation also received the Law and Society Association's dissertation prize in 2008.

Alexandra Huneeus is Assistant Professor of Law and Legal Studies at the University of Wisconsin Law School. Before joining the UW faculty in 2007, Professor Huneeus was a Fellow at Stanford University's Center on Democracy, Development, and the Rule of Law. She received her Ph.D. from University of California, Berkeley (2006), and her J.D. from Boalt Hall, the Berkeley Law School (2001). Her research interests lie in judicial politics, human rights, and legal cultures in Latin America. Recent publications include "Judging from a Guilty Conscience: The Chilean Judiciary's Human Rights Turn" (*Law and Social Inquiry*, 2010). Her Ph.D. dissertation explored the Chilean judiciary's changing attitude toward cases of Pinochet-era human rights violations and the rule of law.

Diana Kapiszewski is Assistant Professor of Political Science at the University of California, Irvine. Her research interests include the role of courts in politics and governance in Latin America, comparative constitutional politics, and qualitative methods. Her dissertation addressed the role of the Argentine and Brazilian high courts in economic governance in the postauthoritarian period. Recent publications include two chapters (one with Samuel P. Handlin) published in *Reorganizing Popular Politics: Participation and the New Interest Regime in Latin America*, edited by Ruth Berins Collier and Samuel P. Handlin (University Park: Penn State University Press, 2009) and "Doing Courts Justice: Studying Judicial Politics in Latin America" (with Matthew M. Taylor, *Perspectives on Politics*, December 2008). She also edited *Encyclopedia of Latin American Politics* (Westport: Greenwood Press, 2002). She holds a Ph.D. in political science from the University of California, Berkeley (2007), and master's degrees in Latin American studies (Georgetown University, 1994) and Spanish (Middlebury College, 1991).

Pablo Rueda is Professor in the faculty of political science at the University of Rosario, Bogota, Colombia, and a researcher at the Observatory of Collective Action Networks of the same university. He is currently finishing his Ph.D. at the University of California, Berkeley. His most recent research explores the relationship between economic and constitutional reforms and social struggles in Colombia, particularly of indigenous movements. Previously, he has published on judges and armed conflict, human rights, and social rights. Among his recent publications are "Hacia una Visión Dinámica de la 'Legalización' de la Política Internacional: Revisión Crítica de la Bibliografía" (*Rev. Desafíos* 10, Bogotá, 2004); "Politica Judicial y Legislativa: La Influencia de la Tutela sobre la Legislacion" (*Rev. Tutela* 43, Bogotá, 2003); "El Acceso de las Parejas Homosexuales al Sistema de Seguridad Social: Derecho al Reconocimiento Judicial" (*Rev. Tutela* 31, 2002); "Jurisprudencia Constitucional y el Conflicto Armado Colombiano" in Antonio Barreto and Daniel Bonilla (eds.), *Derecho Constitucional: Perspectivas Críticas* (Bogotá: Uniandes, 2001); "El Consejo de Seguridad de la ONU y la Proteccion de los Derechos Humanos en la post-Guerra Fria" (*Rev. Desafios* 2, 1999); and "La Corte Penal Internacional y el Conflicto Armado Colombiano" 43 *Colombia Internacional* 45 (Ed. Uniandes Bogotá, 1998).

Rachel Sieder is Research Professor at the Centre for Research and Advanced Study in Social Anthropology (Centro de Investigaciones y Estudios Superiores en Antropología Social, CIESAS) in Mexico City. She is also an Affiliated Senior Researcher at the Christian Michelsen Institute in Bergen, Norway. She was previously Senior Lecturer in Latin American politics at the Institute for the Study of the Americas, University of London, where she remains a Research Associate. Her research interests include indigenous rights, access to justice and judicial reform, indigenous law, and human rights. Among her publications are *The Judicialization of Politics in Latin America* (coedited with Line Schjolden and Alan Angell, New York: Palgrave, 2005); *Multiculturalism in Latin America: Indigenous Rights, Diversity, and Democracy* (ed., New York: Palgrave-Macmillan, 2002); and *Promoting the Rule of Law: Perspectives on Latin America* (London: Institute of Latin American Studies, 2001), coedited with Pilar Domingo. Recent articles include "Derechos indígenas, reformas multiculturales y globalización legal: ¿La construcción del 'Estado de derecho' en Guatemala?" in Juan Manuel Palacio and Magdalena Candioti (comps.), *Justicia, política y derechos en América Latina* (Buenos Aires: Prometeo, 2007) and "The Judiciary and Indigenous Rights in Guatemala" (*International Journal of Constitutional Law*, 2007). Between 1999 and 2008, Sieder was coeditor of the *Journal of Latin American Studies* (Cambridge University Press).

Anne Skjaevestad is a Research Associate at the Christian Michelsen Institute (CMI), University of Bergen. Her master's thesis was titled "The Mapuche People's Battle for Indigenous Land: Possibilities for Litigating on Indigenous Land Rights" (May 2006, University of Bergen). Her research on the Mapuche people forms part of the CMI's ongoing project "Courts and the Poor."

Catalina Smulovitz is Professor and Director of the Department of Political Science and International Studies of the Torcuato Di Tella University in Buenos Aires, Argentina. She is also a researcher of the Argentine National Council of Scientific and Technological Research (CONICET). She has edited, together with Enrique Peruzzotti, *Controlando la Política: Ciudadanos y Medios en las Nuevas Democracias Latinoamericanas* (Madrid: Temas, 2002), published in English as *Enforcing the Rule of Law: Social Accountability in New Latin American Democracies* (Pittsburgh: University of Pittsburgh Press, 2006). Her recent chapters and articles include "How Can the Rule of Law Rule?" in José María Maravall and Adam Przeworksi (eds.), *Democracy and the Rule of Law* (New York: Cambridge University Press, 2003); "The Discovery of the Law: Political Consequences in the Argentine Experience" in Yves Dezalay and Bryant Garth (eds.), *Global Prescriptions: The Production, Exportation, and Importation of a New Legal Orthodoxy* (Ann Arbor: University of Michigan Press, 2002) and "Societal Accountability in Latin America" (*Journal of Democracy*, October, 2000) (with E. Peruzzotti).

PART I

INTRODUCTION

1

Cultures of Legality: Judicialization and Political Activism in Contemporary Latin America

Alexandra Huneeus, Javier Couso, and Rachel Sieder

INTRODUCTION

Legal practices and ideas about law are undergoing dramatic change in Latin America. Today, a turn-of-the-century crop of constitutions grants high courts greater powers; provides long lists of social, economic, and cultural rights; and assigns international treaties constitutional status – or better – within the hierarchy of laws. Judges, in turn, have embraced a new role. In the past, courts were not expected to defend – let alone expand – citizen rights, but to quietly preserve the status quo through formalist interpretation. As one scholar put it only two decades ago, "persistent cultural attitudes" have meant that Latin American judges lack "the values necessary for actively guarding the constitution against popularly elected leaders" (Rosenn 1987). But in recent years several high courts have begun to cast themselves as defenders of rights and to intervene in significant political controversies. And, correspondingly, political claims more often take legal forms. Activists throughout the region increasingly use courts as a stage for their struggles and as a portal through which to import favorable international norms. The growing importance of law, legal discourse and legal institutions in the political arena has led scholars to report that a "judicialization of politics" is underway in the region (Domingo 2004; Sieder, Schjolden, and Angell 2005).

Our volume explores this landscape of changing legal cultures. Starting with the assumption that formalism is no longer a useful concept for describing Latin American legal cultures – and was in any case always an oversimplification[1] – we

[1] For a nuanced discussion of the history of formalism in the region, see Lopez Medina, D. E. (2004). *Teoria Impura del Derecho: La transformacion de la cultura juridica latinoamericana*. Bogota: Legis.

We were fortunate to receive thoughtful and challenging comments on this essay from Daniel Brinks, Alan Angell, Pablo Rueda, and Diana Kapiszewski; we gratefully acknowledge their collegial contributions. Of course responsibility for what follows lies solely with us.

explore the repertoires of legal ideas and practices that accompany, cause, and are a consequence of the judicialization of politics. This volume is the product of an international research effort sponsored by the Law and Society Association, a Ford-LASA Special Projects Grant, and the University of Wisconsin Law School. Over three years and through several meetings, the project gathered leading and emerging scholars of Latin American courts from across disciplines and across continents to debate, reflect on and write about the region's legal cultures and politics.

A focus on the concept of legal cultures offers three distinct contributions to current debates on politics, law, and society. First, it pushes scholars of courts to take seriously the role that ideas, language, and informal practices play in judicial politics. Over the last decade, a new field exploring judicial politics in Latin America has emerged.[2] These analyses, rooted in the methods and models of political science, have sought to answer the questions of where, when, and why law, legal institutions, and legal actors come to influence politics in the region. This nascent body of literature is our starting point, for we share its assertion that law occupies a central role in contemporary Latin American politics. However, these scholars have rarely explored the broader cultural domain. Even those studies that have adopted more historically informed approaches have rarely made explicit the question of the relation between legal cultures and judicialization (Smulovitz 2006; Wilson 2006, 2005; Chavez 2004). Yet law exists in the discursive realm and – perhaps more than other political practices – relies on symbolic practices for its legitimacy. It is therefore revealing to bring out social constructivist understandings of law that pay due attention to the ideas and informal practices of different actors within and without the judiciary. Just as Latin America's "neoliberal turn" during the 1980s cannot be accounted for without considering the role played by ideas about the proper role of markets and the state (Valdez and Goodwin 1995; Schild 2000; Dezalay and Garth 2002), so ideas about things legal held by judges, jurists, attorneys, and different sectors of the public are key to understanding judicialization in Latin America. With this volume, we aim to complement the scholarship rooted in North American political science with the social and cultural focus more characteristic of sociological and anthropological scholarship.

Second, our inquiry pushes the debate on judicialization in Latin America beyond the courts and, more profoundly, beyond the state. We wish to stress that it is not only within the formal state justice system that legal norms and understandings are generated and deployed; these are produced within a huge range of informal, subnational, and transnational spheres, and they shape social interactions that occur

[2] For a comprehensive review of this literature, see Kapiszewski and Taylor (2008).

far afield of the formal legal system. Drawing on the insights of the Law and Society movement, several of the chapters in this volume look beyond national courts to focus on such sites as indigenous movements, the elite legal academy, and the bar. They reveal how these disparate extrajudicial sites contribute to the growing importance of law, legal institutions, and legal actors to politics: Judicialization is a phenomenon that also unfolds outside the formal legal system in ways that shape and influence politics.

Third, by exploring the specific forms judicialization processes take in Latin America, this project teaches us something new about law and politics. In other words, we do not simply take a concept developed in the Northern Hemisphere and see how the Southern Hemisphere conforms or does not conform to it, but rather ask how the unfolding of the relation of law and politics in Latin America forces us to rethink and theorize anew the concept of judicialization. "The judicialization of politics is proceeding apace everywhere," (Comaroff and Comaroff 2006, 148) and it is important to pay attention to the convergence of north and south in this respect. But it is also the case that judicialization in the developing world unfolds in a context in important ways different from that of developed countries with longer histories of centralization of power. Strong legal pluralism, institutionally weak states, recurrent episodes of political instability, developing economies, and increasingly serious challenges to government by organized crime distinguish many Latin American polities from the North American and European settings where the phenomenon of judicialization was first noted, and wherein it has been most studied. Indeed, in some places in the region, a "fetishization of the law" (Comaroff and Comaroff 2006), or a growing use of legal language and forms in social and political life, and a belief in law's potential to assist in the creation of a more just order, co-exists with "the (un)rule of law," or lawless violence and a weak presence of the state, including state justice (Méndez, O'Donnell, and Pinherio 1999). This paradox suggests that Latin America can be a "crucial site for theory-construction" about judicialization (Comaroff and Comaroff 2006: 149), and the chapters that follow take up the challenge.

At its core, this collective volume advances the thesis that ideas and non-strategic action matter to political outcomes, and that judicialization can only be fully understood if legal cultures, too, are considered. However, the conceptual building blocks of this project – legal culture and judicialization – have indeterminate and, in fact, hotly disputed meanings. Before further exploring their relation through the different chapters, we take a step back to examine these disputes. In the following three sections of this introduction, we specify the meaning that we attribute to each concept for the purpose of this volume, and then place our definition in the context of the surrounding debates. The introduction concludes by mapping out the chapters of the volume and by suggesting new agendas for research on law, politics, and legal cultures.

LEGAL CULTURES

In this volume, we place center stage the provocative concept of legal culture or cultures. It is a concept that has elicited academic controversy, with many questioning its analytical value (Cotterell 1997). In part, this is because the concept of legal culture as used in the sociolegal literature and judicial politics literature has tended to imply a fixed set of attitudes, behaviors, aspirations, and beliefs. Such an approach has its roots in scholarly works on comparative legal traditions where the concept of *legal culture* is used loosely to signal the historical, institutional, or doctrinal specificities of non-Western nations' legal systems.[3] It also appears in the works of judicial politics scholars, who, when they do discuss culture in the comparative realm, can depict foreign courts as having a particular character or single value set (Haley 1998; Hilbink 2007; Kapiszewski 2007).

The understanding of legal cultures deployed here stands in contrast to the version of culture traditionally employed by comparative legal scholars (Haley 1998; Merryman 1969). Anthropologists have long criticized the notion of culture as fixed or bounded, pointing instead to the way in which cultural formations are hybrid, contested, and fluid. In a critique of how the term culture is essentialized by transnational human rights discourse, Sally Merry argues that cultures are best viewed as "repertoires of ideas and practices that are not homogenous but continually changing because of contradictions among them or because new ideas and institutions are adopted" (2004: 11). Following the anthropological tradition, we use the term legal cultures to refer to contested and ever-shifting repertoires of ideas and behaviours relating to law, legal justice, and legal systems. Note that the term "repertoires" is not meant to suggest that there is internal cohesion or stability; rather they are the product of accident and history. We understand legal cultures – as with culture more generally – as being porous and characterized by hybridity, as being perpetually produced and re-produced, and as influencing the shape of contests for power, just as it is partly shaped by them. As the contributions to this volume demonstrate, the ideational aspects of legal cultures include representations, ideologies, norms, conceptions, beliefs, values, and discourses about law. The behavioral aspects of the concept of legal cultures discussed in the chapters include language, informal institutions, and symbolic actions (such as mimicry). Further, these sets of ideas and practices can be held and deployed by both legal professionals and other groups and individuals in society.[4]

The related issue of legal pluralism is important here. In their volume on Latin American legal cultures and globalization, Lawrence Friedman and Rogelio

[3] See for example Chiba (1989) on Japan; Potter (2001) on China; or Patrick Glenn (2000) for a general comparative approach.

[4] Our notion encompasses, in other words, both what Lawrence Friedman has dubbed "internal legal culture," or the sets of ideas held by lawyers, judges, and other official actors, and "external legal culture," those held by non-legal actors (Friedman 1997).

Perez-Perdomo speak of the "strictly national character" of legal culture (Friedman and Perez-Perdomo 2003: 2). A restrictive definition and focus on the production of norms by courts, lawyers, parliaments, and councils, however, support a reading of Latin America as a region with a highly unitary legal history. There is another, more socially and historically informed account of law in Latin America, one in which multiple legal orders have coexisted over time in different ways in different countries, and often in quite different ways within the same country. In this alternative account, it is quite difficult to speak of a unitary legal culture as such, except if by legal culture we mean the sum total of these complicated cases of what Boaventura de Santos calls interlegality, his framework of legal pluralism that suggests a radically different ontology of law (Santos 2002).[5] Thus, it is not only within the formal state justice system that legal norms and understandings are generated; these are produced within a huge range of nonformal, subnational, and transnational spheres, spheres that are invariably interconnected. With Santos, we adhere to the pluralist view that Latin America is a region of multiple legal orders that overlap and coexist. We use the plural form *legal cultures* – perhaps testing proper English grammar – as a way to resist sliding back to a more monolithic conception.

Importantly, by adopting this broad and fluid definition of legal cultures, we renounce the concept's utility as an explanatory variable strictly construed. After long debate, we have accepted that legal cultures is not itself a concept that can be fruitfully cast as causing specific, traceable outcomes, or even as the product of specifiable variables in the drama of law and politics. It is too amorphous to occupy an explanatory role within testable hypotheses. That the broad umbrella concept "legal cultures" cannot itself act as an explanatory variable, however, does not mean we have to give up on cultural phenomena as useful to explanation. As Lawrence Friedmanc argues, there are many concepts in the social sciences that are useful, indeed crucial, despite their lack of precision. The term legal cultures works here as an umbrella concept that encompasses a group of phenomena that has been neglected in the field of judicial politics, but which, when carefully delineated and conceptualized, *can* be fruitfully cast as explanatory variables. We keep the term *legal culture* at the centre of this project, despite the controversy surrounding its analytical utility, as a way of pointing to a realm of social phenomena that has been largely neglected by comparative law and politics scholars. With this move we signal that, as lawyers and social scientists, we are interested in exploring aspects of political–legal life that do not seem to be well captured by some of the more traditional studies in our fields – that is, the nonmaterial realm of discourse, norm, and belief, as well as informal practices. As George Steinmetz argues, "Culture seems best able to capture the epistemological, methodological, and substantive distance of these

[5] Santos' conception of interlegality points to the superimposition, interpenetration, and intersection of different legal spaces and orders; interlegality is a highly dynamic process involving a constant interplay between legal structures and human agency (Santos 2002: 437).

[cultural] approaches from the hard materialism and cultural homogenization of objectivistic social sciences" (Steinmetz 1999: 7).

The chapters in this volume, therefore, do not tackle the umbrella concept of legal cultures head-on. Rather, they point us to a diverse range of legal-cultural phenomena and explore their relation to judicialization. The aspects of culture explored in the volume range from "interpretive frameworks," "legal doctrines," "legal meanings," to popularly held ideas about both the nature of law and the demands of judging. The chapters explore debates about legal and constitutional interpretation and the value of international law; about the role of the courts and the relation between law and politics; and about perceptions or beliefs about the intrinsic value of law and practices related to law within society. The authors find legal cultural phenomena in a wide variety of sites, ranging from the courts to social movements and NGOs, the legal academy, the bar and – of course – the general public. Further, these aspects of legal cultures are viewed as explaining changes to politics, just as they are explained to be the product of political and social change. Those chapters that work at a more descriptive level nonetheless suggest ways in which these phenomenon help explain the drama of law and politics in Latin America. Aspects of legal culture are essential to understanding legal processes because they are an "intervening variable in the process of producing legal stasis or change" (Friedman 1997: 34), but, or put differently, also because they are phenomenon that help us understand how social and political life are constructed.

THE JUDICIALIZATION OF POLITICS

Our second conceptual building block, judicialization, has two distinct but related aspects. The first refers to the observation that many courts around the world have embraced a new, higher profile political role that depicts them as defenders of constitutional commitments, advocates of rights, and arbiters of social policy conflicts (Tate and Vallinder 1995). More courts have been granted or have begun exerting the power to review legislation under the constitution, and more courts have assumed a more significant role within important political and social debates that were traditionally left to the elected branches. Correspondingly, the second aspect of judicialization refers to the growing use of law, legal discourse, and litigation by a range of political actors, including politicians, social movements, and individual actors. Increasingly, scholars claim, legislators write laws with the courts' language and opinions in mind (Tate and Vallinder 1995; Stone Sweet 2000); and social movements, individual citizens and the political opposition alike frame their political struggles in the language of rights, and turn to courts to advance them (Comaroff and Comaroff 2006; Sieder et al. 2005). This accelerated recourse to law's language and institutions in political struggles is empirically tied to, but analytically separable from, the first aspect of judicialization: the first refers to the discourse and activity of courts, and the second to that of other political actors, including individual citizens.

Turning to Latin America, we note that the salience of law and courts to the political arena is not only not new, as some have implied, but rather is a founding motif of Latin American politics. As Mark Goodale, quoting Malagón Barceló, reminds us, "America was born beneath the juridical sign" (Goodale 2009: 31). From the papal bulls that formally justified the conquest to the massive bureaucracy that was at the center of colonial government, "law and legal institutions served the Crown's needs of conquest and colonization," acting "as a mechanism of political and cultural hegemony" (Mirow 2004: 11). Steve Stern argues that indigenous "resistance within Spanish juridical frameworks locked the colonials into a social war which hammered away at specific privileges," even as it consolidated the Crown's power in Peru (Stern 1982: 115). Indian litigants challenged Spanish privileges throughout the colonial period in New Spain as well (Taylor 1972: 83).[6] Law's centrality survived independence. Notably, Latin Americans had enacted more than two hundred constitutions prior to the latest wave of constitutionalism (Cordeiro 2008; Loveman 1993), which shows that political elites have always been willing to expend considerable resources on constitutional law as a means of imagining, constructing, and attempting to control the state. Even the use of rights language and of the courts by underprivileged groups to articulate political demands has a long tradition. Historians of the post-colonial eras have shown us how courts and legal discourse were central in postcolonial struggles over slavery (Scott 1985), land reform (Mallon 2000), labor conditions (French 2004; Schjolden 2009), and in the struggle of native peoples for recognition, autonomy, and restitution (Mallon 2000, Rappaport 1994). Well before the recent surge of transnational indigenous resistance, revolutionary leftists in Chile criticized Mapuche rural activists for "*pasarsela juiciando*" (or "living in court") (Mallon 2000: 185).

Indeed, at times one suspects that part of what is "new" about judicialization is only that scholars are now more attuned to the role of courts and law in politics. But we suggest that there are three significant, tangible sets of differences that distinguish law and politics in Latin America today, and that these differences bespeak a process of judicialization: 1) expansion of the domain of social and political life that is articulated in legal language and through legal institutions; 2) the expansion of the number and kinds of legal instruments that have become available for use in political struggles; and 3) ever more frequent recourse to legal language and legal instruments as a strategy within types of political struggles that have traditionally turned to law and courts.

The first difference refers to the by now frequent observation that social and political struggles that in the past would have unfolded in the realm of the political

[6] At one point the Viceroy of New Spain, exasperated by Indian litigiousness, decreed, "I have found it advisable to order that no Indian town can send more than one or two representatives to engage in litigation" at a time (quoted in Taylor 1972: 83). Note that Castilians were also considered to be highly litigious (Mirow 2004).

branches, or would have been otherwise funnelled through non-state channels, now present themselves as legal struggles. Perhaps most notable is the tendency to dress the claims of social justice in the language of social, economic and cultural rights, and to hitch them to legal texts subject to judicial review. In Latin America today there is litigation over access to HIV medicine, marijuana, and the morning after pill; access to education; access to state benefits such as pensions and healthcare; legal recognition of cultural groups (even non-indigenous groups), and access to water and a clean environment, to name a few. Indeed, it has become difficult to imagine a claim for redistribution that would not be stated in rights terms and linked to a legal instrument at some point. Another area of social life that has been judicialized only in recent years is the struggle over authoritarian legacies. In Argentina, Brazil, Chile, El Salvador, Peru, and Uruguay, among others, an important part of the current work of the criminal and civil judges involves adjudication of crimes committed by former members of repressive regimes, so that law's reach into the political domain not only is now wider in the present but stretches further back in time. It also reaches higher into the hierarchy of power. Efforts include trials against heads of state, perhaps culminating in the trials against Augusto Pinochet in Chile and Alberto Fujimori in Peru, wherein law has, for the first time, entangled and condemned former political leaders in the region.

The second difference refers to the ever-expanding toolkit of legal language, instruments, and institutions available for use in social and political struggles. Where constitutions and international treaties used to be seen as laws in a different realm, they have become vernacularized, and lend themselves to any individual or group that can claim a violated right. Democratization in the region has come hand in hand with a generation of new constitutions that tend to emphasize justiciable rights, and many of which create new high courts with stronger review powers. As a result, the Colombian and Costa Rican constitutional courts have become known as liberal beacons, defending the rights of gays, marijuana consumers, street vendors, and other underrepresented groups (Wilson 2007). At the supranational level, today's potential litigants have recourse not only to national legal instruments and institutions, but to a growing plethora of regional and international tools as well (Merry 2006, 2004; Goodale and Merry 2006, 2007; Szablowski 2007). Thus, the International Labor Organization's Convention 169 on the Rights of Indigenous and Tribal Peoples in Independent Countries has been repeatedly, at times successfully, referred to by indigenous groups in struggles against national governments; while in Chile even ex-officers of the Pinochet regime have turned to the Inter-American Commission to redeem their due process rights.

The growing menu of legal tools for political struggle includes new forms of collective litigation such as the Brazilian Constitution's Article 5, which gives legal standing to political parties, unions and organizations; as well as judicially created collective writs of protection in Argentina and Venezuela, and ombudspersons with legal standing throughout the region (Oquendo 2008). Ángel Oquendo argues that Latin America has "launched a true revolution on collective rights, moving beyond the paradigm of group entitlements . . . to that of comprehensive entitlements which generally pertain to society as a whole," but can be claimed by a single litigant (Oquendo 2008). The Ecuadorian and Bolivian constitutions (2008 and 2009, respectively) enshrine a wide range of collective rights for those countries' indigenous populations, reflecting the demands of indigenous movements. Although the previous constitutions (Ecuador 1998, Bolivia 1994) were in part the result of the mobilization of indigenous movements, recognizing as they did a range of collective rights and defining the state as multicultural and pluriethnic, the recent constitutions go much further. In effect, they define their respective nations as "intercultural" and "pluri-national," and recognize the jurisdictional autonomy of indigenous law and its parity with national law.

The third difference is an acceleration in the use of legal language, instruments, and institutions in politics. Within areas of struggle that have traditionally relied on legal forms, such as land redistribution and fundamental rights claims, we believe the turn to law has become more frequent. A darker side of judicialization, for example, is an intensification in use and expansion of the domains of criminal law in governance (Simon 2007). "Criminal violence has become a hieroglyph for thinking about the nightmares that threaten the nation. And everywhere the discourse of disorder displaces attention away from the material and social effects of neoliberalism, blaming its darker undersides on the evils of the underworld" (Comaroff and Comaroff 148). Of course, to claim there is an acceleration in the turn to law is to claim substantial knowledge about the role of law in politics in the past. One conclusion of our project is that more historical work needs to be done on the political role of law and courts in political struggles in Latin American history, as well as the legal history of particular struggles, as will be discussed. Nonetheless, we believe there is ample evidence to sustain these three claims of difference, and that the differences constitute a process of judicialization.

In highlighting that which distinguishes the relationship between law and politics in Latin America today we are not analyzing its causes. Several studies have attempted to encapsulate the reasons underlying judicialization, both in the developing and developed worlds; indeed, the literature on this question is burgeoning. Scholars have pointed to democratization; entrenchment of the rule of law; neo-liberal reform; multiculturalism; globalization and an ensuing diffusion of norms; judicial reform; weak, de-centralized states; heightened expectations about what states owe citizens; erosion of sovereignty; political failure; political competition; recent experiences of authoritarian rule; and the spread of non-governmental organizations, among others (see, for example, Santos 2002; Helmke 2004; Navia and Rios-Figueroa 2005; Sieder, Schjolden, and Angell 2005; Wilson 2006; Comaroff and Comaroff 2008; Benda-Beckmann, Benda-Beckmann, and Griffiths 2009). We understand the causes of judicialization to be complex, multi-determined, and beyond the scope of this introduction: we limit ourselves here to defining judicialization, and allow the chapters to explore the dynamics between legal cultures and judicialization in different settings. We cannot help but note, however, that the three differences outlined above suggest changes in the way people conceive of and practice law, and may also be a product of those changes.

JUDICIAL POLITICS AND LEGAL CULTURES

Many Latin American countries are currently experiencing a change in the dynamics among law, courts, and politics. Correspondingly, a new field of studies examines the judicialization of politics in the region.[7] These studies, focused on the questions of where, when, why and how law matters to politics, generally draw their assumptions and methods from two schools of new institutionalism: rational-choice institutionalism (RI) and historical-institutionalism (HI). RI examines how actors strategically navigate institutional constraints in their quest to maximize their preferences. Thus, for example, Gretchen Helmke argues that Argentina's generally deferential Supreme Court will begin to vote against the government toward the end of an administration when reprisal is less likely to curry favor with the incoming regime (Helmke 2005). Judges are cast as strategic actors who will seize on available opportunities to advance their own power. Such studies have yielded important insights into judicial behaviour and law's political role, indicating, for example, what institutional configurations will yield more assertive courts. As often observed, however, rational actor studies concern themselves mainly with instrumental rationality – how actors choose the means of achieving their ends – and not with other aspects of reason, such as how actors adopt their goals in the first place. Thus, these studies fail to address the possible connections between the form judicialization takes and the way in which the actors involved in such processes actually conceive of or represent law, justice, and the proper role of courts. Absent are the cultural or representational aspects involved in these practices, such as the negotiations and re-negotiations concerning the boundaries between law and politics. Such changes tend to occur gradually and cumulatively and do not fit easily into models which emphasize actors' maximization of their own interests.

HI studies examine how the self-reproducing, historically defined features of institutions shape their political participation. Although HI studies of judicial politics do not define themselves as being about legal culture, they often implicitly address

[7] See note 2. Examples are Brinks (2008), Chavez (2004); Couso (2004); Gargarella, Domingo, and Roux (2006); Gloppen, Gargarella, and Skaar (2004); Helmke (2005); Hilbink (2007); Huneeus (2010); Kapiszewski (2007); Prillaman (2000); Rios Figueroa and Taylor (2006); Scribner (2004); Sieder, Schholden, and Angell (2005); Taylor 2008; Ungar 2002.

how certain ideas, ideologies, or other ideational patterns funnel behavior along path-dependent lines. Lisa Hilbink, for example, has observed how a particular legacy of formal and informal legal practices and ideas inhibits the Chilean judiciary's defense of constitutional rights (Hilbink 2007). Strict hierarchical control, coupled with a conservative ideology within the Supreme Court, has kept the judiciary well out of the constitutional business. Comparing the Argentine and Brazilian high courts, Diana Kapiszewski argues that a court's "character" is the product of naming procedures and other institutional features that, over time, foster a particular manner of working together among judges and of inserting themselves into the political realm (Kapiszewski 2007).

We share with these HI studies a concern with how institutional norms and ideologies shape actors' perceptions and, ultimately, behavior. At the same time, the contributions here extend the HI turn in two ways. First, several chapters give ideas and discourse a more fundamental role in explaining judicial change than do most current HI studies. One of the shortcomings of HI as it has been formulated within judicial politics is that, like its fellow new institutionalisms, it posits a static equilibrium and so struggles to explain change. In HI, ideas and other ideational forms are viewed as passively inherited from the past and bequeathed unaltered to the future, to the point that we lose sight of agency. However, once we view actors as capable of rejecting and reformulating ideas, as well as simply imbibing them, institutions can become less "sticky" (Schmidt 2008). As noted earlier, institutional culture is heterogeneous, not a monolithic whole, and this very variation makes room for change: actors can choose between contesting lines of thought or recombine them in new ways (Campbell 2004). Furthermore, agents are able "to think, speak, and act outside their institutions even as they are inside them, to deliberate about institutional rules . . . and to persuade one another to change those institutions" (Schmidt 2008: 314). In pointing to the explanatory importance of ideas and discourse, this volume aligns with the vision of what some political scientists now refer to as a fourth branch of new institutionalism, called constructivist or discursive institutionalism (Schmidt 2008, Hay 2006). Under this view, institutions are still central to understanding political behavior, but actors are not just ruled by institutions; they play an active, conscious role in the reproduction but also re-creation of institutions through discourse and ideas. This move also puts political science into dialogue with other fields focused on ideas, such as anthropology, sociology, and even philosophy (Schmidt 2008).

Of course, not each chapter in this volume considers itself an exercise in discourse institutionalism, and in any case it is possible to argue that historical institutionalism properly understood anticipates the HI emphasis on ideas and discourse (Hay 2006). Yet this volume is, in part, a call to scholars of comparative law and courts to consider ideas and discourse, as well as inherited scripts and practices, as central to our understanding of judicial behavior and outcomes. Thus, even when the chapters in this volume turn to the more traditional objects of political analysis, such as the work of lawyers and judges (for example, lawsuits and judicial decisions), they point to more cultural domains of that work. Writing about the Colombian Constitutional Court, Pablo Rueda analyzes one specific legal concept developed by the court (that of *mínimo vital*, or subsistence minimum). He reveals the way in which this legal concept generated an emerging theory of social rights in contemporary Colombia that took on a discursive life of its own, far beyond the institutional remit of the Court. In looking at the Mexican Supreme Court, Karina Ansolabehere focuses on judges' shifting and complex ideas about law, suggesting how these conceptions might shape their rulings. There is a second way in which we aim to move beyond existing institutionalist accounts of law and politics. Studies of judicialization in the region to date have tended to be court-centric. By contrast, we borrow from the Law and Society movement the insight that law is created and lived not just in the court and through litigation, but beyond, in the conversations of lawyers and their clients, in social movements, in academia, and in everyday life. Courts are important, of course, but they are only part of the law-and-politics picture. To better understand the causes, contours, and consequences of judicialization, we must look well beyond the judicial arena. It is through the concept of legal cultures that we begin to do so. By using the term *culture* we signal our focus on norm-generating spheres and social practices that tend to be overlooked by scholars of judicialization because they are traditionally – and we believe mistakenly – viewed as not significant to politics; because focus has traditionally been trained on judicial actors or institutions and because their workings and the influences they exert are diffuse or indirect and therefore difficult to capture within causal models.

Thus, Rachel Sieder turns her lens away from the formal institutions of the judiciary and looks at the ways in which a disenfranchised group of indigenous people structures oppositional forms of political and social action by consciously and unconsciously mimicking the state's legal forms. This judicialization of highly localized political protest is, in turn, linked to the spread of "rights talk" and the beliefs in indigenous peoples' collective entitlements, indicative of a wider shift in legal culture(s) outside the formal institutions of the judiciary. Catalina Smulovitz shows us how the life experiences and accumulated specialized knowledge of lawyers can shape court dockets: the rights litigation expertise that Argentine lawyers gained during the dictatorship, she argues, partly accounts for the greater use of courts to advance claims for social justice today in that country. Manuel Gomez reveals how the loyalty of corporate lawyers to their clients survives Chavez's Bolivarian revolution, but transforms these lawyers from well-heeled power brokers to struggling cause lawyers immersed in a high-risk battle against the executive. We should note that scholars in other disciplines have already moved in this direction (see, for example, Goodale 2008 and Snodgrass-Godoy 2006). It is one objective of this volume to put scholars of law and politics and scholars in other disciplines in dialogue with each other.

WHAT LIES AHEAD

Following the introduction, the book is divided along the two dimensions of the concept of judicialization: the articles in Part II refer to the actions of the courts themselves, and those in Part III look beyond the courts to the growing use of law, legal discourse, and litigation by political actors, including politicians, social movements, and individual citizens. The organization of the chapters thus demonstrates how a focus on cultural processes reveals new dimensions of a traditional subject of study (courts), even as it allows us to explore less traditional subjects as sites of judicialization.

The chapters in Part II, "Courts and Judicialization through a Cultural Lens," focus on the most traditional of public law subjects. However, they go beyond institutionalist scholarship by focusing on a little-explored aspect of courts – the legal concepts, frames, and role conceptions on which judges draw. Pablo Rueda focuses on the Colombian Constitutional Court, fixing his gaze on the legal concept of *mínimo vital*, or "subsistence minimum." Rueda argues that in Colombia, this new legal concept developed for the benefit of the marginalized social groups was in fact co-opted into the service of the middle class – subsumed into the maintenance of power dynamics through litigation. Aspects of legal cultures, in this case language, can thus serve to reveal some of the ways in which judicialization may reinforce existing hierarchies of power at the same time as pointing to the transformations of legal consciousness involved in the increasing resort to the courts across Latin America.

Karina Ansolabehere analyzes the changing frameworks through which the Mexican Supreme Court understands and adjudicates rights claims. Looking at freedom of speech, participation, and indigenous rights, she argues that judges' shifting relations with society, the government, and the judiciary itself has altered the way in which judges view rights since the transition to democracy. In her chapter, legal cultures or frameworks play the role of intervening variable: conceptions of rights are changed by the more democratic political and social environment; these change the way in which judges frame their relationship to society and politics have, in turn, fomented the greater protection of certain rights. Turning to the Brazilian Supreme Court, Diana Kapiszewski argues judicial culture must include not only judges' attitudes, but also informal institutions and particular court attributes. She develops a new framework for the analysis of judicial "institutional culture," and applies it to the Brazilian Supreme Court to explore how it contributes to judicialization. Her work is drawn from interviews with justices and observation of the court, allowing her to bring a rich level of detail to her three-pronged framework of analysis about the inner workings of the Brazilian high court.

Alexandra Huneeus' chapter moves our attention from legal institutions at the national to the regional level. Whereas courts have been considered important partners to regional legal integration in the European setting, Huneeus points to several political, institutional, and cultural factors that may mean Latin American courts are playing a different role in the process. At first glance, it might seem that judicialization and regional legal integration are mutually reinforcing phenomena, but through three case studies in which high courts reject rulings by the Inter-American Court, Huneeus suggests that the dynamics are more complex and varied. Factors such as judges' experience with international law, judicial role conceptions, regional politics, and the relationship to the executive can inhibit judges' motivation to comply with Inter-American human rights instruments.

The book's third part, "Judicialization Beyond the Courts," explores the phenomenon of judicialization as it unfolds outside the courts – in a new generation of academic writing and classes (Couso); in the political organizing of indigenous groups (Sieder, Skjævestad); in the metamorphosis of Venezuela's boutique-firm lawyers into ideal-driven cause lawyers; and in the way Argentine lawyers bring their life experience to bear on their practice (Smulovitz). Javier Couso's chapter explores the intellectual and sociological shifts taking place within Latin American law schools in the era of politically prominent courts. In an inversion of the U.S. academia, constitutional law scholars traditionally had not enjoyed a particularly high status among academics. However, with the spread of judicial review and a new emphasis on law's political role, constitutional law has come to be regarded as a central intellectual enterprise in many Latin American countries. This means not only that constitutional scholars are enjoying a higher status, but that scholars and lawyers alike are gaining a more sophisticated understanding of constitutional jurisprudence, and are more likely to turn to it as a source of legal argument, fostering, in turn, further judicialization.

Rachel Sieder's chapter tracks how the indigenous movement in Guatemala has turned to recreating juridical forms outside the context of the state courts in their battle to win recognition and greater autonomy from the state. In recent years, the claims of indigenous groups have become a central political issue and a site of active struggle throughout the region. In light of the tenuous or fraught relationship such groups have to the state, their use of legal and paralegal means seems a particularly rich site through which to study aspects of the relationship among legal concepts, judicialization, and the state. The chapter traces how indigenous communities in Guatemala organized consultation processes in opposition to proposed natural resource exploitation projects. These consultations had contested legal status, but the hope was that by mimicking legal processes of the state, they would have greater political resonance. The chapter thus provides a window on the relationship between the dominant legal culture and bottom-up social movement engagements with law within a highly plural legal environment. It also challenges us to reflect on and perhaps to stretch the definition of judicialization to include the turn not just to law and courts, but to law-like proceedings aspiring to greater impact through mimicry of law.

Turning to the south of Chile, Anne Skjævestad shows how the judiciary's conservatism impedes the defense and advance of Mapuche indigenous claims through the courts. She also argues, however, that the very process of mobilization and experience in the courts served, in turn, to "judicialize" the Mapuche's own "legal consciousness" and understanding of their political battle, giving their movement further momentum. As in Sieder's chapter on Guatemala, we see how legal mobilization alters the self-understanding and practices of a movement.

Manuel Gomez focuses his chapter on Venezuelan lawyers. As the Chavez government radically transforms state institutions and the relationship of old elites to the state, a small group of traditional Venezuelan corporate lawyers have taken on a new and unfamiliar role: cause lawyering. They have taken to defending their traditional clients, now stripped of their access to the government, in their struggle to retain their social position and capital. If the Chavez regime is as dismissive of legality and institutions as its opponents claim, the turn to cause lawyering might appear futile. And, yet, Gomez shows us how even in this setting of politicization of law, legal discourse is the tool of choice of Chavez's opponents, as of the Chavez government itself. The turn to rights language, in other words, seems to transcend particular legal cultures and particular national and subnational scenarios.

In her chapter on judicialization in Argentina, Catalina Smulovitz takes a contrarian view: citizens' ideas about the law, she argues, do not help us explain or understand the greater use of courts by citizens in recent years. Although opinion polls show that perceptions about performance of the judiciary and judges are negative in Argentina, the number of claims and topics that are being brought to the courts has continued to increase. Smulovitz argues that judicialization is not related to ex ante changes in how people evaluate the judiciary. Rather, changes in the opportunity structure for making claims – combined with the existence of a support structure of lawyers specializing in labor rights and a new structure of advocacy nongovernmental organizations (NGOs) – led to the increased resort to courts. Lawyers who had cut their teeth on labor claims found that they could turn their litigation experience to other kinds of demands. In Smulovitz's views, then, it is not the citizenry's ideas about law that matter, so much as the existing resources and, in particular, lawyer's cultural capital.

The final chapter, written by Pilar Domingo, provides a sweeping overview of the legal changes unfolding in Latin America. She shows how legal representations have become more frequently resorted to in instrumental ways by a wide range of actors who, in the past, either were not prominent in the political and social landscape (judges and litigating lawyers); or tended to use other strategies and languages that were not framed in terms of rights of rule of law to advance particular social and political causes (social movements and subaltern actors). She examines three sets of processes related to judicialization in the region. The first is trends in the normative language of rights, law, and legality, or "the power of ideas." The second cluster involves identifying and disaggregating the multi-actor nature of who is driving the process of judicialization. Thirdly, she examines the institutional dimension, looking at the spaces in which the process of juridification is playing out. Domingo's chapter thus suggests a framework for understanding the changes discussed in the preceding chapters.

CONCLUSION

Undoubtedly institutional factors, rational calculations of interests, and shifting opportunity structures explain much about current processes of judicialization. By broadening the study of judicialization to encompass legal cultures, the chapters in this volume reveal the important role that ideas, beliefs, and symbolic and informal practices regarding the law and its power also play. It is our hope that this volume will spur a new research agenda on the relationship between law and politics in Latin America that is sensitive to the importance of the cultural dimensions of processes of judicialization observable in the region. Further, this research agenda should be interdisciplinary. By emphasizing that judicialization is a cultural phenomenon, we signal that the study of judicialization should encompass the use of diverse methodologies, of extrajudicial sites, and of the epistemologies of the various social sciences.

Four areas for further research present themselves in particular. First, we are in need of more historical inquiries into the relation between law and politics in Latin America. To assert that there is a change afoot, and to properly characterize that change, requires knowledge of the past. As noted above, Latin American politics have been steeped in law since the colonial founding. Through historical studies we may well find that there have been prior moments of what we now label judicialization. Further, we may find that judicialization in the past has had different causes, features, and outcomes. Such findings would greatly enrich our understanding of current processes. Second, we are in need of studies that examine politics that have *not* become judicialized. The more politics is judicialized, the more important it becomes to understand the processes that suppress judicialization, be they inclusive political systems that allow citizens to bypass the courts and legal language, or, what is more likely, social exclusion. Who fails to voice their demands in legal language and why, and what does this tell us about judicialization? Third, we are in need of studies that go even further afield of the state judicial system than this volume has done. While Rachel Sieder's chapter ventures beyond the formal justice system entirely, most chapters hew more closely to the state. How does the turn to law play out in everyday life and in legal consciousness? How is law portrayed by the media in Latin America? It would be informative to venture into these neglected sites, and to explore how they connect back to the formal legal system. Eventually, and finally, we are in need of a theoretically and empirically informed account of the politics of producing legal cultures.[8] Who are the key actors and what are the important processes involved in a cultural account of judicialization? Before we get there, however, we need more empirical studies to help us generate theories about the relation between judicialization and cultures. This volume is a first step.

References

Brinks, Daniel. 2007. *The Judicial Response to Police Killings in Latin America: Inequality and the Rule of Law*. Cambridge: Cambridge University Press.

Campbell, John L. 2004. *Institutional Change and Globalization*. Princeton: Princeton University Press.

Chavez, Rebecca Bill. 2004. *The Rule of Law in Nascent Democracies: Judicial Politics in Argentina*. Stanford: Stanford University Press.

Chiba, Masaji. 1989. *Legal Pluralism: Toward a General Theory through Japanese Legal Culture*. Tokyo: Tokai University Press.

Comaroff, Jean and John Comaroff. 2007. "Law and Disorder in the Postcolony." *Social Anthropoloy/Anthropologie Sociale*, 15(2): 133–152.

Cotterell, Roger. 1997. "The Concept of Legal Culture." In *Comparing Legal Cultures*, David Nelken, ed. Aldershot; Brookfield, VT: Dartmouth Publishing Group.

Cordeiro, Jose Luis. July 2008. "Constitutions around the World: A View from Latin America." Institute of Developing Economies Discussion Paper, N° 164.

Couso, Javier. 2004. "Consolidación democrática y Poder Judicial: los riesgos de la judicialización de la política." *Revista de ciencia política*, 24: 29–48.

Domingo, Pilar. 2004. "Judicialization of Politics or Politicization of the Judiciary? Recent Trends in Latin America." *Democratization*, 11(1): 104–26.

French, John. 2004. *Drowning in Laws: Labor Law and Brazilian Political Culture*. Chapel Hill, NC: University of North Carolina Press.

Friedman, Lawrence M. 1997. "The Concept of Legal Culture: A Reply." In *Comparing Legal Cultures*, David Nelken, ed. Hants, UK: Dartmouth Publishing Group.

Friedman, Lawrence M. and Rogelio Pérez-Perdomo, eds. 2003. *Legal Culture in the Age of Globalization: Latin America and Latin Europe*. Stanford: Stanford University Press.

Gargarella, Roberto, Pilar Domingo, and Theunis Roux, eds. 2006. *Courts and Social Transformation in New Democracies: An Institutional Voice for the Poor?* Aldershot, UK and Burlington, VT: Ashgate.

Gloppen, Siri, Roberto Gargarella, and Elin Skaar, eds. 2004. *Democratization and the Judiciary: The Accountability Function of Courts in New Democracies*. London and Portland, OR: Frank Cass.

Goodale, Mark. 2008. *Dilemmas of Modernity: Bolivian Encounters with Law and Liberalism*. Stanford: Stanford University Press.

Goodale, Mark and Sally Merry, eds. 2007. *The Practice of Human Rights: Tracking Law Between the Global and the Local*. Cambridge and New York: Cambridge University Press.

Haley, John Owen. 1998. *The Spirit of Japanese Law*. Athens: The University of Georgia Press.

Hay, Colin. 2006. "Constructivist Institutionalism." In *The Oxford Handbook of Political Institutions*, R. A. W. Rhodes, Sarah A. Binder, and Bert A. Rockman, eds. Oxford: Oxford University Press.

[8] We thank Daniel Brinks for this point.

Helmke, Gretchen. 2005. *Courts Under Constraints: Judges, Generals, and Presidents in Argentina*. Cambridge: Cambridge University Press.
Hilbink, Lisa. 2007. *Judges Beyond Politics in Democracy and Dictatorship: Lessons from Chile*. New York: Cambridge University Press.
Huneeus, Alexandra. 2010. "Judging from a Guilty Conscience: The Chilean Judiciary's Human Rights Turn." *Law and Social Inquiry*, 35(1): 99–135.
Kapiszewski, Diana. 2007. "Challenging Decisions: High Courts and Economic Governance in Argentina and Brazil." *Doctoral dissertation*, University of California, Berkeley.
______ and Matthew Taylor. 2008. "Doing Courts Justice? Studying Judicial Politics in Latin America." *Perspectives on Politics*, 6: 741–67.
Lopez Medina, Diego. 2004. *Teoría Impura del Derecho: La transformación de la cultura jurídica latinoamericana*. Bogota: Legis.
Loveman, Brian. 1993. *The Constitution of Tyranny: Regimes of Exception in Spanish America*. Pittsburgh, PA: University of Pittsburgh Press.
Mallon, Florencia E. 2000. "Land, Morality, and Exploitation in Southern Chile: Rural Conflict and the Discourses of Agrarian Reform in Cautín, 1928–1974." *Political Power and Social Theory*, 14: 143–95.
Méndez, Juan E., Guillermo O'Donnell and Paulo Sérgio Pinheiro, eds. 1999. *The (Un)Rule of Law and the Underprivileged in Latin America*. Notre Dame, IN: University of Notre Dame Press.
Merry, Sally. 2006. *Human Rights and Gender Violence: Translating International Law into Local Justice*. Chicago: University of Chicago Press.
Merryman, John Henry. 1969. *The Civil Law Tradition: An Introduction to the Legal Systems of Western Europe and Latin America*. Stanford: Stanford University Press.
Mirow, Matthew C. 2004. *Latin American Law: A History of Private Law and Institutions in Spanish America*. Austin: University of Texas Press.
Oquendo, Angel. 2008. Upping the Ante: Collective Litigation in Latin America. *Columbia Journal of Transnational Law*, 47: 248–291.
Patrick Glenn, H. 2000. *Legal Traditions of the World*. New York and Oxford: Oxford University Press.
Potter, Pitman B. 2001. *The Chinese Legal System: Globalization and Local Legal Culture*. New York and London: Routledge.
Prillaman, William. 2000. *The Judiciary and Democratic Decay in Latin America: Declining Confidence in the Rule of Law*. Westport, Conn.: Praeger.
Rappaport, Joanna. 1994. *Cumbe Reborn: An Andean Ethnography of History*. Chicago: Chicago University Press.
Ríos Figueroa, Julio and Matthew M. Taylor. 2006. "Institutional Determinants of the Judicialisation of Policy in Brazil and Mexico." *Journal of Latin American Studies*, 38(4): 739–766.
Rosenn, Keith. 1987. "The Protection of Judicial Independence in Latin America." *University of Miami Inter-American Law Review*, 19(1): 1–35.
Santos, Boaventura de Sousa. 2002. *Toward a New Legal Common Sense: Law, Globalization, and Emancipation*. London: Butterworths LexisNexis.
Santos, Boaventura de Sousa and César Rodríguez-Garavito, eds. 2005. *Law and Globalization from Below: Towards a Cosmopolitan Legality*. New York and Cambridge: Cambridge University Press.
Schjolden, Line. 2009. "Sentencing the Social Question: Court-Made Labour Law in Cases of Occupational Accidents in Argentina, 1900–1915." *Journal of Latin American Studies*, 41(1): 91–120.

Schmidt, Vivien A. 2008. "Discursive Institutionalism: The Explanatory Power of Discourse." *Annual Review of Political Science*, 11: 303–26.

Scott, Rebecca. 1985. *Slave Emancipation in Cuba: The Transition to Free Labor, 1860–1899*. Princeton, NJ: Princeton University Press.

Scribner, Druscilla. 2003. Limiting Presidential Power: Supreme Court–Executive Relations in Argentina and Chile. Ph.D. diss., Department of Political Science, University of California, San Diego.

Sieder, Rachel, Line Schjolden, and Alan Angell. 2005. *The Judicialization of Politics in Latin America*. New York: Palgrave Macmillan.

Simon, Jonathon. 2007. *Governing through Crime: How the War on Crime Transformed American Democracy and Created a Culture of Fear*. New York: Oxford University Press.

Smulovitz, Catalina. 2006. "Protest by Other Means: Legal Mobilization in the Argentinian Crisis." In Peruzzotti, Enrique and Catalina Smulovitz, eds., *Enforcing the Rule of Law: Citizens and the Media in Latin America*. Pittsburgh, PA: Pittsburgh University Press.

Snodgrass-Godoy, Angelina. 2006. *Popular Injustice: Violence, Community, and Law in Latin America*. Stanford: Stanford University Press.

Steinmetz, George, ed. 1999. *State/Culture: State/Formation After the Cultural Turn*. Ithaca, NY: Cornell University Press.

Stern, Steve J. 1982. *Peru's Indian Peoples and the Challenge of Spanish Conquest: Humananga to 1640*. Madison, WI: Wisconsin University Press.

Stone Sweet, Alec. 2000. *Governing with Judges: Constitutional Politics in Europe*. Oxford and New York: Oxford University Press.

Szablowski, David. 2007. *Transnational Law and Local Struggles: Mining, Communities, and the World Bank*. Oxford and Portland, OR: Hart Publishing.

Tate, Neal and Torbjorn Vallinder, eds. 1995. *The Global Expansion of Judicial Power*. New York: New York University Press.

Taylor, William B. 1972. *Landlord and Peasant in Colonial Oaxaca*. Stanford: Stanford University Press.

Taylor, Matthew M. 2008. *Judging Policy: Courts and Policy Reform in Democratic Brazil*. Stanford: Stanford University Press.

Unger, Mark. 2002. *Elusive Reform: Democracy and the Rule of Law in Latin America*. Boulder, CO: Lynne Rienner Publishers.

Valdez, Juan Gabriel. 1995. *Pinochet's Economists: The Chicago School of Economics in Chile*. Cambridge and New York: Cambridge University Press.

Wilson, Bruce. 2007. "Claiming Individual Rights Through a Constitutional Court: The Example of Gays in Costa Rica." *I•CON, International Journal of Constitutional Law*, 5: 242–57.

Wilson, Bruce. 2006. "Legal Opportunity Structures and Social Movements: The Effects of Institutional Change on Costa Rican Politics" with Juan Carlos Rodríguez Cordero. *Comparative Political Studies*, 39(3): 325–51.

Wilson, Bruce M. 2005. "Changing Dynamics: The Political Impact of Costa Rica's Constitutional Court." In *The Judicialization of Politics in Latin America*, Rachel Sieder, Line Schjolden, and Alan Angell, eds. New York: Palgrave Macmillan.

PART II

COURTS AND JUDICIALIZATION THROUGH A CULTURAL LENS

2

Legal Language and Social Change during Colombia's Economic Crisis

Pablo Rueda

INTRODUCTION

This chapter addresses the interaction between changes in the language of subsistence rights and the possibilities for greater social inclusion during the economic crisis of the late 1990s in Colombia. One would expect that during economic crises, courts would be deferential to governmental policies and manipulate legal language to serve governmental interests. In such situations, courts would be likely to use the rhetoric of political discretion, sovereignty, and the general interest to legitimize unpopular policies of economic adjustment that cut social spending to appease any popular mobilization against them.

In contrast with this assumption, the evolution of social rights' adjudication before and throughout the Colombian crisis suggests that the function of legal language is not just to legitimize adjustment policies. The language of the courts need not be an epiphenomenon of power politics. In fact, this language can be contested, transformed, mobilized, and used to foster an explosion in litigation that ultimately contributes to activating the political process, even against the explicit interests of the government. However, the case of Colombia also suggests that during times of crisis, and contrary to what some scholars assume, the successful contestation of legal meanings can help to reproduce the status quo instead of producing social change. Because the language of rights is general and abstract, it prevents courts from distinguishing between different people and different types of threats to people's material subsistence. Thus, this language is better equipped to maintain the status quo during crises than to produce any significant social change in situations of social

An earlier version of this paper received an honorable mention as best graduate student paper at the Law and Society Association 2009 Conference in Denver. I greatly appreciate the comments made by people who read it and helped me to improve it substantially. I wish to give special thanks to Pamela Coukos, Javier Couso, Rebecca Currie, Lauren Edelman, Malcolm Feeley, Alexandra Huneeus, David Lieberman, Rachel Sieder, and Martin Shapiro. However, the responsibility for its flaws is entirely mine.

and political stability. Nonetheless, the protection of the economic status quo does not entail that only those economic rights belonging to a propertied class are being protected (but see Hirschl 2004).

As the origin and evolution of subsistence rights in Colombia shows, courts can construct non-textual social rights to protect the dispossessed. However, the Colombian case also shows that instead of constituting an opportunity for the expansion of goods and services to the dispossessed, middle-class litigants used subsistence rights as an opportunity to minimize the effects that the economic crisis had over them. As a result, certain strands of legal meaning of subsistence rights became more salient and the judicial construction of these rights ended up being used in a massive litigation campaign to divert scarce resources from the lower classes to more mainstream, middle-class groups that were being affected by significant fiscal constraints. Moreover, this massive litigation gave the court a prominent role in the whole policy-making process, helping it to activate the formal political process, and "judicializing" the policies of economic recovery. In the meantime, however, the language of subsistence rights did not really achieve its original promises of economic redistribution and social change.

THE ROLE OF LEGAL LANGUAGE IN JUDICIAL POLITICS

There has been a rather small but important group of scholars who have studied the relationship between certain changes in legal language and various social and political processes. The most traditional studies of this sort claimed that legal language and especially legal meanings are inherent properties of the rules and standards that are contained in statutes and judicial opinions. More recently, however, this notion has been abandoned, and the meanings of legal concepts have been seen as the results of social processes (Mitchell 1990; Weissbourd and Mertz 1985). According to this view, concepts are the object of continuous social contestation and manipulation. Some have seen these processes of contestation and manipulation as phenomena occurring mainly outside of the courthouses and the legal process proper (Mertz 1994), whereas others have claimed that courts do have an important role in defining the meaning of legal concepts (Wahlbeck 1998).

In any case, regardless of where the changes in the meaning of legal concepts occur, the levels of contestation of legal meanings do not remain constant. As a result, the meanings of legal concepts tend to become more settled over time. This process of achieving greater legal determinacy, which Phillips and Grattet have called "meaning settling," represents a form of "institutionalization" in the way Berger and Luckman conceptualized the term (Phillips and Grattet 2000). In other words, the settling of legal meanings is the social process through which the relevant actors in a specific social process (in this case litigation and the activities around it) come to see a given meaning as appropriate, commonsensical, and natural (Berger and Luckman 1966). In their view, the process of meaning settling has a specific sequence, which they describe as having two independent stages: construct elaboration and domain expansion. In the first stage, the relevant legal actors (judges, lawyers, legal scholars, etc.) settle and refine the meaning of legal concepts. Once these meanings have achieved a certain level of determinacy, and the relevant actors have embedded and legitimized them, courts start to expand (or define) the domain of social categories and situations to which the concepts are applied. They claim that "as a concept becomes more embedded, courts appear to shift attention from elaborating a concept to expand it to encompass new behavior and circumstances" (Phillips and Grattet 2000: 582).

The dynamic model that Phillips and Grattet use to describe the settling of legal meanings as a social process represents an advancement over more static models. However, it still tends to depict meaning-making in the legal realm as a one-way process. Moreover, they regard construct elaboration – that is, the definition of the meaning of the concepts – as a stage that is previous to and independent of the stage in which the legal actors expand the domain of cases and social categories to which the concepts are applied. By considering these as two separate and independent stages, they tend to divorce the process of meaning settling from the social and political reality that sets in motion the whole process. Therefore, their model is unable to explain the mechanisms and processes through which social actors (the "who") influence the adoption of particular meanings of legal concepts in the discourse of courts. Furthermore, by that same token, these authors overstate the effects of the institutionalization of legal meanings. Their model fails to see that although the contestation of legal meanings tends to diminish through time, leading to greater legal determinacy, the whole process may be reversed and legal meanings can be "unsettled" once again. In particular, I will show in this chapter that legal meanings may be unsettled whenever two conditions are present: first, when the semantic field of the legal concept is linguistically rich and provides enough strands of meanings for litigants to use, and second, the courts are under sufficient pressure to expand its meaning. Moreover, as we will see later on, the processes of settling and unsettling of the meanings of a legal concept cannot be separated from the types of situations in which they are used and the social groups that use them. However, what happens when the meaning of a legal concept is unsettled?

Another related problem that the literature on legal language has addressed is establishing the social effects of changes in legal concepts. Particularly, the issue has been whether changes in legal concepts can bring about any kind of social or political change. In this respect, the literature can be divided into two different groups: those that say that changes in legal concepts can bring about social change, and those that say they cannot. Among those scholars who say that changes in the meaning of legal concepts can have a social impact, some focus on the moment of interaction between social movements and government officials, and the way a "constitutional culture" transforms the understandings that legal officials have of certain constitutional clauses. However plausible this claim may be, it defines social change in rather narrow and legalistic terms, understanding social change as the "popular and professional understandings of the constitution" (Siegel 2006: 1325). Other scholars studying legal language have conceptualized social and political change in broader terms that go beyond issues of legal interpretation. Keith Syrett, for example, has asserted that a change from the common law language of "privileges" and "immunities" to one of "collective rights" partly allowed labor unions in the United Kingdom to win the media and public image battle initiated by the Thatcherites (Syrett 1998). In his view, although linguistic change is not a panacea, it has important psychological and political effects. In particular, the adequate framing of a legal issue allows greater linguistic economy, shifts the burden of explanation and justification to the counterpart, sets the terms of the debate, and enables the advancement of policy. The links among cognitive frames, the shifts in the burden of justification, and the furtherance of policy have been addressed by cognitive scientists (Lakoff 1990, 2007) and there is substantive evidence supporting Syrett's claim. However, even accepting his claim, policy change does not always lead to social change. In particular, the mobilization leading to policy-making during times of economic or social change may be directed toward the maintenance of the status quo, and in these cases, one can justly question the existence of a direct correlation between linguistic and social change during economic crises. As I will show, judicial responsiveness to the contestation of legal concepts and the resulting expansion of the meaning of those concepts may end up hindering social change instead of fostering it. In particular, this is likely to occur during economic crises when certain social groups see their subsistence or their way of life as being threatened, and they resort to a rich linguistic framework that facilitates, or even invites, litigation.

RESEARCH STRATEGY, MEASUREMENT, AND THEORETICAL ASSUMPTIONS

Case Selection

The case of social rights' adjudication during the economic crisis of the late 1990s and early 2000s conforms to what Harry Eckstein, following Popper, called a "crucial case" (Eckstein 1975) or, more specifically, a "least likely case" (Gerring 2001: 219–20). A crucial case is one in which the variation in the dependent variable drastically contradicts the expectations created by the accumulated knowledge in the field. In other words, a case in which the actual outcome is the least expected one. Focusing on these cases is an extremely helpful research strategy because it maximizes the theory-generating and theory-testing power of case studies. This is especially helpful in areas like judicial politics where there are very few cases available to generate testable hypotheses (Shapiro and Stone Sweet 2002: 209). In this vein, even though the findings of the present study are limited to the Colombian case, this is a crucial case because it contradicts the outcomes expected by the literature on at least three dimensions. First, given the powerlessness of courts, during an economic crisis one would expect courts to abstain from any active form of policy-making and allow the political branches to act. Second, as mentioned in the introduction, the powerlessness of courts would lead one to expect that their use of language during times of economic crises are going to be used to maintain the legitimacy of unpopular governmental decisions. In fact, one would expect legal language and argument to be highly formalistic and rigid, leaving little room for innovation and contestation of legal meanings. In other words, in a crisis, one would expect the legal system as a whole to be unresponsive to social claims, and the legal language used by the courts should reflect this lack of responsiveness. Third, one would expect that any eventual judicial responsiveness to the contestation of legal meanings during a time of crisis should produce social change. Nonetheless, as we will see, the Colombian case defies these three expected outcomes.

The Unit of Analysis

Traditional studies of judicial behavior regard patterns of court decisions or individual votes as outcomes that can be explained by relating them to a series of potential independent variables, mainly, social, economic, and political factors presumably linked to judicial attitudes toward specific problems. I am interested in explaining how changes in the meaning of legal language affect the behavior of a wide array of social and political actors, including the courts themselves. My main concern here is with the way changes in the legal language of courts relate to social, economic, and political factors. Thus, in this chapter, I depart from traditional judicial behavior approaches: because I am not interested in explaining changes in judicial behavior, I focus on the content of court opinions instead of analyzing judicial decisions. However, given the ambiguity of terms like "language" and "discourse" (Conley and O'Barr 2005: 8), studying the language of courts may prove an impossible task, requiring that one use a unit of analysis that permits the investigation of changes in meaning in an orderly way. For this purpose, I focus on a specific legal concept, *minimo vital*, which has been used by the Colombian Constitutional Court (CCC) to adjudicate social rights. I use this concept as a unit of analysis, and measure the way its meaning has changed over time by observing the variations in the networks of relations that the court constructs between *minimo vital* and other concepts. To put it in linguistic terms, this chapter analyzes the diachronic (historical) transformations in the focal point (most usual meaning) of the semantic field (network of relations between concepts) of the concept of *minimo vital*.

Theoretical Assumptions

The analysis done in this chapter is not limited to the linguistic aspects of judicial opinions. On the contrary, it assumes that both courts and claimants use language in specific ways to advance rather concrete political goals. Thus, this analysis seeks to connect the transformations in the meaning of concepts to the changes in the social, economic, and political context in which they are used. It attempts to illustrate the ways in which different social groups contest and manipulate key legal concepts. In using language, social groups tend to highlight specific strands of meaning or to establish connections between terms, redefining the semantic field of certain concepts that are very important in their social and political struggles. Some strands of meaning survive, others change, and still others disappear because of the outcomes of the struggles carried out by these social groups. Thus, the version of "conceptual history" used here primarily analyzes the ways in which legal language helps to describe, legitimize, or question social and political reality, by affecting individual perception and judgment (Koselleck 1995: 62; 2002: 24). However, it also studies how, under certain circumstances, language can contribute to changing that reality. The fact that language can contribute to transform social and political reality does not mean that language determines that reality. One of the proponents of this type of analysis has aptly framed the issue in the following way: "[c]oncepts, by defining extra-linguistic structures, condition political events. Yet as concepts, whatever their variations, continue to be applicable, their use is also affected by extra-linguistic forces, such as structures, which cannot be transformed overnight" (Koselleck 1995: 67).

Data Gathering, Selection, and Classification of the Cases

The analysis of the opinions of the CCC was done in two different stages. In 2002, I conducted a content analysis of 313 opinions along with other researchers at Los Andes University in Colombia. This analysis included all the opinions involving social rights' adjudication from 1992 to 1998, and a selection of opinions from 1999 to 2001. Because the purpose of the study was analyzing legal language and not voting patterns, the opinions that we analyzed during this second period were those that announced a new rule, consequently excluding all those opinions in which the court was simply reiterating what it had said in previous decisions. Later on, during 2005, I complemented this study with a content analysis of a selection of opinions during the years 2002–4 employing the same criteria used in selecting the opinions from 1999 to 2001.

The classification of the opinions included various criteria, mainly, general topic, type of social rights claimed, type of service or good that was being claimed, type of claimant (e.g., age, sex, employment, physical condition, etc.), type of defendant (public or private entity), type of relation between claimant and defendant (e.g., employment, family, contract, statutory, etc.), and finally, rules explicitly announced by the court. In turn, the content analysis of the opinions was complemented and contrasted with a more formal analysis that tried to establish whether the patterns of citations of the court were merely rhetorical or whether the court actually followed the rules announced in previous opinions. In this chapter I complement these analyses of judicial opinions with the follow-up of the repercussions that the court's rulings had over political outcomes (policies) and process in three cases: long-term housing financial policy (UPAC-UVR), the freeze the salaries of public employees, and the extension of a value-added tax to basic necessities.

TOP-DOWN CONSTRUCTION OF LEGAL LANGUAGE

An Introduction (1992–1998)

The dynamics of the construction of legal language in this period is driven top-down by the court's supply of an expansive social rights' language at a time when Colombia's Gross Domestic Product (GDP) was growing substantially. During the early 1990s, Colombia was living a period of relative economic stability and growth, combined with a political turmoil that had given rise to a significant institutional transformation. This context helped the newly created constitutional court to assume an active political role in the protection of social rights and the development of its own policy, assuming some of the powers that were previously held by congress and the administration. In sum, economic stability and institutional turmoil greatly contributed to this first stage in the "judicialization" of politics. In particular, the first stage of the process of judicialization of subsistence rights corresponds to a transformation in three interrelated dimensions: the *meaning* of legal terms, the types of *claimants*, and the types of *cases* that the court decided.

The first transformation corresponds to a change in the meaning of the key legal concept used to adjudicate social rights as fundamental rights: the concept of *minimo vital* or subsistence minimum. Although social rights were adjudicated using the concept of *minimo vital* throughout this whole period, the meaning of this concept changed significantly. As originally conceived, *minimo vital* was tantamount to a right to subsistence, but by 1998 it came to entail the provision of any goods and services necessary to "preserve the dignity and equality of an individual." With regard to the change in the types of subjects being protected, the CCC went from protecting individuals structurally marginalized from the market and other mechanisms of distribution of goods and services, to a protection of particularly vulnerable social groups and then to a general protection of the middle classes. Finally, the types of cases changed from being exceptional, factually complex (and usually dramatic) situations in which the lack of certain goods or services entailed an imminent risk to life and limb, to a broader array of everyday circumstances in which a specific act or omission allegedly affected the dignity and equality of individuals. However, to understand the ways in which the economic context constituted an opportunity for the expansion of the meaning of subsistence rights in these three dimensions, and how in turn this favored a massive wave of social rights' litigation during the crisis, we must first briefly examine the political and economic context of Colombia during the 1990s.

Contextualizing "Judicialization": Social, Political, and Institutional Background

In 1991, when Colombia adopted a new constitution, it was going through a period of acute political turmoil. Yet, at that time, the country was enjoying a period of relative economic stability and prosperity. During the last half of the 1980s, Colombia was experiencing the most violent period of its recent history. The government was leading a bloody war against the Medellín cartel, one of the four recently demobilized guerrilla groups that was being massacred by the thousands, institutions and political elites were largely discredited, and four presidential candidates had been assassinated. This situation threatened to destabilize the entire political system. In this context, a student movement supported by the government and various prestigious intellectuals started promoting a solution with a clearly "law-centered" view of the political problem: they demanded a call to a constituent assembly (Dugas 2001: 809). They achieved their goal, the call to a constituent assembly was approved, and a new constitution was created.

The 1991 constitution strengthened the mechanism of abstract judicial review that had been open to citizens since 1910[1] and created a writ for the protection of fundamental constitutional rights called *tutela*. This writ can be claimed directly upon any judge without the need of an attorney, but it is only available whenever claimants have no other mechanism of judicial protection or when the mechanisms formally available do not provide a prompt and effective protection. This writ is decided through an expeditious procedure: first instance judges have ten days to decide, appeal judges have twenty, and all judicial decisions are subject to a discretionary review by the constitutional court.

Although the constitution does not explicitly classify rights, the most widespread understanding in the legal profession at the time was that only certain civil and political rights were fundamental. Social rights, then, were definitely not regarded as fundamental, and thus, they were arguably excluded from any form of protection through tutela. Formally, the new constitutional court adhered to this traditional liberal view, declaring that the otherwise generous catalogue of social rights established in the 1991 constitution was to be gradually developed by the legislature and the administration to the extent that the country's material resources permitted the extension of social rights, services, and welfare.

At the time, Colombia's economy was growing at a relatively high rate, as were other Latin American economies, and the perspectives for an expansion of welfare rights for less privileged groups was not inconceivable. Foreign investment was increasing, benefiting greatly from the country's recent economic liberalization,

[1] Judicial review was created in Colombia in 1863. Initially, and until 1910, they were limited to a form of veto that allowed the president or the legislatures of the states to ask the Supreme Court to declare the unconstitutionality of any law enacted by Congress (during the time when Colombia had a federalist constitutional system).

and it was enhancing the amount of private assets available. Public capital was also on the rise. This was in part because of the large-scale privatizations of government-owned companies, the opening of state monopolies, the granting of state licenses to operate the sectors of services and telecommunications, and the investments produced by newly discovered oil fields. Thus, by 1992, when the new constitutional court started to operate, the country's GDP was growing more than 4 percent per year. In 1993, it increased to 5.2 percent, then in 1994 it also increased, reaching 5.5 percent, and in 1995, it was growing at a rate of 5.1 percent.

However, as we will see throughout the following subsections, despite continued economic growth, the promises of a legislatively enacted expansion of social rights were not carried out and the CCC started expanding them on their own.

Top-Down Expansion of Social Rights: From the Subsistence of the Marginalized to the Dignity and Equality of the Middle Classes

As Table 2.1 illustrates, during this first stage in the development of *minimo vital*, we can observe changes in the types of cases, the claimants, and in the focal point of the semantic field or most common meaning of *minimo vital*. Throughout the 1990s, the types of cases became factually simpler, and yet they diversified to various rights, issues, and areas. The types of claimants during the first part of the 1990s were individuals whose complex personal circumstances permanently marginalized them from the market system. However, judicial verification of these circumstances was too burdensome and casuistic. Thus, the court created simpler categories of individuals who were especially vulnerable, and ended up protecting individuals who were only occasionally affected by specific market dysfunctions like workers who were not receiving their wages or maternity leaves because of the bad financial situation of their employers or their pension funds. Finally, the typical language associated with the concept of *minimo vital* also shifted, from the concrete and descriptive aspects like protecting the life, subsistence, or physical integrity of individuals to more abstract and normative aspects like protecting human dignity, attaining greater social solidarity, human equality, or fulfilling the promises of an "*estado social*" (a kind of social democratic welfare state).

This whole process had various consequences. It simplified the rules of adjudication of *minimo vital*, expanded them to various realms, and opened the possibility to new interpretative avenues. In turn, these factors constituted an incentive for litigation among increasingly more mainstream social groups, enhanced the court's discretion to grant protection in such cases, and at the same time, made court intervention in social issues more frequent than before. In the following section, then, I will describe the way in which these changes took place.

In one of its first decisions in 1992, the CCC created a new fundamental right to subsistence called *minimo vital*, which is not explicit in the constitution. This unenumerated fundamental social right was based on a very similar concept, the

TABLE 2.1. *The first stage of the judicialization of* minimo vital

<table>
<tr><td>Year</td><td colspan="8">1992–1999</td></tr>
<tr><td>Argument for protection</td><td colspan="4">Connectivity doctrine as main argument</td><td colspan="4">Framework of minimo vital as main argument</td></tr>
<tr><td rowspan="2">Areas of the semantic field most directly associated with minimo vital</td><td colspan="4">Empirical and concrete strands of meaning</td><td colspan="4">Normative and abstract strands of meaning</td></tr>
<tr><td>Life and subsistence</td><td>Physical integrity</td><td>Mental integrity</td><td>Individual autonomy</td><td>Human dignity</td><td>Equality principle</td><td>Social solidarity</td><td>“Estado social”</td></tr>
<tr><td>Types of claimants</td><td colspan="3">Structurally marginalized from the market</td><td colspan="3">Special categories of vulnerable individuals</td><td colspan="2">Occasionally affected individuals</td></tr>
<tr><td>Types of cases</td><td colspan="4">Factually complex and protection to a highly valued right</td><td colspan="4">Factually simplified and direct protection to minimo vital</td></tr>
<tr><td>Nature of CCC’s intervention</td><td colspan="3">Exceptional protection</td><td colspan="3">Special protection</td><td colspan="2">Ordinary intervention</td></tr>
</table>

Existenzminimum, created by the German Federal Administrative Tribunal shortly after World War II.[2] In its Colombian version, this right has been defined in various ways: as the right to a minimum of material conditions "necessary for subsistence," going through more abstract and rhetorical formulations, as "the minimum conditions necessary to have an autonomous and dignified life, according to the possibilities of the state," and in a more actively reformist vein as a right that "seeks to guarantee equal opportunities and social justice in a country that has been historically unjust and inequitable, with cultural and economic factors that converge to create a 'social deficit.'"[3]

In many respects, the way in which the court framed the arguments in its first opinion on *minimo vital* is a typical example of the discursive tendency of its subsequent opinions during the three years that followed. The court's opinion was constructed upon a two-tiered argument: one tier is entirely rhetorical, while the other also includes an empirical component. The first part of the argument seeks to legitimize the construction of this nontextual right based on an extensive textual foundation. Its strategy was to establish as many discursive connections as possible between the newly created right and the text of the constitution. This strategy can be analogized to securing the incorporation of *minimo vital* into the constitution by knitting it into a dense textual web, and establishing rhetorical connections with as many articles of the constitution as possible.

To legitimize the judicial creation of a nontextual right, the CCC argued that the right to a *minimo vital*, although not expressly established in the constitution, could be inferred from a "systematic interpretation" of its text. Among the articles of the constitution that the court tied to *minimo vital* were those that refer to the rights to life, bodily integrity, work, health, social security, the right to receive assistance from the state, and the right to have a shelter, among others. However, the court also anchored this new fundamental right on a series of constitutional principles like human dignity, social solidarity, and individual autonomy. Finally, the CCC tied the *minimo vital* to organizational and structural principles established in the constitution, and particularly, to the "*estado social*" constitutional clause, which the CCC interpreted as establishing a social-democratic welfare state. In ascertaining these discursive relations and creating a whole doctrinal framework around it, the court laid out a great part of the semantic field of the concept that it had just created. It defined a series of structural relations between basic human ideals (e.g., dignity, autonomy, solidarity), a model of state-society relations (i.e., the *estado social*, literally a "social state"), a series of instruments to pursue these ideals (i.e., social rights), and at the center of this frame, it placed a unifying device: the *minimo vital*.

However, by 1992, the idea that a social right could be fundamental in and of itself was not widespread and the tutela writ was designed to protect only fundamental

2 Bundesverwaltungsgericht (BVerwGE) 1, 159, 161 ff.

3 CCC, Decision T-426/92.

rights. Thus, the CCC created a doctrine that allowed it to connect social rights to other rights that were indisputably fundamental, and at the same time, it helped to limit the scope of goods and services provided through tutela. According to this "connectivity" doctrine, social rights were not inherently fundamental but they became so whenever (and to the extent that) their protection was necessary to safeguard fundamental rights. In such cases, health services, salaries, or pensions, were protected only whenever, and to the extent that, they were necessary to protect the life or bodily integrity of individuals. However, as we will see further on, proving that the lack of a specific good or service threatens a fundamental right was almost impossible in the short period of time that judges had to decide tutela cases. For this reason, the CCC started using legal presumptions, and in doing so, it started creating new general legal rules. This had the effect of lowering the burden of proof for claimants and constructing even more simplified and broader templates of cases and categories of subjects deserving protection through *minimo vital*. Because the CCC could no longer legitimize its function on the complex factual drama of the cases, the rhetorical tier of the language became the standard legitimation tool. However, during its first three years of existence, the court entrenched *minimo vital* by using both the rhetorical and the factual (connectivity) arguments. A description of the first cases and the court's arguments seem helpful in illustrating this.

Initial Stages in the Evolution of Minimo Vital: *Overview of Some Exemplary Cases*

The facts of the first *minimo vital* case are rather dramatic, and they illustrate the general approach that the court had to social rights' adjudication during this first period. An elderly man requested his right to receive a pension to the appropriate public institution. A year after his request, the institution had not answered. In the meantime, the man had been driven into indigence because he could not pay the rent and had no other means of subsistence. Moreover, he was also ill and needed to undergo surgery, but he had no means to pay for it. Thus, the claimant requested that the court issue an injunction ordering the relevant public institution to recognize his pension. The CCC reviewed the lower court's judgment and granted the claimant the right to receive his pension. This *minimo vital* case, as the ones that the CCC decided throughout the following three years, can be characterized as having two basic features: a complex factual situation and the possible affectation of a highly valued right. The typical factual situation is one in which multiple factors converge to produce two results: place the claimant under an imminent risk and make him or her helpless to confront it. This risk is one likely to affect a highly valued right generally regarded as fundamental; namely, his or her life or bodily integrity. In the first decision, for example, the claimant was poor, elderly, ill, unemployed, and had been thrown out of his home. Because he was elderly and ill, he could not find a job easily. Therefore, he could not do anything to help himself resolve his situation of marginalization and impotency, which threatened to become even worse if he did not receive his pension. Not only were the claimant's life and physical integrity at risk; given his age, he was excluded from the labor market and thus from any possibility of self-help.

As noted earlier, in general terms the former pension case is a template for subsistence rights adjudication during the following years; although from 1992 to 1995, the court only reviewed six *minimo vital* cases.[4] During those years, when the claimants could not prove that their situation was absolutely desperate and that they were incapable of self-help, the court did not grant protection of their right to a *minimo vital*. The following year after the right to a *minimo vital* was created by the CCC, for example, the CCC reviewed the case of a child who was in a coma and was being released from the hospital because his mother could not afford to pay for the hospital bill. His mother, a single parent, filed a tutela writ requesting that the hospital, which was a public institution, continue rendering the services to her child. The court denied the protection arguing that the mother should show solidarity with other patients who needed the services provided by the hospital more urgently, and that the constitutional protection of social rights depended on the availability of fiscal resources.[5] The assumption of the court was that in this specific situation the mother could – and should – provide the care that her minor son needed for his subsistence.

In its next decision, the CCC denied the claim in favor of an arguably indigent soldier with schizophrenia. Third parties interested in the soldier's situation claimed that the army hospital should keep him institutionalized on its premises because there was nobody to take care of him and he was homeless. The court denied the injunction because there was not enough evidence that the soldier was at risk of indigence when released from the hospital.[6] Thus, at this very early stage, the court only protected the *minimo vital* when the factual situation imminently entailed a risk to the life or integrity of the claimant and he or she was impotent to overcome such risk.

However, the CCC also expanded the context of application of subsistence rights. The initial standards required to grant protection through *minimo vital* were to be gradually softened in the years to follow, loosening the evidentiary burden imposed by the connectivity criterion. In the following years (1995–9), perhaps because the concept of *minimo vital* was gradually consolidating and expanding, the court started framing its arguments based more directly on the "right" to a *minimo vital*. In a way, the concept of *minimo vital* was gaining a discursive autonomy from the connectivity criterion. For a start, the CCC started granting injunctions in cases that

4 In 1992, the court revised two cases, in 1993, three cases, and in 1994, only one. As we will see these numbers contrast not only with the total number of cases that the court reviewed in those years, but more importantly with the number of *minimo vital* cases that the court would review in the following years. See Fig. 2.2.

5 CCC, Decision T-527/93.

6 CCC, Decision T-384/93.

were less dramatic and complex. In the same way, the standard of what constituted an imminent risk, which the claimants had to prove to obtain protection, became less burdensome. Finally, the court also started connecting social rights with other fundamental rights besides life and bodily integrity, and this shift helped it to expand and diversify the types of issues in which it granted the injunctions. It expanded its docket of pension cases, and started getting involved with patterns of firings of pregnant women, failures to pay maternity leave and salaries, medical treatments not covered by public health plans, food and health conditions in prisons, and others.

Furthermore, not only did the CCC start expanding the kinds of situations in which it considered it necessary to protect *minimo vital*, but also it started becoming more generous. The way the court expanded the coverage of public and private health plans exemplifies this trend. As we saw, the court started granting protection whenever the services or medications were necessary to preserve the life of the claimant. Shortly thereafter, however, the CCC extended the coverage to whenever these services were necessary to secure claimants a *dignified* life. Thus, it included a large and diverse amount of treatments and services, from AIDS treatments to palliatives for pain, adult diapers, and erectile dysfunction medications. To be sure, the expansion of the protection to social rights via the addition of the notion of "dignity" to the right to life was full of contradictions and zigzags. During this period, the court inexplicably decided similar cases in different ways, and there was at least one serious attempt to curtail the concept of *minimo vital*.[7] However, the general pattern during this stage was the expansion and diversification of *minimo vital* cases.

As the court started expanding and diversifying the issues that it reviewed, it also increased its own docket of cases. However, this was not just a consequence of the fact that the court was granting injunctions in new issues. Rather, it happened because the CCC had to reaffirm to reticent lower judges that its new doctrines and rules were mandatory. Partly because the court's initial approach was too casuistic and contradictory, the factual situations it studied were too complex, and evidentiary standards too burdensome for a lower judge to study in ten or twenty days, lower judges were not following the CCC's doctrines. Instead, they decided not to get involved in the adjudication of social rights, a task that they considered essentially administrative. In response to this situation, the CCC decided to review all those cases where lower judges did not follow its precedents. Thus, because the court was diversifying the *minimo vital* doctrine to completely new sets of circumstances, and because its docket was increasing, the CCC had to define in more general terms what types of cases and claimants were protected by *minimo vital*.

7 This is the case of Decision SU-111/97, in which the court argued that the executive and the legislature were the organs responsible for addressing structural situations of inequality and injustice and the progressive development of social rights. The judiciary, the CCC contended in this decision, did not have the necessary means to get involved in the administration of scarce resources.

Of course, during this period the types of claimants being protected by the courts also began to change. The changes in the types of claimants are closely related to the changes in the types of cases that the court studied. Although there is no simple conceptual category that captures the social types initially protected by the court, one can say that they were individuals who were both marginalized from the market and incapable of self-help. As the court describes them, the types of claimants for which the court awards protection are those "defenseless individuals (who would otherwise) succumb upon their own impotency."

From 1995 onward, however, the court started intervening more directly in the economy by protecting individuals who were inserted in the market. It gradually started including individuals who were part of the labor market as subjects of the special protection awarded through the concept of *minimo vital*. In order to do this, the court started using various devices. One of them was to simplify the complex factual circumstances in which it awarded injunctions by using simpler conceptual categories of "vulnerable subjects." Thus, the court started protecting the elderly, the disabled, fired pregnant women, workers, ill minors, and so on. However, neither the courts nor these new types of claimants could easily prove that their subsistence was at risk. Thus, as mentioned earlier, the court created a second device to solve this problem: it started using legal presumptions according to which certain categories of people that fell into certain situations or categories, that had previously defined by the court had their subsistence at risk. These presumptions exempted the claimants and the courts from having to establish the risk over life or health as a matter of fact. In other words, it transformed the factual determination of risk into a legal issue. In this way, the CCC achieved two goals: it gave lower judges clearer rules and simpler evidentiary standards to solve *minimo vital* cases in the ten or twenty days that they had to do so, and it expanded (and clarified) the scope of protection.

Finally, during this period the language used by both the court and the claimants also started changing drastically. As stated earlier, the conceptual framework of *minimo vital* no longer was attached to the criterion of connectivity. The court no longer relied on the existence of a factual connection between the protection of life, bodily integrity, or some other fundamental right to protect social rights. Instead, it started relying more and more on a direct protection of *minimo vital* as an autonomous fundamental right. However, this change did not mean that the right to life disappeared from the court's social rights' language; it just meant that the court broadened the meaning of "life." The *empirical* life was qualified with the term "dignified." This expression places "human dignity" toward the center of the semantic field of the concept of *minimo vital*, displacing life, bodily integrity, and subsistence from the central role that they formerly had. This shift can be seen in the following phrase, which exemplifies the court's language at this period: "The *minimo vital*... presupposes a fundamental constitutional right to life, understood not as mere existence, but as a dignified existence that has all the necessary conditions to develop human faculties as much as possible."[8]

This trend toward highlighting the most abstract and normative strands of the semantic field of *minimo vital* also appealed to other concepts besides dignity. The CCC also started using the idea of equality, social solidarity, or the *estado social*, (literally a "social state") as standard rhetorical devices. At this point, *minimo vital*, which was initially a concept that connected the individual to his or her material needs, started being connected to more complex notions involving equality, redistribution, and solidarity. Thus, the social character of *minimo vital* started becoming more salient and the court's social rights' language started being more closely linked to the notion of an egalitarian society. At the same time, the *minimo vital* started being conceived as a right belonging to families, not just to individuals, situating *minimo vital* more toward the mainstream of Colombian social life. From then on, the ideal of state-society relations encapsulated in the concept of the *estado social* became inseparable from social rights' adjudication. However, more importantly, linking *minimo vital* to the more abstract and normative parts of its semantic field allowed the CCC to expand the protection of social rights more freely. In addition, as we will see, the vagueness of the term *dignity* gave the CCC greater discretion to determine what acts or policies breached *minimo vital* and constituted an incentive for litigants to use, contest, and manipulate one or another strand of meaning of the concept.

BOTTOM-UP CONSTRUCTION OF LEGAL LANGUAGE: THE MIDDLE CLASSES RUSH TO COURT (1998–2004)

As we saw during the first stage, *minimo vital* served as a corrective created and controlled by the CCC to extend the benefits of a relatively functional economy to marginalized categories of individuals. In the second stage, however, the function of *minimo vital* radically changed. When the economy crashed, there was a massive wave of litigation that transformed *minimo vital* into a mechanism of economic intervention aimed at protecting the middle classes. Scarce economic resources started being redirected to prevent the decay of the middle class by judicial fiat. Moreover, during this period the CCC helped to motivate both congress and the administration into creating a policy that protected the middle classes and, for better or for worse, it established the guidelines (in some cases even the wording and mathematical formulae) of such policies. Furthermore, the court was also able to "export" its language into the political process proper, significantly transforming the political preferences of legislators in congress. In fact, the legislature refused to reissue a presidential legislative initiative that created a value-added tax for basic necessities. In rejecting this initiative, congress explicitly argued that the CCC

[8] CCC, Dec. T-283/98.

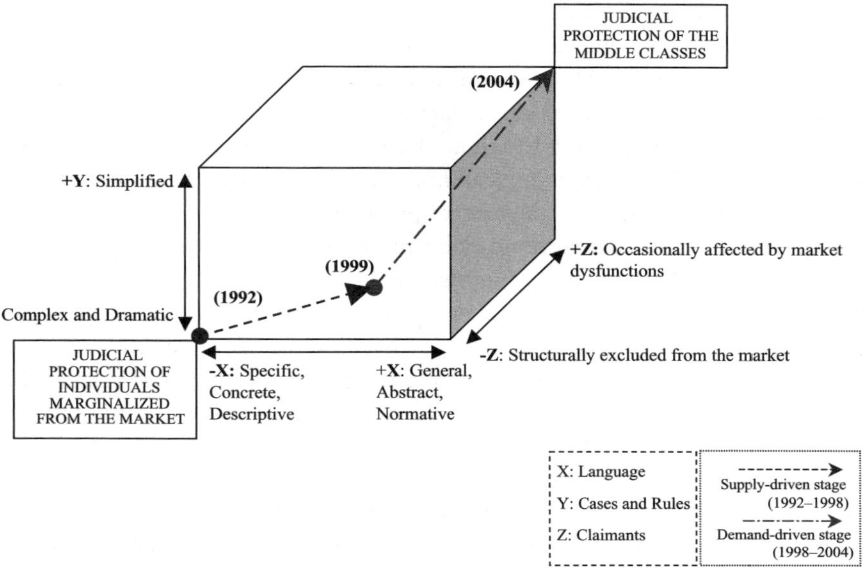

FIGURE 2.1. Judicialization of social rights in Colombia (1992–2004).

had previously declared that taxing basic necessities during an economic crisis is unconstitutional and that it violated the right to a *minimo vital*.

Figure 2.1 illustrates the process of judicialization of social rights in Colombia. In this process, the intense middle-class litigation triggered by the economic crisis of 1999 marks a breakpoint. At that point, judicialization and construction of the meaning of *minimo vital* went from being a top-down process to one that was driven from the bottom up. Alternatively, to put it in economic terms, this process went from being supply-driven to being demand-driven. To respond agilely to the litigation explosion caused by the crisis, the court further simplified the types of cases and the rules used to adjudicate social rights (Y axis). It also gave a more general, abstract, and normative meaning to the concept of *minimo vital* (X axis), and at the same time, it started benefiting claimants who were not structurally excluded from the market but occasionally affected by market dysfunctions resulting from the crisis (Z axis). However, to understand the nature of Colombia's economic crisis, and the structural and institutional weaknesses that made this crisis especially difficult for the middle classes, I will introduce some of the economic and political background surrounding it.

Introduction: The Economic and Political Background of the Second Period

Roughly, until 1995, Colombia was experiencing a period of stable economic growth. However, by 1996, several political and economic factors were starting to change this situation. Drug-related corruption scandals involving President Ernesto Samper threatened the country's political and economic stability. The situation worsened when the international economic crisis that had affected other Latin American countries, like Mexico, Brazil, and Argentina, arrived in Colombia. In combination with certain institutional and structural weaknesses, the crisis severely affected the middle classes in this country; and they resorted to the courts for protection. Under these circumstances, one would expect the CCC to back down in its social policy-making role and allow the administration enough freedom to formulate the policies of economic recovery. However, instead of doing this, the CCC was responsive to the claims of the middle classes, becoming an active player in the formulation of policies directed toward avoiding the fall of the middle classes. In doing so, it redirected the initial goal of *minimo vital* from a device for expanding state services to marginal groups to a strategy that helped to maintain the economic status quo that the middle classes enjoyed before the crisis.

In fact, even before the 1990s, Colombia had enjoyed a long period of sustained economic growth throughout the 1970s and 1980s; a trend that was exceptional for Latin American standards. In the late 1980s, Colombia started a process of economic liberalization that was launched full-scale in 1990. The government dismantled long-held subsidies in certain sectors, privatized various state-owned companies, licensed certain economic activities to private investors, especially in the service sector, and opened its internal market to imported products and services. This whole process attracted foreign and domestic investment, increasing the country's GDP and favoring its fiscal balance. However, this process of economic liberalization did not entail the reduction of the size of the state apparatus. On the contrary, liberalization paralleled the establishment of a new constitution that created a series of major political and institutional reforms that significantly increased state expenditures.

For a start, the new constitution consolidated a process of decentralization of political and administrative power. Municipalities and regions could now elect their own mayors and governors, and they had greater control over their administration. Regional and municipal governments could now use their economic resources more freely, and they could acquire public and private debts without significant control from the central government. They also acquired greater leeway to increase their personnel and to decide how to distribute public resources. Indeed, they exercised their new autonomy by increasing their expenditures from 8.1 percent of the GDP in 1990 to 13.6 percent in 2000. However, these governments were not the only ones that increased their expenditures; the size and the array of activities of the central government also increased, and the expenditures of the central government went from 20.4 percent of the GDP in 1990 to 37.7 percent in 2000. The 1991 constitution created a more robust judiciary, a centralized system of prosecutors, and an ombudsman. In the context of these newly acquired functions, increased freedom, and relative economic prosperity, the public and private sectors increased their levels of consumption and indebtedness (Correa 2000; Kalmanovitz 2001: 9).

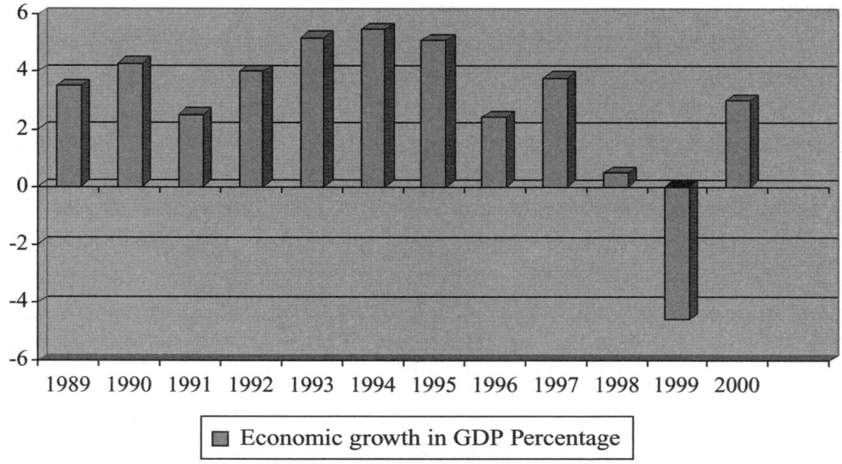

FIGURE 2.2. Economic growth in Colombia (*Source*: Kalmanovitz 2001).

There was, at the time, what some have called a boom of consumption (Echeverry 1999).

The economic crisis came in the midst of these high levels of public and private indebtedness and consumption. In this situation, economic growth went from a positive 5.5 percent in 1994 to a negative 4.6 percent in 1999; the worst crisis that the country had gone through since the 1930s (Kalmanovitz 2001: 23). The obvious response of highly indebted public and private employers would have been to reduce labor costs by reducing personnel. However, although unemployment increased significantly, Colombian labor laws are protective of workers' stability and establish relatively high economic penalties for firing employees. Firing public employees is even more difficult and it usually requires a previous administrative procedure. Thus, on the one hand, unemployment increased significantly,[9] and on the other, public and private employers that could not fire their employees simply stopped paying their salaries, health care affiliations, and pensions. To complete this scenario, inflation was still high for a time of crisis. Thus, the Colombian central bank decided to raise the country's prime interest rate from 24 percent to 35 percent to control it, and in this same vein, the government decided to freeze the salaries of all public employees.

The Litigation Explosion as a Determinant of Judicial Policy-Making

The occasional market dysfunctions, against which the CCC had protected individuals belonging to vulnerable categories, had now become a systemic problem affecting various social strata. As Figure 2.2 shows, there was a significant increase in

[9] From 9% in 1995 to more than 20% in 2000.

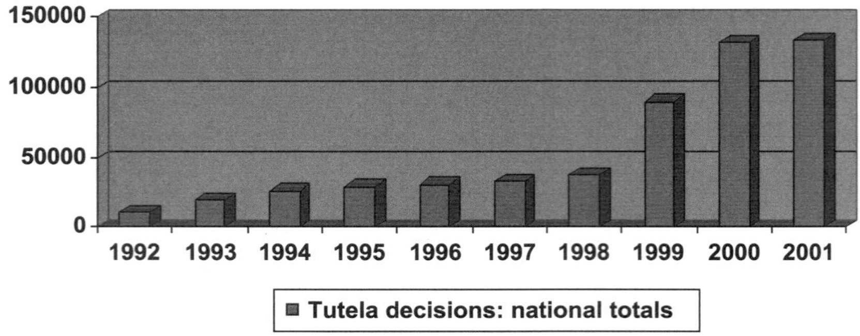

FIGURE 2.3. Amount of tutela decisions nationwide (*Source*: CCC).

the amount of tutela decisions during this period. The amount of tutela decisions nationwide went from more than 38,000 in 1998 to more than 90,000 in 1999 and to around 132,000 in 2000. There is no data available regarding the percentage of the tutelas nationwide that specifically involved *minimo vital*. As Figure 2.4, illustrates available data do show a significant increase in both the percentages and the totals of *minimo vital* decisions reviewed by the CCC from 1999 onward. The trends shown in Figures 2.3 and 2.4 suggest something rather paradoxical. Seven years before, the general understanding in Colombia was that social rights were not fundamental. Situations that affected those rights were perceived as failures in the economy or the bureaucratic system. Occasionally these situations gave rise to political protests, but for the most part people had to "lump them." By 1999, however, important segments of the Colombian population had come to perceive the consequences of the

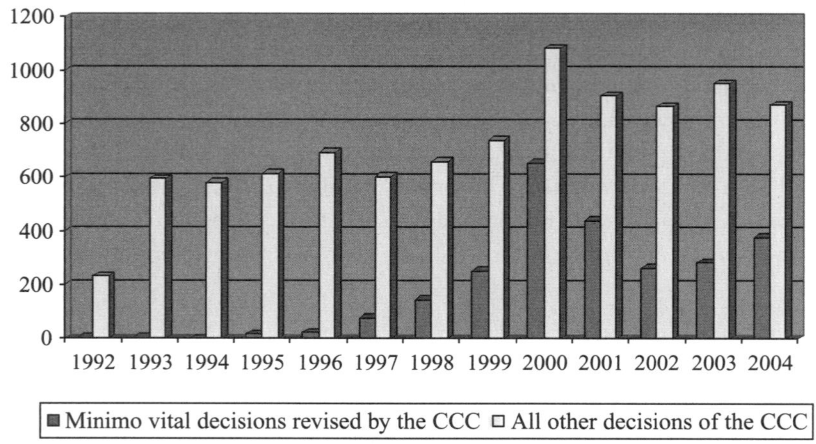

FIGURE 2.4. *Minimo vital* decisions vs. all other decisions issued by the CCC. (*Source*: CCC).

economic crisis as breaches of their fundamental rights. Social rights had acquired a wholly different status and people resorted to the courts en masse.

At this point, the CCC had already defined a series of relatively clear and simple rules regarding the most common breaches to the *minimo vital*. Moreover, lower judges usually decided according to the rules established by the CCC. However, the protection granted by *minimo vital* did not cover the whole range of situations to which claimants were exposed during the crisis. Even if lower judges followed the court's rulings, the consequences of the economic crisis were quantitatively and qualitatively beyond what the judiciary as a whole could possibly cope with through a mechanism of concrete individualized review like tutela. Even if the judiciary could protect some individuals, this would only constitute a palliative, but it would leave the institutional and structural causes of the crisis untouched. Moreover, *minimo vital* rhetoric had relied heavily on the vulnerability of certain special categories of subjects. Now, the subjects affected by the crisis were individuals who increasingly belonged to the middle classes. Finally, even though the court had used *minimo vital* to protect the middle class against exceptional market dysfunctions, it had done so by focusing on the ways in which these dysfunctions affected existing contractual obligations (e.g., employers that stopped paying salaries or pensions, providers that had not provided health care services). The consequences of this crisis went beyond simple individual breaches of contract, and they required more than just acting on the fringes of the system to correct eventual market deficiencies. If the CCC was to do anything at all to protect social rights against the effects of the crisis, it had to do so by acting directly as a policy-maker at a more macro level.

To be sure, the CCC had already realized the limits of social rights' policy-making through tutela, and in 1997, it had devised the doctrine of the "unconstitutional state of affairs." This was a legal construct that the court applied when it was obvious that the situation of a single claimant affected a whole class, and was caused, not by a specific action or omission of a public or private entity, but by a structural factor that required the design of a public policy. In those cases, the CCC ordered the competent authority to address the situation and gave a series of guidelines for this purpose. Through this mechanism, the court had addressed the situations of health services, food, prison conditions, bureaucratic inefficiency in social security entities, and the adaptation of public transportation vehicles for people with disabilities. However, in those circumstances the CCC only gave very loose policy guidelines to the defendants (generally governmental entities) and the results of its experiment with this mechanism were mixed. Under these circumstances, the best available option was to address the problem through abstract judicial review.

The first case in which the CCC addressed the consequences of the crisis through abstract review was the case of the "UPAC decisions." Since the early 1970s, the government had designed a system to finance long-term housing loans known under its Spanish acronym UPAC (Unit of Constant Purchasing Power). To maintain constant monetary values, this mechanism initially used a mathematical formula that was tied to inflation. However, in 1993, the government changed this formula and tied it to the prime interest rate, which is established by the Colombian central bank. When the crisis started, the central bank raised the interest rates to protect the banks, but a great number of middle-class families had to give their houses back to the banks because they could not afford the increase in monthly payments. Many people resorted to the courts through tutela. However, when these cases were selected for review, the CCC denied the injunctions, arguing that an eventual breach of the right to housing was not enough to award protection through *minimo vital*. Instead, the claimants "should resort to an alternative mechanism of judicial protection." They did exactly that. The people who were losing their houses raised abstract review claims against long-term housing laws, focusing on the unconstitutionality of the 1993 mathematical formula that tied the loans to the prime rate. The CCC called a public hearing in which it heard the opinions and analyses of at least twenty important economists who were experts in housing finance, including various ministers and government officials, senior researchers at the central bank, and university professors. Some time after the hearing, the CCC declared that the laws regulating these loans were unconstitutional, but not without previously devising a comprehensive plan of action. The first feature of its decision was that the court deferred the effects of its decision until congress had issued a new law to minimize the financial chaos its decision would produce. Second, the court engaged in full-scale policymaking requiring that the new law complied with a very detailed list of conditions, knowing that the congress would have to meet the court's requirements eventually. There would inevitably be someone who disliked the new law, whether that person represented the banks, developers, homeowners, or some other interest group. In addition, because filing abstract unconstitutionality claims in Colombia does not require legal representation, standing is open to all citizens regardless of whether they have a private cause of action, and filing a claim does not entail any major costs, people who did not like the new law would be likely to file a new claim of unconstitutionality against it. Thus, the CCC was able to monitor whether congress complied with its conditions. The court went even further and established that the banks should recalculate the interest rates to the homeowners retrospectively, delegating the monitoring of these arrangements on the lower courts.

The second case of abstract review in which the CCC addressed the consequences of the crisis was the salaries of public employees.[10] As a mechanism to control the growing fiscal deficit and rising inflation, the administration decided to freeze all public salaries for 2000 without recognizing the depreciation of money according to historic inflation. Thus, it did not include the necessary funds in the budget law for that fiscal year. Initially, more than five thousand public employees filed tutelas, claiming violations to their *minimo vital*. These levels of litigation were

[10] CCC, Decision C-1433/2000.

unprecedented in Colombia, and they showed a growing attitude of rights' consciousness and legal mobilization, especially if one considers that freezing public salaries was not historically uncommon in Colombia. Although the CCC selected all these cases for review, it decided not to grant the protection to the claimants' *minimo vital* in any of them. It argued that the effect that the freeze had on each individual's subsistence could not be established and that issuing an injunction would be unfair to those other public employees who had not filed claims. Other public employees had already filed claims of abstract review against the 2000 budget law. When the CCC ruled on the abstract review case it decided to "protect the rights of public employees" and design a policy of redistribution of the social costs of Colombia's inflationary economy. It declared the unconstitutionality of the law and ordered the administration to appropriate the necessary funds to maintain the purchase capacity of the public employees whose salaries were below a certain level. Public employees with salaries above that level would receive a decreasing fraction of inflation, and as their salaries increased, they would reach a certain salary level where the administration no longer had such an obligation.[11]

A third major case of social rights policy-making through abstract review involves the CCC's ruling over a law that extended a value-added tax to basic necessities. In adopting the two decisions mentioned earlier, the CCC was confronting the relatively unpopular administration of President Pastrana in circumstances of an acute economic crisis. In contrast, the administration of President Uribe has always been highly popular, and the country was starting to recover from the crisis.[12] In 2003, while the country was still recovering, Uribe proposed a bill that extended value-added tax to basic necessities. Congress passed the bill without any significant debate. Soon after the law was enacted, the CCC declared the unconstitutionality of this tax based on two arguments. According to the first argument, tax reforms since the 1960s had increasingly relied on indirect taxation and the accumulated effect of this pattern had overburdened the most economically vulnerable segments of society. Regressive taxes and taxes on basic necessities became unconstitutional in circumstances of economic crisis when the government could return to more balanced tax policies that did not affect the *minimo vital* of the least economically capable. Thus, the CCC decided the unconstitutionality of a specific tax based not on a specific feature of the text of the law, but on an evaluation of the circumstance in which it was to be implemented (as defined by the historic orientation of taxation in general, in combination with the effects of the contemporary economic crisis).

[11] In the budget law for the next year, which had already been passed by the time the court decided, the administration once again failed to include the necessary funds. This time, a new court (seven out of nine justices had changed) reiterated the ruling of the previous year, but established a series of exceptional circumstances under which the administration could decide not to level salaries to inflation. CCC, Decision C-1064/2000.

[12] Uribe has maintained a minimum of 70% favorable opinion throughout his two terms and has continuously controlled congress.

The second reason why the CCC declared the tax unconstitutional was that it had been approved without any significant debate in congress, and this had frustrated the constitutional rule of no taxation without representation. Shortly thereafter, the administration defied the court's ruling by introducing a bill with the same value-added tax for basic necessities. In this case, though, congress actually did debate the measure and overwhelmingly rejected the bill proposed by the president. It argued, among other issues, that extending a value-added tax to basic necessities affected the *minimo vital* of the most economically vulnerable segments of the population. Thus, in this case there was a judicialization of politics in at least two different ways. For a start, there was a direct enhancement of the power of the court over policy outcomes (i.e., the rejection of the tax), and secondly, there was a penetration of legal language and argument into the formal political process in the legislature.[13]

CONCLUSIONS

As demonstrated earlier, the dynamics of judicialization in Colombia started with the "supply" of an expansive social rights' language aimed at achieving social change, particularly toward incorporating social groups that were excluded from the market. In the context of a growing and stable economy and an unresponsive political system, the expansive character of this language gave rise to an increase in subsistence rights' litigation and to a series of new social claims. At the same time that subsistence rights' litigation increased and the types of claims diversified, the kinds of individuals making such claims also changed. The richness of linguistic connections between *minimo vital* and other concepts was being increasingly exploited, not by marginalized individuals, but by more mainstream and middle-class social groups. These groups started claiming social rights via *minimo vital* and this made certain strands of meaning of this concept more salient, whereas others were forgotten.

At this point, then, the dynamics of the process of judicialization became more "demand-driven" and the language of *minimo vital* started being contested and constructed mostly bottom-up by the myriad claimants that were resorting to the courts. The CCC had lost an important part of its agency in guiding the direction of its judicial social policy-making. As a result, during the economic crisis the CCC was no longer extending social benefits to individuals and groups that were marginalized from the market economy, but protecting the middle classes from the failures of an economy in crisis to which they were integrated. This reversed the trend that the CCC had started some years before of directing social expenditure toward the people who were structurally marginalized from the market. Instead of protecting

[13] Another case of adoption of the *minimo vital* language into congressional debates and policies was the adoption of a law protecting the families of kidnapped persons against the consequences arising from previously acquired debts. In this case, congress adopted all the rules that the CCC had established. CCC, Dec. T-402/2001.

the unemployed and the lower classes, subsistence rights' adjudication redirected social expenditure redistributing state funds toward more middle-class groups that had been affected by the economic crisis.

Therefore, the bottom-up character of the process of construction of legal language highlights two important issues. First, it shows the ways in which the legal language used by the court affects the types of claims and the types of claimants that resort to the courts. In this case, a rights-based language expanded the types of claims and claimants, but it did so at the cost of simplifying and flattening the kinds of narratives of social exclusion that gave rise to the concept of *minimo vital*. Moreover, the unintended consequences of the *minimo vital* also highlight the importance that economic, social, and political structures have in transforming the functions of courts while showing the limits of their agency as policy-makers. Finally, it shows how judicial responsiveness to social claims and the successful contestation of legal meanings cannot be automatically associated with social change even when the courts are able to influence the formal political process. More research is needed regarding the way in which law, legal language, and social movements interact in situations of crisis to understand the complex relation between courts and social change better.

References

Berger, Peter and Thomas Luckman. 1966. *The Social Construction of Reality: A Treatise in the Sociology of Knowledge*. Garden City, NY: Doubleday.

Correa, Patricia. 2000. "Public Debt, Public Debt Market, and Monetary Policy in Colombia." *Borradores de Economía*, 147, Bogotá, Colombia: Banco de la República.

Conley, John M. and William M. O'Barr. 2005. *Just Words: Law, Language, and Power* (2nd ed.). Chicago: Chicago University Press.

Dugas, John C. 2001. "The Origin, Impact, and Demise of the 1989–1990 Colombian Student Movement: Insights from Student Movement Theory." *Journal of Latin American Studies*, 33: 807–37.

Echeverry, Juan Carlos. 1999. UPAC: Evolution and Crisis of a Model of Development, *Archivos de Economía* 129. Bogota, Colombia: NPD.

Eckstein, Harry. 1975. "Case Studies and Theory in Political Science." In *Handbook of Political Science*, vii. F. Greenstein and N. Polsby, eds. Reading, MA: Addison-Wesley.

Gerring, John. 2001. *Social Science Methodology: A Criterial Framework*. Cambridge: Cambridge University Press.

Hirschl, Ran. 2004. *Toward Juristocracy: The Origins and Consequences of the New Constitutionalism*. Cambridge, MA: Harvard University Press.

Kalmanovitz, Salomón. 2001. Constitución y Modelo Económico, Paper presented at the ILSA Seminar on the 10th Anniversary of the Colombian Constitution. Bogota, Colombia: Universidad Nacional de Colombia.

Koselleck, Reinhart. 2002. *The Practice of Conceptual History: Timing History, Spacing Concepts*. Stanford: Stanford University Press.

Koselleck, Reinhart. 1995. "A Response to Comments on the Geschichtliche Grundbegriffe." In *The Meaning of Historical Terms and Concepts: New Studies on Begriffsgeschichte*, Hartmut Lehman and Melvin Richter, eds. Washington D.C.: German Historical Institute.

Lakoff, George. 2007. *Whose Freedom? The Battle over America's Most Important Idea*. New York: Farrar, Straus, and Giroux.
______. 1990. *Women, Fire, and Dangerous Things: What Categories Reveal about the Mind*. Chicago: University of Chicago Press.
Mitchell, Timothy. 1990. "Everyday Metaphors of Power." *Theory and Society*, 19: 545–77.
Mertz, Elizabeth. 1994. "A New Social Constructivism for Sociolegal Studies." *Law and Society Review*, 1243–65.
Phillips, Scott and Ryken Grattet. 2000. "Judicial Rhetoric, Meaning Making, and the Institutionalization of Hate Crime Law." *Law and Society Review*, 34: 567–606.
Shapiro, Martin and Alec Stone Sweet. 2002. "Testing, Comparison, Prediction." In *On Law, Politics and Judicialization*, Martin Shapiro and Alec Stone Sweet, eds. Oxford: Oxford University Press.
Siegel, Reva B. 2006. "Constitutional Culture, Social Movement Conflict, and the Constitutional Change: The Case of the de facto ERA – 2005–06 Brennan Center Symposium Lecture." *California Law Review*, 94: 1323.
Stone Sweet, Alec. 2002. "The Success of Judicial Review and Democracy." In *On Law, Politics, and Judicialization*, Martin Shapiro and Alec Stone Sweet, eds. Oxford: Oxford University Press.
Syrett, Keith. 1998. "'Immunity,' 'Privilege,' and 'Right': British Trade Unions and the Language of Labor Reform." *Journal of Law and Society*, 25: 388–406.
Wahlbeck, Paul J. 1998. "The Development of a Legal Rule: The Federal Common Law of Public Nuisance." *Law and Society Review*, 32: 613–38.
Weissbourd, Bernard and Elizabeth Mertz. 1985. "Rule Centrism Versus Legal Creativity: The Skewing of Legal Ideology Through Language." *Law and Society Review*, 19: 623–59.

3

How Courts Work: Institutions, Culture, and the Brazilian *Supremo Tribunal Federal*

Diana Kapiszewski

INTRODUCTION

Since the mid-twentieth century, courts have begun to play a more important role in politics and policy-making in a range of polities. However, this "global expansion of judicial power" (Tate and Vallinder 1995) has been uneven: courts in many countries remain quite timid, and even the most crusading courts challenge the exercise of government power only selectively. As scholars have turned to examine the causes, contours, and consequences of the halting process of judicialization, the comparative judicial politics literature has blossomed. Since the main way courts become involved in politics is through their rulings, a central question in the literature concerns why courts decide politically crucial cases as they do.

Three main lines of argumentation have emerged to answer that question in Latin American cases: the strategic, the institutional, and the cultural approaches. The strategic approach suggests that judges' decisions are guided by opportunities and constraints in the broader political system, in particular those tied to the configuration and preferences of the elected branches (e.g., Helmke 2005) or the level of popular support a court enjoys (e.g., Staton 2006). Yet strategic accounts essentially identify the political conditions under which courts *will be able to* play a more salient role in politics and policy-making – for instance, in a context of political fragmentation or divided government. As scholars have begun to note (Hilbink 2009; Ingram 2009), just because courts *can* assume a more important political role does not mean that they *will do* so. Moreover, such accounts tell us relatively little about *how* courts will play a role in politics.

The institutional approach holds that a court's enduring institutional features and its position within the political system influence its rulings (Whittington 2000:

I am very grateful to the editors of this volume and to Matthew C. Ingram for their thoughtful comments on several versions of this chapter.

608, 617). To some degree, this account of judicial behavior is marked by the same weakness as the strategic approach: just because courts are given particular powers (for instance, the ability to carry out judicial review or grab cases from lower courts), or are positioned in a particular way in the institutional super-structure, does not mean that they will use those powers or take advantage of that positioning to play a more active role in politics. And their powers and positioning alone may not account for *how* they will play any political role they adopt. Furthermore, much of the literature has focused on *formal* institutions. While these set crucial ground rules and boundaries, particularly (although certainly not only) in institutionally insecure developing democracies such as many in Latin America, consideration of how *informal* judicial institutions affect the process of judicialization is also important.

Traditionally, scholars of Latin American courts who adopted a cultural approach to account for judicial behavior limited their accounts to demonstrating how judges' "formalism" or "apoliticism" impeded political activism. Some of the newest scholarship in the cultural vein (see Hilbink 2007, Huneeus 2010) has broadened the cultural lens, showing how particular judicial practices, as well as judges' views of their role, of other judges and courts, and of the relationship they ought to maintain with society, might matter for judicialization. Yet despite courts being the main protagonists in the literature on judicialization in Latin America, relatively few scholars have looked closely at "how courts work" on the inside to explain their role in politics.

This chapter argues that *combining* the institutional and cultural accounts of judicial behavior can offer considerable insight into why and how courts become engaged in politics. That is, it seeks to demonstrate that institutions and culture work *in tandem* to influence the process of judicialization. The chapter begins by suggesting various ways in which high courts' *external institutions* (e.g., those created by elected leaders) – in particular the formal rules and informal norms guiding the composition, independence, access to and powers of high courts – influence high courts' internal culture and judicialization. The chapter then shows how high courts' *internal culture* – an interactive phenomenon comprising multiple judicial ideas and practices – both shapes the way that high courts engage in politics and policy-making *and* conditions the effect of external institutions on the judicialization process.

To illustrate these points, the chapter analyzes Brazil's apex court, the Supreme Federal Tribunal (*Supremo Tribunal Federal*, STF) and its decision-making on a set of politically crucial cases between 1985 and 2004. Brazil has undergone a significant judicialization of politics since transitioning to democracy in 1985 and in particular since the promulgation of the 1988 constitution. In turn, political scientists have begun to analyze the STF's decision-making, especially its assertiveness vis-à-vis elected leaders. While scholars have analyzed what are referred to here as the Court's external institutions (e.g., Taylor 2008), little has been written about the STF's internal culture or how it influences the Court's engagement in politics.

Furthermore, the present analysis aims to move beyond the specific question of how often high courts challenge elected leaders to demonstrate how other facets of the STF's political engagement – for example, its "clientele" and how it times its rulings – are influenced by high court external institutions and internal culture in tandem.

Of course, external judicial institutions and internal court culture are not the causal "be all and end all." A range of political, constitutional, social, and economic factors in the broader context in which courts operate influence judicialization in any polity. Nonetheless, it seems indisputable that the way in which those broader dynamics influence courts' performance in politics and policy-making is mediated to some degree by judicial institutions and culture. Understanding courts' institutions and culture may thus also have implications for those theories that point to factors in the broader context to explain judicialization.

EXTERNAL HIGH COURT INSTITUTIONS

The literature analyzing judicial politics in Latin America includes many studies that examine how external formal high court institutions (those established by elected leaders and formalized in law) affect judicialization (e.g., Wilson 2005, Taylor 2008). These studies represent a crucial first step. However, the literature has not sufficiently appreciated the role that external institutions can play in shaping internal high court culture, or the degree to which their effects on judicialization are *conditioned* by high court culture. Further, scholars of comparative politics increasingly argue that focusing exclusively on formal rules and procedures – those that are "created, communicated, and enforced through channels that are widely accepted to be official" (Helmke and Levitsky 2006: 5) – when studying politics in developing democracies "can yield an incomplete if not wholly inaccurate picture of how politics works" (O'Donnell 2006: 287; see also Helmke and Levitsky 2004). *Informal* institutions – unofficial norms and practices that have become routinized through time and repetition[1] – may also affect judicialization.

This section discusses, both in the abstract and specifically in the case of the STF, a delimited but suggestive set of external high court institutions (both formal and informal) that might shape internal high court culture, and (conditioned by that culture) influence judicialization. To clarify the first claim, the notion is not that internal culture is a "product" of external institutions; many dynamics (including, almost certainly, history) combine to produce internal judicial culture. The claim is simply that external institutions *contribute* to shaping internal culture in important ways, and that their effect on the judicialization process is conditioned by that culture.

[1] The definition of informal institutions is contested. As understood here, both formal and informal institutions entail a degree of consistency (Helmke and Levitsky 2006: 6).

External Institutions

The "profiles" of the justices who compose a Court (that is, their legal training and focus and their political and judicial backgrounds) are shaped by a number of factors including how rigorous the requirements to become a justice are, the appointment process, who participates in that process and how (see Brinks 2005), and whether a judicial career exists and reaches the high court. Those profiles, in turn, likely influence various aspects of high court internal culture such as justices' role perceptions and interjustice collegiality, which can undoubtedly affect how a Court will engage in politics. Likewise, the rules and informal practices guiding justices' tenure; on what formal and informal grounds and by whom justices can be dismissed; and whether the rules regarding Court size are stipulated in the constitution or by law can influence two aspects of internal high court culture in particular: how secure justices feel in their positions and how well-institutionalized a Court is (that is, the degree of separation that exists between the institution itself and the justices who compose it). In turn, these qualities can affect, for instance, how assertive justices will be in their decision-making, and how they will time their most politically crucial rulings.[2] A high court's size can also influence its internal organization, the practices justices develop to review and decide cases and who participates in decision-making. These facets of internal culture also have important implications for the timing and content of high court rulings.

Further, what formal constitutional guarantees of independence exist, and what informal practices elected leaders have adopted to threaten or manipulate a Court (if any), have implications for internal high court culture and (conditioned by that culture) for judicialization. Several scholars have studied judicial independence and its consequences for judicial decision-making (see Larkins 1996; Colon 2003; Santiso 2004; Wilson 2005; Ríos-Figueroa 2006; Finkel 2008).[3] For instance, Couso (2005) suggests that a "reasonable" degree of independence from government is a prerequisite for judicial assess vis-à-vis elected leaders in Latin America. And Chavez illustrates how in Argentina, the "informal institutions and practices" that presidents use to control courts often trump guarantees of judicial independence in the constitution (Chavez 2004: 23). Yet external institutions concerning high court independence can also affect justices' beliefs regarding their security, the way they interact with each other and the practices they adopt to do their job. These facets of internal high court culture may have important effects on judicialization, for instance, on the decisions at which justices arrive and on whether their relations with elected leaders are productive or contentious.

[2] Many of these rules and procedures are addressed piecemeal in studies of the region's high courts; see Navia and Ríos-Figueroa (2005) for a systematization of certain aspects.

[3] Formal (de jure) judicial independence is relatively easy to evaluate on the basis of formal rules guiding the appointment and removal processes, salary changes, budgetary autonomy, etc.; actual (de facto) judicial independence is notoriously difficult to operationalize and measure.

Finally, several external institutions related to judicial power and accessibility can also impact internal high court culture, and their effect on judicial production is likely conditioned by that culture. Again, most scholars who have studied external institutions related to high court power and accessibility have highlighted their effect on judicial production (see Cepeda Espinosa 2005; Wilson 2005; Ríos-Figueroa and Taylor 2006; Wilson and Rodríguez Cordero 2006). Yet external institutions such as the jurisdiction and judicial review powers that are awarded to Courts, what mechanisms are available to reach them (and how permissive the appeals structure is), and whether a Court can control its docket, [4] in large part through their effects on the size of a Court's caseload, can affect its internal organization and the practices justices adopt to review and decide cases – as well as the content of its decisions. To offer just one example, an immense caseload may encourage justices to develop "ducking" practices to avoid (or, indeed, to play) a certain role in politics. Likewise, a Court's ability to issue temporary rulings (referred to as "injunctions") may allow or encourage it to adopt particular decision-making practices (for instance, stalling final rulings) with concomitant implications for how it becomes involved in politics.

The STF's External Institutions

Few formal rules guide appointments to the Brazilian high court. The 1988 constitution stipulates that STF justices must be Brazilian citizens between the ages of 36 and 64 when appointed, must possess outstanding judicial knowledge, and must have an impeccable reputation (Article 101). Appointment entails nomination by the president, public (and largely symbolic, Ballard 1999, note 216) senate confirmation hearings, and approval by an absolute majority of the senate (Article 52). Although Brazil's elected leaders have developed some informal appointment practices, they have tended to be nonpartisan and generally augmented (rather than undermined) formal rules. Presidents seek a balanced geographic representation on the Court, and it generally includes at least one justice who formally served on the state Supreme Court of São Paulo. In addition, following President Cardoso's (1995–2003) appointment of the first woman to the Court (Justice Ellen Gracie Northfleet in 2000) and President Lula's (2003–present) appointment of the first Afro-Brazilian (Joaquím Barbosa in 2003), future configurations of the Court will likely include at least one woman and one Afro-Brazilian.

Consequently, most justices who have sat on the STF through the posttransition period have had a relatively strong professional profile, and few have been popularly identified with any political party.[5] Eleven of the twenty-one justices appointed to

[4] See Colon 2003; Navia and Ríos-Figueroa 2005; and Ríos-Figueroa 2006 for detailed analyses of institutional and constitutional design.

[5] Justices with ties to the Workers' Party (*Partido dos Trabalhadores*, PT) appointed by President Lula (of the PT) represent an exception.

the high court between 1985 and 2009 had held significant posts in the judiciary prior to being appointed to the Court;[6] eight had held posts within the federal prosecutorial organ, nine had held an important post in the executive branch of the federal government, four had been a deputy or senator in the national congress, and many were considered eminent jurists.[7]

The 1988 constitution allows for qualified life tenure: justices must retire at the age of 70 but are "irremovable" before that point (Article 95). Although the charter does not describe the processes of impeachment or dismissal in detail, it does indicate that the senate is responsible for trying and deciding cases in which justices are accused of misconduct (*crimes de responsabilidade*), and that the senate can also impeach and remove justices (Article 52). However, in contrast to what has occurred in other Latin American countries (for instance, in Argentina or Peru), no justice has been tried for misconduct, induced to step down, or removed since well before 1985. Finally, the number of STF justices – eleven since 1969 – is established in the constitution (Article 101) rather than by law, making even more difficult the manipulation of the Court's composition.

The 1988 constitution granted the judiciary unprecedented financial and administrative (i.e., "formal") independence vis-à-vis the other branches of government (Articles 96 and 99). In addition to the tenure guarantees just mentioned, courts elaborate their own budgets (within limits determined by the other branches of government) and organize internally as they choose; moreover, judges' salaries are "irreducible" (Article 95).[8] The difficulty of amending the constitution sets these guarantees even more firmly in place.[9] Additionally, elected leaders have developed few informal tactics to compromise the STF's independence or hold it accountable for its rulings (Sadek 1995: 11; Arantes 1997; Santiso 2004; Taylor 2004: 338; Brinks 2005). The Court was not replaced on transition to democracy, and because its size has not changed since that point, only President Lula has been able to appoint more than a handful of justices.[10] Although it is not uncommon for the Attorney General to "visit" and "converse" with justices to clarify the government's point of view on a particular case, such contact is handled delicately, and only on special occasions do other cabinet ministers visit the Court – deputies and senators would never "dare" to do so

6 The Brazilian federal judiciary contains the elite of the legal profession (judges must pass rigorous and competitive entrance exams and are promoted on merit); justices' ascendance through the judiciary is thus a testament to their preparedness and training.

7 This discussion draws on Kapiszewski (2007, Appendix 3.5).

8 In addition, the STF penned (per stipulations in Article 93 of the 1988 constitution) the broad law on judicial administration and decisions (*Estatuto da Magistratura*).

9 Amendments may be proposed by the executive, by one-third of the chamber or senate, or by more than one-half of the state legislatures; they require the approval, in two successive votes, of at least three-fifths of the chamber and senate (Rosenn 1990: 783). Certain provisions of the charter (*cláusulas pétreas*) cannot be amended.

10 President Lula had appointed eight justices by 2009.

(EC-13, EC-28, EC-29).[11] Further, while the government has often taken advantage of the multiple mechanisms that exist to appeal certain STF decisions (frequently in an effort to delay a final ruling), an STF ruling has rarely been overturned or significantly modified.

As outlined in the constitution, the STF's jurisdiction is quite broad, including original,[12] as well as ordinary and extraordinary appeals jurisdictions (Article 102).[13] The Court's judicial review powers are also quite extensive. The STF has been empowered to carry out concrete constitutional review since 1891, and has had some abstract review powers since the mid-1960s.[14] The 1988 constitution enhanced the STF's abstract review powers and limited its jurisdiction to constitutional matters, such that since the 1990s it has essentially served as a constitutional court although it is not designated as such.[15] The Court can both declare norms unconstitutional and declare unconstitutional administrative, regulatory or legislative lapses that prevent the full exercise of a constitutional right or full application of a constitutional principle (Rocha and Paulo 2003: 18–19). When the STF carries out concrete constitutional review, the immediate effects of its decisions are *inter partes*; its abstract review decisions have *erga omnes* and more immediate effects.

A wide array of mechanisms can be used to reach the STF. Abstract review cases, which are filed directly with the Court and may only be initiated by a few actors (outlined in Article 103 of the 1988 constitution and Laws 9.868 and 9.882 of 1999), make up a tiny subset of its caseload.[16] The vast majority of STF cases are appeals

[11] One data source for this chapter is a set of interviews carried out by the author with a range of political and judicial actors in Brazil in 2004 and 2005. Respondents' names are not mentioned to protect confidentiality. Instead, each interview is assigned a particular code: citations with the prefix "I" were informational interviews; "EG" denotes general expert interviews; "CSE" denotes case selection interviews; "CSM" or "JG" denotes interviews with justices; "EC" denotes expert interviews regarding economic policy cases; and "AS" denotes interviews with high court clerks.

[12] Abstract review cases regarding the constitutionality of active federal, state, or local norms passed after 1988, certain cases involving high state officials, the nation or a Brazilian territory/state and conflicts of competency between superior courts or between any superior court and any other court are filed directly with the STF.

[13] The STF's ordinary appeals jurisdiction includes cases in which a constitutional right has been denied by one of the superior courts and cases involving political crimes. Its extraordinary appeals jurisdiction includes cases decided by lower courts in which the appealed decision either contradicts a constitutional clause, declares unconstitutional a treaty or federal law, declares valid a municipal law or government act whose constitutionality was questioned or deals with conflicts between municipal and state law.

[14] Judicial review is *diffuse* or *decentralized*: the constitution of 1891 empowered all federal and state courts to carry out concrete judicial review (Dolinger 1990: 812). See Arantes (1997) regarding Brazil's "hybrid" judicial review system.

[15] In an institutional innovation, the 1988 constitution established an "everything-but-constitutional" court – the Supreme Tribunal of Justice (*Superior Tribunal de Justiça*, STJ) – which hears appeals of nonconstitutional cases, leaving the STF as a constitutional court by default. Note, however, that the STF may only engage in *a posteriori* review.

[16] Four abstract review mechanisms exist to reach the high court. The one most often used is the Direct Act of Unconstitutionality (*Ação Direta de Inconstitucionalidade*, ADIn), which allows plaintiffs to

of lower court rulings.[17] Brazil's appeals structure is quite permissive, many appeals mechanisms exist, and prior to 2004 the Court essentially lacked docket control: it had to rule on every case it received even if that ruling was simply a dismissal on the basis of some technical flaw (Taylor 2004: 113, 135).[18] Given the Court's broad jurisdiction and the ease of appeal, the STF receives and decides an extraordinary number of cases: 163,950 cases were filed with the high court during the 1980s; 326,493 cases were filed in the 1990s; and the Court received *more than a million* cases between January 2000 and November 2009. For a time, the Court had a drive-through window in the basement to facilitate case-filing.

Since the mid-1990s, most STF cases are decided by a single justice.[19] Either single justices, one chamber, or the full Court (i.e., sitting *en banc*) may issue preliminary rulings as well as hand down rulings on the merits. Preliminary rulings (*injunções*) generally entail an expedited decision-making process, and temporarily suspend application of all or part of a law until its constitutionality has been determined. There are no rules regarding how soon after issuing an injunction the Court must render a final ruling on a case, and no requirement that the two be in the same direction (JG-02). The STF sitting en banc may also emit summary rulings (*súmulas*), general statements, or doctrine abstracted from one or a series of related cases that articulate how the STF understands and interprets a particular theme or issue (Rosenn 1984: 34).[20] Judicial reform of December 2004 (Constitutional Amendment No. 45) instituted the binding summary ruling (*súmula vinculante*, a legal instrument similar to binding precedent in common law systems) which allows the STF to designate certain summary rulings as binding on itself and on judges at all levels when deciding similar cases.

question the constitutionality of federal or state norms issued by the executive and legislature or administrative decisions issued by courts since 1988.

17 Since the early 1990s more than 90 percent of the STF's case load has consisted of two types of appeals: extraordinary appeals (*recursos extraordinarios*, REs, broadly applicable to lower court rulings) or interlocutory appeals (*agravos de instrumento*, AGs, filed when the court just prior to the STF denies the use of an RE). All data drawn from http://www.stf.jus.br/portal/cms/verTexto.asp?servico=estatistica&pagina=movimentoProcessual (July 6, 2009).

18 Constitutional Reform No. 45 of 2004 included one formal step toward docket control – the creation of the institution of "broad repercussion" (*repercussão geral*), which requires plaintiffs filing REs or AGs to demonstrate the broad political, economic, or social "relevance" of the constitutional questions their cases raise. The reform allows the STF to accept technically deficient cases it considers important and to dismiss technically sound cases it deems unimportant, thereby acknowledging its political role.

19 Historically, the only rulings justices could perform individually were case dismissals due to technical flaws. Law 8.038 (1990) empowered single justices to dismiss cases that questioned jurisprudence that had been consolidated in one of the STF's summary rulings (*súmulas*). In 1994 (and again in 1998), following explosions in the STF's caseload, the Civil Procedural Code (Article 557) was reformed to allow justices to make decisions on their own when applying any set (*passificada*) jurisprudence of the high court.

20 Cases brought to the STF that contradict súmulas are rejected (unless the Court desires to change the *súmula*).

INTERNAL HIGH COURT CULTURE

Judges' ideas about law and the judicial endeavor, and the practices they develop as they do their job, are at the heart of the cultural approach to explaining judicial decision-making.[21] Much early work on Latin American courts adopted a cultural approach, arguing that the formalistic nature of legal culture in the region impeded judicial assertiveness (e.g., Karst and Rosenn 1975; Frühling 1984). Only a small subset of the work produced since the field of comparative judicial politics began to blossom in the early 1990s points to legal or judicial culture to explain judicialization in Latin America. That work focuses disproportionately on Chile and mainly seeks to account for Chilean courts' *lack* of involvement in politics or policy-making (the opposite of judicialization). Hilbink (2007), for example, examines how Chilean judges' "apolitical" ideology and insularity (reinforced and recycled through judicial rules and structure) prevented them from defending liberal democratic principles into the mid-1990s.[22] Huneeus (2010), by contrast, argues that judicial culture is nonmonolithic and identifies circumstances under which its heterogeneity became manifest in Chile in connection with judging in the area of human rights. And Couso (2002) argues that Chilean courts tempered their decision-making in the constitutional arena to preserve their power to fulfill what they saw as their fundamental role: deciding more mundane struggles in the legal realm.[23]

Yet a court's internal culture arguably includes an even more diverse range of judicial views and routines. This section develops a multifaceted notion of internal judicial culture and discusses how different aspects of that culture may help to account for judicial involvement in politics and policy-making. Like the editors of this volume (and departing from studies that limit culture to the ideational realm), it suggests that the ideas *and the practices* that judges and justices develop as they do their job (be they formally established or routinized through repetition), are illustrative of and can be meaningfully included in the notion of judicial culture. Indeed, considering judicial rules and practices, which might be thought of as internal institutions, as constitutive of culture is another way that this chapter (and the volume) approximate the cultural and institutional approaches

[21] Given the cultural model's concern with judges' views on the nature of law and the constitution, their institution and their mandate (that is, with "legal ideology"), it has some affinities with the attitudinal model of judicial behavior, which argues that judges' *political* ideology and policy preferences affect their decision-making (Segal and Spaeth 1993). Developed to account for judicial decision-making on the U.S. Supreme Court, the attitudinal model is seldom employed to explain judicialization in the Latin American context.

[22] Note that in using institutional and cultural factors to explain judicialization, Hilbink's approach is similar to the one employed here.

[23] To give one non-Chilean example, Miller (1997) proposes that the particular "sociology of judicial review" courts develop can influence the degree to which courts are willing and able to constrain elected leaders.

to explaining judicialization. The Brazilian STF is used to illustrate the section's points.

Internal Culture

How secure justices feel in their roles and how vulnerable they believe their institution is to elected-branch attack can affect judicial production. For instance, Helmke (2005) suggests that in insecure settings (such as Argentina), justices may challenge elected leaders more often as those leaders lose their grip on power, in order to distance the Court from incumbents and to ingratiate it with the incoming administration. An aspect of high court internal culture closely related to security that could affect, for instance, how much justices strive to "make a statement" with their rulings or challenge powerful actors is the degree to which the institution stands separate from the justices who populate it at any point in time. For instance, Argentine justices are known to indicate in their rulings that the rulings represent the thinking of the Court "in its current configuration," emphasizing that a different set of justices would likely issue a different decision. Such statements suggest relatively little differentiation between justices and Court: the Court becomes the justices who sit upon it.[24]

How strong a Court's leadership is – either less formal "intellectual" leadership or more formal appointed or elected leadership – might condition judicialization by affecting the unanimity of rulings or the final vote on rulings on close cases. More generally, a Court's internal organization (for instance, if it is divided into chambers) can affect who will participate in deciding different cases, with implications for what kinds of rulings the Court will hand down. Furthermore, the more professionalized the Court's staff, particularly if clerks are involved in writing opinions, the better grounded a Court's rulings may be, perhaps increasing the forcefulness of its decisions.

The views justices hold about the role their institution should play in general and in politics, and how it should carry out judicial review (arguably the most political of judicial roles) likely have their roots in justices' professional profiles, as noted previously. Role perceptions affect justices' views about the relationship their Court should maintain with society – how transparent its operations should be and how open it should be to societal input. Justices' role perceptions may also affect the potential for interjustice collaboration, as well as the development of internal rifts that could impinge on the ease and fluidity of the Court's decision-making. In sum,

24 The question is one of degree: even a high court as institutionalized as the U.S. Supreme Court is strongly identified with its current composition. Yet in the U.S., differentiation remains between the justices of the day and the Court as an institution – in part because the fundamental features of the latter are decidedly not open to change. Moreover, the U.S. Supreme Court rarely includes in its opinions an acknowledgement that another set of justices would have ruled differently.

all of these facets of internal culture have implications for how the Court engages in politics.

The practices that Courts develop to manage their caseload, review cases, and issue rulings are also crucial aspects of their internal culture, all of which can affect judicialization in a number of ways. Most generally, how consistently a Court appears to follow procedures and how much discretion they allow (and the Court exercises) can influence its actual and perceived reliability, which in turn may affect how and when it will be approached to participate in politics (and how it will do so). Also, in what order cases are reviewed, what case review entails and whether it is written or oral, who participates in decision-making and to what degree deliberation occurs, and how opinion authorship is determined all influence when and how a Court delves into politics. To give just one example, if justices generally wait until full-Court deliberations to discuss cases and always proffer votes in the same order, early voters could wield more influence over the Court's political engagement, while different decision-making rules and norms might generate more opportunities for coordination, bargaining and logrolling among justices (Helmke 2000). Finally, we might anticipate that the more justices value and seek to foment transparency and openness, the more trust their Court might instill in the populace, or the more influence societal actors may believe they can have on its rulings, encouraging them to file cases, thus hastening judicialization.

The STF's Internal Culture

This section describes the internal culture of the contemporary STF.[25] The STF sits at the head of a federal judiciary consisting of highly professional, well-trained judges (Rosenn 1984: 29–30). That professionalism, combined with collegiality and segmentation, consistency and discretion, create the STF's eclectic internal culture.

Security, Leadership, and Internal Organization

Due to the STF's institutional stability, a sense of security permeates the Court. In no interview that I conducted did a justice, either retired or current, appear concerned about the permanence of justices on the Court or about its institutional future.[26] By the same token, the Court (as an institution) seems to stand apart from the justices who populate it at any moment: the STF retains a sense of itself that is larger than its momentary composition. For instance, by Brazilian standards, a good

[25] Few of the judicial reforms introduced through the 1988 constitution or Constitutional Amendment No. 45 in December 2004 directly affected the STF; those related to its internal culture are discussed here. Unless otherwise indicated, all of the information in this section was garnered during interviews the author held with high court clerks.

[26] In Argentina, by contrast, justices' concern for their own future and the future of their institution served as the tacit background for analogous interviews.

deal of pomp and circumstance surround the STF: the justices wear dramatic capes when the Court meets en banc, a tradition that reinforces on a weekly basis the STF's institutional importance. Moreover, interviews with past and current justices revealed their respect for their institution and the role it plays in governing Brazil.

Two types of meaningful leadership coexist on the STF. The formal presidency, with a term of two years, rotates among the Court's members, and no justice may serve more than one term. Although the Court's internal rules stipulate that justices elect the Court president, the informal (but consistently followed) norm is that every two years the justice who has sat on the STF for the longest (and has not yet been president) assumes the role. Clerks and justices alike emphasized the ethical upside of this arrangement. The lack of "real elections" for STF president obviates internal campaigning which, along with being anathema to the Court's aspirations of transparency, could lead justices to engage in "deal-making" or engender conflicts among justices aligned with competing candidates (AS-01, AS-04, JG-03). The president represents the Court in official functions and serves as its public face, decides certain types of cases, and sets the agenda for and manages the Court's en banc sessions. The role of high court president is recognized and respected: justices, legal scholars and politicians alike often intimated a link between the presidency of certain justices and certain rulings (CSE-23). The STF also has a less-formal intellectual leader (a "dean of Court" or "*decano*," generally the justice who has sat on the Court the longest) to whom the Court turns for direction; justices and legal scholars were generally consistent in identifying these intellectual leaders. I found no evidence of conflicts between the Court's two types of leadership.

As with many of the Court's internal rules, the STF's internal structure is formalized in its procedural manual, the *Regimento Interno*. The Court has operated in two chambers since 1931 and each chamber has included five justices (the president belongs to neither) since 1965. Justices and clerks disagreed about the degree of informal segmentation that marks the STF, however. Some intimated that the STF is quite internally segmented. They described different justices' chambers as "islands" (AS-01, AS-04, JG-03) and suggested that justices have developed and follow different procedures when ruling on cases individually (again, the vast majority of the Court's rulings since 2000 have been decided by a single justice). Other respondents suggested more interaction. They noted that the STF's clerks have created their own association and request help and information from each other frequently (AS-02, AS-03), and that justices periodically communicate in administrative sessions and are often in touch with each other on a daily basis.

Staffing individual justice's chambers (*gabinetes*) is one chief of staff (*chefe de gabinete*, who performs administrative tasks), five clerks, and twenty-odd administrative staff.[27] Clerks must have a law background, but there is no public competition

[27] These staff hail from within (*servidores*) and without (*tercerizados*) the STF personnel pool; they tend to work in a justice's chambers briefly and have no impact on the formulation of case summaries (*relatorios*) or decisions.

for clerkships – justices can hire whomever they like. In the early post-transition period, justices generally chose outstanding members of the administrative staff to be their clerks, and clerks stayed with "their" justice through his or her entire time on the Court. Since the early 2000s, however, clerks have more frequently been young superstars with strong academic backgrounds who stay less time in the Court and who see clerking as a stepping stone to a high-powered career. Clerks' duties vary from one justice's chambers to another; they may be more or less involved in writing summaries (*relatorios*) of cases, researching and developing draft opinions (AS-01, AS-02, AS-03). In most cases, they perform initial triage, identifying important cases for the justices. My interviews with clerks revealed them to be consistently professional and knowledgeable (and exceedingly patient teachers).

Justice Role Perception and Collegiality

Judicial role perceptions are difficult to assess: they are unlikely to be clearly reflected in written opinions or faithfully conveyed in conversations. Nonetheless, despite their disparate professional profiles (reviewed earlier), practically every justice interviewed in connection with this project answered "to protect rights" or "to defend the constitution" (or both) when questioned about the STF's primary function. Interviews with STF justices and experts (plus a review of the justices' individual votes on politically crucial cases) suggested the coexistence of two views of *how* the Court should go about protecting the constitution, however. Those views aligned relatively well with the individual justices' professional profiles. Some justices (often those with more experience in politics) were more open to considering the political or economic consequences of their decisions (and were thus sometimes referred to as "*consequencialistas*"), whereas others (often those with more experience in the judiciary) focused primarily on legal considerations when issuing rulings (and were thus nicknamed "*legalistas*") (CSE-04, CSM-01, EC-33).

One question at the heart of this volume concerns *evolution* in legal culture. While little has been written on STF justices' role perceptions prior to the contemporary period, the framework employed in this chapter offers some clues about the STF's more historic internal culture. On the one hand, as suggested earlier, prior to 1988, the STF's jurisdiction extended far beyond constitutional matters. Given the multiple responsibilities that accrued to the Court, there was likely weaker consensus among justices on the Court's role. By the same token, Brazilian leaders have been appointing justices with a mix of backgrounds (that is, with significant experience in the elected branches and in the Brazilian judiciary) since at least the 1930s (see Kapiszewski 2007). Thus, the institutional underpinnings for a consequencialista / legalista divide have existed for decades. And although that underlying divide likely manifested itself differently prior to 1988 given the Court's previously broader mandate, by 1950 (far before the expansion of its judicial review powers), the Court was already sufficiently involved in political matters to become a target for the press and for congress (Viotti da Costa 2001: 155).

In the contemporary period, consequencialistas often took a more holistic approach to decision-making, highlighting the necessity of protecting the institutional system laid out in the constitution, while their legalista colleagues were more likely to emphasize the importance of defending the constitutional articles and clauses most relevant to a case. Consequencialistas thus found it easier to justify upholding laws or presidential decrees containing crucial government policies that contradicted one or two constitutional clauses (to avoid potentially system-threatening political or economic turmoil), while their legalista counterparts were more willing to invalidate such norms (see Kapiszewski 2007). This divide implies that STF justices must continuously negotiate the boundaries of law and politics with each other. For example, while Minister Nelson Jobim (1997–2006) came to be identified as the "leader of the government in the Court" (I-7),[28] Justice Marco Aurélio (1990–present) has been known to brandish "*o livrinho*" (the constitution) during the STF's deliberations as a reminder of the STF's fundamental function.[29] In sum, consensus on how the Court should carry out its role (that is, judicial review) is weaker than it might be, for instance, on a Court composed completely of justices who hail from the lower echelons of the judiciary (such as the Supreme Court in Chile).

Despite this rift, justices emphasized the Court's collegiality (CSM-03, JG-03). In fact, collegiality is apparent from the moment one enters the STF's bright, modern "annexes": people nod and exchange salutations in the hallways, and upon opening the door to a justice's chambers, a visitor is immediately exposed to the cheerful hubbub of the young administrative staff who sit at the front. The Court's case review procedures also reflect a relatively collaborative style. Rather than reviewing cases through a written process, as occurs in other Latin American countries, the STF sits en banc to deliberate and decide the most important cases it receives. The Court's twice-weekly sessions are highly interactive, and while they can feature quite heated debate, disagreement does not seem to dent the Court's overall collaborative spirit.

Furthermore, according to clerks, justices rarely miss high court sessions and rarely invoke the reasons at their disposal to justify not voting on any particular case. Moreover, until the early 2000s, only one justice (the lead justice, or *relator*) was familiar with most cases prior to their being considered by the Court sitting en banc; case summaries were not distributed. Therefore, the Court's deliberations and decisions on most cases were based on a single justice's summary and interpretation

[28] While appointed by President Cardoso, Minister Jobim maintained the nickname even after President Lula assumed power; that is, the justice was essentially progovernment rather than a puppet of his appointer.

[29] Another potentially explosive rift remained latent: no STF justice was removed with regime transition in 1985, and it was not until 2003 that all of the justices who sat on the Court at the time of transition had retired. Brazil thus spent the early posttransition period with a Court consisting of justices used to defending (and by some accounts still loyal to (JG-06)) a different institutional system.

of the case (and his or her suggested ruling). This practice required justices to rely heavily on their colleagues – reliance that would have been difficult without (and likely encouraged) collegiality.[30] Collaborative intra-Court relations are likely also encouraged by the justices' professional backgrounds and the fact that elected leaders have neither manipulated nor sought to politicize the Court.

Consistency, Discretion, Transparency, and Openness

A consensual set of rules and norms guide the operation of Brazil's federal courts (Taylor 2004: 7), and procedural continuity also marks the STF's operation (despite some inconsistencies in justices' decision-making practices when they are ruling on cases individually). The Court's written manual (*Regimento Interno*) outlines its internal rules and procedures, and decision-making on cases considered by the full Court (*plenario*) appears to adhere closely to the rules laid out there, in the constitution and in two laws regulating consideration of abstract review cases (Law 9.868 and Law 9.882, both of 1999). Indeed, clerks of five sitting justices gave strikingly similar responses to my questions regarding Court procedure, and whenever they were not sure of a particular detail, they consulted the *Regimento Interno*, the constitution or these laws, copies of which every clerk had at hand.

Each case that arrives at the Court is first randomly assigned (*distribuido*) by computer to a particular justice, who becomes the lead justice for the case. The following procedures are then followed for cases that go to the full Court for resolution: the justice to whom a case was originally assigned (and his or her clerks) analyze the case and write a case summary and draft vote. The justice then advises the Court president that the case is ready to go to the full Court. The STF president sets the Court's agenda, choosing which cases it will hear and in what order they will be heard. Decision-making begins with the lead justice's oral presentation of the case summary and draft vote. Next, oral arguments are offered and genuine debate occurs. Following deliberations, each justice votes orally in reverse order of seniority: the justice who has sat on the Court for the least time votes first and the most senior justice votes last.[31] The STF president then interprets the direction of each justice's vote and announces the ruling on the case.[32] If the case was decided in the direction that the lead justice argued, he or she writes the final opinion; if not, another justice is chosen by the president. The transcription of each justice's vote becomes his or her formal vote (included in the final written decision); the

30 Since the early 2000s, materials regarding many cases are distributed prior to the session in which those cases will be considered.

31 Justices may ask the president for permission to vote out of order or to add comments before or after they have voted.

32 "Defining" justices' votes in this way, particularly in close cases, and especially given that justices' oral votes can be lengthy and vague and can deal with multiple discrete constitutional issues, gives the Court president great power.

Court's most important rulings often include lengthy, separate concurrences and dissents.

Despite this orderly process, the STF retains significant decision-making discretion and room for informal innovation. For instance, the Court possesses significant latitude with respect to the timing of its decisions: there are no rules concerning either the order in which it must decide cases or how quickly it must do so, and no formal requirement that the STF president include on the Court's agenda the cases that have been in the Court the longest.[33] The STF's astronomical caseload provides the Court a ready justification for long decision times, further facilitating delay.[34] Also, at any point before the final votes on a case are cast, justices may request time to study the case in greater detail (*pedir vista*). Granting the request suspends voting on the case until the justice "returns" it. Although written rules regulate when justices should return ADIns they request to study, it is easy, both formally and tacitly, to extend the review period. Justices have been known to hold onto cases they requested for long periods of time, due to case complexity, to the Court's huge caseload and to political considerations (AS-02).

Finally, STF justices and their clerks have sought to create a culture of transparency on the Court. All Court personnel assured (and reassured) me that neither the lead justice on a case nor his or her clerks ever discuss draft opinions with other justices or clerks before those opinions are read before the full Court. Doing so, they said, could suggest a practice of unethical deal-making outside of Court sessions. Also, all of the Court's full sessions and those of its two chambers have been public since the Court's inception, and have been televised live on the dedicated judiciary channel, *TV Justiça*, since August 2002.[35] In addition, the Court publishes a weekly electronic newsletter outlining its most important decisions (*Informativo STF*), and its web site (www.stf.jus.br) contains a wealth of information about the STF and its work, including statistics, opinions, past and future decision-making schedules, and so forth.

The multitude of mechanisms available to file cases with the Court make it formally accessible, and justices have developed additional formal and informal practices to open the Court to external input. Unlike in many other Latin American high courts, Brazilian lawyers argue their cases before the STF when it sits en banc. Also, the Court accepts a variety of written briefs from various sources regarding

[33] Moreover, a law can be declared unconstitutional at any point – even decades – after it went into effect; no statute of limitations exists (Rocha and Paulo 2003: 58).

[34] In certain abstract review cases, the STF can even decide whether its decision will be prospective or retrospective, and can indicate the exact point in time from which a law declared unconstitutional will be considered without effect.

[35] Although justices' individual decision-making is obviously not public, as noted previously, justices may only rule on their own when the high court's jurisprudence is "set" on the issue in question; that jurisprudence setting is done by the full Court and thus public.

cases.[36] And justices and clerks alike emphasized that when the STF is examining a socially visible dispute, justices can receive hundreds or thousands of e-mails regarding the case, in general from citizens (AS-03; JG-07). In addition, the Court has recently begun to hold public hearings prior to deciding socially significant cases.[37]

Summing Up

Table 3.1 summarizes the analysis of the STF's external institutions and internal culture. For each external institution, the table highlights whether the institution is formal (written in an official document) or informal (routinized through practice over time). As scholars have noted, formal and informal institutions interact in a variety of ways, including reinforcing, negating or competing with each other (see Helmke and Levitsky 2004, 2006; Lauth 2005; Tsai 2006). While external institutions tend to be formal, when formal and informal institutions act together, they tend to complement each other. For instance, the informal appointment practices elected leaders have adopted essentially served to supplement and extend formal rules, rather than undermine them. The overall image of the STF that emerges on the basis of its external institutions is one of a stable, independent, powerful, and relatively accessible – and consequently overburdened – institution.

For the Court's internal culture, Table 3.1 discriminates between ideational and practical elements of culture, which interact and shape each other. On the inside, justices seem secure in their posts, yet are simultaneously aware that their institution is something greater than themselves. The Court has two meaningful forms of leadership, and justices employ superstar clerks whose stays are increasingly fleeting. Some degree of consensus on role perception exists (although the tactics justices would use to carry out an overall strategy of constitutional defense differ), and the atmosphere on the Court is generally collaborative. Despite the discretion their posts and extant procedures afford them, STF justices seem rule-bound. Finally, transparency and openness have emerged as important aspects of the Court's culture.

INSTITUTIONS, CULTURE, AND JUDICIALIZATION

The analysis thus far has suggested ways in which a Court's external institutions can shape its internal culture, and ways in which a Court's internal culture both influences judicialization and conditions how external institutions do so. The chapter's

36 In particular, the institution of *amicus curiae*, which allows any organ, entity, or interested lawyer to provide the Court with technical briefs on abstract review cases, was established in 1999 (Law 9.868) with the express intent of opening the STF's deliberation process to more input.

37 On an anecdotal comparative note, it was significantly easier to schedule interviews with Brazilian high court justices than it was with Argentine justices, and interviews tended to last longer in Brazil.

TABLE 3.1. *Summary of the Brazilian STF's external institutions and internal culture*

External institutions	Formal or informal	Evaluation of STF
Rules guiding eligibility	F	Few but rigorous formal requirements
Rules guiding appointments	F and I	Presidential nominations approved by senate; informal practices exist but do not undermine formal rules
RESULT: Profile of justices	I	Most with significant judicial and political experience; relatively few ties to appointing presidents
Rules guiding tenure/dismissal	F	Mandatory retirement at age 70; constitution outlines clear criteria but vague process for impeachment
Rules regarding size	F	Size of high court (eleven members) stipulated in the constitution
Rules guiding independence from elected leaders	F	STF constitutionally designed as independent institution; elected leaders have not established informal practices to undermine that independence
Rules guiding jurisdiction	F	Very broad; includes original, ordinary, and appellate
Judicial review powers	F	Very broad; abstract and concrete, established in constitution and a series of laws
Mechanisms to reach Court	F	Many ways to access the Court
Rules guiding appeal	F	Permissive appeals structure
Rules regarding docket control	F	STF traditionally could not control docket; weak form of control established with judicial reform in 2004
RESULT: Caseload size	I	Extraordinary caseload; many repeat cases
Rules re: types of decisions	F	Most cases decided by one justice; full Court can issue preliminary, final, and "summary" rulings
Internal culture	**Idea or practice**	**Evaluation of STF**
Beliefs regarding security	I	Most justices evinced security
Institutional differentiation	I	STF justices differentiated from the STF as institution
Leadership designation	P	Two types, elected and intellectual
Internal organization	P	Two chambers; chamber organization differs
Profile of staff	P	No public competition for clerkships; increasingly, clerks are young academic superstars who stay less time in the Court
Role perception (views on judicial review)	I	Relative consensus on role (defend the constitution), but carrying it out means different things to different justices

Internal culture	Idea or practice	Evaluation of STF
Collegiality	P	Atmosphere is mainly collaborative
Consistency/discretion in case review & decision procedures: full Court	P	*Regimento Interno* written to systematize high court functioning; lead justice writes case summary and draft opinion to present to full Court; *Transparency*, STF president sets agenda; decision-making oral and deliberative in form; process is consistent but allows for discretion
Consistency/discretion in case review & decision procedures: individual justices	P	Less consistency in individual justices' decision-making procedures, but also less decision-making discretion as they must follow the full Court's jurisprudence
Transparency	I and P	Court seeks to project an image of transparency
Openness	I and P	Court has established several paths for external inputs

final section illustrates these points using the Brazilian case, demonstrating how the STF's external institutions and internal culture shaped the role it has played in politics and policy-making – and *how* it has played that role – since the 1985 transition to democracy.

Since 1985, and in particular since the promulgation of the 1988 constitution, the STF has been called on to decide a broad range of politically important cases.[38] This analysis examines its decision-making on a systematically selected sample of fifty-five such cases,[39] which while quite diverse, can be loosely organized into three subsets.[40] In one subset, the STF distributed power among the branches of government by rationalizing the new institutional system outlined in the 1988 constitution and by mediating a series of national-level political disputes. In a second subset, the constitutionality of a variety of national economic policies – privatizations, social security reform and retirement benefits, salary adjustments and taxation regulations – was questioned. Finally, a few salient cases regarding rights reached the high court.

The particular range of mechanisms available for cases to reach the STF (and its lack of docket control during the time period under study) likely played important roles in producing this mix of cases. Yet who the justices were and how they saw their

[38] "Politically important" cases are understood as cases in which a Court had the opportunity to endorse or challenge the exercise of government power in a significant way.

[39] My case selection strategy entailed triangulating case mentions three sources: (1) twenty-five expert interviews in which respondents were asked to identify politically important cases; (2) articles on the STF and its rulings drawn from every issue of *O Estado de São Paulo* from 1985 to 2004 inclusively; and (3) a bibliography of local scholarly work on the high court and its rulings. Cases had to be mentioned a certain number of times in each source to enter the sample.

[40] Kapiszewski (2009) discusses these fifty-five cases in more detail.

role likely conditioned the way those mechanisms were employed. Had the justices not been of mixed judicial *and* political backgrounds, for instance, opposition and government leaders might have been more reluctant to use those mechanisms to file politically crucial cases with the Court. Likewise, had the Court lacked meaningful leadership with whom elected leaders could negotiate the outcome of such cases, they might not have consistently filed appeals with the STF, despite the permissivity of the appeals structure.

The fifty-five cases were filed by a diverse range of actors. Although some facet of the state was a party in practically every case in the sample, the original plaintiffs included opposition parties (almost 30 percent of cases), unions (16 percent of cases), the Bar Association (11 percent of cases), individuals (9 percent of cases), governors or states (7 percent of cases), businesses (7 percent of cases) and the public prosecutor (5 percent of cases). Each case was obviously driven by its own dynamics. Yet several of the STF's external institutions (for instance, the mechanisms that potential claimants can use to reach the Court and its broad jurisdiction and judicial review powers), as well as certain aspects of the Court's internal culture (such as its efforts at transparency and openness) likely encouraged this varied set of actors to involve the Court in a diverse range of politically important cases.

With regard to how the STF ruled on these cases, first, the Court issued injunctions on thirty-two of the fifty-five cases in the sample (or 58 percent of the time). On the one hand, the Court's ability to issue injunctions (an external institution) *allowed* it to engage in politics cautiously and selectively; on the other, the political savvy and role perceptions of some of its justices (facets of internal culture) *motivated* it to do so. As Faro de Castro (1997) has asserted, the STF sometimes uses injunctions, which have a narrower reach than do decisions on the merits of a case, to gauge reaction to a particular ruling or to send a "soft signal" to elected leaders that they may ultimately lose a particular case.[41] An injunction may have been used in this way, for example, in ADIn 2010, in which the Court struck down key aspects of public-sector pension reform, a critical government initiative. The full bench issued an injunction in late September 1999 and issued a partial ruling in June 2002, but did not issue a final ruling until March 2004.

Although most injunctions were issued by the Court sitting en banc (twenty-four out of the thirty-two injunctions, or 75 percent), individual justices' ability to issue injunctions under certain conditions offers each STF member the ability to drive the Court's involvement in politics, if only briefly. For example, in 1993 Justice Marco Aurelio Mello issued an injunction suspending the installation of a plebiscite regarding the form and system of government (ADIn 829, ADIn 830), and in 1996, he temporarily suspended significant congressional deliberations on social security

[41] A justice interviewed in connection with this project suggested that the STF might use more political criteria when issuing an injunction, while making a final decision on the merits requires judging "according to the Constitution and the law" (JG-01).

reform (MS 22503). Although the full Court quickly vacated both injunctions, crucial political processes ground to a halt as a result of these suspensions.

The amount of time the STF took to decide the cases in the sample also varied wildly, from twelve days (ADIn 913) to more than a decade (ADIn 295), emblematic of a more general trend in the Court's decision-making. Certainly the Court's slow decision-making on some cases was associated with the sheer number and complexity of the cases on its docket. Yet its external institutions and internal culture likely also contributed to this variation. For instance, the rules regulating access to the Court allowed elected leaders to appeal high court rulings, delaying final rulings and their execution in eight of the fifty-five politically crucial cases under study (15 percent of the sample). Further, the discretion the Court has developed with regard to case review and decision-making allowed STF presidents, motivated by their backgrounds and role perceptions, to delay or accelerate decisions on "more important cases" (AS-03) or otherwise seek the "most opportune" moment to hand down rulings (AS-02; CSE-02; JG-04).[42]

With regard to the direction of the Court's rulings, most scholars of the STF depart from the premise that the Court is very assertive with respect to the elected branches (Arantes 1997; Sadek 1999; Werneck Vianna et al. 1999; Taylor 2004; cf. Koerner 2006). The sample of cases under analysis here suggest a mixed picture: the Court both challenged *and* endorsed the exercise of government power in four cases (8 percent of the time)[43] and endorsed the exercise of government in twenty-six out of forty-eight cases (or 54 percent of the time).[44] The Court's will and ability to challenge elected leaders at all likely have their roots in the STF's formal and de facto independence, as well as in justices' belief that their tenure on the Court and the institution itself are relatively secure from attack by elected leaders. Furthermore, the profiles of the justices and their role perceptions likely go a long way in explaining the particular distribution of rulings.[45] As noted earlier, the Court includes justices with strong backgrounds in the federal judiciary and justices with significant experience in government, with correspondingly contrasting views of the STF's role and of how politically crucial cases should be resolved. This legalista / consequencialista divide was indubitably activated when the Court was ruling on politically crucial cases, and

[42] It bears noting that, overall, the STF is a relatively efficient institution, in contrast to the rest of the federal judiciary (Arantes 2005; Taylor 2006, 2008): it manages to resolve annually practically the same number of cases it receives (STF web site). The Court's internal culture – its procedural consistency, organization into two chambers, and the skill and professionalism of its clerks – likely contributed to this outcome, as did justices' ability to decide cases individually (an external institution).

[43] The parties on both sides of the case were government actors.

[44] The N is 48 rather than 55 due to characteristics of the sample: in two sets of cases the STF issued the same decision (those decisions are only included in the total once); three cases involved the behavior of state or municipal government; and the STF has not issued a final decision on two cases.

[45] To repeat, partisanship does not explain the direction of the Court's rulings: most justices are not identified with any political party, and even the justices appointed by President Lula with strong ties to the PT have not voted consistently to support the interests of the party.

the decisions under study suggest that each position prevailed approximately half the time (that is, the former when the Court challenged the exercise of government power and the later when it endorsed that exercise).

As to the justices' votes on the cases under study, in almost half (twenty-seven out of fifty-five cases), the STF's primary ruling (a longstanding injunction or final decision) was either unanimous or had just one dissent;[46] the Court was badly split (6–5 or 7–4) on less than one-third of the rulings. Two competing internal cultural dynamics contributed to this outcome. On the one hand, the legalista / consequencialista divide made either conflict (and badly split decisions) or compromise (leading to rulings with which most justices could live) inevitable when the Court was deciding politically crucial cases. With the Court's appreciation of the gravity of its role, the mutual respect among its justices, and its overall collegiality, however, compromise became the default decision-making logic, allowing the STF to arrive at "middle of the road" rulings (referred to as *decisões "Salomónicas"* by Brazilian constitutional scholars) that could garner most justices' backing.

Of course, the Court's legalista / consequencialista divide sometimes shone through, even in its compromise rulings. One example is a case in which plaintiffs claimed a particular type of bank account they held had suffered losses with the imposition of five economic stabilization plans (RE 226855). The STF's compromise ruling – that the workers' accounts would be adjusted to compensate for losses generated by the imposition of two of the five plans – was in fact badly divided. Justices with the most previous experience in government formed part of the majority in the 6–4 ruling, while all four dissenting justices had strong backgrounds in the judiciary or the Office of the Public Prosecutor (*Ministerio Público*). Nonetheless, due at least in part to elements of the STF's internal culture beyond role perception, the vote on only a minority of the Court's rulings clearly reflected the legalista / consequencialista divide.

It also bears noting that in a number of the rulings under study, the Court actively sought to limit its role in politics. These rulings are emblematic of a more general dynamic in the Court's decision-making that justices referred to as "defensive jurisprudence." Defensive jurisprudence entails batting away certain cases in an effort to delineate the types of cases the Court will hear, and issuing decisions (or failing to do so) with the intent of discouraging the filing of certain types of cases (AS-02). For instance, in early rulings on a type of concrete review case that practically calls on the STF to fill legislative or regulatory voids (e.g., MI 107),[47] the STF indicated that it would limit itself to notifying the legislature or relevant administrative agency that failure to produce the legislation or regulation for which

[46] More often than not, that one dissent was penned by Justice Marco Aurelio Mello, who was eventually given the nickname "the defeated justice" (*o ministro vencido*) because of the number of times he formed part of the minority or was the single dissenting vote.

[47] The case type is an injunctive writ (*Mandado de Injunção*, MI).

the plaintiff called was unacceptable. Such rulings made the writ a less effective instrument for contesting legislative omissions.[48] Also, because the 1988 constitution's description of the types of civil society groups that may file ADIns (Article 103) did not correspond to an extant juridical category, the STF elaborated its own restrictive standing criteria, likely discouraging civil society groups from filing ADIns (Rocha and Paulo 2003; EG-02). What external institutions or elements of internal culture would lead the STF to dissuade the filing of cases?

The Court's lack of formal docket control, the numerous mechanisms available to access it (which together produced its massive caseload), and its procedural decision-making discretion both encouraged and allowed the development of defensive jurisprudence. Moreover, justices on less-empowered or less-secure Courts may be reluctant to bat away particular types of cases. Such justices might consider the frequency with which political actors and society turn to them as an insurance policy (hoping elected leaders will not threaten an institution whose services they – or their constituents – employ frequently), or might interpret the raw number of decisions they proffer as a reflection of their power. The more secure STF, by contrast, neither hesitated to bat away cases nor needed to receive and decide more and more cases to feel "powerful."

In sum, several of the STF's external institutions and elements of its internal culture discussed in the previous section conditioned and shaped the role the STF played in politics and policy-making and how it played that role during the first two posttransition decades. To be sure, the present analysis is somewhat impressionistic: drawing stronger and potentially generalizable inferences would require further research and careful process tracing to tease out precisely how Courts' external institutions and internal culture shape judicialization in Latin America. Nonetheless, this account is suggestive of the potential that combined institutional and cultural explanations hold for explaining various facets of the judicialization process.

CONCLUSIONS AND IMPLICATIONS

Over the past twenty-five years in Latin America, transitions from authoritarian rule, the turn to neoliberal economic policies and judicial reform efforts have combined to produce a dramatic expansion in the number of disputes potentially subject to adjudication and the potential of judiciaries to resolve them. As a result, today myriad political conflicts are being argued, considered, and resolved in the region's courts of law. Yet we have only begun to understand the ideas and practices that underpin the way judge and justices do their job and the growing importance of courts to politics and policy-making.

48 In subsequent cases (e.g., MI 232 and MI 283), the STF was a bit more assertive, indicating how the legislative void could be filled if the responsible organ were not to do so.

This chapter argued that examining "how courts work" – considering *both* their external institutions and internal culture – can help us to explain why and how they become engaged in politics. The chapter applied this institutional-cultural framework for analyzing courts to the Brazilian Supreme Federal Tribunal. First, it showed how the Court's external institutions helped to shape its internal culture. Then, basing the analysis on a set of politically important cases the STF received between 1985 and 2004, it traced potential connections between the STF's external institutions and internal culture, on the one hand, and several aspects of its engagement in politics, on the other. The analysis sought to demonstrate both how internal culture influenced the way the STF got involved in politics *and* how culture conditioned the effect that external judicial institutions had on the Court's political engagement. Examining these dynamics cross-nationally could help explain variation in "judicialization" across the region.

The framework and findings have two implications for the study of courts and judicialization in Latin America. One promising avenue for future cross-national inquiry is more systematic exploration of high courts' internal culture, and of how the external institutions created by elected leaders to regulate how Courts work shape that culture, both intentionally and unintentionally. The findings resulting from such an analysis could have important implications for institutional design and for judicial reform initiatives. Further research could also be carried out on how informal judicial institutions – both external and internal to courts – develop and what relationships they maintain with related formal institutions. "Law-on-the-books" versus "law-in-action" dichotomies suggest that informal practices develop when formal rules are vague, insufficient, or flexible, yet we can imagine that they may also develop when formal rules are perfectly clear and relatively inflexible, and that each situation has different implications for judicial behavior. Moreover, as noted earlier, once informal institutions are established, many types of relationships may form between them and formal institutions, from subversion to complementarity. While the latter scenario sounds more promising than the former, it may not be. And even in the former, it seems unreasonable to assume that formal institutions are automatically superior. In short, further study of the relationships between formal and informal institutions, and how they influence each other and the judicialization process, seems warranted.

Second, in any context, broader institutional, social, political, and economic forces also affect judicialization: the institutional-cultural approach introduced here certainly does not tell the complete causal story. Nonetheless, the high court institutional-cultural matrix discussed in this chapter certainly mediates the effect such forces have on judicialization. For instance, considering how two courts differ with regard to their external institutions and internal culture could help to account for variation in judicialization across quite similar strategic environments (which a strategic account of judicial behavior might be at a loss to explain). In short, the institutional-cultural approach can help us better account for seemingly anomalous situations in which high courts positioned in relatively similar institutional or political opportunity structures behave differently.

External judicial institutions and internal judicial culture are likely important pieces of the judicialization causal puzzle in many contexts. Further exploration of these judicial features, how they interact and how those interactions influence judicialization may reveal latent yet crucial synergies between the institutional and cultural approaches to explaining judicial behavior. As Stone Sweet (1999: 150–1) has highlighted, how quintessential culturalists such as Eckstein (1988) view culture is not so different from how quintessential institutionalists such as North (1990) view institutions: both facilitate human interaction by narrowing, and investing with meaning, the available choices for conduct. Given what is at stake when high courts rule on politically significant cases, we need to better understand the degree to which "how courts work" guides how they become involved in politics and policy-making in contemporary Latin America.

References

Arantes, Rogério Bastos. 1997. *Judiciário e política no Brasil*. São Paulo: IDESP.

Arantes, Rogério Bastos. 2005. "Constitutionalism, the Expansion of Justice, and the Judicialization of Politics in Brazil." In *The Judicialization of Politics in Latin America*, Rachel Sieder, Line Schjolden, and Alan Angell, eds. New York: Palgrave. 231–62.

Ballard, Megan J. 1999. "The Clash Between Local Courts and Global Economics: The Politics of Judicial Reform in Brazil." *Berkeley Journal of International Law*, 17:230–76.

Brinks, Daniel. 2005. "Judicial Reform and Independence in Brazil and Argentina: The Beginning of New Millennium?" *Texas International Law Journal*, 40:595–622.

Cepeda Espinosa, Manuel J. 2005. "The Judicialization of Politics in Colombia: The Old and the New." In *The Judicialization of Politics in Latin America*, Rachel Sieder, Line Schjolden, and Alan Angell, eds. New York: Palgrave. 67–103.

Chavez, Rebecca. 2004. *Rule of Law in Nascent Democracies: Judicial Politics in Argentina*. Stanford: Stanford University Press.

Colon, Edgardo. 2003. "The State of Judicial Independence of Latin America: A Framework for Evaluating Judicial Independence and the Success or Failure of Judicial Reforms." Ph.D. Dissertation, University of Houston.

Couso, Javier A. 2002. "The Politics of Judicial Review in Latin America: Chile in Comparative Perspective." Ph.D. Dissertation, University of California, Berkeley.

Couso, Javier A. 2005. "Judicial Independence in Latin America: The Lessons of History in the Search for an Always Elusive Ideal." In *Institutions and Public Law: Comparative Approaches*, Tom Ginsburg and Robert A. Kagan, eds. New York: Peter Lang. 203–24.

Dolinger, Jacob. 1990. "The Influence of American Constitutional Law on the Brazilian Legal System." *The American Journal of Comparative Law*, 38:803–37.

Eckstein, Harry. 1988. "A Culturalist Theory of Political Change." *American Political Science Review*, 82:789–804.

Faro de Castro, Marcus. 1997. "The Courts, Law, and Democracy in Brazil." *International Social Science Journal*, 49:241–52.

Finkel, Jodi. 2008. *Judicial Reform as Political Insurance: Argentina, Peru, and Mexico in the 1990s*. Stanford: Stanford University Press.

Frühling, Hugo. 1984. "Law in Society: Social Transformation and the Crisis of Law in Chile, 1830–1970." Ph.D. Dissertation, Harvard University School of Law.

Helmke, Gretchen. 2000. "Ruling Against the Rulers: Court-Executive Relations in Argentina under Dictatorship and Democracy." Ph.D. Dissertation, University of Chicago.

Helmke, Gretchen. 2005. *Courts under Constraints: Judges, Generals, and Presidents in Argentina*. Cambridge: Cambridge University Press.

Helmke, Gretchen, and Stephen Levitsky. 2004. "Informal Institutions and Comparative Politics: A Research Agenda," *Perspectives on Politics*, 2:725–40.

Helmke, Gretchen, and Stephen Levitsky, eds. 2006. *Informal Institutions and Democracy: Lessons from Latin America*. Baltimore: John Hopkins University Press.

Hilbink, Lisa. 2007. *The Politics of Judicial Apoliticism: Chile in Comparative Perspective*. Cambridge: Cambridge University Press.

Hilbink, Lisa. 2009. "The Origins of Positive Judicial Independence." Paper delivered at the Congress of the Latin American Studies Association, June 11–14, Rio de Janeiro, Brazil.

Huneeus, Alexandra. 2010. "Judging with a Guilty Conscience: The Chilean Judiciary's Human Rights Turn," *Law & Social Inquiry*, 35:1.

Ingram, Matthew. 2009. "Not All Courts Are Created Equal(ly): A Causal Logics Approach to Clarifying Causation in Judicial Politics." Paper presented at the annual meeting of the American Political Science Association, September 3–6, Toronto, Canada.

Kapiszewski, Diana. 2007. "Challenging Decisions: High Courts and Economic Governance in Argentina and Brazil." Ph.D. Dissertation, University of California, Berkeley.

Kapiszewski, Diana. 2009. Powerbroker, Policymaker, or Rights Protector? The Brazilian *Supremo Tribunal Federal* in Transition. Paper presented at the annual meeting of the American Political Science Association, September 2–6, Toronto, Canada.

Karst, Kenneth L,. and Keith S. Rosenn. 1975. *Law and Development in Latin America*. Berkeley: University of California Press.

Koerner, Andrei. 2006. "Decisão judicial, instituições e estrutura socioeconômica por uma análise política do pensamento jurídico brasileiro." In *História da Justiça Penal no Brasil Pesquisas e Análises*, Andrei Koerner, ed. São Paulo: IBCCRIM. 259–81.

Larkins, Christopher M. 1996. "Judicial Independence and Democratization: A Theoretical and Conceptual Analysis." *American Journal of Comparative Law*, 44:605–26.

Lauth, Han-Joachim. 2005. The Impact of Informal Institutions on Democratic Performance: Theoretical Reflections and Empirical Findings. Paper presented at the annual meeting of the American Political Science Association, September 1–4, Washington, D.C.

Miller, Jonathan. 1997. "Judicial Review and Constitutional Stability: A Sociology of the U.S. Model and its Collapse in Argentina." *Hastings International and Comparative Law Journal*, 21:77–176.

Navia, Patricio, and Julio Ríos-Figueroa. 2005. "The Constitutional Adjudication Mosaic of Latin America." *Comparative Political Studies*, 38:189–217.

North, Douglass C. 1990. *Institutions, Institutional Change, and Economic Performance*. New York: Cambridge University Press.

O'Donnell, Guillermo. 2006. "On Informal Institutions, Once Again." In *Informal Institutions and Democracy: Lessons from Latin America*, Gretchen Helmke and Steven Levitsky, eds. Baltimore: John Hopkins University Press. 285–9.

Ríos-Figueroa, Julio. 2006. "Institutional Models of Judicial Independence and Corruption in Latin America." Ph.D. Dissertation, New York University.

Ríos-Figueroa, Julio, and Matthew M. Taylor. 2006. "Institutional Determinants of the Judicialization of Policy in Brazil and Mexico." *Journal of Latin American Studies*, 38:739–66.

Rocha, Zélio Maia da, and Vicente Paulo. 2003. *O controle de constitucionalidade nos concursos públicos*. Brasília: Vestcon.

Rosenn, Keith S. 1984. "Brazil's Legal Culture: The Jeito Revisited." *Florida International Law Journal*, 1:1–43.

Rosenn, Keith S. 1990. "Brazil's New Constitution: An Exercise in Transient Constitutionalism for a Transitional Society." *American Journal of Comparative Law*, 38(4): 773–802.

Sadek, Mara Teresa. 1995. "A crise do judiciário vista pelos juízes: Resultados da pesquisa quantitativa." In *Uma introdução ao estudo da justiça*, Maria Teresa Sadek, ed. São Paulo: Editora Sumaré. 17–23.

Sadek, Mara Teresa. 1999. "O Poder Judiciário na Reforma do Estado." In *Sociedade e Estado em Transformação*, Luiz Carlos Bresser Pereira, Jorge Wilheim, and Lourdes Sola, eds. São Paulo Editora UNESP. 293–324.

Santiso, Carlos. 2004. "Economic Reform and Judicial Governance in Brazil: Balancing Independence with Accountability." In *Democratization and the Judiciary: The Accountability Function of Courts in New Democracies*, Siri Gloppen, Robert Gargarella, and Elin Skaar, eds. London: Frank Cass. 161–80.

Segal, Jeffrey A., and Harold J. Spaeth. 1993. *The Supreme Court and the Attitudinal Model*. Cambridge: Cambridge University Press.

Staton, Jeffrey. 2006. "Constitutional Review and the Selective Promotion of Case Results." *American Journal of Political Science*, 50(1): 98–112.

Stone Sweet, Alec. 1999. "Judicialization and the Construction of Governance." *Comparative Political Studies*, 23:147–84.

Tate, C. Neal, and Torbjörn Vallinder, eds. 1995. *The Global Expansion of Judicial Power*. New York: New York University Press.

Taylor, Matthew. 2004. "Activating Judges: Courts, Institutional Structure, and the Judicialization of Policy Reform in Brazil, 1988–2002." Ph.D. Dissertation, Georgetown University.

Taylor, Matthew. 2006. "Courts, Policy Contestation, and the Legitimation of Economic Reform under Cardoso." In *Statecraft and Monetary Authority: Democracy and Financial Order in Brazil*, Lourdes Sola and Laurence Whitehead, eds. Oxford: Centre for Brazilian Studies. 205–36.

Taylor, Matthew. 2008. *Judging Policy: Courts and Policy Reform in Democratic Brazil*. Stanford: Stanford University Press.

Tsai, Kellee S. 2006. "Adaptive Informal Institutions and Endogenous Institutional Change in China." *World Politics*, 59: 116.

Viotti da Costa, Emilia. 2001. *STF: O Supremo Tribunal Federal e a Constração da Cidadania*. São Paulo: Instituto de Estudios Jurídicos e Económicos SC Ltda.

Werneck Vianna, Luiz, Maria Alice Rezende de Carvalho, Manuel Palacios Cunha Melo and Marcelo Baumann Burgos. 1999. "*A judicialização da política e das relações sociais no Brasil.*" Rio de Janeiro: Editora Revan.

Whittington, Keith. 2000. "Once More Unto the Breach: Post-Behavioral Approaches to Judicial Politics." *Law and Social Inquiry* 25:601–32.

Wilson, Bruce M. 2005. "Changing Dynamics: The Political Impact of Costa Rica's Constitutional Court." In *The Judicialization of Politics in Latin America*. Rachel Sieder, Line Schjolden, and Alan Angell, eds. New York: Palgrave. 47–65.

Wilson, Bruce M., and Juan C. Rodríguez Cordero. 2006. "Legal Opportunity Structures and Social Movements: The Effects of Institutional Change on Costa Rican Politics." *Comparative Political Studies*, 39:325–51.

4

More Power, More Rights? The Supreme Court and Society in Mexico

Karina Ansolabehere

INTRODUCTION

Under what conditions does an increase in the power of supreme courts to control other branches of government translate into greater protection of citizens' rights? In order to understand this process, we should consider not only the ability of the court to control the other branches, but also changes in the relationship between the court and the rest of the judiciary, and between the court and society. This chapter focuses on the case of Mexico, analyzing the interpretative framework developed by the Mexican Supreme Court on freedom of expression, freedom of association, and indigenous rights between 1988 and 2007.[1]

A number of constitutional reforms after 1988, together with changes in the political and social context that modified the role of the Supreme Court in Mexican society, meant that the court became more politically powerful, more socially visible, and less omnipotent within the judiciary. The mandate of the high court to resolve conflicts between branches of government and to rule on the constitutionality or unconstitutionality of laws (judicial review) was strengthened. At the same time, the resolution of other cases, such as violations of citizens' individual rights, was progressively delegated to the appeals tribunals (*Tribunales Colegiados de Circuito* or TCC). Similarly, the power of the court to manage the judiciary was slowly curtailed though the creation of two key bodies: the Federal Council of the Judiciary (*Consejo de la Judicatura Federal*), created in 1994, and the Electoral Tribunal of the Federal Judiciary (*Tribunal Electoral del Poder Judicial de la Federación*), created

[1] The year 1988 was selected as the starting point of this analysis because it was in that year that a constitutional reform was implemented that increased the Supreme Court's powers of constitutional control to resolve conflicts between the different branches of government.

in 1996.[2] In 2002, the Law of Transparency and Access to Public Information was approved, giving the court greater public visibility.[3]

The institutional reforms were aimed at converting the Court into an arbiter of political conflicts between majorities and minorities within the legislature and between the political branches in Mexico's nascent democracy.[4] The Supreme Court ceased being a court of the government and became instead a court for politicians: its functions are more for the political class than for the citizenry. Even as the reforms made the Court more visible, they did not alter the rules of standing to make the Court more accessible to citizens in individual rights' cases. This could be considered a possible cause of the low level of judicialization in rights' cases within the Court's jurisdiction (the Court has developed a mere thirty-eight main doctrines, or "*criterios*,"[5] with respect to rights' issues in twenty years). During the period under examination, however, there has been an increase in *criterios* relative to the rights considered here. This increase in the Court's attention to rights has led to the establishment of rights-favorable interpretative frameworks in some instances, and rights-restrictive frameworks in others.

The goal of this chapter is to analyze the manner in which the consolidation of the Mexican Supreme Court (*Suprema Corte de Justicia*) as a political arbiter, together with the appearance of weak counterweights within the judiciary and society, have helped shape the Court's interpretative frameworks on citizenship rights. The chapter hypothesizes that a close relationship exists between the interpretative frameworks developed by the court, on the one hand, and the relations of the court with the executive and legislature, the judiciary, and ordinary citizens, on the other.

The chapter is divided into four sections. The first sets out the analytical model applied. The second analyzes the characteristics of the Supreme Court's relations with the political branches and society at large from 1988 to the present. The third contains a description of the interpretative frameworks developed by the court with regards to freedom of expression, freedom of association, and indigenous rights. The final section analyzes the relationship between the changing socio-political relations of the court and its emerging rights jurisprudence.

2 The constitutional reform in electoral matters carried out in 2007 laid out the powers of constitutional interpretation of the Electoral Tribunal of the Federal Judiciary. From that moment onward the monopoly of the Supreme Court over constitutional interpretation was broken.

3 Sentences are publicly available and a judicial channel was created allowing citizens to follow debates on live television.

4 Mexico was governed by the Partido Revolucionario Institucional (PRI) for more than seventy years, in a form of presidentialism exercised by a hegemonic party, wherein the president exercised broad powers of political control over the other branches of government and over the states of the federal republic (Weldon 2002; Valdés Ugalde 2002).

5 In Mexico, the term *criterios* refers to the main rules established in "thesis of jurisprudence" (*tesis de jurisprudencia*). The Mexican Supreme Court, after a sentence, selects the main rules that it develops. Its rules are criteria that are followed by lower courts in its decisions and used by lawyers to build their arguments.

ANALYTICAL APPROACHES

Post-transition democratic processes have shown that the guarantee and protection of fundamental rights is not an automatic consequence of changes in political regime, nor of an increase in judicial power. A mosaic of situations exists in this respect in Latin America, with wide variations between countries. If we accept that the judiciary and especially high courts ideally exercise the role of protecting rights, the regional picture is one of uncertainty. In some supreme courts or constitutional courts we can perhaps talk about a *rights* revolution – the active promotion of citizens' rights by the judiciary (Epp 1998). The cases of Costa Rica (Wilson 2007) and Colombia (Wilson 2007; Cepeda Espinoza 2005) are paradigmatic in this respect. There are powerful courts that have not undergone a rights revolution, such as the Argentine Supreme Court (*Asociación para los derechos civiles* 2008; Ansolabehere 2008), and powerful courts that have explicitly rejected a "rights-active" stance, the most characteristic example being the Chilean Supreme Court (Couso 2005; Hilbink 2007).

In analyzing the relationship between courts and rights, two approaches have been developed in recent years that attempt to identify the factors favoring a rights revolution. These are (1) those emphasizing support structures for legal mobilization, and (2) those emphasizing institutional factors that increase access to justice.

The key reference for the support structure school of explanation is Charles Epp's seminal work, *The Rights Revolution* (1998). Epp argued that the determinant factor permitting a "rights revolution" was the existence of support structures for legal mobilization. Support structures involve the following elements: strategic organization of litigating lawyers, litigating lawyers who are specialists in rights, and resources to finance strategic litigation. In this view, the explanation for rights revolutions in different common-law countries lies in the capacity of civil society to develop a support structure. It is civil society, rather than the nature of the law or of the justice system, that produces this kind of change. Epp argues that the judiciary, especially supreme courts or their equivalents, admitting rights cases is related to repeated litigation on similar issues over time, and that this can only be achieved through a legal support structure with sufficient resources.[6]

When the high courts have discretion over their caseload, they choose those cases that will become key issues for the judiciary as a whole. For this reason, it is important not just to litigate, but to litigate in a sustained manner to establish precedents and to open new avenues of interpretation. However, court cases are expensive and slow, and their successful prosecution requires trained lawyers with sufficient incentives to take them on. Be they a lawyer or an ordinary citizen, it is very expensive for individuals to take rights cases to court.[7] Strategic rights litigation can only exist

[6] Epp focuses principally on civil rights and individual freedoms.

[7] It is for this reason that firms and corporations, rather than individuals, have tended to use the judiciary to achieve their objectives: they have sufficient resources to enable them to do this, and the expected benefits for them outweigh the costs of litigation.

where there are organizations that promote it over the long term, and that receive governmental or nongovernmental support to do so.[8]

The second approach focuses not on the capacities of civil society but rather on the reduction in barriers to access to constitutional jurisdiction that may facilitate a rights revolution. The cases of Costa Rica and Colombia serve to illustrate this point (Wilson 2007; Cepeda Espinoza 2005). In the late 1980s and early 1990s, both countries carried out pro-rights constitutional and judicial reforms. The rights of historically excluded groups were explicitly recognized and constitutional courts or their equivalents were established.

Although there is no evidence of a significant support structure for legal mobilization in either country (Wilson 2007), there has been an exponential increase in the judicialization of rights issues and a pro-rights tendency on the part of the courts subsequent to these reforms. The main explanatory factor is access to justice. The reforms removed barriers to access to the Court's jurisdiction over constitutional rights issues. Neither the Colombian figure of the *tutela* nor the Costa Rican *amparo*, mechanisms designed to protect individual rights, require the support of a lawyer to file a claim and they can be presented at any time.

Both approaches concur that changes in courts' interpretative frameworks of rights are linked to the ability of groups in society to pressure the judiciary. This pressure can be organized, as in the case of support structures for legal mobilization, or individual, as in the case of access (most access-driven cases are individual appeals, although not exclusively so). Nonetheless, both explanations relegate the relations of the court itself with the political branches and with the rest of the judiciary to second place. In Mexico, political and legal changes have increased expectations about law (Fix Fierro and López Ayllón 2002). As mentioned earlier, while institutional reforms have been carried out that have modified the position of Supreme Court of justice, they have not necessarily made the Court more accessible to citizens (Magaloni and Saldívar 2007). Consequently, groups and individuals do not enjoy the kind of access necessary to exert pressure on the judiciary to develop a more pro-rights jurisprudence.

At the same time, the explanation of legal support structures (Epp 1998, 2005) is plausible for the case of political parties and corporate interest groups. Some 66 percent of jurisprudential doctrines, or *criterios*, developed by the Court between 1988 and 2007 are a response to cases promoted by political parties and other organizations, while only 34 percent originated with individual rights' claims. The Mexican case demonstrates an increase in judicial consideration of rights. This development, however, is not associated with a massive increase in litigation and a dialogue on the conflicts raised in those cases.

It is not only legal mobilization or access, but also the broader context of the Court's relations and its opportunity structures that facilitate or impede modifications to its

[8] For reasons of space the issue of the conditions that facilitate the emergence of these kinds of support structures is not addressed here, but it is of course an important comparative question.

interpretative frameworks. In this sense, this study endorses the "political regime" approach to studying judicial power (Gillman 2004; Dahl 1957). One of the main strengths of this approach is that it promotes a movement away from studies centered on judges toward studies concerned with the "political construction of judicial power" (Gillman 2004: 5). According to Gillman, courts are not only "a mechanism to promote judges' preferences, but also to promote the goals of non-judicial actors" (2004: 5). From this perspective, the wider political and social relations of supreme courts matter, and the jurisprudential criteria they develop are not independent of these.

Many studies have analyzed changes in the role of the judiciary in democratic regimes, such as the growing judicialization of social and political conflicts (Sieder et al., 2005; Ansolabehere 2005). Some of this research identifies judicial culture, or in broader terms, legal cultures as an important element in explaining the success of institutional reforms to the judiciary (Pásara 2004; Domingo 2005; Friedman, 1997). Some even consider judicialization an indicator of changes in legal culture. However, although many studies make reference to legal culture, there is no unanimously accepted definition of the concept (Nelken 1997; Friedman 1997; Cotterrell 1997; Pérez Perdomo and Friedman 2003; Hertogh 2004). The most commonly cited definition makes reference to the attitudes, ideas, expectations, and values that people have with respect to their legal systems, institutions and rules (Friedman 2003). The lack of conceptual definition of legal culture reflects debates around the concept of culture in general and political culture in particular, the latter being particularly illustrative: political culture is a controversial, complex, and all-encompassing term (Almond and Verba 1963, 1980; Peruzzotti 1997) and no consensus exists about its causal role in political phenomena (Knight 2008; Cleary and Stokes 2006).

In this chapter I have chosen to analyze interpretative frameworks around rights rather than referring to legal culture. An interpretative framework (Snow and Benford, 1988) points to the process of construction of meanings to define conceptions about different subgroups of rights and the main issues linked to each one. According to this line of interpretation, this process of the construction of meanings is the product of the place of the court within the political regime. The process reflects the interplay among interests (of judges and other actors), institutions, relations, social roles, and resources, and, in turn, it affects these factors. Nevertheless, the focus here is on the type of relations that the court maintains within the judiciary (with the lower echelons of the judiciary and other bodies) and with elements outside the judiciary (with the political branches and with citizens), and how these relations influence the development of an interpretative framework about rights. The interpretative framework is understood as the outcome of a process through which a rights-relevant issue is constructed on the basis of jurisprudential thesis, or *criterios*, bringing together meanings and the substantive issues associated with those meanings. The following sections analyze the ways in which changes in the relations of the Mexican Court with external actors correlated with shifts in the interpretative framework around the three groups of rights considered here.

TABLE 4.1. *Scheme of relationship*

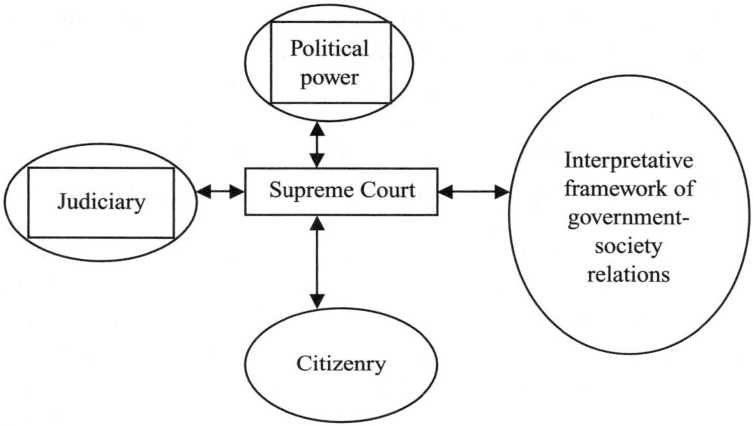

The main advantage of this perspective is that it emphasizes intermediate-level factors (relations), rather than macro-level factors (political or social context) or micro-level factors (judges' preferences), with the aim of analyze medium-term tendencies in the interpretative criteria developed by the courts. Instead of analyzing specific decisions, a focus on tendencies or interpretative frameworks allows us to identify elements of movement or change in the courts' criteria that are not just linked to the preferences of judges. Building on previous work (Ansolabehere 2007, 2006, 2005), I propose the scheme of table 4.1 for the purposes of empirical analysis:

Although capturing the relation between these different elements is a complex process, three elements in particular deserve attention: 1) the capacity of supreme courts and political branches to control each other; 2) the relations between the supreme court and the judiciary as a whole; and 3) the degree of fluidity in relations between the supreme court and society. With respect to the third element, the focus is restricted to the degree of visibility and accessibility of the court to citizens. To the extent that the Court's decisions are mandatory for the parties involved, the degree of control the court has over society is a constant. However, changes in this capacity to control society are linked to the ways the court uses judicial action to shape relations between government and society. Changes in counterweights also imply changes in the Court's opportunity structures[9] and with the ways rights are conceived. (See Annex 1 to a description of all possible relationships)

The doctrines or *criterios* established by courts are derived not only from the mechanical application of the law, but also from the opportunity structure in which those courts are situated. For example, it is assumed that high courts are interested

[9] This concept is drawn from social movement theory (McAdam 1996), which proposes that processes of contentious collective action are facilitated by the existence of a political opportunity structure when mobilized social actors identify favorable conditions to advance their demands.

in securing a high degree of social support for their actions. Higher visibility allows court decisions to be more widely known, which in turn affects the degree of support the court receives. The capacity of each of the parties in a relationship to control the other is conceptualized in the following manner:

1) Relationship Between the Court and the Political Branches

Mutual control is strong when the courts have concentrated judicial review power; and when the political branches can modify the key rules governing the court's functions, such as the number of justices or budgetary allocations, through a parliamentary majority. Mutual control is weak when constitutional control is not exclusively exercised by the Supreme Court or constitutional court (diffuse control); when the judicial ruling does not set precedent; and when the political branches can neither modify the key rules governing the court's functions (because these rules are themselves set out in the constitution) nor affect the court's budgetary allocation (where the court has budgetary autonomy). Two other combinations are possible: strong control of the court over the political branches and weak control of the latter over the court, and conversely, strong control of the political branches over the court that, in turn, is weak vis-á-vis the political branches.

2) Relationship Between the Court and the Judiciary

Mutual control is strong when the court controls the appointment of judges and their promotions; when rules exist establishing the mandatory application of the court's jurisprudence by the lower courts; and when the lower echelons of the judiciary have strong professional organizations. Weak mutual control exists when the court does not appoint judges; when there are no rules stipulating the mandatory application of the court's jurisprudence; and when the lower instances of the judiciary lack strong professional organizations. Two additional combinations are possible: strong control of the court over the judiciary and weak control of the judiciary over the court, and the inverse – strong control of the judiciary over the court and weak control of the court over the judiciary.

3) Relationship Between the Court and Society

This relation is considered to be fluid when constitutional appeals to the Supreme Court are easily accessible for citizens, and when the decision-making process and governance of the judiciary are visible. It is considered to be nonfluid when the opposite conditions prevail. The other possible combinations are a visible but non-accessible court and an accessible court with low social visibility.

Table 4.2 presents the different combinations of possible links in each dimension of the analysis.

In relation to the other dimension of the relationship – the court's interpretative frameworks regarding rights – the focus here is on the development of how rights are understood. The following elements are taken into account: the tendency of the jurisprudence, including whether it is pro-rights or restrictive of rights; the substantive issue and the corresponding right invoked; and the meaning associated with the decision. The interpretative framework is the sum of these three dimensions. To characterize the tendency of the jurisprudential criteria, each right in question was defined on the basis of specialist literature or specific documents. In the case of (a) freedom of expression, the main meaning is the free circulation of ideas, opinions, and information (which includes various subissues, such as freedom of the press, right to information, and ownership of the mass media) (Loreti 2006; Álvarez 2006). With respect to (b) freedom of association, the central meaning is the ability of people to meet and form associations in pursuit of individual and collective political, trade union, and other objectives, without impediments, above and beyond the rights established by the laws of a democratic society (Asamblea General de la Organización de Estados Americanos, 1970. American Convention of Human Rights, Art. 16). Finally, with respect to indigenous rights, the central meanings are those of self-determination, the use and ownership of land, and the preservation of culture (Asamblea General de Naciones Unidas, 2007 Declaration on the Rights of Indigenous Peoples 2007). A jurisprudential criterion is considered pro-rights when it comes closest to the meaning on which the right focuses; it is considered rights restrictive when it establishes exceptions regarding the right in question.

Second, issues related to each right developed by the court were identified for the period under study on the basis of empirical analysis, together with the contents associated with those decisions, to allow for the tracking of changes over time. To guarantee the viability of the classification, a control was carried out that involved the classification of the same content on different occasions in the same manner (Weber 1990). The following section analyzes the changes in the relations of the Mexican Supreme Court during the period under study. Finally, tendencies in the interpretative framework are considered according to the previously discussed outline.

THE MEXICAN SUPREME COURT AND ITS BROADER RELATIONS

The Mexican Supreme Court (*Suprema Corte*) has been closely associated with politics: it has not established a clear division between its jurisdictional function and its political role; and, at the same time, through the country's democratic transition it has gained broader powers to resolve political conflicts (Ansolabehere

TABLE 4.2. *Characteristics of the relations in each dimension of the analysis*

Relations	Characteristics of mutual control			
Relationship between the Supreme Court and the political branches	Strong-strong Heteronomous	Strong-weak Judicial autonomy	Weak-strong Political autonomy	Weak-weak Autonomous
Relationship between the Supreme Court and the judiciary	Strong-strong Heteronomous	Strong-weak Absolute sovereignty	Weak-strong *Primus internares*	Weak-weak Autonomous
Relationship between the Supreme Court and citizens	Visible-accessible Fluid	Visible-inaccessible Informative	Nonvisible-accessible Jurisdictional	Low visibility, inaccessible Nonfluid
Profile	Powerful with strong political, judicial, and social counterweights Arbiter of political conflicts, and arbiter of rights-related conflicts	Powerful with weak political, judicial, and social counterweights Arbiter of political process	Weak with strong counterweights Arbiter of rights-related conflicts	Weak with weak counterweights Weak arbiter

2007; Domingo 2000; Magaloni 2003; Fix Fierro 1999).[10] The institutional design of the Mexican democratic transition created a constitutional tribunal that serves politicians before citizens by allowing the court to intervene in the resolution of political conflicts and transferring its responsibilities related to the violation of individual rights to the appeals tribunals (*Tribunales Colegiados de Circuito*).[11] On the one hand, the mechanisms created to increase access to the court's jurisdiction and to present a constitutional challenge are for the exclusive benefit of different federal and local agencies, political minorities, and political parties in matters of electoral questions (Art. 105 of the constitution). On the other hand, the Court's powers to resolve *amparo* appeals (a mechanism that allows individuals to present a legal claim against the state for violation of their individual guarantees) have been progressively delegated to the appeals tribunals, although the Court reserves the right to decide on cases it considers relevant.

The period 1988–2007 was one of great change for the relations of the Mexican Supreme Court. It was characterized by the following elements:

- An increase in the Court's independence vis-á-vis the political branches
- An increase in the ability of the Court to control the political branches
- A reduction in the political branches' control over the judiciary
- An increase in the fluidity of the Court's relationship with society.

During the last twenty years, the Court went from being politically weak, socially invisible, and sovereign over the judiciary to being more politically powerful, more socially visible, and less sovereign over the judiciary. This trend occurred within the broader context of an increase in political pluralism.[12] In the terms set out in Table 4.2, the court ceased being a weak court with strong counterweights and moved closer to being a strong court with weak political, legal, and social counterweights. Between 1988 and 2007, three phases of the court's relations can be discerned. The first phase extends from 1988 to 1994, the second from 1995 to 2003, and the third from 2003 to 2007.

[10] The high degree of mobility of justices until the 1994 reforms is a good example. The annual reports presented by the president of the court indicate the number of permissions that were granted to judges for them to take on political offices. The court was not the last stage in justices' careers, but rather a stepping stone that enabled them to be appointed to a political post.

[11] These are equivalent to appeals tribunals and are composed of three judges.

[12] México fue gobernado por casi 70 años por el mismo partido, el Partido Revolucionario Institucional, constituyendo lo que Giovanni Sartori calificó como un sistema de partido hegemónico. Si bien no hay estricto acuerdo sobre la fecha exacta, una mayoría de trabajos coinciden en señalar a 1977 como año de comienzo de un proceso de liberalización política y posteriormente de transición a la democracia, que a través de reformas electorales sucesivas, aumentó considerablemente el pluralismo político en las instituciones representativas. En 1997, por primera vez el PRI perdió la mayoría en la Cámara de Diputados, y en 2000 por primera vez perdió la elección presidencial.

First Phase: After the 1987 constitutional reform,[13] the Court became strong and had strong political counterweights. This responds to the heteronymous nature of its relationship with the political branches, although this was also linked to its complete sovereignty over the judiciary and the fact that it maintained a relatively static relationship with society. In terms of the relationship between the Court and the political branches, the reform established the absolute control of the Court over issues of constitutionality, and developed mechanisms that reduced the ability of the political branches to intervene. With respect to the relationship with the judiciary, there were no notable changes: the Court retained its powers to appoint and remove judges and magistrates, and its jurisprudence is mandatory for the lower courts, where it retains control of legality. Finally, in its relationship with society, to the extent that the Court's judgments were not public, the only mechanism available to increase awareness of its actions was through the annual report that the president of the Court presents every 15th of December. The Court became more powerful within a broader context of increase in political competition (Lujambio 2000; Merino 2003).

Second Phase: After the 1994 constitutional reform,[14] the Court consolidated its role as an arbiter of political conflicts (becoming stronger) and lost counterweights within the political branches, chiefly because of changes in the rules of designation and requirements to access the Court. These changes, plus shifts in the broader political context, meant that the control of the Court over the judiciary declined at the same time as its relationship with society remained static. The 1995 reform that extended the Court's constitutional jurisdiction not only increased the kinds of conflicts between the political branches in which the Court could intervene, but also created a constitutional challenge that allowed political minorities, political parties (for electoral matters), and other state agencies to recur to the Court to question the legality of laws and regulations (Art. 105 of the constitution). With regard to the relationship between the Supreme Court and the judiciary, the 1995 reform created the Federal Judicial Council (*Consejo de la Judicatura Federal*), which was awarded powers to designate, remove, and promote judges, and to carry out administrative tasks relating to the operation of the judiciary. The Court, then, was made more politically powerful within a broader context of the consolidation of political competition. In line with Jodi Finkel's work (1998; 2004), we might

13 *Publicada en el Diario Oficial de la Federación* el 10/08/1987.

14 Published in the *Diario Oficial de la Federación*, December 31, 1994. Reforms were also carried out in 1993, although these were less important for the overall model of the judiciary. These reforms were related to the competencies of the ordinary and federal courts, as well as with the procedures for *amparo* cases. They established that all such controversies presented to the lower courts within the federal judiciary would be subject to the procedures established in accordance with the Constitution. They also specified that the Supreme Court had exclusive competence over controversies between one or more states of the republic and the capital (known as the Federal District), between the branches of government within any given state, and between the organs of government within the Federal District.

conclude that these changes are indeed a product of the political opening. At the same time, a growing judicialization of political conflict was observable (Ríos 2004).

Third Phase: The approval of the Federal Law of Transparency and Access in 2003 produced a new shift in the Court's relations.[15] This law set out the obligations of the different state branches to provide public access to information, for example the publication of definitive sentences, the curriculum vitae of ministers, and the budget. The Court simultaneously drew up a set of internal regulations about transparency and public access to information, and created a judicial TV channel that transmitted the Court's sessions live. This measure increased the visibility of the Court for citizens in general, at the same time as it lost political counterweights. In short, the Court maintained its autonomy with respect to the political branches, became less sovereign over the judiciary, and more socially visible. Its relationship with the judiciary and the political branches remained stable, without major transformations, but its relationship with society changed. It became more visible, although it was no more accessible to citizens.[16] Today, we have a powerful Court with weak judicial, political, and social counterweights in a context of increased political competition and a greater degree of legal mobilization on the part of actors within the political branches.

Table 4.3 synthesizes the changes identified.

How did these changes affect the interpretative framework on the rights issues identified as the focus of the study?

RIGHTS DECISIONS OF THE MEXICAN SUPREME COURT

The first element that should be emphasized is that the Mexican Supreme Court has established few criteria related to the group of rights under consideration here (freedom of expression, freedom of association, and indigenous rights). As noted earlier, the institutional design restricted the jurisdiction of the court rather than extend it to the protection of rights. The units of analysis used here are the jurisprudential theses (*criterios*)[17] and isolated thesis (*tesis aisladas*)[18] developed by the Supreme Court

[15] It is important to note that a new change occurred with regard to access to public information. On July 20, 2007, a reform of Article 6 of the Constitution was approved, establishing more precise parameters and principles governing access to information. The principle of "maximum publicity" (fraction I) and the availability of information to whomever requests it, without them necessarily having a legal interest (fraction III) are important in this respect.

[16] A new change occurred in relations between the court and citizens. According to agreement 2/2008, the Supreme Court established guidelines for public hearings for issues considered of national interest or judicial interest. Given the newness of this disposition, it has not been included in the framework presented here; it is not yet possible to evaluate its impact.

[17] Jurisprudential theses are binding on lower courts. The Amparo Act established that a thesis becomes jurisprudence (mandatory) when used five times without interruption in similar cases.

[18] Isolated rulings show the theses derived from the previous decisions that the Court agrees to make reference to. These criteria are not obligatory for the lower courts but do become part of the broader parameters for their decisions.

TABLE 4.3. *Evolution of the relations of the Mexican Supreme Court of Justice*

	Before 1987	1988–1994	1995–2002	2003–2007
Relations between the court and the political branches	Weak	Political autonomy	Greater political autonomy	Political autonomy
Relations between the court and the judiciary	Absolute sovereignty	Absolute sovereignty	Moderate sovereignty	Moderate sovereignty
Relations between the court and citizens	Not fluid	Invisible	Invisible	Informative
Profile	Weak with strong political counterweights	Powerful with weak political counterweights Arbiter of political conflicts	Powerful with weak political and judicial counterweights Consolidation of role as arbiter of political conflicts	Powerful with weak political, judicial, and social counterweights Visible arbiter

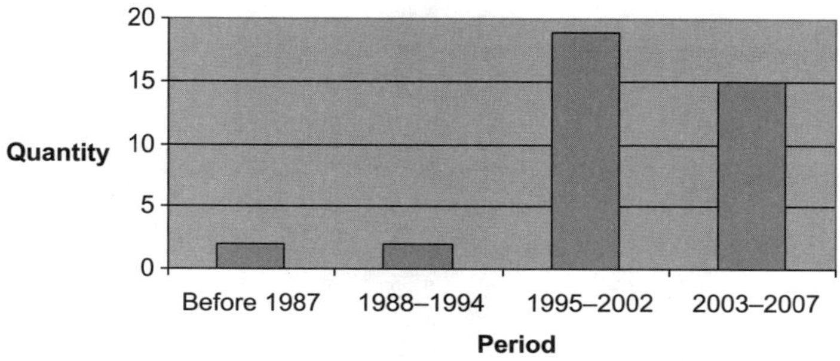

FIGURE 4.1. Evolution of the criteria from 1917 to 2007.

(both in full sitting and in its respective chambers) relative to the rights under consideration. These theses show the criteria deployed by the court when it wishes to transcend specific decisions and establish precedent for future decisions. A selection was carried out through searches in the database of jurisprudence and isolated thesis (rulings) available on the Supreme Court's web site, as well as in the different versions of the IUS database, officialy produced for the Supreme Court for public and legal practitioners.[19] The universe of cases contained thirty-eight theses (criteria) relative to the three groups of rights under consideration. Two of the thirty-eight did not correspond to the period under study. The decision to restrict the universe of cases was made on the basis of comparability. In the seventy years between 1917 and 1987, only two theses (criteria) make specific reference to these rights. The evolution of jurisprudential theses or *criterios* is shown in Figure 4.1.

Figure 4.1 shows that few jurisprudential theses were published on these issues; an average of less than two during a twenty-year period. Most notably, the court has set few precedents with respect to the rights issues under consideration here. However, it is also clear that when the Court loses political counterweights – when its powers over the political branches increase – and acquires other counterweights, the number of rulings increases exponentially, indicating an epochal shift in these issues. How are the rulings distributed between the different rights in question?

Evidently, from 1995 to 2002, it is no longer only the political branches that restrain the Court's actions (see Figure 4.2). During this period, the Court became more powerful, but acquired new, albeit weak, counterweights within the judiciary. This moment marked the beginning of a period in which the Court's reflection on rights became more dynamic, as evidenced by an increase in the production of

[19] The terms used for this search were: freedom of expression, freedom of association, freedom of trade union association, indigenous rights, uses and customs (*usos y costumbres*), indigenous communities, in addition to the numbers of the constitutional articles that make express mention of these rights (Articles 1 and 2 on indigenous rights, Articles 6 and 7 on freedom of expression, and Article 9 on freedom of association).

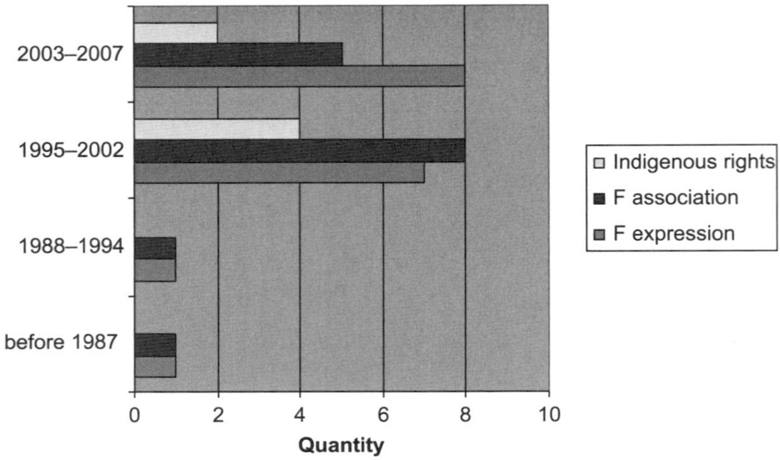

FIGURE 4.2. Evolution of the criteria for right.

jurisprudential criteria on these issues. In this sense, it is also important to emphasize that indigenous rights were considered by the Court for the first time ever as a direct consequence of the 2001 constitutional reforms on the issue. The Court was strengthened (and acquired moderate counterparts) and political representation became more plural. As Rios has demonstrated (2004), this affected decision-making on constitutional cases, where there was a growing tendency for decisions against the Partido Revolucionario Institucional (PRI), the hegemonic party until 1997. What were the characteristics of the interpretative framework developed by the Court? Using the baseline defined earlier, have the Court's rulings been pro-rights or restrictive of rights? What issues and meanings are they linked to?

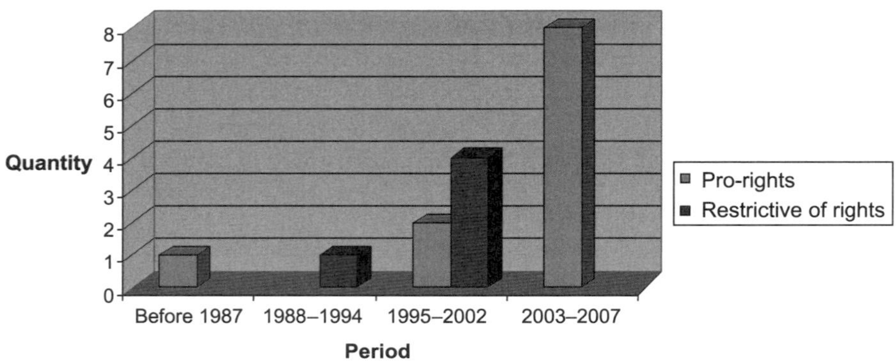

FIGURE 4.3. Way the criteria linked to freedom of expression.

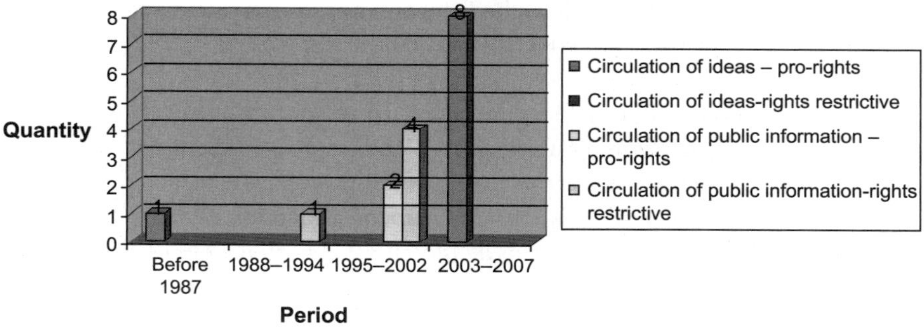

FIGURE 4.4. Meaning and issues of the criteria linked to freedom of expression.

Freedom of Expression

The golden age of freedom of expression came after the approval of the Law of Transparency and Access to Public Information in 2003, as Figure 4.3 shows. Also, as demonstrated by the data, an increase in the Court's visibility coincided with a changed conception of the circulation of ideas, from one where public information was restricted to preserve the state to one that promoted the circulation of ideas and opinions as necessary for democratic government.

In terms of tendency, the theses, or *criterios*, have evolved from a restrictive formalist interpretation of law toward a pro-rights interpretation that corresponds to the change in the Court's relations with society. The issue that cuts across the criteria is the circulation of ideas, opinions, and other information. There are two dimensions to the Court's rulings: a) the circulation of ideas, particularly those of a political or commercial nature,[20] and b) the circulation of public information (from the different branches of government), specifically access to public information by citizens.[21] Although the former coincides with the period characterized by the increase in the Court's social visibility, the latter coincides with the consolidation of the Court as an arbiter of the political process. In the first case, the Court's interpretation is fundamentally pro-rights. In the second case, it is rights-restrictive (see Figure 4.4).

Freedom of expression is considered a necessary condition for democracy because it is crucial to the formation of public opinion:

> . . . In this sense, these fundamental rights of free expression of ideas and of communication and access to information are indispensable for the formation of public

[20] Thesis: PJ 25/2007; PJ 27/2007; 24/2007; 26/2007; 1aLIX/2007; 1a. CLXVI/2004; 1a. CLXV/2004; PJ 3/2004; P. XXXVI/2002; Sem Jud XXXVIII 224.

[21] Thesis: P. LXI/2000; P. XLV/2000; P. LX/2000; PXLVII/2000; PLVI/2000; PLXXXIX/1996; 2ª. I/1992.

> opinion, a necessary component for the functioning of a representative democracy. (Suprema Corte de Justicia, Tesis, 24/2007)

The Court's interpretation of the prohibition on prior censorship as an explicit rule expresses a similar line of argument, a standard that different Mexican legal arrangements should respect. For this reason, if a disposition is considered to be prior censorship, then that disposition is considered unconstitutional (1st thesis. LIX/2007). In line with this interpretation, there is a difference between the circulation of ideas that form the basis of public opinion and other kinds of information such as that on criminal organizations or commercial data:

> In some cases and under certain circumstances, publicity can be a contribution to public debate about public affairs, and can contribute to the diffusion and shaping of ideas which can and should be part of public debate. However, in the majority of cases, commercial discourses are simply a collection of messages which propose the realization of a commercial contract and, to this extent, their production can be regulated by a legislator within much broader limits than if it were a case of the exercise of freedom of expression in political matters . . . in the majority of occasions this [circulation of ideas] only complements the free exercise of a commercial activity, and therefore legal and constitutional limits are applicable . . . The legislator, therefore, by considering the advertising as a message which provides information about commercial supply can subject it to the limits of truthfulness and clarity which are required in this realm. (Suprema Corte de Justicia Tesis, 1ra. CLXV/2004)

However, with respect to the circulation of public information, the theses developed by the Court are restrictive.[22] In cases where citizens demand information from the state, the Court's theses favor the restriction of information rather than its circulation:

> . . . the result of the sessions of the [municipal] councils, set out in the registers of those organs of government and municipal administration, involve the discussion and resolution of different interests (municipal, state, national, social and individual), and for this reason their circulation cannot be indiscriminate or generalized, nor can it occur simply to satisfy the curiosity of the citizen; there must be a legitimate interest or relationship between the person soliciting [the information] and the desired information [itself], and the diffusion of this information, even in limited contexts, must not prejudice the public interest. (Suprema Corte de Justicia, Tesis, P. LXI/2000)

[22] This will probably tend to change on the basis of the standards relative to access to public information established in the reform of Article 6 of the Constitution, approved on July 20, 2007.

With regard to public information, the court also developed criteria establishing truthfulness as a fundamental condition of information provided by public authorities for citizens. The meaning displays a somewhat tutelary perspective toward citizens to the extent that it establishes that public authorities exercise an exemplary function with respect to citizens:

> . . . If the public authorities, elected and appointed to serve and defend society, display attitudes that permit charges of unethical behavior [to be laid against them], by giving the community information that is manipulated, incomplete, [or] dependent on the interests of groups or people, [and] which [therefore] prevents [citizens] from knowing the truth in order to freely participate in the formation of the general will, then they are in grave violation of the individual guarantees set out in article 97 of the constitution (Honorable Cámara de Diputados, 2008), paragraph 2, because their actions lead one to believe that they tend to include in our political life what we might call a "culture of trickery," of manipulation and secrecy, instead of . . . taking rapid and efficient actions to arrive [at the truth] and make this known to citizens. (Suprema Corte de Justicia Tesis, P. LXXXIX/1996)

On this point, it is important to note that these criteria were developed prior to the approval of the Law of Transparency and Access to Public Information. It seems that the legislative reforms were significant, particularly given that they created a federal body, the Institute of Access to Public Information (*Instituto de Acceso a la Información Pública*, or IFAI). In sum, we can say that in relation to freedom of information two clearly defined moments coincide with two profiles of the court. First, after the consolidation of the court's role as arbiter of political conflicts in 1995, the issue was the circulation of public information and the tendency to preserve state secrets. Information was considered a good that needed to be restricted to preserve the "public interest." Second, when the court became more visible to society after 2003 (when the issue of transparency and access to information acquired an unprecedented prominence in the public agenda), we observe a shift in the meaning of the right. Information, opinion, and ideas should circulate because these are considered vital for democracy. The interpretative framework around freedom of expression has shifted from considering the circulation of information as a danger to government to understanding it as a condition of good, democratic government.

Freedom of Association

Freedom of association is also essential for democracy. As in the case of freedom of information, the key period of development of criteria relative to this right coincides with the consolidation of the Court as an arbiter of the political process after 1995. With respect to the interpretative framework relative to this right, the tendency

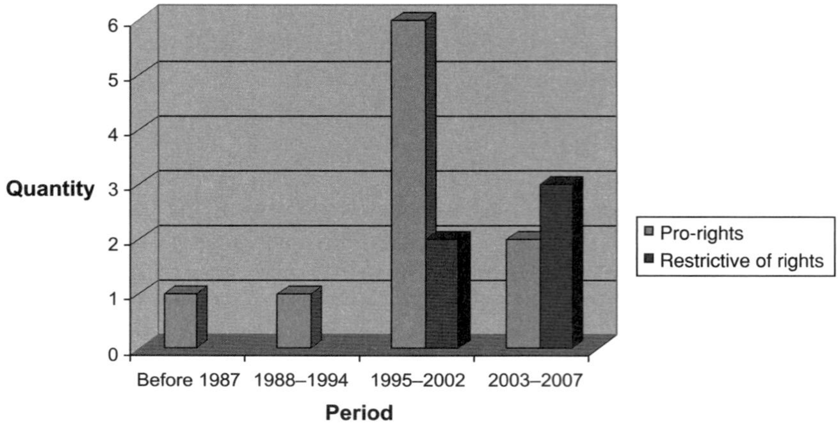

FIGURE 4.5. Evolution of the way of criteria linked to freedom of expression.

is contrary to that in the case of freedom of expression (Figure 4.5). The criteria favorable to freedom of association coincide with the consolidation of the Court as an arbiter of the political process, but as the Court becomes more visible the tendency is reversed.

The different criteria, all related to the right to associate (or not to associate) with others, make clear reference to three types of organizations: interest groups (including business and professional associations, and trade unions), financial associations, and political parties. Two issues cut across these three types: a) freedom to join (or not to join) an organization,[23] and b) the requirements for establishing an organization.[24] The Court's interpretation with respect to the former issue has been pro-rights and is linked to free association, something particularly important because it established the doctrine to break with so-called Mexican corporatism.[25] Interpretation with respect to the second issue has been rights-restrictive, signaling the existence of different types of barriers to the creation of organizations, mainly of the financial, professional, and political type (Figure 4.6).

In relation to the first issue, the Court established that an obligation to join trade unions (the "closed shop") or business associations was contrary to freedom of association to the extent that the right includes the possibility of joining or not joining, or leaving an organization:

[23] Thesis: P. LIII/99; PJ 43/; P. XLV/99; P. I/97; P. CII/92, Sem Judicial de la Federación, Quinta parte. VII pág 99.

[24] Thesis: CXXXVIII/2007; PJ 41/2004; PJ 40/2004; 2a. CLVIII/2002; PJ 48/2001; P. CXXXV/2000; P. CXXV/2000.

[25] Mexican corporativism was called a socio-political system that had its roots in the control of the unions, business association, and civil society organization by the state and the hegemonic party.

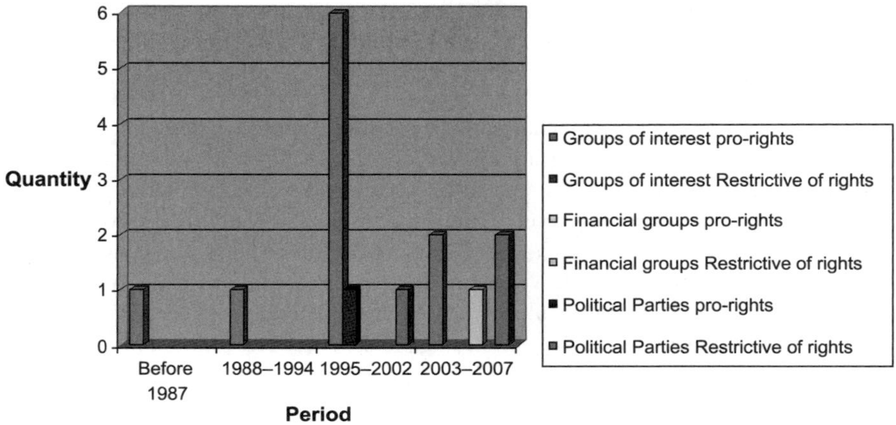

FIGURE 4.6. Issues linked to freedom of association.

> ... Article 123 of the Constitution establishes trade union freedom as a universal principle ... This freedom should be understood with respect to its three fundamental aspects: 1. A positive aspect which consists in the worker's right to join an already existing trade union or to constitute a new one; 2. A negative aspect which implies the possibility of not joining a given trade union and of not associating oneself with any trade union, and 3. The freedom to leave a trade union. The stipulation that a sole trade union for government workers should exist for each government agency, established in article 42 of the cited legislation, violates the guarantee of free association of workers set out in article 123, section B, fraction X of the General Constitution of the Republic, as it restricts the freedom of association of workers in defense of their interests. (Suprema Corte de Justicia, Tesis P. LIII/99)

This tendency could be explained in the following terms. Between 1988 and 94 and between 1995 and 2002, most of the theses or *criterios* show the Court's contribution to breaking with Mexican corporatism, which was based on the existence of a single trade union or business association for each area of economic activity. Membership in these unions and associations was mandatory. The Court endorsed freedom of business and trade union association. This decision reaffirmed the attempt by Mexican President Ernesto Zedillo to strengthen territorial representation within the PRI (representation within the PRI was previously corporate, by sector). Independent of the reasons behind the ruling, these criteria consolidated an interpretative framework that was clearly favorable to freedom of association for interest groups.

The rights-restrictive decisions after 2003 deal with barriers to constituting organizations and the state's requirements for their establishment. The jurisprudential theses developed with respect to political parties are of particular interest, as the

Court delegated to the legislature the power to establish the conditions for the creation of new political parties in line with criteria of reasonableness.[26]

> . . . Therefore, on the basis of a harmonious interpretation of articles 9, 35 fraction III and 41, fraction I of the Constitution, we conclude that freedom of association is not absolute for political parties, but rather is affected by a constitutional precept: participation in electoral processes is subject to [the rules] established by ordinary legislation. In short, it is up to the legislature, whether federal or state legislatures, to establish laws governing the ways in which citizens can politically organize, in line with criteria of reasonableness which allows for the free exercise of that fundamental right, as well as the achievement of the objectives pursued by political parties. (Suprema Corte de Justicia, Thesis PJ 40/2004)

Positions allowing for "reasonable" barriers to access have been established in theses relative to the formation of financial and professional associations. With respect to freedom of association, two interpretative frameworks coexist: one that we could call freedom of affiliation and a second that we could call barriers to access. Together these comprise an interpretative framework that on the one hand favors individuals' rights of association (a citizen can join, not join, or leave the organization they choose and obligatory affiliation clauses are deemed unconstitutional), but subsequently favors barriers to access for the formation of new organizations. In this sense, the barriers to the creation of political parties maintain the status quo. In this case, the greater social visibility of the Court did not translate into an interpretation favoring the creation of new organizations, but rather led to an interpretation concerned with establishing the conditions governing their creation. The framework promotes free association of individuals and existing organizations, but favors control over the formation of new ones.

It is worth highlighting the question of access barriers and conditions to form new organizations because they are considered one of the main contemporary problems related to freedom of association. The Inter-American Human Rights Commission has stated:

> States have the power to regulate the inscription, monitoring and control of organizations within its jurisdiction, including human rights organizations. However, the right of free association without interference mandates states to guarantee that those legal requirements not impede, delay, or limit the creation or functioning of those organizations, or they will be in breach of their international obligations. (Comisión Interamericana de Derechos Humanos, cited in Cejil 2006)

[26] The law established that a political party cannot be set up without the existence of a national political group, effectively prohibiting the formation of subnational or regional parties.

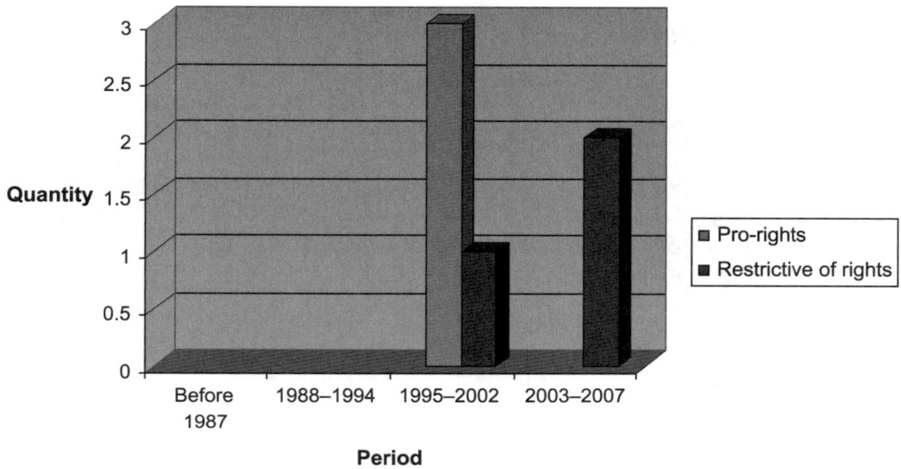

FIGURE 4.7. Evolution of the way criteria linked to indigenous rights.

Indigenous Rights

The constitutionalization of this group of rights was far from accidental (Ansolabehere 2006). The constitutional reform of 2001 was the product of a powerful mobilization by an indigenous movement led by the Zapatista National Liberation Army (Ejército Zapatista de Liberación Nacional, or EZLN), and independent of the content of the decisions, signaled the inclusion of these rights in the Court's agenda (Figure 4.7). Before 2001, conflicts involving indigenous people did not appear as such (they were instead linked to agrarian issues).

Here again the temporal distribution of the theses or *criterios* would seem to be counterintuitive. When the court became more socially visible, the *criterios* are more rights-restrictive; yet, in the preceding period, coinciding with the Zapatistas' march to the center of Mexico City, the tendency of the *criterios* is pro-rights.[27] Three issues cut across the court's considerations: a) the recognition of uses and customs (*usos y costumbres*) in determining access to justice,[28] b) the allocation of land and natural resources,[29] and 3) the issue of harmonization between federal and local laws on

[27] Nonetheless, although these did not appear as indigenous rights issues but rather were linked to questions of judicial review, more than three hundred indigenous municipalities presented constitutional appeals against the process of constitutional reform used to approve the constitutionalization of indigenous rights in 2001. In this sense, the indigenous movement deployed a strategy of judicialization of conflict as a means of signaling its disagreement with the decisions adopted by the constituent assembly.

[28] Thesis: XXXVIII/2003; 1a. XXXIX/2003; 2a. CXLI/2002.

[29] Thesis. CXXXVII/2002.

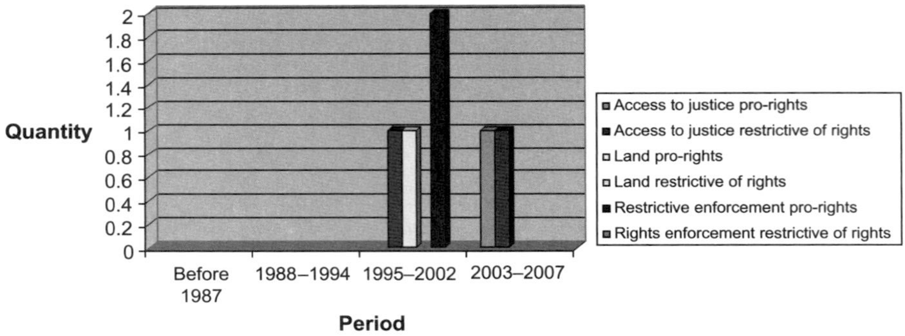

FIGURE 4.8. Issues linked to indigenous rights.

indigenous rights.[30] In this case, a restrictive tendency is clearly observable in the *criterios* related to the issues of access to justice (Figure 4.8).

Recognition of cultural diversity in access to justice – clearly a point of tension between universalism and group-specific rights – was resolved through a formalist, restrictive reading. The Court recognized cultural specificity, but only within highly restricted parameters, or "formalities" in the Court's terms. According to these parameters, for example, there is no mandatory obligation to have anthropological expert opinion (*peritaje antropológico*) – this is at the judge's discretion. In addition, the obligation to provide a translator when the accused does not speak Spanish is meant to make the accused aware of his or her rights rather than to provide an integral defense of those rights in his or her native language.

> ... establishes that with regards to access to state jurisdiction the customs and cultural specificities of indigenous ethnicities should be taken into account, with the right to assistance in court proceedings from interpreters and public defenders who know their language and culture; rights which are respected by the impugned articles in question, given that these establish different formalities which should be observed in favor of said ethnicities, consisting of: that penal procedures against a member of any ethnic group should take that person's ethnic group into account (72, fraction II); that recourse should be made to expert testimony that enables the judge better to know the nature of the accused and be aware of his or her cultural differences with regard to the national norm or average (165 bis); members of the ethnic group of the accused may serve as de facto expert witnesses (171); when the accused is indigenous and does not speak or understand sufficient Spanish, a translator will be assigned who will communicate their basic rights to them (269 fraction IV); public officials will take into account all observations they have received about the nature of the accused and the ethnic group they pertain to, either at the time of committing the crime, during their detention, or during the investigatory phase

30 Thesis CXXXIX/2002; 2ª. CXL/2002.

> (285). The preparatory declaration should specify the indigenous group the accused belongs to, and whether or not they speak and understand sufficient Spanish (209); during the trial, the court procedures should take into account, amongst other things, the ethnic affiliation of the accused to an indigenous group and the practices and characteristics of that group (296 bis). Therefore, if the aforementioned legal requirements contained in the legal precepts which are currently disputed tend to guarantee that indigenous people are not without adequate legal defense in criminal proceedings against them, this demonstrates that they are in line with the guarantee of access to justice cited. (Suprema Corte de Justicia, Tesis 1ra XXXVIII/2003)

With respect to land and natural resources, the content of the court's interpretation restricts the self-determination and autonomy of indigenous peoples to the administration of their territories within the municipality.

> . . . On the basis of the above, this precept (the reform of article 2 of the constitution) enshrines the territorial principle of indigenous peoples, recognizing their unity with the territories they inhabit and their habitat and, therefore, their right to exploit this according to the manner and customs of land ownership which they decide with respect to their internal forms of economic organization, in line with those established by the Federal Constitution and relevant secondary legislation, for the purposes of which the possibility of coordination and association of indigenous communities within the municipal sphere is established. This should be part of the constitutional framework which stipulates respect for the rights of third parties and members of the community. (Suprema Corte de Justicia, Tesis 2da. CXXXIX/2002)

Finally, with respect to the extent of indigenous rights, the Court was clear in establishing that the reform of the Constitution served as a minimum baseline for all state constitutions, whether these expressed a pro-rights or a more restrictive framework. With regard to the interpretative framework on indigenous rights, we can conclude that the Court has developed contents that recognize group rights (in a narrow way), the unity of indigenous peoples and their territory, and that in this sense it endorses a "restrictive" autonomy. It considers the rights set out in the federal constitution as a minimum not a maximum level for the guarantee of those rights in Mexico, and finally it is restrictive and formalist in recognizing cultural difference in access to justice. As is the case with other rights, it seems that the key point with respect to a pro-rights interpretation was the moment when the Court consolidated its role as a political arbiter, which occurred at the same time as a process of massive social mobilization in favor of indigenous rights. It is a framework that recognizes group rights outside the judicial sphere, but those rights are not easily exercised as individual rights by members of the ethnic group in question.

TABLE 4.4. *Principal comparative characteristics of the court's interpretative framework*

	Period	Content	Framework
Freedom of expression	2003–2007: powerful with weak political, legal, and social counterweights (visible court) 1995–2002: powerful court with weak counterweights Restrictive of the circulation of public information Access to information is a danger for the government	Favorable to the circulation of ideas and opinions favoring the formation of public opinion Circulation of ideas a condition for democracy	Shifts from the viewing the circulation of public information as a danger to government to seeing the circulation of information, ideas, and opinions as a necessary condition for democracy
Freedom of association	1995–2002: Powerful court with weak political and legal counterweights 2003–2007: Powerful court with weak political, legal, and social counterweights	People can join or not join the organizations of their choosing Freedom of affiliation to different organizations is a fundamental component of freedom of association<anchor id="c04ind0116" rid="ind0289::687"/> Freedom of association<anchor id="c04ind0117" rid="ind0289::688"/> is not tied to access barriers for new organizations	The freedom of individuals to affiliate to organizations is a component of freedom of association; access barriers and requirements for the creation of new organizations (including political parties) is not tied to this freedom of association

Indigenous rights	1995–2002: Powerful court with weak political and legal counterweights	Political constitution as a minimum baseline for the recognition of indigenous rights Autonomy for indigenous groups in the administration of territory and natural resources The observance of minimum requirements with respect to access to state law for individuals belonging to indigenous groups is sufficient to ensure that those individuals are not without adequate legal defense and that this right is guaranteed	Recognition of the group dimension of indigenous rights in a restrictive way Tension between individual and group rights for members of those groups
	2003–2007: Powerful court with weak political, legal, and social counterweights	The observance of minimum requirements with respect to access to state law for individuals belonging to indigenous groups is sufficient to ensure that those individuals are not without adequate legal defense and that this right is guaranteed. Recognition of the group dimension of indigenous rights Tension between individual and group rights for members of those groups	

Comparative Results

This section presents a comparative analysis of the characteristics of the various interpretative frameworks on the different groups of rights. Here the political and social context is prioritized, together with the predominant interpretative framework and the characteristics of the votes.

- Freedom of expression, with respect to the circulation of ideas, opinions, and information is clearly a new topic, which acquires prominence at the same time as the Court acquires greater social visibility. This issue is in line with the content of the criteria and appears to signal not only a tendency toward a pro-rights interpretative framework, but also expresses a change in legal ideology, to the extent that it makes the right a condition of democratic government.
- The two periods of interpretation of this right can be understood as a shift by the Court toward a new interpretative paradigm around the circulation of ideas and opinions and the relationship between the state and citizens.
- With regard to freedom of association, we can also observe two periods that coincide with changes in the Court's profile. However, in contrast to the previous right, the contents of these two periods do not indicate a shift in the interpretative framework. In the first period it is established that freedom of affiliation of individuals is a fundamental component of the right, while in the second period it is established that the setting of requirements for the formation of new organizations is not contradictory to freedom of association. This second issue is particularly linked to the requirements to create new political parties.
- Finally, with regard to indigenous rights, the appearance of this issue before the Court was linked to the August 2001 constitutional reform. The framework endorses the group dimension of indigenous rights, recognizing in a limited[31] view of the autonomy of groups to administer their territory. However, the framework is restrictive of the individual dimension of indigenous rights, limiting its reading of the right to access of justice to the formal minimum requirements. In this case the greater power of the Court, together with the constitutionalization of indigenous rights, provided a favorable context for the development of an interpretative framework that recognizes the group dimension of these rights, although it does not clearly recognize the individual dimension.
- The consolidation of the Court as an arbiter of the political process and its increased power coincided with a greater engagement with rights, although the contents of that engagement was not necessarily favorable to the different issues related to those rights. In interpreting freedom of expression the Court moved toward an interpretative framework clearly favorable to that right. In

[31] It is important to sign that there are, and were, a strong debate about the scope of the indigenous rights reform in the country.

the other two cases, however, the frameworks combine rights-enhancing and rights-restrictive aspects.

- In line with the legal support structures perspective, we can see that plaintiffs before the Court are organizations, mainly political parties and interest groups (66% of the criteria derive from actions promoted by these kinds of organizations) and the rulings were specially supportives of them.

CONCLUSIONS

The principal conclusion is that the changes in the Court's relations, and thus its role vis-á-vis the political branches and citizens, are linked to the appearance of rights cases before the Court. In addition to the Court consolidating its role as political arbiter, different actors with access to its jurisdiction begin to take rights cases to court, and as a result the Court increased the number of jurisprudential theses issued on rights-related themes. This is particularly notable with respect to freedom of expression and freedom of association – rights that are included in the text of the 1917 Constitution – and on which the Court had barely made any pronouncements until it changed its relations with the political branches.

However, the interpretative frameworks the Court develops are heterogeneous, combining both pro-rights and rights-restrictive criteria. In this sense, the frameworks developed by the Court open up certain topics and close others. This feature allows for a questioning of some of the democratic theory that links democratic consolidation with judicial independence and theories of constitutional democracy that associate processes of constitutionalization of rights and the existence of strong constitutional tribunals with greater observance and guarantee of rights. The Mexican Supreme Court has become more independent of the political branches and has stronger powers to control the actions of those branches. However, it has not necessarily become a stronger guarantor of rights, even though it has reflected on them at greater length. This more powerful court is not necessarily a more "progressive" court, at least not with respect to all the rights issues discussed here.

Finally, for the case of Mexico, changes in the Court's relations from a top-down perspective (increase in the Court's powers but without legal or social counterweights) have correlated with changes in the interpretative framework of rights, although the direction of those changes is not always rights-friendly. In light of this consideration, strengthening the bottom-up dimensions of the Court's relations – including strengthening legal and social counterweights and increasing access to the Court's jurisdiction – could contribute to making it more of a court for citizens and less of a court for politicians (as it was originally conceived). Future research on the ways in which these interpretative frameworks on rights developed by the Court affect the Court's relations with the political branches, the judiciary, and society will increase our understanding of these dynamics.

ANNEX 1. *Relationship between the Supreme Court and the political branches*[32]

Dimensions	Indicators	Possibilities	Index	Powers of mutual control
Court's control over political branches[33]	Type of judicial review a) degree of concentration of powers of constitutional review b) reach of the court's constitutional rulings	1 - Concentrated 2 - Diffuse 3 - General and abstract 4 - Particular and concrete	1 + 3 = Strong control of the court over the political branches 1 + 4 = Moderate control of the court over the political branches 2 + 3 = Not possible 2 + 4 = Weak control of the court over the political branches	Strong(Cs)/strong(P): Heteronymous Strong(Cs)/weak (Ps): judicial autonomy Weak (Cs)/strong(Ps): political autonomy Weak(Cs)/weak(Ps): autonomous
Political branches powers of control over the Supreme Court[34]	a) rigidity in the rules governing the functioning of the judiciary b) budgetary autonomy	1 - Rigid 2 - Flexible 3 - Autonomous 4 - Not autonomous	1 + 3 = Limited control of political branches over the court 1+4 = Weak control of political branches over the court 2+3 = Moderate control of political branches over the court 2+4 = Strong control of political branches over the court	

Note: Taken from Ansolabehere (2007), *La política desde la justicia. Cortes Supremas, gobierno y democracia en Argentina y México*, México: FLACSO y Fontamara.

[32] The relationship between the Supreme Court and the political branches is reconstructed according to two dimensions of analysis: a) the court's veto power over the decisions of the political branches (the court's power to control the political branches), and b) the political branches' power to influence the rules governing the functioning of the judiciary (the political branches' power to control the court and the judiciary). The first relates to the strategic component of a decision, the possibility of the courts' vetoing the decisions of the political branches. The second takes into account the conditions guaranteeing the insulation of judges from pressures from the political branches.

[33] This focuses on the characteristics of the institution charged with judicial review regarding the power of the judiciary to overrule decisions by the political branches (laws, regulations, dispositions, and so forth). Two characteristics of regimes of judicial review are taken into account: concentration and reach. *Concentration* refers to whether judicial review powers are diffuse (they can be carried out by any court) or concentrated (they can only be exercised by the Supreme Court of a constitutional tribunal). *Reach* refers to the general applicability of a given sentence, distinguishing decisions that set general precedents from those where the rulings apply only to the case in question (Guarnieri y Pederzoli 1999, Nino 1989).

[34] This considers two elements: a) the ability of the political branches to modify the rules governing the judiciary, and b) the degree of influence the political branches exercise in defining the judiciary's budgetary allocation. The first element refers to the stipulation (or its absence) within the Constitution of the number of judges of the court, as well as the requirements for their candidacy and their powers. It is hypothesized that in the absence of an explicit constitutional mandate on these issues, there are greater possibilities to manipulate the Supreme Court (as these elements can be changed by a simple parliamentary majority). On the question of the budget, the existence or absence of norms guaranteeing autonomy in the administration of the judicial budget is a key factor.

ANNEX 1 (cont.). *Relationship between the Supreme Court and the judiciary*[35]

Dimensions	Indicators	Possibilities	Index	Powers of mutual control
Court's control over the judiciary[36]	a) court's control over the judicial career b) norms governing the use of the court's jurisprudence by lower courts	1 - Strong control 2 - Weak control 3 - Mandatory 4 - Nonmandatory	$1+3/1+4/2+3=$ Strong control of the court over the lower ranks of the judiciary $2+4=$ Weak control of the court over the lower ranks of the judiciary	Strong(Cs)/strong (Pj)Heteronymous Strong(Cs)/Weak(Pj): absolute sovereignty Weak (Cs)/ Strong(Pj): *primus interpares* Weak (Cs)/Weak (Pj): autonomous
Lower courts can act as a counter-weight to the power of the Supreme Court[37]	Strength of professional associations within the judiciary	1 - Strong 2 - Weak	1 - De facto counterweight: ability of the lower ranks of the judiciary to act as a strong counterweight 2 - No counterweight: ability of the lower courts to act as a counterweight is weak	

Source: Ansolabehere (2007).

[35] Two dimensions of analysis are considered here: a) the court's powers to influence the decisions of judges (the court's degree of control over the lower courts) and b) the ability of the lower courts to function as an institution that constrains the actions of the Supreme Court (the possibility that the lower courts can operate as a counterweight to the Supreme Court). The different combinations between these two dimensions allow for a matrix of the relationship between the Supreme Court and the lower courts to be drawn. It is hypothesized that the relationship of the court with the lower courts will affect their understandings of policy issues. The aim here is to map changes in this relationship, assuming that while the Supreme Court is always in a position of authority vis-á-vis the lower courts and judicial employees, this link can be articulated in different ways. The metaphor of *primus interpares*, or the absolute sovereign, illustrates the inertias in this relationship.

[36] This takes into account: a) the means by which supreme courts influence the judicial career, specifically powers to name, promote, or remove judges, and b) the existence of norms governing the use of the court's jurisprudence by judges. It is hypothesized that a court that has exclusive control over the appointment and removal of judges will have greater formal and informal powers of control over their careers and thus a greater ability to control the lower ranks of the judiciary. In other words, such an arrangement will favor less autonomy on the part of judges. At the same time, it is hypothesized that the existence of rules that mandate the use of the court's jurisprudence in all courts will lead to less autonomy on the part of judges, while the absence of this kind of mandate will favor greater judicial autonomy.

[37] This refers to the importance of organizations or associations of judges. It is hypothesized that the existence of strong professional associations (strength understood as percentage of judges who comprise these associations and the areas of judicial policy that they deal with) to which are delegated, for example, tasks related to training and representation of the judiciary, making them a de facto internal counterweight in relation to the court. In the inverse situation, where there are no strong professional associations within the judiciary, they will not constitute a strong counterweight to the court's decisions. These organizations can act as a veto, de-legitimizing the role of the Supreme Court within the judiciary itself, but if they are weak they cannot be considered an actor with veto powers.

ANNEX 1 (cont.). *Relationship between the Supreme Court and society*

Dimensions	Indicators	Possibilities	Index	Powers of mutual control
Relationship between the court and citizens[38]	Degree of publicity surrounding court proceedings and policy with respect to the judiciary[39] Accessibility of the Caurl's jurisdiction	1 - High 2 - Low 3 - Simple 4 - Complex	1+3: Open 1+4: Inaccessible 2+3: Accessible 2+4: Closed	Visible and accessible: fluid Visible and inaccessible: informative Nonvisible and accessible: jurisdictional Nonvisible and nonaccessible: nonfluid

References

Almond, Gabriel and Verba, Sidney. 1963. *The Civic Culture: Political Attitudes and Democracy in Five Nations*. New Jersey: Princeton University Press.

———. 1980. *The Civic Culture Revisited: An Analytic Study*. Boston: Little, Brown.

Álvarez, Ignacio. 2006. "Libertad de Expresión en América Latina," Programa de Cooperación en Derechos Humanos México-Unión Europea (2006). Mexico: SER-Unión Europea.

Ansolabehere, Karina. 2008. "*Más poder ¿más derechos? Control de constitucionalidad y ciudadanía*." Mexico: Mimeo.

———. 2007. *La política desde la justicia. Cortes Supremas, gobierno y democracia en Argentina y México*. Mexico: FLACSO-Fontamara.

———. 2006. "Diversidad Retórica: Suprema Corte de Justicia y Diversidad Cultural," paper presented to the VI Congress of the Red Latinoamérica de Antropología Jurídica, Oaxtepec, Mexico.

———. 2005. "Jueces, política y derecho: particularidades y alcances de la politización de la Justicia." *Isonomía*, 22(Abril): 39–64. México, ITAM.

Asociación para los derechos Civiles. 2008. *La corte y los derechos*, Buenos Aires, Siglo XXI.

Avritzer, Leonardo. 2002. *Democracy And The Public Space In Latin America*. Princeton: Princeton University Press.

Cepeda Espinosa, Manuel. 2005. "The Judicialization of Politics in Colombia: The Old and the New." In *The Judicialization of Politics in Latin America*, Sieder, Rachel, Schjolden, Line, and Alan Angell, eds. 67–104. London: Palgrave Macmillan.

38 In contrast to my previous work, this dimension of analysis is considered a fundamental component in the construction of the profile of supreme courts in contexts where significant changes in the relations between state and society are taking place. Transitions to democracy and posttransitions are associated with processes of revitalization of civil society (Cohen and Arato 2001; Olvera 2003 etc.). At the same time, a revalorization of the social dimensions of democracy is occurring (Avritzer 2002). Given these transformations, this relationship must be considered in any analysis of supreme courts.

39 When access to judicial decisions is easy, and where their decision-making processes are visible to society (for example, through TV broadcasts or transcripts of debates available to the public) then high publicity exists; low publicity prevails in the absence of such mechanisms.

Cleary, Matthew and Stokes, Susan. 2006. *Democracy and the Culture of Skepticism: Political Trust in Argentina and Mexico*. New York: Russell Sage Foundation.

Cohen, Jean; Arato, Andrew. 2001. *Sociedad civil y teoría política*. Mexico: Fondo de Cultura Económica.

Cotterrell, Roger. 1997. "The Concept of Legal Culture." In *Comparing Legal Cultures*, Nelken, David, ed. 13–32. Aldershot: Darmouth.

Couso, Javier. 2005. "The Judicialization of Chilean Politics: The Rights Revolution That Never Was." In *The Judicialization of Politics in Latin America*, Sieder, Rachel, Schjolden, Line, and Alan Angell, eds. London: Palgrave Macmillan.

Dahl, Robert. 1957. "Decision Making in a Democracy: The Supreme Court as a National Policy Maker." *Journal of Public Law*, 6: 278–99.

Domingo Villegas, Pilar. 2005. "Judicialization of Politics: The Changing Political Role of the Judiciary in Mexico." In *The Judicialization of Politics in Latin America*, Sieder, Rachel, Schjolden, Line, and Alan Angell, eds. London: Palgrave Macmillan.

______. 2000. "Judicial Independence: The Politics of the Supreme Court in Mexico." In *Journal of Latin American Studies, VolII, Part III, Oct*: 705–735. Cambridge: Cambridge University Press.

Epp, Charles. 2005. "Courts and the Rights Revolution." In *The Judicial Branch*, Hall, Kermit and Mcguire, Kevin, eds. Oxford: Oxford University Press.

Epp, Charles. 1998. *The Rights Revolution: Lawyers, Activists, and Supreme Courts in Comparative Perspective*. Chicago, London: University of Chicago Press.

Finkel, Jodi. 2004. "Judicial reform in Argentina in the 90s: How electoral incentives shape electoral change," *Latin American Research Review*, 39(3): 56–80.

______. 1998. *Judicial reform in Latin America: market economies, self interested politicians and judicial independence*. Chicago: Mimeo.

Fix Fierro, Héctor. 1999. "El poder judicial." In *Transiciones y diseños institucionales*, Gonzáles, M. y López Ayllón, S. (coord). México: UNAM.

Fix Fierro, Héctor and López Ayllón, Sergio. 2002. "Legitimidad contra legalidad. Los dilemas de la transición jurídica y el estado de derecho en México." In *Estado de derecho. Concepto, fundamentos y democratización en América Latina*. Carbonell, Miguel, Orozco, Wistano, and Vázquez, Rodolfo, coord. 329–71. México: UNAM-ITAM-Siglo XXI.

Friedman, Lawrence. 1997. "The Concept of Legal Culture: A Reply." In *Comparing Legal Cultures*, Nelken, David, ed. 33–40. Aldershot: Dartmouth.

Gillman, Howard. 2004. "Elements of New Regime Politics Approach to the Study of Judicial Politics," paper presented in the annual congress of the American Political Science Association, Chicago.

Guarnieri, C. and Pederzoli, P. 1999. *Los jueces y la política. Poder judicial y democracia*. Madrid: Taurus.

Hertogh, Marc. 2004. "A European Conception of Legal Consciousness: Rediscovering Eugen Ehrlich." *Journal of Law and Society*, 31(4: 457 481).

Hilbink, Lisa. 2007. *Judges beyond Politics in Democracy and Dictatorship: Lessons from Chile*. Cambridge: Cambridge University Press.

Knight, Alan. 2008. "La cultura política mexicana." In *La conflictiva y nunca acabada construcción de la democracia deseada. México en perspectiva histórica y comparada*, Knight, Alan, Schedler, Andreas, Whitehead, Lawrence, Rabasa, Emilio, eds. 1–30. México: Porrúa-Tecnológico de Monterrey.

Loreti, Damián. 2006. "Estándares internacionales en materia de libertad de expression," Programa de Cooperación en Derechos Humanos México-Unión Europea (2006), México: SER-Unión Europea.

Lujambio, A. 2000. *El Poder Compartido un ensayo sobre la democratización mexicana*. México: Océano.
Mc Adam, D. 1996. "Political Opportunities: Conceptual Origins, Current Problems, Future Directions." In *Comparative Perspectives on Social Movements*, McAdam et al. eds. 23–40. Cambridge: Cambridge University Press.
Magaloni, Ana Laura, Zaldívar, Arturo. 2006. "El ciudadano olvidado." In *Nexos*, Nro 342, Junio, México: Ed. Nexos.
Magaloni, Beatriz. 2003. "Authoritarianism, Democracy, and the Suprema Court: Horizontal Exchange and the Rule of Law in México." In *Democratic Accountability in Latin America*, Mainwaring, Scott and Welna, Christopher, eds. 266–306. Oxford: Oxford University Press.
Merino, Mauricio. 2003. *La Transición Votada*. México: Fondo de Cultura Económica.
Nelken, David. 1997. "Puzzling Out Legal Culture: A Comment on Blankenburg." In *Comparing Legal Cultures*, Nelken, David, ed. Aldershot: Dartmouth.
Nino, Carlos. 1989. "La Filosofía del Control Judicial de Constitucionalidad," *Revista del Centro de Estudios Constitucionales*, 4: 79–88.
Olvera, Alberto. 2003. *Sociedad Civil, Esfera Pública y democratización en América Latina*. Mexico: Universidad Veracruzana/Fondo de Cultura Económica.
Pásara, Luis. (Comp.). 2004. *En Busca de una Justicia Distinta: Experiencias de Reforma en América Latina*. México: Instituto de Investigaciones Jurídicas, UNAM.
Pérez Perdomo, Rogelio and Lawrence Friedman. 2003. "Latin Legal Cultures in the Age of Globalization." In *Legal Culture in the Age of Globalization: Latin America and Latin Europe*, Friedman, Lawrence and Pérez Perdomo, Rogelio, eds. 1–19. Stanford: Stanford University Press.
Peruzzotti, Enrique. 1997. *The Legacy of the Politics of Human Rights in Post-Dictatorial Latin America: Social Movements and Cultural Innovation in Argentina*, Documento de trabajo, Nro. 42: Buenos Aires, Universidad Torcuato Di Tella.
Ríos Figueroa, Julio. 2004. "El surgimiento de un poder judicial efectivo en México: gobierno dividido y toma de decisiones en la Suprema Corte de Justicia, 1994–2002." In *El poder judicial en la transición y consolidación democrática en México*, pp. 11–36, México, IFE.
Rachel Sieder; Line Schjolden, and Alan Angell. 2005. *The judicialization of politics iLatin America*. London: Palgrave Macmillan.
Snow, David and Benford, Robert. 1988. "Ideology, Frame Resonance, and Participant Mobilization." *International Social Movement Research*, 1: 197–217.
Valdés Ugalde, F. 2002. *Problemas del cambio constitucional en México*, paper presented at the 1st Latin American Congress of Political Science, Salamanca.
Weldon, Jeffrey. 2002. "Las fuentes políticas del presidencialismo en México." In *Presidencialismo y democracia en América Latina*, Mainwaring, Scott y Matthew Soberg Schugart, comps. Buenos Aires: Paidós.
Weber, Robert. 1990. *Basic Content Analysis*. London: Sage.
Wilson, Bruce. 2007. "Rights Revolutions in Unlikely Places," paper presented at Latin American Studies Association Congress, Montreal.

Documents Consulted

Asamblea General de Naciones Unidas. 2007. Declaración de Derechos de los pueblos indígenas, Nueva York.
Honorable Cámara de Diputados. 2008. *Constitución política de los Estados Unidos Mexicanos*, Mexico.
Organización de Estados Americanos. 1970. *Convención Americana de Derechos Humanos*.

Cejil. 2006. "CEJIL expresa preocupación por proyecto de ley enVenezuela," http://www.cejil.org/comunicados.cfm?id=738.
Suprema Corte de Justicia. 2007. Tesis 25/2007. México: www.scjn.gob.mx
Suprema Corte de Justicia. 2007. Tesis 27/2007. México: www.scjn.gob.mx
Suprema Corte de Justicia. 2007. Tesis 24/2007. México: www.scjn.gob.mx
Suprema Corte de Justicia. 2007. Tesis 26/2007. México: www.scjn.gob.mx
Suprema Corte de Justicia. 2007. Tesis 1ra LIX/2007. México: www.scjn.gob.mx
Suprema Corte de Justicia. 2007. Tesis 1ra CCXXXVII/2007. México: www.scjn.gob.mx
Suprema Corte de Justicia. 2005. Tesis 2nd LVII/2005. México: www.scjn.gob.mx
Suprema Corte de Justicia. 2004. Tesis PJ 41/2004. México: www.scjn.gob.mx
Suprema Corte de Justicia. 2004. Tesis PJ 40/2004. México: www.scjn.gob.mx
Suprema Corte de Justicia. 2004. Tesis 1ra CLXVI/2004. México: www.scjn.gob.mx
Suprema Corte de Justicia. 2004. Tesis 1ra. CLXV/2004. México: www.scjn.gob.mx
Suprema Corte de Justicia. 2004. Tesis PJ 3/2004. México: www.scjn.gob.mx
Suprema Corte de Justicia. 2003. Tesis 1ra. XXXVIII/2003. México: www.scjn.gob.mx
Suprema Corte de Justicia. 2003. Tesis 1ra. XXXIX/2003. México: www.scjn.gob.mx
Suprema Corte de Justicia. 2002. Tesis 2da. CXXXVIII/2002. México: www.scjn.gob.mx
Suprema Corte de Justicia. 2002. Tesis 2da CXXXIX/2002. México: www.scjn.gob.mx
Suprema Corte de Justicia. 2002. Tesis 2da. CXL/2002. México: www.scjn.gob.mx
Suprema Corte de Justicia. 2002. Tesis P. XXVI/2002. México: www.scjn.gob.mx
Suprema Corte de Justicia. 2002. Tesis 2da CLVIII/2002. México: www.scjn.gob.mx
Suprema Corte de Justicia. 2002. Tesis 2da CXLI/2002. México: www.scjn.gob.mx
Suprema Corte de Justicia. 2001. Tesis PJ 48/2001. México: www.scjn.gob.mx
Suprema Corte de Justicia. 2000. Tesis P. LXI/2000. México: www.scjn.gob.mx
Suprema Corte de Justicia. 2000. Tesis P. XLV/2000. México: www.scjn.gob.mx
Suprema Corte de Justicia. 2000. Tesis P. LX/2000. México: www.scjn.gob.mx
Suprema Corte de Justicia. 2000. Tesis P. XLVI/2000. México: www.scjn.gob.mx
Suprema Corte de Justicia. 2000. Tesis P. CXXXV/2000. México: www.scjn.gob.mx
Suprema Corte de Justicia. 2000. Tesis P. CXXV/2000. México: www.scjn.gob.mx
Suprema Corte de Justicia. 1999. Tesis P. LIII/99. México: www.scjn.gob.mx
Suprema Corte de Justicia. 1999. Tesis P. J 43/99. México: www.scjn.gob.mx
Suprema Corte de Justicia. 1999. Tesis P. XLV/99. México: www.scjn.gob.mx
Suprema Corte de Justicia. 1997. Tesis P. I/97. México: www.scjn.gob.mx
Suprema Corte de Justicia. 1996. Tesis P. LXXXIX/1996. México: www.scjn.gob.mx
Suprema Corte de Justicia. 1992. Tesis 2da. I/92. México: www.scjn.gob.mx
Suprema Corte de Justicia. 1992. Tesis P. CII/92. México: www.scjn.gob.mx

5

Rejecting the Inter-American Court: Judicialization, National Courts, and Regional Human Rights

Alexandra Huneeus

INTRODUCTION

At first glance, one might assume that judicialization at the national level would enhance the influence of the Inter-American Court of Human Rights (IACtHR). The Inter-American Human Rights System provides national courts with a ready-made arsenal of global legitimacy – in the form of treaty law and court opinions – with which to enter political battles. As politics is displaced from the legislature and the public square into the courts, and as social and political demands more frequently take on the form of an adversarial rights claim, it seems plausible that national judges will deploy this arsenal more frequently, fomenting, in turn, the Inter-American Court's influence. Scholarship on the European regional systems indeed suggests that national courts have played a pivotal role in regional legal integration (Alter 2001).

Conversely, it could also be that stronger, more politically savvy high courts will be jealous of their power, sidelining the supranational instance so as to retain final arbiter status. The U.S. Supreme Court, one of the world's most politically prominent tribunals, has a reputation for rejecting the jurisprudence of foreign courts. Most recently, it announced that the rulings of the International Court of Justice (ICJ) are not directly binding on national courts and that the ICJ's interpretation of international treaties is not definitive.[1] Furthermore, even as courts in Europe have been crucial to the integration of the European Union (EU) system, there have been backlashes. High courts in particular at times try to avoid review by the European Court of Justice, disagree with its rulings, and discourage referrals. In this scenario, judicialization and regional integration are not mutually reinforcing phenomena but, rather, in competition.

[1] See *Medellín v. Texas* 552 US 491 (2008) and *Sanchez-Llama v. Oregon*, 548 U.S. 331 (2006).

There is much to learn, in other words, about when national courts foment regional legal integration, as in the virtuous circle scenario, and when they do not. Furthermore, the question has been little explored in the context of the Latin American human rights system, which presents a different structure from that of the regional European systems, as well as differences in national court structures, laws, and traditions. This chapter takes on a piece of this puzzle by generating theories about when high courts comply with Inter-American Court rulings. In about one-half of the rulings it has issued since it began its work in 1979, the IACtHR issues orders that require action by national courts. Further, it has increasingly taken on a role of reviewing whether national practices of judicial independence and due process comply with the American Convention on Human Rights. This chapter seeks to discern the factors that influence how national courts respond to this incursion into their turf, and whether they act as a partner in regional legal integration by complying with the IACtHR's decisions. It focuses exclusively on high courts, acknowledging that lower courts have a significant but very different role to play in this dynamic (Naddeo 2009; Alter 2001).

The chapter proceeds by examining recent instances in which the high courts of Argentina, Chile, and Venezuela rejected a ruling of the Inter-American Court. All three countries have experienced the expansion of legal forms into the sphere of politics over the past two decades. However, they present settings with very different high court political roles. Indeed, these three settings are in some ways emblematic of legal-political dynamics in the region today: Argentina is considered a leading example of the "new constitutionalism," a trend, originating in Europe, of enacting constitutions that not only establish the competence of the branches of government but also include "high levels of substantive norms" that commit the state to "particular objectives" and, correspondingly, a more substantive jurisprudence (Carbonell 2007: 10; see also Couso in this volume). Argentine courts have routinely taken center stage in important political battles, and civil actors have increasingly focused their strategies on the courts (Smulovitz 2005). Chile presents a more traditional setting. Although its constitution was conceived of as a guardian of Pinochet's neoliberal economic reforms (Couso 2004), its courts have tended to avoid challenging the government on rights issues (Couso 2005; Hilbink 2007), save in the very specific realm of Pinochet-era claims (Huneeus 2010). Venezuela, of course, is a participant of and in many ways the leader of Latin America's Left. Venezuelan courts were granted greater powers by the 1999 Constitution, and have since participated more fully in political battles. At the same time, the courts now view themselves as participants in the social transformation of Venezuela under the Chavez government's Bolivarian Revolution. Critics argue that they are increasingly dependent on an executive who uses them to advance political ends (Allen-Brewers 2009; Gomez in this volume; Perez Perdomo 2005).

Amid these contrasts, rejection of Inter-American rulings provides the common ground for the cases here examined. High courts often comply with the

Inter-American Court, and the Argentine Supreme Court is one of its greatest allies in the region. However, the focus on rejection brings out the contrasts in the different courts' relation to the IACtHR. This is in part because confronting an international court is a difficult step to take, and following Dworkin's idea that hard cases best serve to elucidate judicial philosophies (Dworkin 1986), these rejections reveal a great deal about judges' ideas about the relation between the Inter-American and national systems, and about their own role as actors within the international and national systems. Furthermore, the focus on rejection brings to light the fragility of the Inter-American System. A few recent studies emphasize the influence and successes of the Court and Commission (Hawkins and Jacoby 2008; Sikkink 2004; Stacey 2009). However, it is important to keep in view that the system is susceptible to the varying responses of national actors and the vicissitudes of regional politics – more so than its European counterpart. Gerald Neuman argues that the Inter-American Court needs to be more strategic and give greater "consideration to the consent of the regional community of states as a factor" in its interpretive strategy (Neuman 2008: 101). One might add that the Court could do more to win over the region's high court judges (Parra 2009), and understanding the dynamics of court rejection is a first step.

By tracing high court responses to recent Court rulings in these vastly different environments, then, we can begin to generate theories about how the changing role of courts locally may create opportunities for the Court to exert greater power in the region. This study draws from and contributes to scholarship that asks how supranational legal institutions come to exert influence on state actors. Until now, the field has focused on the European legal system, with little attention to the Inter-American System, let alone the human rights institutions of the African Union. The studies that do look at the Inter-American System have focused on state-level compliance, without disaggregating and looking at separate state actors, such as the courts (Hawkins and Jacoby 2008). The study also informs the question of the relation between legal cultures and judicialization. To date, most studies of comparative judicial politics have employed the models and presumptions of rational choice institutionalism (see Introduction). In generating theories about what factors shape high courts into good interlocutors for the Inter-American Court, however, I also consider ideas and discourse as independent variables. That is, I am interested in how conceptions judges have about their role in the political system generally, and in linking the international and national legal regimes specifically, can enhance or diminish the power of the Inter-American Court.

The following section discusses what the scholarship on the role of courts in fomenting regional court power has said in the context of the European Court of Justice (ECJ), the European Court of Human Rights (ECHR), and the Tribunal of Justice of the Andean Community (AJ). After a brief description of the Inter-American System, the essay moves on to present the three case studies of rejection of the Inter-American Court by local high courts. Finally, drawing from the case studies, it proposes five hypotheses about when high courts act as a partner to the Inter-American Court, and suggests avenues for further study.

NATIONAL COURTS AND REGIONAL INTEGRATION

Under neofunctionalist theories of the rise of the European legal system, "the self-interests of private litigants, national judges, and the ECJ [European Court of Justice] align such that the mutual pursuit of 'instrumental self-interest' leads to the expansion and penetration of European law into the domestic realm" (Alter 2001: 106).[2] Thus, it is not just state interests that matter, as in the realist theories of European integration. The system is structured such that the strategic actions of subnational actors – judges and litigants – enhance ECJ power. An important mechanism underlying this dynamic is the preliminary ruling mechanism, which allows national courts to refer cases that bring up EU-level legal issues to the ECJ. The case then returns to the national court for further adjudication. Thus, lower courts are able to bypass their own hierarchical superiors on many important questions when they deem it convenient (Alter 2001).

Recent findings raise questions about how far we can generalize from the ECJ experience to other regional settings. In the first place, many of the mechanisms available to the European agents – such as trade incentives and direct referral by lower court judges – are absent in the regional human rights systems. It is unclear, for example, to what extent systems with different structures, such as the European Council System or the Inter-American System, put in place incentives for national judges to comply with and cite to regional court rulings. Summarizing a series of country studies on the ECHR, Helen Keller and Alec Stone Sweet find that national judges do, indeed, play an important role in the reception process: "In many states, the courts have taken the lead in incorporating the Convention, and in strengthening other quasi-constitutional mechanisms of reception" (Keller and Stone Sweet 2008: 687). However, we do not yet know why they do so, and the question is all the more vexing because, as Keller and Stone Sweet note, high courts often promote the ECHR at the expense of their own power (Keller and Stone Sweet 2008: 688).

In the second place, even in those regional settings where the same mechanisms are in place as in the EU, national courts do not necessarily play the role of enhancing the regional court. Laurence Helfer and Karen Alter write that the Andean Tribunal of Justice (ATJ) is the world's third most active international court. Furthermore, it is modeled after the ECJ, including the preliminary ruling mechanism. However, despite its structural similarities to the European system, they find

[2] For a summary and critique of neofunctionalist theories of EU, see Andrew Morackvsic, 2005, "The European Constitutional Compromise and the Neo-Functionalist Legacy." *Journal of European Public Policy*, 12(2): 349–86.

that judges have not been important to fomenting ATJ power: "National courts are mostly reluctant and passive intermediaries that rarely submit references on issues Andean law outside of IP and generally refrain from using the Andean legal system to expand their authority" (Helfer and Alter 2009: 4). Alter and Helfer find that domestic administrative agencies have played a very active role in referring cases to the ATJ, concluding that we must pay attention to other domestic actors as robust interlocutors for international courts.

Alter and Helfer, then, do have an explanation for why the ATJ gained power despite "reluctant and passive" national courts: other domestic actors took on that role. However, they do not have an explanation for why national courts would be reticent to enter into a dialogue that would enhance their own power. Judges seem to be avoiding strategic behavior and instead "refrain from using the Andean legal system as a tool to aggrandize their authority" (Helfer and Alter 2009). It is implicit in Alter and Helfer's argument that the way judges conceive of their role might be a factor influencing their choices: "National courts' judges have a limited conception of their relationship with the ATJ" (Helfer and Alter 2009: 6). They also note that judges seem to misunderstand the ATJ, and they point to the stickiness of these misconceptions that cause them to act non-strategically.

In turning to the Inter-American System, this chapter draws two lessons from this scholarship on the relation of regional and national courts. First, we need to be on the lookout for factors that can create mutually beneficial incentives, such that judges use the Inter-American Court to gain more power, and, in so doing, enhance the Court's power. Secondly, and reading between the lines, ideas and conceptions seem to be part of the story of whether and how national judges act to enhance the international system's influence. We need to be aware that judges are not only self-interested actors looking to aggrandize their own power. They are also embedded actors who participate in and help create institutional ideologies, including ideas about their role at the intersection of national and international realms. These ideas, in turn, may at times guide action.

The Inter-American System

The Inter-American System for the protection of human rights is a creation of the Organization of American States (OAS), a regional institution formed at the close of World War II, when optimism about multilateral cooperation in creating a new world order ran high.[3] The signatories immediately adopted the American Declaration of the Rights and Duties of Man (hereinafter "Declaration"), which predates by roughly six months the UN Declaration of the Rights and Duties of Man. Like the UN Declaration, which resembles it in scope and content, the

[3] Few Latin American countries directly participated in World War II, but the region's countries sided with the Allies, and supported the war effort in various ways.

American Declaration was not created to be binding but aspirational.[4] In 1960, the OAS gave birth to a binding human rights treaty, the American Convention on Human Rights (hereinafter "Convention"). The Convention created a new list of rights, strengthened the powers of the Commission, and created the Inter-American Court. Today, twenty-one members have ratified the Convention, and all of these have conceded jurisdiction to the Inter-American Court (which requires a separate step from that of ratifying the Convention). Excluded are the United States, Canada, Cuba, and most of the Caribbean.[5] Together the Declaration and Convention are the primary human rights instruments of the Inter-American System for the protection of human rights.

The two main regional organs for the protection of human rights are the Commission and the Court. Today the Commission, situated in Washington D.C., carries out quasijudicial and nonjudicial functions, and is in many ways much more active and influential than the Court.[6] It appears before the Court in all cases to argue that a violation has taken place.[7] Its work can be divided into three general areas. The first is that of monitoring OAS states. Indeed, its most influential role has been that of pressuring governments and informing the world about human rights violations through its country reports. Secondly, and most relevant to this chapter, it is charged with investigating petitions alleging human rights violations filed by States' Parties and individuals. It attempts to resolve the case on its own, submitting a list of recommendations to a State Party if a violation is found. The Commission then refers cases to the Court if the State Party fails to comply, or if it deems the case to have a particular legal or political salience. It appears before the Court in all cases to argue that a violation has taken place.[8] Finally, the Commission is charged with educating the public about human rights.

The Court, created by the Convention, began its work in 1979. It has both adjudicatory and advisory functions, as it is charged with both enforcing the provisions of the American Convention of Human Rights as well as interpreting regional human

[4] Nonetheless, the Court and Commission have both declared it to be indirectly binding, through the American Charter, and through the concept of an evolving system of human rights. I/A Court H.R., *Interpretation of the American Declaration of the Rights and Duties of Man within the Framework of Article 64 of the American Convention on Human Rights*, Advisory Opinion OC-10/89 of July 14, 1989, Series A No. 10.

[5] Several Caribbean countries, originally signatories, renounced the Convention on the question of death penalty.

[6] The U.S. State Department web site concedes, "Through private persuasion and published reports on human rights infringements, the IACHR has been instrumental in improving OAS members' human rights practices and has helped to resolve conflicts."

[7] Under a recent reform, individual claimants now also appear before the Court, representing themselves, so that the Court hears the arguments of the individual petitioner, the Commission, and then the State in each case.

[8] Previously, it was conceived of as an advocate for the claimant. Under a recent reform, individual claimants now also appear before the Court, representing themselves, so that the Court hears the arguments of the individual petitioner, the Commission, and then the State in each case.

rights law. Under the adjudicatory function, the Court decides cases between States' Parties, or between individuals and a State Party, referred to it by the Commission or a State Party. Individuals cannot refer cases directly to the Court. Furthermore, it has jurisdiction only over states that have voluntarily acceded jurisdiction. Under the advisory function, OAS bodies or member states can request the Court to issue opinions on legal interpretation of regional human rights instruments or on questions of whether local laws are compatible with the Convention. Seven judges sit on the bench, elected on their individual capacity by State Parties to the Convention.

Although the Court has been successful at creating a coherent, oft-cited body of jurisprudence through its roughly one hundred contentious cases, it faces many challenges, including a low budget, a tense relationship with the Commission, and frequent criticism from national governments. Caseload has been a particularly difficult issue. In 2008, the Court issued nine final judgments in contentious cases. Compared to the European Court of Human Rights (ECHR), and even to the work of the Commission, this is a pittance. The ECHR, which has jurisdiction over forty-seven States Parties to the European Convention, issued 1,881 judgments in 2008.[9] The Commission, for its part, reports that it published seventy reports (including forty-nine cases found admissible; ten reports on petitions found inadmissible; four reports on friendly settlements; and seven reports on the merits).[10] The Inter-American Court is working to increase its low caseload, which it rightly views as an important step towards consolidation of its regime.

Compliance has been another challenge. A study comparing compliance to the ECHR and the Inter-American Court found that compliance to the Inter-American Court had been previously understated; while only 9 percent of cases receive full compliance, a more nuanced view of compliance reveals that 76 percent of cases receive partial compliance (Hawkins and Jacoby 2008). Cavallaro and Brewer argue that the Court will be unlikely to gain a high compliance rate given the political challenges of the governments it oversees, but garnering compliance should not be the Court's only goal; it should also focus on giving social movements jurisprudence relevant to their particular, local human rights struggles (Cavallaro and Brewer 2008). None of these recent studies, however, specifically considers the Inter-American Court's relation to, and ability to garner compliance and support from, high courts. This seems a particularly important question in light of Felipe Gonzalez's observation that, during the past decade, the Inter-American Court's orders increasingly address themselves to the judicial branch (Gonzalez 2009). Because of the requirement to exhaust local resources unless those resources are somehow inadequate, the Inter-American Court often ends up judging local

9 Survey of Activities 2008 Registry of the European Court of Human Rights 2008 http://www.echr.coe.int/NR/rdonlyres/D5B2847D-640D-4A09-A70A-7A1BE66563BB/0/ANNUAL_REPORT_2008.pdf.

10 Annual Report of The Inter-American Commission for Human Rights 2008. http://www.cidh.org/annualrep/2008eng/TOC.htm.

judiciaries.[11] In addition, claimants often turn to the Inter-American System with claims of due process violations, and the Inter-American Court has repeatedly asked national courts to reopen closed cases.

To begin the discussion about the Inter-American Court's relation to local courts, the following sections examine the recent rejection of Inter-American Court rulings by three national high courts, those of Chile, Argentina, and Venezuela. I begin by briefly examining the relation of law and politics in each country and then present the Inter-American Court ruling in question, and examine its reception by the national high court.

THE CHILE CASE

Law and Politics in Chile

Chile moved from authoritarianism to democracy in 1990, the year General Pinochet stepped down as head of government. In the subsequent seventeen years, democracy has flourished. Political party competition is strong. Corruption is low.[12] Vestiges of authoritarian power have slowly but steadily been cast out. Indeed, Chile is one of the highest performers in comparative studies of democracies beyond the North–West quadrant.[13]

In the midst of these momentous legal and political shifts and exposure to outside influence, however, sits a politically cautious, change-averse judiciary. Even as the Chilean state underwent dramatic political and economic shifts and international human rights law was partly reshaped by Pinochet-related litigation, the Chilean judiciary has remained shy of controversy, ducking politically salient issues despite growing public demand (Couso 2004). Gomez and Correa found that the courts avoided reviewing government action in 98 percent of cases that presented cases of acts that were legal according to legislation, but not necessarily under the Chilean constitution.[14] Another study found that, although courts around the world have recently gained in political prominence (Tate and Vallinder 1995), with some democracies experiencing judicial "rights revolutions" (Epp 1998), Chilean "courts have never expanded – let alone contributed to – constitutional rights" (Couso 2005). During the 1990s, courts avoided reviewing the constitutionality of 98 percent of cases that challenged government action as not permitted under the Chilean constitution (Couso 2004: 79). For constitutional claims that did secure judicial review, "Decisions were as likely to limit constitutionalist principles as they were to uphold

[11] Before the age of democracies in the region, the Court and Commission were more willing to forego the requirement to first exhaust local resources.

[12] Chile ranks just under the United States in Transparency International's corruption index. See: http://www.transparency.org/cpi/2004/cpi2004.en.html#cpi2004.

[13] Guillermo O'Donnell's term for the United States, Canada, and Western Europe (1999).

[14] This study is cited in Couso (2005).

them" (Hilbink 2007). That is why, one scholar concludes, "Minorities have no real reason to feel protected" by their access to judicial review (Atria 2000: 374).[15] One recent paper suggests that ideological change is afoot in the Chilean justice system (Couso and Hilbink 2009). But the authors point to the lower judges and the Constitutional Tribunal rather than the Supreme Court). The judicialization of politics has likewise been muted in the realm of civil society. Although Chile had a powerful and law-centered human rights movement during the dictatorship, this did not translate into a vibrant nor legally mobilized civil society after the transition to democracy. Indeed, most of its members were absorbed by the new government, and foreign funding quickly dried up. In contrast to Argentina, the human rights movement of the 1980s, which focused on the violations of fundamental rights such as torture and disappearance, did not spill over into other areas of rights. The dictatorship-era nongovernmental organizations (NGOs) have only in recent years taken on new kinds of causes.

Almonacid v. Chile. In September of 2006, the Inter-American Court issued rulings against the Chilean state on two consecutive Tuesdays. The first was *Caso Claude Reyes y otros v. Chile* (Sentencia de 19 de septiembre de 2006. Serie C No. 151), in which the Court found that the State of Chile lacked transparency, and had to reform its public information regime. The second case, issued a week later, was *Caso Almonacid Arellano y otros v. Chile*, a case of a Pinochet-era disappearance that the Supreme Court had closed under the 1978 Amnesty Decree (Sentencia sobre Excepciones Preliminares, Fondo, Reparaciones y Costas. Sentencia de 26 de septiembre de 2006. Serie C No. 154.) Arellano Almonacid was one of more than one thousand persons who disappeared during the military regime led by Augusto Pinochet (1973–90). In 1998, the Supreme Court affirmed a ruling granting amnesty to the perpetrators of the crime, and closed the case despite the fact that the investigation had still not uncovered what, exactly, had happened to Almonacid. His family pursued the case, submitting it to the Inter-American Commission, and the Commission, in turn, referred it to the Inter-American Court in July of 2005. The Court held that the Chilean Amnesty Decree of 1978 was in violation of the American Convention. It demanded that the State of Chile repeal the Amnesty Decree, reopen the investigation of the *Almonacid* case, and punish those responsible.

Together the cases piqued the Chilean media's interest in matters Inter-American. Each touched on a matter high on the public agenda at the time. Freedom of information was a salient issue in part because President Bachelet had campaigned on a platform including greater citizen and civil society participation in the policy-making process, and in part because actors of the Lagos governments stood accused of corruption charges in a handful of cases making headlines for several years in a row. The legacy of Pinochet-era human rights violations has been a central

[15] Whenever I quote a Spanish language source, I use my own translation.

political controversy ever since the transition to democracy, and particularly since the Pinochet detention in London sparked a wave of prosecutions that unfolds to this day. Legally, the question of what to do about the 1978 Amnesty Decree in case of disappearance had only been resolved by the Supreme Court for the first time in 2004.[16] In that case, the Court said the Amnesty did not apply to cases of disappearance in which the body had not been found. Now the Inter-American Court stepped in with a much more sweeping argument: the Amnesty Decree was invalid. Public attention to the cases was, however, fleeting, and most Chileans would not know what "*Almonacid*" refers to today.

Reception of Almonacid

Almonacid makes five separate demands of the Chilean state: 1) The State must ascertain that the Amnesty Decree does not impede the investigation of the extrajudicial killing of Almonacid, nor the identification and punishment of those responsible for his death; 2) The State must also ascertain that the Amnesty not impede prosecution of other like violations that occurred in Chile; 3) Within one year, the state must pay the family for the cost of litigation; 4) The State must publish the findings contained in the Inter-American Court ruling within six months in a newspaper of wide circulation; and 5) Within a year, the State must issue a report to the Court about the measures it has taken to comply with the ruling.

Note that the Court ruling does not distinguish between the organs within the state that must respond. However, under the Constitution, it is the judiciary that is charged with the functions of investigation of a crime, adjudication, and sentencing. It is thus to the judicial branch, and specifically to the Supreme Court as final arbiter and head of the judiciary, that the Inter-American Court addresses itself when it says that the *Almonacid* case must be reopened and investigated, and that those responsible must be sentenced. Furthermore, other cases of like violations must be investigated and sentences issued. The Amnesty Decree may never again be applied. Arguably, the Inter-American Court is saying that even the cases in which the Supreme Court or other court had reached a final judgment and applied the Amnesty during the 1970s must be reopened, upending years of final judgments.

Within two weeks of the ruling, the president of the Supreme Court publicly declared to the press that *Almonacid v. Chile* was not binding, but merely a guide. In addition, he said that the courts do not intervene in the discussion of laws. In other words, the Supreme Court has no power to rescind the Amnesty; that is the work of the legislature.[17] Judges merely apply the laws. With his statements, the

[16] Many cases had been permanently closed under the Amnesty Decree. However, the argument that cases of disappearance were different had not been resolved by the court until its ruling in Sandoval.

[17] "Presidente de la Suprema: fallo de Corte Interamericana de DDHH no es vinculante," *La Tercera*, October 16, 2006.

Supreme Court president signalled the inevitable breach of at least the first requirement of *Almonacid v. Chile*, that the Almonacid case itself be reopened. For even if Congress repealed the Amnesty retroactively, it would be for the Court to decide whether this case should be reopened. Needless to say, *Almonacid* has not been reopened, nor have other cases that had reached a final decision. Arguably, if the Congress repealed the Amnesty Decree, the courts would no longer apply it to any other cases. However, the decision of whether to do so would still reside with the courts themselves, as they must decide on the question of the retroactivity of penal laws. The President's statement also misstates the law. Chile has already given binding jurisdiction to the Court, and thus its rulings are binding not advisory.

President Bachelet's public response to the ruling stood in direct contrast to that of the Supreme Court. At a public event commemorating a Pinochet-era torture center, she announced, "My duty as President is to make sure Chile follows the rulings of the Inter-American Court of Human Rights."[18] Francisco Cox, a Chilean lawyer seasoned in Inter-American litigation, reports that for the first time he received calls as never before from the government about how to comply with the ruling.[19] There was a sense among human rights lawyers familiar with the Inter-American System that the Bachelet government was seriously committed, more so than any of its democratic predecessors.

Nonetheless, the Court's second stipulation has not been met. A bill was submitted to the congress on December 13, 2007, that would tell the courts not to apply the Amnesty Decree. In May, the president vowed to give "a new impulse to the bill that reinterprets Article 93 of the Penal Code,"[20] but the legislation has not advanced in congress.[21] Even members of the Center party, the Christian Democrats, were reluctant to back such a piece of legislation, Inter-American Court notwithstanding.[22] The demand that the Amnesty Decree not impede any case from going forward was not met by the deadline of September 26, 2007.

On the face of it then, we have a flagrant, declared repudiation of an Inter-American Court ruling by the Chilean Supreme Court, coupled by an empty promise of fulfillment by the executive. On closer look, however, we find that the Supreme Court's press release was not the whole story. On December 13, 2006, almost two months after *Almonacid* and only three days after Pinochet's death, the Supreme Court issued a landmark ruling on an Amnesty case. For the first time, the

[18] "Chile: President Bachelet – 'My Duty as President is to Make Sure Chile Follows the Rulings of The Inter-American Court of Human Rights,'" October 14, 2006, *U.S. Fed News*.

[19] Interview with Francisco Cox, January 6, 2007, Santiago, Chile.

[20] Organizaciones de DDHH emplazan a Michelle Bachelet durante visita a Suiza. El Mostrador.cl, 1 de Junio de 2007.

[21] See: http://sil.senado.cl/pags/index.html.

[22] Indeed, one prominent politician argued that *Almonacid* is the reason that Chile has not yet ratified ICC ratification: the right-wing parties saw it as a negative example of international court incursion into national affairs. 19 de Enero de 2007 Ex senador José Antonio Viera-Gallo: 'Derecha se opone al TPI por fallo contra aplicación de la ley de Amnistía' por Macarena López M.

Supreme Court grounded a ruling in which it did not apply the Amnesty Decree on international law rather than domestic law. Furthermore, it cited *Almonacid v. Chile*. The courts had long been citing international law, especially the Geneva Conventions, but also Inter-American jurisprudence. Suddenly, however, this was the foundation of their decision. It was a victory for the Inter-American Court, but one that was hidden behind the Supreme Court president's vehement response to *Almonacid v. Chile*. The Supreme Court has also complied with *Almonacid* in that the Amnesty Decree has not been applied by the Supreme Court since the Inter-American Court's ruling in *Almonacid*.

It is important to note, however, that this is the direction that the Chilean courts have been heading since 1998. Rare was the judge who applied the Amnesty Decree in cases of disappearance and extrajudicial killing. Some had even allowed torture cases to move forward, an action that could only be justified under international law. The few cases to which the Amnesty Decree was applied were usually reversed at the Supreme Court level. The reliance on international law was a milestone, but one in a string of many. Thus, it is impossible to attribute this switch to the Inter-American Court's single decision, or even its line of decisions. Rather, the Inter-American Court provided one more tool in the kit of those arguing against the Amnesty Decree, and it made it that much more inconceivable for the Supreme Court to apply the Amnesty Decree in the cases that it had not already closed.

THE ARGENTINE CASE

Law and Politics in Argentina

Since the transition from dictatorship to democracy in Argentina in 1983, the relation between law and politics has become more judicialized. As Pilar Domingo argues, "The experience of the break with military rule was critical in propelling not only a political discourse of rights but also societal consciousness of the need to embrace constitutional democracy and rule of law – moving away from the old logic of populism" (Domingo 2004). One of the first acts of the new government was to put junta members on trial. Catalina Smulovitz argues that civil society in Argentina turned to law in great part because of the drama and symbolism of these trials (Smulovitz 2002). Civil actors responded by bringing cases to the courts. Between 1991 and 2002, the Supreme Court's caseload grew by more than six times, and the federal court caseload doubled (Smulovitz 2005). The most prominent example of this cycle of civil society's turn to the courts and greater activism by the courts was the deluge of legal claims against the government during the 2002 financial collapse. At the height of the crisis, the courts challenged the government on the constitutionality of the *corralito*, or the freezing of the bank accounts to stem devaluation of the currency.

The courts, in turn, did not disappoint, at least at first. Under Alfonsin, "the Supreme Court rendered controversial decisions on various issues. It liberalized society's laws on divorce, drugs, and other issues... It also frustrated several of Alfonsin's important policies" (Larkins 1998: 427). In 1992, it even ruled that ratified human rights treaties were *directly* applicable within the domestic sphere.[23] This is clearly an example of judicialization enhancing Inter-American Court influence. In 1994, under Menem, a new constitution was promulgated that adopted and further specified this monist conception of the relationship between international and domestic law. Although the constituent assembly was convened under circumstances that were viewed with skepticism by the public (Levit 1999), the resulting document gave the courts greater discretion. Article 75 stipulates that all treaties ratified by Argentina are superior to domestic laws, and that certain human rights treaties, including the American Declaration of the Rights and Duties of Man and the American Convention, have constitutional status. Given that the Constitution also grants judges the power of constitutional review, it thus grants judges power to strike down any law they may deem in violation of certain human rights treaties.

Nonetheless, this cycle of judicialization in Argentina did not necessarily yield greater autonomous court power. President Menem, in particular, had a penchant for intervention into judicial affairs. Most notably he packed the Supreme Court in 1990, expanding it from five to nine, and filled it with his supporters. A string of subsequent rulings made evident the Court's slavish loyalty to Menem (Larkins 1998). The Court lost legitimacy (Domingo 2004; Smulovitz 2005) even as demand for political intervention by the courts, continued.

Bueno Alvez v. Argentina. On April 5, 1988, Mr. Bueno Alvez was illegally detained by Argentine federal police investigators, who then proceeded to torture him so as to force from him a statement against his lawyer. Bueno Alvez subsequently filed suit in federal court, but the criminal investigation of his case was never completed and, in 2004, an Argentina appellate court ruled that the statute of limitations had run out on the case. Bueno Alvez submitted the case to the Inter-American Commission under the argument that torture constitutes a crime against humanity, and therefore no statute of limitations can apply. In its report, the Commission found that Argentina had violated Bueno Alvez's rights under the American Convention and Declaration. It subsequently submitted the case to the Inter-American Court. The Court ruled against the State on May 11, 2007, demanding that the State pay damages, publish the Inter-American Court opinion in the public media, and reopen the investigation (Corte IDH. Caso Bueno Alves vs. Argentina. Sentencia sobre el fondo, reparaciones y costas de 11 de mayo de 2007. Serie C No. 164). Although the Court agreed that the crime did not classify as a crime against humanity, the lack of investigation was a denial of justice and an ongoing wrong that needed remedy.

[23] Corte Suprema de Justicia de la Nacion [CSJN], 7/7/1992, "Ekmekdjian, Miguel Angel c/ Sofovich, Gerardo y otros," Fallos (1992-315-1492) (Arg.).

Reception of Bueno Alvez

After *Bueno Alvez* came down, the government accepted its international responsibility and vowed to pay the victim as the Court demanded. The Supreme Court, by contrast, issued a ruling in direct contradiction to that of the Inter-American Court in August. It reviewed the decision to close the case on an extraordinary writ, but then reaffirmed the finding that as the underlying crime was not a crime against humanity, the statute of limitations had run out, and the case had to be closed. The Supreme Court relies on a Public Ministry opinion on the case that speaks directly to the question of the Inter-American Court's role. Although the Public Ministry opinion pre-dates *Bueno Alvez v. Argentina*, the Supreme Court's reliance on it amounts to a direct affront to the Inter-American ruling:[24]

> [T]he obligation to investigate and punish the violation of human rights exists within the frame and with the tools of the rule of law, and does not stand above them (Derecho, René Jesús s/incidente de prescripción de la acción penal Causa No. 24.079C, para VI).

With this ruling, the Supreme Court places its own judgment above that of the Inter-American Court: indeed, it seems to imply that the Inter-American Court ruling prioritizes the investigation and punishment of violations of human rights above the rule of law itself.

To understand this defiance, it is important to recall that the Constitution of 1994 explicitly brought the Inter-American Declaration into national law, at the level of constitutional law. However, the difficulty is that the Declaration does not trump constitutional law, but must be read to complement it. Article 75 also holds that the American Convention and Declaration, "have constitutional hierarchy, do not repeal any section of the First Part of this Constitution and are to be understood as complementing the rights and guarantees recognized herein." Since 1994, the Supreme Court of Argentina has been struggling to figure out what this Article of the Constitution means on the ground:

> Deconstructing the core tenets of this constitutional provision has been one of the paramount endeavors undertaken by the Supreme Court of Argentina since 1994. By simultaneously deferring to the opinion of supranational adjudicatory bodies, but still conferring the last word regarding the compatibility of relevant regional case law with its core text to the domestic judiciary, the Constitution of Argentina crafted a theoretically compelling, institutionally complex tool to promote compliance with international – and regional – human rights law. (Naddeo 2007: 34)

Furthermore, this was not the first time that the Inter-American Court ordered the Argentine Supreme Court to reopen a case on which a statute of limitation had run

[24] I owe this observation to Cecilia Naddeo.

out and to punish those responsible. The *Bulacio* case had presented similar facts of a torture and extrajudicial killing on which the domestic courts ruled the statute of limitations had run out (Corte IDH. *Caso Bulacio vs. Argentina*. Sentencia de 18 de Septiembre de 2003. Serie C No. 100). Criminal lawyers were very critical of the *Bulacio* ruling, claiming that the Court had gone overboard in prioritizing the right of a victim in an ordinary criminal case to have a transgressor punished over the constitutionally enshrined due process rights of the accused. In that case, however, the Supreme Court reluctantly submitted to the Inter-American Court. In this case, it rebeled.

With *Bueno Alvez*, then, the Argentina Supreme Court announced a new solution to the problems posed by Article 75. Prior to the ruling, the situation seemed to be that there were two final arbiters (Naddeo 2007: Levit 1999). Now the Supreme Court displaced the Inter-American Court and appointed itself the final arbiter in "harmonizing" or interpreting the fundamental rights enshrined in international treaties, in the Argentine Constitution, and in the very jurisprudence of the Inter-American Court. Argentina is bound by the Inter-American Declaration, but not by the Inter-American Court's interpretation of the Declaration when that interpretation creates a conflict with constitutional law.

THE VENEZUELA CASE

Law and Politics in Venezuela

Since the 1990s, Venezuelan political battles have increasingly taken judicial forms (Perez Perdomo 2005). As politics grew more contentious in the 1990s, and as Venezuela's traditional social networks and political pacts began to unravel (Gomez in this volume), political struggles that would previously have been resolved behind closed doors began arriving on court dockets. Since the start of the Chavez administration in 1998, moreover, this judicialization has accelerated. Chavez began his presidency with a constitutional overhaul, and the language of constitutionalism and rights suffuses his discourse. At the same time, former elites increasingly challenge the Chavez government's political program in the courts (Perez Perdomo 2005) as it is the only political channel available to them. Indeed, Manuel Gomez argues in this volume that the separation of law and politics has blurred under the Chavez regime.

Even as courts became a crucial site of contestation, they were also targeted by Chavez's reformist efforts, and accordingly they have come under greater political control. After assuming the presidency in 1998, Hugo Chavez called for the creation of a new constitution that would re-found the Venezuelan state. He invoked elections for a National Constituent Assembly, which first convened in 1999 with a strong pro-Chavez majority. The Assembly immediately declared that the judicial branch was in crisis and created a Judicial Emergency Commission to purge corrupt judges and rewrite the rules governing the judiciary. The new constitution, enacted in December of 1999, called for the creation of a new high court, the *Tribunal Supremo de Justicia*, with more expansive powers than the traditional Supreme Court. The new court was constituted provisionally in 2000, and the permanent members were appointed in 2001.

The Constitution also called for the creation of judicial disciplinary tribunals, which would be governed by a new Code of Ethics. Furthermore, in its transitional articles, the Constitution called for the creation of the *Comisión de Funcionamiento y Reestructuración del Sistema Judicial* (CFRSJ), which would be charged with disciplinary matters until the new code of ethics was promulgated. The CFRSJ was created within a year. Since its creation, many judges have been dismissed, and critics argue that Chavez was able to use the CJRSJ, staffed with provisional officers, to selectively purge judges not favorable to his government's politics.[25] In addition, many of the judges replacing the purged judges have themselves been named provisionally. Judicial independence in Venezuela has thus become a crucial and contested political issue, and so it is perhaps not surprising that it became the focus of an Inter-American Court ruling.

Apitz v. Venezuela. In *Caso Apitz*, the Inter-American Court reviewed the dismissal of three Venezuelan judges under the Convention's procedural guarantees. Officially, the judges had been dismissed for "inexcusable judicial error" in their ruling on a case having to do with the registration of a real estate transaction. The judges appealed to the Inter-American System on the grounds that their dismissal was politically motivated. The three served on an important appellate court that reviews administrative acts. They claimed that the Chavez government, which had publicly called for the removal of the three judges, had been unhappy with several of their rulings, and wanted to make room for pro-government judges. The Court ruled in August of 2008 that the procedure to remove the judges had violated their right to an impartial hearing, among other due process guarantees under the Convention. It ordered the State to: 1) pay reparations to the deposed judges; 2) reinstate the judges to a position comparable in rank to the one they last held; and 3) within a year, approve a new ethics code and end the regime of provisional judges. The Court did not find that the evidence sufficed to establish that Venezuela's Supreme Court or judiciary as a whole lacked independence, as the plaintiffs had argued.

The *Apitz* case posed a significant challenge to the Chavez administration because it brought to public light the regime of reforms of the judicial system. In particular, the fact that many judges in Venezuela, as well as those in charge of disciplinary matters, hold a provisional and therefore more vulnerable status was placed under scrutiny. The case is also significant in that it reflects a trend, noted earlier, by the

[25] The Inter-American Court agreed, calling for an end to the provisional regime. *Caso Apitz*.

Inter-American Commission and Court of moving into the business of judging judicial systems. The opinion is basically a technical review of procedures for appointing and removing judges.

Reception of Apitz

In December of 2008, responding to a government petition, the Venezuela Supreme Court ruled that the *Apitz* ruling could not be executed: The ruling clashes with Venezuelan constitutional law, it proclaimed, and in any case the Inter-American Court had overstepped the bounds of its authority. The Venezuelan court concludes, remarkably, by calling on the executive to withdraw Venezuela from the American Convention of Human Rights.

Three aspects of the Venezuelan Court's ruling, which provoked both national and international criticism, deserve comment. First, the ruling seems to alter the constitutional status of the Inter-American Convention and Court in Venezuela. Under the Venezuelan Constitution, international treaties are directly applicable and have constitutional status. The Supreme Court is the official arbiter of conflicts between constitutional provisions. However, Article 23 provides that human rights conventions hold a higher hierarchical status if they establish a more favorable rights regime than that provided by the Constitution. This doctrine of greater deference to human rights is called the *progressive principle* (Brewer-Carías 2009). In reviewing the *Apitz* ruling, however, the Venezuelan Court does not grant the Convention's provisions this greater level of deference. Rather, it treats the conflict it sees between the *Apitz* ruling and the Constitution as a conflict of provisions of equal status (Brewer-Carias 2009).

Second, the Venezuelan Court openly describes its own interpretations as in service to a political project: "Law is a normative theory at the service of the politics underlying the axiological project of the Constitution" (2008: 11). This interpretive philosophy leads the Court to conclude that human rights cannot be treated as absolute or ahistorical, but must be fitted to the needs of that political project. In other words, "Constitutional norms that privilege the general interest and the common good" should prevail, as should those dispositions that "privilege collective interests over particular interests" (2008: 11). Here, the interests of the three ex-judges are trumped by the public interest (in the finality of Supreme Court decisions and in not upsetting the appointments and removals made under the provisional system). Note, however, that the Venezuelan Court echoes the Inter-American Court's call for the legislature to pass a new Code of Ethics and thereby end the system of provisional judges.

But perhaps the most remarkable aspect of the ruling is its request to the executive that Venezuela withdraw from the American Convention. The reason given is that the Inter-American Court has overstepped its bounds and is meddling in internal legal matters. However, there seems to be no legal foothold for the request. The single-authored dissent argues that the Venezuelan Court overstepped its authority: decisions on foreign affairs lie exclusively with the executive. The Venezuelan tribunal's rejection stirred controversy within and without Venezuela. Twelve local human rights' NGOs together issued a declaration stating that the ruling "weakens human rights guarantees for persons in the country and in the hemisphere."[26] Apitz himself made the rounds of opposition radio and television talk shows, arguing that the Supreme Court was a Chavez lackey. International human rights organizations such as Amnesty International and Human Rights Watch condemned the ruling as undermining human rights in the region.

Meanwhile, the three judges have not been reinstated, nor have they received compensation, and a new code of ethics has yet to be passed. Arguably the ruling makes it easier for the Chavez administration to withdraw from the Inter-American human rights system by providing him with a high court opinion in support of such a move. It is interesting to note, however, that lately the Venezuelan government often cites Inter-American rulings for support. In March of 2009, the Inter-American Court again ruled against the Venezuelan government.[27] Although the Court found that the government had failed to provide adequate protection for journalists, it did not find that the Chavez government had violated the right to freedom of expression under the Convention. The government has frequently referred to that case to argue that there is freedom of expression in Venezuela, just as it has referred to the *Apitz* case to say that the Inter-American Court did not find that the judiciary as a whole lacked independence. This reliance on Inter-American Court rulings amounts to an implicit legitimation of the Inter-American System.[28]

ANALYSIS OF THE CASES

This chapter explores synchronicities between regional legal integration and judicialization by looking at when and how high courts comply with the commands of the Inter-American Court. The preceding sections presented three cases of high courts rejecting the Court. In this section I compare the three rejections, and then use the differences to generate a list of factors that may predict whether high courts will comply with or reject the commands of the IACtHR, and how they will do so. At this early stage of social scientific studies of the Inter-American System, we are still in need of theory-generating studies.

[26] "Foro por la Vida Foro por la Vida rechaza sentencia de TSJ sobre el Sistema Interamericano de Derechos Humanos," Caracas, January 13, 2009. http://www.espaciopublico.info/index.php?option=com_content&task=view&id=275&Itemid=30 (July 27, 2009).

[27] Corte IDH. *Caso Perozo y otros vs. Venezuela*. Excepciones Preliminares, Fondo, Reparaciones y Costas. Sentencia de 28 de enero de 2009. Serie C No. 195.

[28] See, for example, the fact sheets of the Venezuelan Embassy in the United States: http://www.embavenez-us.org/factsheet/FS-CorteIDH2.pdf (July 27, 2009).

Comparing the Rejections

Even as they are united in defying the Inter-American Court, the Supreme Courts could not be more different from each other in terms of the relationship they articulate among the Supreme Court, the Inter-American Court, and the national political sphere. The Chilean Supreme Court acts through a nonjudicial forum to announce its noncompliance. It does not dignify the Inter-American Court ruling with a judicial response. The Chilean Court thus misses an opportunity to enter into dialogue with the Inter-American Court and other national courts in the Inter-American System, and to further develop Latin American doctrine on the relation between the Inter-American Court and domestic judiciaries. Furthermore, the Supreme Court president announced that Inter-American Court rulings are only advisory, thereby rendering meaningless the distinction between the Court's advisory and contentious jurisdiction, and reducing the status of its interpretations to that of soft law. Enrique Tapia also argued that domestic courts have no power to change the laws, equating the act of reinterpreting the Amnesty Decree to rewriting it. Only the legislature, then, is empowered to bring Chile into compliance with international law. The Supreme Court thus erects a dualist regime in which the legislature is supreme, and stands between the Inter-American Court and the Chilean judiciary. Without legislative action, the Inter-American Court is legally powerless within Chile. The Supreme Court does not entirely reject *Almonacid*. It does occasionally cite *Almonacid*, and it refrains from applying the Amnesty Decree to cases not already closed. However, this was already the direction it had moved in since 1998.

The Argentine Supreme Court, by contrast, announces its noncompliance in a judicial decision. Thus, it participates in the making of Inter-American jurisprudence, as it has been actively doing since 1992. Moreover, in this decision the Argentine Supreme Court announces a very different hierarchy than does the Chilean Supreme Court. Although it places itself as final arbiter of laws in the national regime, it conceives of international treaties and constitutional law as equal in the hierarchy of laws, as is enshrined in the Argentina Constitution. Thus, it enunciates a monist conception of international law even as it anoints itself final arbiter of how the Inter-American treaties and jurisprudence will be interpreted within Argentina (at least insofar as they are deemed to conflict with constitutional law). Under this hierarchy, Inter-America Court rulings can have direct effect, subject to Supreme Court approval. Even as it rejects the IACtHR's ruling, then, the Supreme Court further develops a conversation that the Chilean court shut down, and keeps open the door to international law that it had itself opened in 1992 (and which the Chilean Supreme Court shut with its nonjuridical refusal to reopen *Almonacid*).

At the same time, the Argentine Supreme Court's defiance can also be read as a backlash. Since 1992, the Supreme Court has given the Inter-American Court a growing voice in Argentine affairs by announcing a monist regime and by frequently citing Inter-American instruments and jurisprudence (Naddeo 2007). After the *Bulacio* Inter-American ruling, it even reopened a closed criminal case, to much local criticism. Here, the Supreme Court reverses course and puts itself above the Inter-American Court. Once a monist regime is established, it seems, domestic courts will come into more direct competition with international courts over power in the domestic sphere. As Alter writes, "A virtuous circle, where successful litigation encourages more cases to be raised and more references to the ECJ may certainly emerge, but it is not the only possibility. Negative feedback loops may also emerge" (Alter 2001: 128).

Like the Argentine Supreme Court, the Venezuelan Tribunal dignified the Inter-American Court ruling with a judicial response. Five months after the Inter-American ruling, it issued an opinion complete with cites to Inter-American instruments and to the Peruvian Supreme Court's jurisprudence on the Court. It thus joined the Inter-American Court dialogue on the Inter-American Court's status in the realm. Furthermore, unlike the Chilean Supreme Court president, it acknowledged that, under the American Convention, the Court's rulings have binding authority over Venezuela. Yet, of the three, its ruling deals the hardest blow. Its claim that it is not constitutionally bound to follow the Inter-American Court echoes that of the Argentine Supreme Court. However, in doing so it announced a new, lower status for all Inter-American instruments within the hierarchy of laws than what the Venezuelan Constitution, on its face, seems to demand. Even more damagingly, by calling on the government to withdraw from the Convention and jurisdiction of the Inter-American Court, the tribunal undermined the legitimacy of the Inter-American System, revealing the weak foundations of supranational judicial power.

Factors Contributing to Inter-American Court Power

From these cases, five factors emerge as potentially fruitful hypotheses about when high courts comply with or reject Inter-American rulings, and, more generally, when national courts foment or diminish Inter-American Court influence. These factors are familiar from the judicial politics literature on judicial behaviour. However, they have not been considered in the Inter-American setting and applied to the relation between high courts and the Inter-American Court. I briefly discuss each in turn.

1) JUDICIAL INDEPENDENCE FROM THE EXECUTIVE. The three case studies raise an interesting set of questions about executive–judicial relations and the international sphere. Current scholarship suggests that settings in which democracy and the rule of law is generally respected coincide with greater regional court power (Cavallaro and Brewer 2008; Helfer and Slaughter 1997). Further, international relations scholars

have shown that new democracies are particularly keen on performing compliance with international human rights norms so as to legitimate themselves in the international sphere (Simmons 2009). In the case of Chile and Argentina, both presidents welcomed the Inter-American ruling and immediately promised to follow its orders. Both presidents were survivors of the repression of the military dictatorships, committed to human rights discourse, and eager to perform compliance. The Chilean and Argentine courts, in this sense, thwarted their executives' efforts to uphold the Inter-American System. The cases suggest that judiciaries will not always defer to the international human rights agenda of their executives. This raises the possibility that national settings of democratic governments with a strong human rights agenda coupled with greater judicial independence does not necessarily yield high courts receptive to Inter-American rulings.

2) REGIONAL POLITICS AND THE NEW LEFT. Regional politics affect national politics, and may play a role in judges' actions. The Chavez regime is in important ways the leader of a movement of governments of Latin America under which executives with strong popular appeal adopt a socialist program even as they alter the constitution and funnel political power toward the executive branch (and away from judiciaries). Under a regional politics thesis, which is an extension of the judicial independence thesis, courts within a country participating in the New Left movement will be less likely to foment Inter-American Court influence. Courts in these regimes will be hard put to use Inter-American rulings to stand up to popular presidents. Further, these governments, which include the governments of Bolivia, Ecuador, and Nicaragua, often directly challenge the Inter-American System. The leaders of the "New Left" embrace the language of human rights, and emphasize social, cultural, and economic rights in particular. Both Chavez and Evo Morales, president of Bolivia, have raised the possibility of creating an alternative regional human rights body under the auspices of the Bolivarian Alliance for the People of Our Americas ALBA or the Union of South American Nations (Unasur), two regional bodies initiated by Chavez.[29] Chavez has continually criticized the OAS as a U.S. puppet and has threatened to withdraw from the system in general, and from the Court's jurisdiction in particular.

In the *Apitz* scenario, Chavez had publicly called for the removal of the three judges at issue in the IACtHR ruling and publicly spoke out against the IACtHR ruling. In its sentence, the Venezuelan Court openly declares that its jurisprudence is informed by the Socialist–Democratic spirit of the 1999 Constitution, enacted under Chavez. Furthermore, it calls on the government to do what it has already indicated

[29] Respectively, Bolivarian Alliance for the People of Our Americas, which includes Bolivia, Cuba, Ecuador, Honduras, Nicaragua, and Venezuela, among others; and the Union of South American Nations, which includes twelve South American nations.

it is considering doing – withdraw from the treaty. It thereby gives withdrawal a judicial imprimatur.

3) IDEAS ABOUT JUDGING. This study is not based on interviews with high courts judges, and cannot reveal how, exactly, judges conceive of their role vis-à-vis the international sphere. We do have studies, however, on how Chilean judges view their interpretive role (Hilbink 2007; Huneeus 2009), and I suggest this may be a significant factor in determining how a high court works with or against the Inter-American Court.

I argue elsewhere that the Chilean judges' turn to litigation of Pinochet-era claims stems not from an embrace of international human rights norms, but rather an effort to atone for past complicity with the Pinochet regime (Huneeus 2010). Judges describe themselves as protagonists in the judiciary's turn toward litigation of Pinochet-era cases, and this protagonism serves to relegimate the judiciary from its past collusion with a repressive regime. Thus, it is a strategy aimed at a national audience, undertaken almost entirely with national legal instruments, and focused exclusively on Pinochet-era cases. The Chilean judges are reluctant to acknowledge the international sphere's role in the prosecutorial turn, failing to mention even the detention of Pinochet in London as influencing their own actions (Hilbink 2007; Huneeus 2006). While acceding to *Almonacid*'s demands would open up many more cases for prosecution, it would also take away from judges' self-described role as protagonists in the prosecutorial turn. It is possible, then, that the nationalist understanding judges have of their role in the prosecution of Pinochet cases accounts for the Supreme Court's ignoring *Almonacid*'s commands, just as it has made them ground the majority of their Pinochet-era rulings on national rather than international law.

Studies of judges' conceptions of their role in cases invoking human rights could be fruitful in explaining when high courts promote regional integration. The judicial culture of the Venezuelan judiciary, in particular, has undergone change during the past two decades, moving from an embrace of formalism to a more purposive view of judicial interpretation: "The formalist and timid attitude predominant in the former Supreme Court has been replaced by an interpretive boldness and a clear desire to renew the legal order under the new supreme tribunal, in particular its Sala Constitucional" (Perez Perdomo 2005: 141). The ruling of the Venezuelan Court indeed openly judges as participants in the Bolivarian Revolution, and as having its social and political program as an explicit end. The Bolivarian Revolution, as its name suggests, is not limited to the national sphere: it has Pan-American aspirations. However, as noted earlier, it prioritizes the common good over individual rights, and the Venezuelan Court accordingly claims an interpretive philosophy in which social and political ends trump the protections of individual civil and due process rights. Inter-American jurisprudence, by contrast, emphasizes individual civil and political rights.

Turning to Argentina, the new constitutionalism emerges as a possibly significant feature of judicial culture. Argentina is considered to be a leading example of the new constitutionalism (Carbonell 2007; Landau 2005), a concept that refers not just to texts, but to theories of interpretation and jurisprudential practices (Carbonell 2007; Couso in this volume). In particular, the new constitutionalism is linked to a more substantive jurisprudence that incorporates consideration of principles and values, proportionality tests, reasonability tests, and other constitutional doctrines that ultimately grant judges a large dose of discretion (Carbonell 2007: 10). Surprisingly, the link between the new constitutionalism and the international realm has not been a focus of scholarship (Pisarello 2007: 159). Clearly, however, the new practices and theories, which emphasize fundamental rights, have important implications for the interpretation of the status and content of international human rights treaties. We are in need of a study on whether these new theories of interpretation spill over and influence how judges conceptualize the content of international rights, the status of treaties in the national sphere, and their own role in articulating the relation between the international and national spheres.

4) PATH DEPENDENCY: FAMILIARITY OF HIGH COURT WITH RIGHTS AND INTERNATIONAL LAW. As noted in the case study sections, the Argentine Supreme Court has participated in much substantive reasoning based on rights provisions in recent years. It is also accustomed to being at the center of political controversy. It is quite plausible that this experience makes the judges more comfortable with and willing to participate in adjudication under international treaties. This argument echoes the argument made by Catalina Smulovitz in this volume that experience with rights litigation made Argentina's lawyers more likely to bring such claims to the courts. Judges, in turn, have gained experience with rights-based public law litigation. This experience might make them more likely to handle rights cases under international law.

However, this path-dependent argument fails to explain the reception of *Almonacid* in Chile and *Apitz* in Venezuela. If there is one area where Chilean courts have been assertive and have gained experience in defending rights, it is in the resolution of Pinochet-era cases of human rights violations after 1998. Furthermore, litigants have argued for decades that Pinochet-era human rights crimes fall under international law. Yet the Chilean Supreme Court has been very slow to draw on international instruments to decide cases, preferring to decide under national law even when this means twisting existing doctrine in new directions. In this case, experience with rights adjudication and greater court assertiveness has not enhanced Inter-American Court power. Similarly, the Venezuelan Court has seen an increasing amount of politically charged rights litigation arrive at its docket in recent years, but this has not made it a proponent of the Inter-American Court.

Familiarity, of course, comes not just from practical experience but also through education. The Chilean justice's misstatement of Inter-American Court law raises the possibility that education in international law affects how judges respond to the Inter-American Court. Arnulf Becker argues that while international law was once considered an important political language in the region, it was drained of its salience during the era of dictatorships (Becker 2006). He observes that many Latin American international law textbooks model themselves after European texts and refer to the Inter-American System in only a few pages "in a subchapter of a section dealing with international organizations, and usually after a description of the U.N. System" (Becker 2006: 289). As Keller and Stone have noted in the context of the ECHR (Keller and Stone Sweet 2008), comparative study of the varying positions the Inter-American System occupies in legal education, including judicial training, might shed light on the question of when national courts promote regional integration.

5) THE LEGALIST THESIS AND THE NEW CONSTITUTIONS. The legalist thesis posits that the law itself actually influences outcomes: law constrains judges and determines outcomes. Applied here, it is significant that the Argentine and Venezuelan constitutions are of more recent vintage than the Chilean, and directly address the question of the status and effect of human rights treaties in the national realm. Article 76 of the Argentine Constitution provides that the Inter-American Convention is directly applicable in the domestic sphere and carries the status of constitutional law. The Venezuelan Constitution similarly provides that human rights treaties are directly applicable, and carry the status of constitutional law (Article 23). By contrast, the Chilean Constitution, ratified in 1980 – under the Pinochet regime and only one year after the Inter-American Court came online – does not provide that human rights treaties are directly applicable, nor does it specify the status they occupy within the national regime. It thus leaves Chilean courts with an ambiguous mandate. This difference may help explain why the Chilean Supreme Court ignores the order to reopen the sentence of *Almonacid*, without directly addressing the IACtHR's ruling. Explicit constitutional language likely corresponds with a more direct engagement.

Conclusion: Judicialization and Human Rights

It is noteworthy that Inter-American Court rulings have been openly rejected by high courts at least three times in recent years. This resonates with the findings of Alter and Helfer, who note with surprise that the recent empowerment of national courts in Latin America does not seem to have made a difference to courts' willingness to refer courts to the Andean Tribunal of Justice:

> [R]ecent institutional reforms have increased the assertiveness of many courts in Latin America, especially in the area of individual rights, with the result that judges in the region are exerting more independence and influence over executive branch officials and legislatures. This trend has not, however, spilled over to national court interactions with the ATJ.

However, if we look closely at these instances of rejection of the Inter-American Court, we see important differences in the manner of rejection, and in the consequences of the manner of rejection, and these, in turn, are suggestive of factors that help us understand when courts will enhance Inter-American Court power. The rejections suggest that it would be fruitful to further explore the consequences of executive–judicial relations, of regional politics, of judges' ideas about and experience with the particular human rights violations they are reviewing, of legal education, and of constitutional texts' treaty provisions..

Stepping back, it is interesting, if speculative, to reflect on the link between, on the one hand, the type of relation between law and politics within each country, and, on the other hand, the manner of rejection of the Inter-American Court. I noted in the introduction that the three countries in some ways are representative of current trends in the region, with Argentina as an example of the new constitutionalism, Chile as an example of a more traditional, formalist legal culture, and Venezuela as an example of the New Left, wherein law is viewed as participating in the socialist transformation of the state. These differences in legal–political dynamics are reflected in the manner in which the high courts reject the Inter-American Court, and whether they view the Inter-American Court as a threat to the national political project or as a partner in developing regional human rights norms. In other words, the case studies suggest that, with more data, one could construct a typology that links the manner in which the boundary between law and politics is articulated in a particular national setting to the manner in which the relation between the international and national spheres is articulated.

In closing, I note that the discussion here has focused on the first kind of judicialization in Latin America, the greater participation of courts in politically salient public issues. Another next step would be to examine the subtler but likely more pervasive effects of the second aspect of judicialization presented in this volume's introduction, that of dressing social demands in the language and forms of law: Does the turn toward legal language in political claims enhance the influence of the Inter-American System in national politics?

References

Brewers-Carías, Allan R. 2009. La Interrelación entre los Tribunales Constitucionales de América Latina y la Corte Interamericana de Derechos Humanos, y la Cuestión de la Inejectuabilidad de sus Decisiones en Venezuela. (On file with author).

Atria, Fernando. 2000. "Revisión Judicial: Sindrome de la Víctima Insatisfecha." *Estudios Publicos*, 79: 347–402.

Alter, Karen. 2001. *Establishing the Supremacy of European Law: The Making of an International Rule of Law in Europe*. Oxford: Oxford University Press.

Becker Lorca, Arnulf. 2006. "International Law in Latin America or Latin American International Law? Rise, Fall, and Retrieval of a Tradition of Legal Thinking and Political Imagination." *Harvard International Law Journal*, 47(1): 283–305.

Brewer-Carias, Allan R. 2009. "La Interrelación entre los Tribunales Constitucionales de Américan Latina y la Corte Interamericana de Derechos Humanos, y la Cuestión de la Inejecutabilidad de sus Decisiones en Venezuela." Paper presented at a conference at the Universidad Carlos III de Madrid, March 30.

Carbonell, Miguel ed. 2007. *Teoría del neoconstitucionalismo: Ensayos escogidos*. Madrid: Editorial Trotta.

Cavallaro, James L. and Stephanie Erin Brewer. 2008. "Reevaluating Regional Human Rights Litigation in the Twenty-first Century: The Case of the Inter-American Court." *American Journal of International Law*, 102(4): 768–827.

Couso, Javier. 2004. "The Politics of Judicial Review in Chile in the Era of Democratic Transition, 1990–2002." In *Democratization and the Judiciary: The Accountability Function of Courts in the New Democracies*, Siri Gloppen, Roberto Gargarella and Elin Skaar, eds. Portland, OR: Frank Cass Publishers.

______. 2005. "The Judicialization of Chilean Politics: The Rights Revolution That Never Was." In *The Judicialization of Politics in Latin America*, Rachel Sieder, Line Schholden and Alan Angell, eds. 105–29. New York: Palgrave Macmillan.

______ and Lisa Hilbink. 2009. "Is Change on Its Way in Chile? Institutional Reforms and New Developments in Rights Adjudication in Chile." Paper presented at the Annual Meeting of the Law and Society Association, May 28–31, Denver, Colorado.

Domingo, Pilar. 2004. "Judicialization of Politics, or Politicization of the Judiciary? Recent Trends in Latin America." *Democratization*, 11(1): 104–26.

Dworkin, Ronald. 1986. *Law's Empire*. Boston: Harvard University Press.

Epp, Charles. 1998. *The Rights Revolution: Lawyers, Activists, and Supreme Courts in Comparative Perspective*. Chicago: University of Chicago Press.

Gonzalez, Felipe. 2009. "The Experience of the Inter-American Human Rights System." Paper delivered at the University of Wisconsin Law School, March 30.

Hawkins, Darren and Wade Jacoby. 2008. "Partial Compliance: A Comparison of the European and Inter-American Courts of Human Rights." Paper presented at Annual Meeting of the American Political Science Association, Boston MA, August 28–31.

Helfer, Laurence R. and Karen J. Alter. 2009. "The Andean Tribunal of Justice and its Interlocutors: Understanding Preliminary Reference Patterns in the Andean Community." *NYU Journal of International Law and Politics*, 41.

______ and Anne-Marie Slaughter. 1997. "Toward a Theory of Effective Supranational Adjudication." *Yale Law Journal*, 107 (2): 273.

Hilbink, Lisa. 2007. *Judges beyond Politics in Democracy and Dictatorship: Lessons from Chile*. New York: Cambridge University Press.

Huneeus, Alexandra. 2010. "Judging from a Guilty Conscience: The Chilean Judiciary's Human Rights Turn." *Law and Social Inquiry*, 35(1): 99–135.

______. 2006. The Dynamics of Judicial Stasis: Judges, Pinochet-Era Claims, and Judicial Legitimacy in Chile (1998–2005). Ph.D. Dissertation. University of California, Berkeley.

Keller, Helen and Alex Stone Sweet, eds. 2008. *A Europe of Rights: The Impact of the ECHR on National Legal Systems*. Oxford: Oxford University Press.

Landau, David. 2005. "The Two Discourses in Colombian Constitutional Jurisprudence: A New Approach to Modeling Judicial Behavior in Latin America." In *George Washington International Law Review*, 37: 687–744.

Larkins, Christopher. 1998. "The Judiciary and Delegative Democracy in Argentina." *Comparative Politics*, 30(4): 423–42.

Levit, Janet Koven. 1999. "The Constitutionalization of Human Rights in Argentina: Problem or Promise?" *Columbia Journal of Transnational Law*, 37: 281.

Melish, Tara. 2002. *Protecting Economic, Social, and Cultural Rights in the Inter-American Human Rights System: A Manual on Presenting Claims*. New Haven: Schell Jr. Center for International Human Rights.

Neuman, Gerald L. 2008. "Import, Export, and Regional Consent in the Inter-American Court of Human Rights." *The European Journal of International Law*, 19(1): 101–23.

Naddeo, Cecilia. 2007. Co-Adjudicating Human Rights Conflicts: The Supreme Court of Argentina and the Inter-American System of Human Rights. Master's thesis, Stanford Leland University.

———. 2009. Untitled paper presented at the Annual Meeting of the Law and Society Association, May 28–31, Denver, Colorado.

O'Donnell, Guillermo. 1999. *Counterpoints: Selected Essays on Authoritarianism and Democratization*. Notre Dame, IN: Notre Dame University Press.

Parra, Oscar. 2009. Untitled paper presented at the Annual Meeting of the Law and Society Association, May 28–31, Denver, Colorado.

Pérez Perdomo, Rogelio. 2005. Judicialization and Regime Transformation: The Venezuelan Supreme Court. In *The Judicialization of Politics in Latin America*, Rachel Sieder, Alan Angell and Line Schholden, eds. 263–92. New York: Palgrave Macmillan.

Pisarello, Gerardo. 2007. "Globalización, Constitucionalismo, y Derecho." In *Teoría del Neoconstitucionalismo: Ensayos Escogidos*, Miguel Carbonell (ed.). Madrid: Editorial Trotta.

Sikkink, Kathryn. 2004. *Mixed Signals: U.S. Human Rights Policy and Latin America*. Ithaca and London: Cornell University Press.

Simmons, Beth. 2009. *Mobilizing for Human Rights: International Law in Domestic Politics*. New York: Cambridge University Press.

Stacey, Helen. 2009. *Human Rights for the 21st Century: Sovereignty, Civil Society, Culture*. Stanford: Stanford University Press.

Smulovitz, Catalina. 2002. "The Discovery of Law: Political Consequences in the Argentine Experience." In *Global Prescriptions: The Production, Exportation, and Importation of a New Legal Orthodoxy*, Bryant Garth and Yves Dezalay, eds. Ann Arbor: University of Michigan Press, 249–75.

———. 2005. "Petitioning and Creating Rights: Judicialization in Argentina. The Judicialization of Politics in Latin America." In *The Judicialization of Politics in Latin America*, Rachel Sieder, Alan Angell and Line Schholden, eds. 263–92. New York: Palgrave Macmillan.

Tate, Nate, and Torbjorn Vallinder, eds. 1995. *The Global Expansion of Judicial Power*. New York: New York University Press.

Tribunal Supremo de Justicia, Venezuela. 2008. Caso Gustavo Álvarez Arias y otros). December 18, 2008. http://www.tsj.gov.ve/decisiones/scon/diciembre/1939-181208-2008-08-1572.html. (December 18, 2009).

PART III

JUDICIALIZATION BEYOND THE COURTS

6

The Transformation of Constitutional Discourse and the Judicialization of Politics in Latin America

Javier Couso

INTRODUCTION

Implicit in the assertion of a connection between *legal culture* and the *judicialization of politics* in Latin America is the notion that both concepts relate to relevant practices in this area of the world. As it turns out, however, neither is uncontroversial. Some scholars do not recognize the notion of legal culture as a meaningful or useful category, because they reduce social reality to rationally motivated individual actors operating under the constraint of different structures. Others dismiss the idea of a judicialization of politics in Latin America as unsuitable to the region.

Building on the growing body of literature that has documented the emergence of judicialization of politics in Latin America (Ríos-Figueroa and Taylor 2006; Taylor 2006; Sieder et al. 2005; Gloppen et al. 2004; Domingo 2004; Smulovitz 2002; Helmke 2005), this chapter takes legal culture to be a useful analytical category to make sense of the behavior of judges, lawyers, and even society at large. It then proceeds to explore the connection between judicialization and legal culture in the region. Furthermore, it suggests that in addition to structural factors such as the introduction of constitutional courts, the grant of judicial review powers to high courts, or the emergence of support structures, important changes in the internal legal culture of the region have been crucial for the emergence of judicialization of politics in Latin America.[1] Specifically, the chapter traces the role that legal scholarship – in particular, constitutional theory – has played in transforming the region's legal culture.

The focus on legal scholarship as a factor contributing to the shape of the legal cultures of Latin America derives from the conviction that it represents one of the most important sites for the configuration of an understanding of the nature, sources, and role of the law, as well as conceptions about the judiciary and legal interpretation.

[1] To use the by-now canonical taxonomy introduced by Lawrence Friedman (1975).

This is particularly the case in a region where – like other places with a civil law background – legal scholarship, or *la doctrina*, is considered a formal source of law, and where it plays a critical role in socializing students into the legal field. Not all scholarship on law carries this formal status; only scholarship that specifically interprets and develops legal doctrine. Thus, as will be further elaborated later on, when I refer to legal scholarship in this chapter, I refer to the narrower meaning encompassed by the civil law understanding of *la doctrina*.[2]

Thus, in what follows, an effort is made to trace the evolution of the constitutional scholarship of Latin America as it has played out in Chile, a country with a long and rich history of legal scholarship. This exercise reveals that constitutional discourse experienced a revolutionary transformation over the last few decades. I argue that this dramatic shift facilitated the introduction of processes of judicialization of politics in the region by changing traditional understandings of the status of legislated law and the role of the courts in a democracy.

THE JUDICIALIZATION OF POLITICS IN LATIN AMERICA

Several definitions exist of judicialization of politics (Shapiro and Stone Sweet 2002; Tate and Vallinder 1995; Holland 1991). For all this variety, however, they share a core meaning that includes the expansion of judicial power into policy domains formerly left to the executive and legislative branches. Furthermore, there is agreement that this kind of empowerment of the courts usually goes hand in hand with an assertive interpretation of the constitution that expands or creates new individual rights (Epp 1998).

Over the last two decades, Latin America has experienced a fair amount of rights-enhancing judicialization of politics, both at the national and international levels, the latter within the Inter-American Human Rights system (Sikkink 1996; Huneeus in this volume). The emergence of judicialization in a region where courts have traditionally been deferent to the elected branches of government and consequently reluctant to overrule legal norms on grounds of unconstitutionality, calls for explanation. Any analysis of the rise of the judicialization of politics in Latin America should start by recognizing that it is correlated with structural changes introduced to the political systems of most countries of the region. Among others, the introduction of constitutional courts (Chile, in 1981; Colombia, 1991; Peru; 1993; Bolivia, 1998; Ecuador, 1996), the granting of constitutional review powers to high courts (Costa Rica, 1989; Brazil, 1988), the incorporation of jurisdictional mechanisms aimed at providing justiciability to the rights clauses of the constitution (Chile, 1976; Argentina, 1994), and the emergence of support structures facilitating the access of growing groups of citizens to the courts (Smulovitz in this volume).

[2] "Doctrine" and "*la doctrina*" are false cognates. The proper word for "doctrine" in Spanish is "*jurisprudencia*" (itself a false cognate of sorts). There is no proper word for "*la doctrina*" although in this chapter I refer to it at times as legal scholarship, at others as theory.

While recognizing the significance of these structural elements in furthering judicialization, I argue that they are not in themselves enough to explain its emergence in Latin America. This, incidentally, is compatible with what the comparative study of judicialization has revealed, specifically, that the latter can happen even in the absence of structural factors such as the introduction of constitutional courts or a bill of rights, as was the case in the United States (Nelson 2000), France (Stone 1992), and Israel (Edelman 1994). If this is so, and such structural elements are neither necessary nor sufficient conditions for judicialization to emerge, perhaps legal culture might play a role in this story.

LEGAL SCHOLARSHIP AS LEGAL CULTURE

The very idea of culture questions approaches that see social reality as exclusively driven by rational individuals pursuing their self-interest under the constraint of structures. Indeed, any appeal to culture implies that shared meanings and understandings can move people to act in ways not determined by either their self-interest or structural features. The power of culture becomes apparent when an observer is confronted with situations in which actors facing similar incentive-structures nonetheless exhibit radically different behavior. To make sense of such disparate ways of acting in the presence of the same options, it seems appropriate to search for other explanatory factors beyond incentive-structures. This residual is often labeled as culture, a notion that most people take to refer to deeply rooted conceptions of the self, what is deemed right and wrong, and so forth.

As is the case with other complex concepts, even when it is accepted, the idea of legal culture resists a simple definition. Thus, some equate it to notions like legal consciousness, legal values, or legal ideology. Given the complexity and indeterminacy of this concept, it is important to stipulate as clearly as possible the way in which such terms will be used in this chapter. I take *legal culture* to express the conceptions of the law, the legal system, and their relationships with politics, held by both individuals repeatedly exposed to it (internal legal culture), as well as by those who have more distant or occasional relationship with the legal system (external legal culture). The conception of legal culture adopted here is meant to capture the symbolic representation of things legal by both the central actors of the legal process (judges, lawyers, jurists) as well as by people with a less direct relationship to it. Furthermore, the ideas and representations just mentioned translate into patterned practices (Introduction in this volume). As cultural artifacts do, legal culture helps to stabilize expectations through the constraint of the behavior of the relevant actors, in this case, legal actors.

Once a definition of legal culture is stipulated, the problem is to identify indicators or elements in which the legal culture expresses itself. However, this is not an easy matter. One strategy is to make use of surveys and other techniques of this type to inquire about the conceptions of the law and the legal system held by representative samples of the general population or of the legal actors. Another possible path is the kind of qualitative research common within ethnography, which emphasizes in-depth interviews of relevant actors and participant observation of legal practices. However, here I use the lens of legal scholarship to examine the changing legal culture of Latin America, in particular constitutional scholarship, which represents a particularly valuable way to get at the internal legal culture of the region, because of the relevance that it has both in the training of lawyers and judges and within legal practice.

By *legal scholarship* I refer to the form of legal discourse that is elaborated to clarify the meaning of legal norms and decisions made by the courts. In countries with a civil law tradition, legal scholarship is produced through a systematic conceptualization of legal materials such as codes, constitutional clauses, statutes, and judicial decisions. The relevance of legal scholarship in the legal life of countries associated with the Continental European legal tradition (such as those of Latin America) derives from the fact that it is one of the most important factors shaping the conceptions of the law and the universe within which legal actors operate. The following account of the role of legal scholarship in Italy by Cappelletti, Merryman, and Perillo (1967) mirrors the role it plays in Latin America:

> (The) professor-scholar is the inheritor of a proud tradition reaching back to the Glossators (. . .). His work, published in the form of textbooks, treatises, commentaries, monographs, and articles, constitutes what Italians call 'the doctrine.' (. . .). Doctrine is not law in Italy in the way that legislation and judicial decisions are law, but it pervades the legal process, strongly influencing legislators and judges, who tend to conform to the doctrinal model not only of what law is but of what their functions are.[3]

As this passage indicates, legal scholarship in civil law countries is not merely a heuristic tool but – more importantly – a way of shaping the representation that legal actors maintain concerning the very nature of the enterprise of law. This is typically implicit because –while explaining the law of the country – jurists help to constitute a discourse about the very nature of law and of the legal system. This discourse is then transmitted to judges, legal academics, and litigants through the medium of legal education, which in civil law regimes makes an intensive use of legal scholarship as a pedagogical tool.

In spite of its relevance for the legal culture of Latin America, recent comparative scholarship on law and politics has made surprisingly little use of legal scholarship. Instead, it is common to encounter studies that claim to be analyzing legal culture, but that do this through analyses of the number of lawyers or degree of litigiousness in a given country,[4] factors that are better conceptualized as either sources or

[3] See Mauro Cappelletti, John H. Merryman, and Joseph M. Perillo (1967: 166–7).

[4] See for example, Lawrence Friedman and Rogelio Pérez-Perdomo (2002), where many of the contributors to that edited volume use these type of elements as a proxy for legal culture.

consequences of changes in the legal culture, but not elements of it. The lack of attention to legal scholarship in the field of Latin American judicial politics is a reflection of the little consideration that law in general gets in the numerous studies that have been published on the judicialization of politics in the region. This gap in the literature has been criticized recently by two specialists in Latin American law and politics, Diana Kapiszewski and Matthew Taylor (2008):

> We suggest that greater advances could be made in our understanding of judicial politics in Latin America if law itself were to become a more prominent consideration in our analyses. We are not suggesting that political scientists become legal scholars. Rather, we simply believe that in our analyses of the judicialization of politics, of the courts' increasing involvement in policy-making, and of their willingness and ability to assert power, we keep in mind that constitutions and laws are the fundamental background for judicial behavior: even in weakly institutionalized settings, they motivate, enable, and constrain judicial actors.[5]

Coinciding with this call for incorporating legal analysis into efforts to understand the judicial politics of Latin America, this chapter addresses a critical element of law in the region, legal scholarship. At any rate, the decision to focus on legal scholarship as itself a subject of inquiry is not idiosyncratic. In fact, it has recently sparked the interest of an array of legal scholars working on Latin American law. One of them, Diego López Medina (2004), highlights that the legal imagination of some of the most important Latin American legal actors has been profoundly shaped by legal scholarship:

> At least from a theoretical point of view, law can be interpreted as a network of theories, texts, and practices (. . .) giving form to the imaginary of lawyers, judges, law professors, and students (. . .), something which in turn has an autonomous influence (from the material culture) on the way people understand and use law. The pursuit of the interrelations between texts and ideas can be seen as a form of 'cultural study of law.'[6]

As López Medina points out, the discursive nature of law makes scholarship an important factor in the configuration of the legal imagination of relevant actors. This explains why the study of constitutional theory has played an important role in ascertaining the state and evolution of the legal culture of the United States, as the work of scholars such as Howard Gillman (1993), Rodger Smith (1990), and Keith Whittington (2007) have shown.

In spite of its relevance for sociolegal studies, however, legal scholarship has so far failed to capture the attention of most scholars working on Latin America. One of the reasons for such neglect might lay in the presumption that there is not much of it to study, and that of the little there is, most merely reproduces European

[5] See Diana Kapiszewski and Matthew Taylor (2008: 5).

[6] See López Medina (2004: 86–7). Translation from Spanish by the author.

and North American scholarship. Such an approach, however, ignores the fact that in peripheral countries jurists do engage in doctrinal work aimed at guiding the actions of the rest of the members of the legal domain. Indeed, although much of the *doctrina* articulated in the region represents a mixture of misreadings and appropriations borrowed from more prestigious jurisdictions, it plays an important role in the configuration of the legal ideology of Latin America.

Having said this, it is of course true that paying attention to the evolution of legal culture through the study of legal scholarship does not preclude the need to be fully aware that – as it happens with other rhetorical practices – they often have little connection with what happens on the ground. This danger, however, should not prevent us from exploring the ways in which legal scholarship can shape the representations of law and the legal system in ways not predicted by those who ushered it in.

THE TRANSFORMATION OF CONSTITUTIONAL SCHOLARSHIP IN LATIN AMERICA

From Marginality to Centrality

As stated earlier, to make sense of transformations within the legal culture(s) of Latin America which are relevant for the emergence of judicialization of politics, we need to focus on changes at the level of the constitutional scholarship of the region because of the connections between constitutional discourse and judicialization processes. Furthermore, constitutional scholarship is particularly well suited to make sense of the legal culture(s) of a given place, because one of its main tasks is precisely to draw the limits and relationships between law and politics.

When looking at Latin America's constitutional scholarship, the first element that stands out is the sea change that it has experienced over the last two to three decades, both in terms of its status within the legal field and of its content. Indeed, after more than a century in which it paled in comparison with private law,[7] constitutional scholarship has become the most important and vibrant legal subject in the region,

[7] The decay of constitutional law in Latin American legal academy started fifty to sixty years after independence from Spain (which happened between 1810 and 1825). Up to that point it had been a fairly active field, due to requirements of postcolonial politics and specifically the need to organize the new republics by introducing new constitutional charters. Analyzing doctrinal production during the nineteenth century, Rogelio Pérez-Perdomo states: "In the subject of constitutional law, there was also an important production, which attempted to adapt the political and constitutional science developed in Europe to the constitutional charters and social structure of Latin America." See Rogelio Pérez-Perdomo (2004: 144). In Chile, there was very dynamic constitutional law literature up until the late nineteenth century. Among others, it is worth mentioning the work of Jorge Huneeus (1880), Manuel Carrasco Albano (1858), José Victorino Lastarria (1865), and Joaquín Rodríguez Bravo (1888).

to the point that it has started to colonize other legal subjects, in what some jurists call the "constitutionalization of law" (Aldunate 2009; Bauer 1998).[8]

Although the new preeminence of constitutional discourse in Latin America is most apparent in countries such as Colombia, Costa Rica, and Argentina – which are at the frontline of judicialization of politics – it can also be noticed in other countries of the region with more limited processes of judicialization. Thus, for example, in Chile the status of constitutional law has experienced a dramatic rise when compared with twenty years ago. The increased relevance of constitutional discourse in Chile can be first appreciated from the academic production of books on this subject, which has been booming over the last two decades (more than three hundred books were published in the period 1989–2009, compared to less than a hundred in the much longer period of 1924–89). This sharp increase in the publication of constitutional law books is all the more significant in a context in which the elaboration of works in other legal subjects has remained relatively constant. Second, there was a sharp increase in the number of journals dedicated to constitutional scholarship, from just two before the 1970s to ten in 2007.[9]

In addition to the increment in the number of works published in the field of constitutional law, the subject has become far more prestigious. An indicator of the growing status of constitutional law within the Chilean legal field can be ascertained by the unprecedented numbers of deans of law schools who are constitutional law scholars. In fact, whereas in the first century of university-level legal education constitutional law scholars were elected to a deanship only once, it is now fairly common to see scholars from this field being promoted to lead law schools.[10]

8 After its vibrant start in the early nineteenth century, constitutional law and theory gradually lost its protagonism within the legal field, to the point that by the mid-twentieth century it had become a marginal and little developed subject, paling in front of civil law, which since the era of codification – toward the mid-nineteenth century – had become the central legal subject in Latin American law. The marginal status of constitutional law during most of the twentieth century in Chile was confirmed by noted constitutional scholar Alejandro Silva Bascuñán, who relates how in the 1930s the Dean of the Law School of Universidad de Chile, Fernando Alessandri, told him to try to provide more density to the field of constitutional law, which in his opinion was technically unsophisticated (Interview with the author, 2000).

9 Until 1970 there were only two academic journals with a substantial interest in constitutional law: the *Revista de Derecho Público* (edited by the Universidad de Chile), and the *Revista de Derecho* (edited by the Universidad de Concepción). By 2009, eight more such journals were in existence: *Estudios Constitucionales* (Universidad de Talca); *Revista Chilena de Derecho* (Universidad Católica de Chile); *Ius et Praxis* (Universidad de Talca); *Revista de Derecho Público* (Universidad Católica de Valparaíso); *Revista de Derecho* (Universidad Austral); *Revista de Ciencias Sociales* (Universidad de Valparaíso); *Revista de Derecho* (Universidad Católica del Norte); *Revista Derecho y Humanidades* (Universidad de Chile).

10 Throughout the twentieth century, most deans of Chile's law schools were scholars specializing in private or criminal law (the University of Chile and the Catholic University of Chile – the oldest and most traditional – had over thirty deans specialized in such subjects and just one who was a constitutional law professor). Over the last two decades, the presence of constitutional law scholars

Another indicator of the new relevance attained by constitutional scholarship in Chile is the sharp growth in the number of research projects that get funding from the National Commission for Scientific and Technological Research (CONICYT). Whereas up to the mid-1990s constitutional law projects represented around 10 percent of all law-related projects funded, by the late 2000s they had doubled that level (to around 20 percent of the total), a sign of the current academic prestige and sense of relevance attained by constitutional law.[11]

As the data of this sections suggest, the traditional marginality of constitutional discourse has been completely transformed over the last two decades, to the point that it has become one of the most vibrant subjects in the legal field, attracting the best and the brightest scholars and students.

The Sources of the Doctrinal Revolution

Parallel to becoming more productive and prestigious, constitutional discourse in Latin America was experiencing a revolutionary transformation that would completely transform its outlook in the space of just a few years. Consequently, the traditional paradigm prescribing a formalist interpretation of law and a complete subordination of judges to legislation was substituted by another encouraging a value-oriented jurisprudence exerted by activist judges and characterized by the notion that legislated law should be subordinated to the courts' interpretation of the Constitution (Landau 2005). This paradigm shift owes much to the reception in Latin America of a global doctrine affirming that human rights constitute the central category of constitutionalism. Furthermore, it is also the result of the importation to the region of doctrines legitimizing judicial control of the constitutionality of law, either in its Continental European version (i.e., through the introduction of constitutional courts) or in its American version (which gives that power to the regular courts). In the case of the reception of the European model, the borrowing was to some extent natural, as the latter had been the regular source of doctrinal change in Latin America. In the case of the U.S. model of judicial review, the inspiration came from the scores of Latin American legal academics who started to pursue graduate training in law in the United States

heading law schools in Chile rose dramatically, to the point that it is now common to see such academics serving as deans or directors. These have included Jorge Correa Sutil (who served as Dean of the Law School of the Universidad Diego Portales in the 1980s and early 1990s); Raúl Bertelsen (who served as Dean of the Law School of the Universidad de los Andes during the 1990s); Rodrigo Correa (Universidad Adolfo Ibáñez); Patricio Zapata (Universidad de las Américas and previously Universidad Andrés Bello); Manuel Núñez (Universidad Católica del Norte). Carlos Peña (who served as Dean at Universidad Diego Portales from the mid-1990s through the mid-2000s) is considered an expert in both private and constitutional law.

[11] The figures were prepared by the author based on the data provided by Fondecyt, the research program at National Commission for Scientific and Technological Research (CONICYT). http://www.conicyt.cl/bases/fondecyt/disciplina/.

in the late 1970s,[12] where they were socialized by their liberal North American law professors into the virtues of the legendary Warren Court (Couso 2007).

Moreover, the new constitutional theories started to penetrate the legal field as most of the countries in Latin America were leaving behind the wave of brutal military regimes that had affected the region in the 1960s and 1970s. This coincidence made the reception of the new constitutional theories all the more feasible, because the very formalism and judicial deference to legislated law that characterized the previous paradigm was being blamed for the passivity exhibited by the judiciaries in the face of the massive human rights violations perpetrated during the authoritarian wave. Thus, the antiformalism and judicial activism promoted by the new constitutional paradigm encountered little opposition from those scholars who had invested in more traditional understandings of constitutional law.

For all the previous facts, and in spite of the radical change that it implied, the new constitutional orthodoxy was soon consolidated to the point that it became dominant. The unprecedented academic contact between constitutional scholars from the region and prestigious scholars from Europe and North America helped to cement adherence to the new constitutional creed among Latin American constitutional scholars. One important site of confluence was (and continues to be) the conferences regularly organized since 1981 by the International Association of Constitutional Law (IACL), an organization that gathers some of the most prominent constitutional scholars of the world.

As we have seen, the transformation of Latin American constitutional doctrine signaled the abandonment of the strong legal formalism that had dominated throughout the previous century and a half. The traditional insistence on the superiority of codified and statutory law and the prescription of a modest role for the judiciary (to apply the law without scrutinizing its fairness) was suddenly replaced by a constitutional discourse emphasizing the relevance of human rights, constitutional principles, and value-oriented judges. To illustrate this remarkable transformation, in the next section I analyze constitutional textbooks and treatise before and after this momentous change.

The Old Constitutional Discourse

The roots of Latin America's adherence to legal formalism and the notion of the supremacy of legislated law lie in the reception in the early nineteenth century of the French Revolution's mistrust of judges. These ideas were embraced and disseminated throughout the region by Andrés Bello, who was the most influential legal scholar in the region. The Civil Code Bello drafted for Chile (which was also adopted by Colombia, Ecuador, El Salvador, Venezuela, Nicaragua, and

[12] See Dezaley and Garth (2003: 479).

Honduras)[13] emphasized the role legislated law played in the life of a republican system as well as the imperative that each and every person obey it.[14] This call to submit to legislation was directed not only to the public or the government, but especially to the judiciary itself. Given his insistence in the majesty of legislated law, Bello's Civil Code explicitly denied any legal value to the judicial decisions, stating that: "Judicial decisions would only apply to the cases at hand . . . Only the legislator can explain or interpret the law in a generally obligatory way."[15]

The emphasis that Bello gave to the supremacy of legislation and the subordination of the courts would have a long-lasting effect in the region. Following this theory, Luis Claro Solar, a highly influential Chilean legal scholar writing a few decades after Bello, toward the turn of the century, fully embraced the formalist and deferential paradigm introduced by Andrés Bello. He wrote:

> Even if the law exhibits a notorious injustice, the judge ought to apply it as it is: 'Dura lex sed lex' (tough law is nonetheless law). If we allow judges to correct the injustice of legislation, these would be replaced according to the conscience of the judge, and individuals would not know what to do, since each person has his own ways to understand fairness, and fairness would then inspire the most anomalous and contradictory decisions.[16]

As we can see from this passage, the defense of legal formalism and the subordination of judges to legislated law were complete and unapologetic. Even if unjust, statutory law would have to be applied by the courts. It was better to risk a discrete injustice through the strict application of the law than to expose the whole legal system to the discretion of the judges.

While both Bello and Claro Solar were civil law scholars (the core subject in the field of law for most of Latin America's history), the same traditional conception of law and the role of judges was endorsed in the few constitutional law treatises that started to appear toward the mid-twentieth century. One example of this trend was a treatise by Chile's most noted constitutional scholar of that century, Alejandro Silva Bascuñán who, in spite of his proclaimed adherence to natural law, adamantly rejected the idea of giving judges the power to overrule legislation deemed to violate the constitution (and, presumably natural law). He wrote:

> The risks of giving [the power to guard the constitution] to the courts are apparent to even the most ardent proponents of this formula. The main danger is that – in spite of all the theoretical precautions – the judicial body will make its decision [on the constitutionality of law] inspired by political considerations (. . .). When that happens, the court assumes such high and effective power as to become the

[13] See Rogelio Pérez-Perdomo (2004: 120).
[14] Iván Jacksic's account of Andrés Bello's intellectual trajectory concludes that: "Bello's purpose was to enshrine legislated law as the core value of the republican system." See Jaksic (2001: 211).
[15] Article 3 of the Chilean Civil Code. Translation from Spanish by the author.
[16] Cited in López Medina (2004: 190). Translation from Spanish by the author.

> superior authority of the state, transforming the political regime in a government of the judges that participate in the court, when they have not been elected nor called to take the highest place on the direction of the collectivity.[17]

The hegemony of this traditional constitutional theory was not confined to legal treatises. In fact, it was the working theory embraced by members of the judiciary as well. This is apparent in a study conducted in the late 1970s on the perception of law and its relationship with the political system among high court judges (Cuneo 1980). The study, which was based on public speeches by the head of the Supreme Court during the period 1971–9, found that the legal conceptions of the justices expressed "the most primitive sort of formalist legal positivism,"[18] especially regarding their notion that codified and statutory law was so clear as to make interpretation superfluous. Furthermore, the justices' public statements reproduced to the letter the modest role prescribed for the judiciary by constitutional theory:

> The mission of the Court is to defend the current legal order. We lack – as is evident – the power to alter the latter through interpretation (. . .). The renovation of the legal order can only be pursued through new legislation. Therefore the violation – directly or indirectly – of legality is unacceptable, because without law there is no justice (. . .). Judges ought to act strictly within the framework of existing legality.[19]

What is interesting about these statements by Chile's top court is that they were consistent amidst a period of unprecedented political conflict, that is, the government of Salvador Allende (1970–3) and the military dictatorship that followed it. The main features of this discourse were a formalist attitude toward legal interpretation (textualism, originalism, and so forth), accompanied by a strong opposition to judge-created law. This last point was consistent with an understanding of the theory of separation of powers that translated into judicial deference to the legislative branch. Finally, the theory had a clear preference for procedural values over substantive justice, in spite of the occasional statement defending – in the abstract – the importance of natural law theories.[20]

The formalist character of the constitutional theory prevalent in Latin America for most of the twentieth century explains that the syllabus of constitutional law courses were mostly devoted to the treatment of what was called the "organic" section of the

[17] Silva Bascuñán (1963: 89). Translation from Spanish by the author.

[18] Cuneo (1980: 74). Translation from Spanish by the author.

[19] Cuneo (1980: 77). Tranlation from Spanish by the author.

[20] Summarizing the main traits of the legal and judicial philosophy exhibited by the Chief Justices of the Chilean Supreme Court, the author of the study, Cuneo, had this to say: "In sum, law amounts to legal rules ('*el derecho es la ley*'), independent of whether or not it expresses values, that is, of its fairness or unfairness. Law is to be found in statutory norms and not in social life. The task of the courts vis-à-vis the law is not to assess whether or not it is just or appropriate to the historical circumstances." Cuneo (1980: 76).

Constitution (that is, those establishing the different branches of governments, their powers, and their reciprocal relationships), while the treatment of the "dogmatic" section of the Constitution (that dealing with individuals' rights) was reduced to a mere enumeration of the Bill of Rights, without much analysis.

Summing up this point, the analysis of the relatively scarce literature on constitutional theory available up to the 1980s shows that the dominance of legal positivism and a deferential understanding of the role of the courts vis-à-vis the political system was absolute.

The New Orthodoxy: From Legal Formalism to Neoconstitutionalism

Given the hold that formalism traditionally had in Latin America's legal scholarship in general – and in constitutional discourse in particular – the dramatic transformation of constitutional theory over the last two decades represents nothing short of a conceptual revolution. Although it is impossible to date it precisely, it is clear that by the late 1980s the new orthodoxy was rapidly penetrating the region's constitutional scene. A clear indication of the paradigmatic shift experienced by constitutional theory in Latin America can be appreciated in an influential treatise by Carlos Nino (1992), an Argentine scholar with strong connections with Yale Law School. The book, entitled *Fundamentos de Derecho Constitucional. Análisis filosófico, jurídico y politológico de la práctica constitucional* (*The Basis of Constitutional Law: A Philosophical, Legal, and Politological Analysis of Constitutional Practice*), was radically different – in both form and substance – from everything that had previously been published on the subject in Latin America. Among other innovations, Nino brought to his constitutional law analysis an array of Anglo-American scholars who were largely unknown in Latin America's legal audience, such as Ronald Dworkin, John Rawls, Bruce Ackerman, Alexander Bickel, Jules Coleman, Robert Dahl, H. L. A. Hart, Amartya Sen, Charles Taylor, and Michael Walzer.

In addition to the new authors Nino analyzed to elaborate his constitutional theory, the treatise represented a substantial innovation in that it gave preeminence to the analysis of fundamental rights (what used to be called the "*dogmatic*" section of the Constitution) vis-à-vis the study of the organization of power characteristic of the "*organic*" part of the Constitution. Furthermore, it was remarkable in the attention that it devoted to discussing judicial control of the Constitution, a subject that traditional theory had confined to a discrete place. In his treatment of this subject, Nino unambiguously supported judicial review of the constitutionality of legislation:

> Through the control of the constitutionality [of law], judges can be central actors in the search for a profound consensus around principles guaranteeing the legitimacy and stability of our constitutional practice.[21]

[21] Nino (1992: 658–9). Translation from Spanish by the autor.

Note that in addition to endorsing judicial review, Nino expressed an extremely different understanding of the nature of constitutional law. In a language with strong Dworkinean overtones, he supports the notion that judges ought to perform their judicial review tasks by engaging in rational deliberation over principles with other societal actors. This conception of the constitutionalism and the role of a judge in a democratic society could not be more distant to that of legal traditionalism.

In Chile, this new type of constitutionalism found echo within a group of scholars in close contact with Nino and his colleagues from Argentina. Among others, the work of Carlos Peña, a scholar at Universidad Diego Portales, did much to spread the virtues of the new constitutional creed. In advancing his position, Peña (1996) issued a devastating critique of traditionalist constitutional theory. He wrote:

> I think that – as in the rest of Latin America – the constitutional history of our country exhibits a certain gap between that which is proclaimed in the constitutional texts and the way in which the political system actually functions. Without exaggeration, I believe – to paraphrase the title of a famous work – we have not taken our Constitution seriously. One of the most marked features of the political development of Latin American countries – and ours is no exception to that rule – is the discordance between its institutional domain, that is, the domain of norms, and the domain of culture, which is, in fact, the one that motivates our political behavior. Even though the ideals of a strong constitutionalism have been present at the rhetorical level, they haven seldom existed at the level of reality.[22]

It is interesting to note that – in defending the new constitutional discourse – Peña goes as far as to condemn the whole trajectory of Latin American constitutionalism, arguing that it had been a façade, hiding a lawless political reality. With this statement, he was not merely calling for improving a constitutional theory that had become outdated, but questioning the relevance that the old paradigm had for the political life of the continent. After issuing a subtle wink to Ronald Dworkin's highly influential *Taking Rights Seriously* (1977), Peña goes on to advocate the ideals of a "strong constitutionalism," the code word for a constitutional theory contemplating judicial control of the constitutionality of legislation by courts willing to engage in an interpretive practice that would enable them to creatively addressing novel constitutional issues. In his words:

> The constitution is not exhausted by the mere words of its clauses. From the point of view of the institutions, a constitution amounts to the practices which those who interpret it create. Those who interpret the constitution – as the constitutional experience of the USA and of Europe in the postwar era demonstrate – are the ones who draw the lines which makes life together possible. They are also the ones who signal when the rights of minorities are being violated, and furthermore, the precise moment when politics has overcome law ("*el derecho*").[23]

[22] Peña (1999: 15). Translation from Spanish by the author.
[23] Peña (1999: 12).Translation from Spanish by the author.

The works of scholars such as Nino, Peña, and others introduced into Latin America what Alec Stone Sweet (2000) has labeled "higher law constitutionalism"; that is, a theory that regards the Constitution as embodying universal principles (human rights) deemed to be above any statutory law and susceptible to be directly applied by the judiciary, even at the cost of trumping the sovereign decisions of the democratically elected branches of government.[24] This approach, continues Stone Sweet, amounts to a postmodern version of natural law thinking.[25]

The radical departure from the past implied by the adoption of "higher law constitutionalism" benefited from the fact that the constitutional discourse of France and Spain (the countries that had historically been most influential in the development of Latin American legal theory) were themselves finishing their own conversion to the new orthodoxy, which took the label of neoconstitutionalism in Spain.

At this point, it is useful to summarize what the proponents of this new constitutional orthodoxy take to be the core elements of it. For this, we turn to the account of it by a Spanish constitutional scholar who has articulated it in a publication directed at a Latin American legal audience. In the words of Alfonso García Figueroa (2003):

> [Neoconstitutionalism] designates a theory or group of theories which have provided a conceptual and/or normative basis to the constitutionalization of the legal system in non-positivistic terms. In the development of this type of constitutionalism, there are some implicit elements of the constitutionalization of law which have had a strong influence. Among others, there are material, structural, functional, and political aspects that should be highlighted (. . .). The material aspect of the constitutionalization of the legal system consists in the reception by the legal system of certain moral demands imposed through the form of fundamental rights. In other words, law has acquired a strong axiological character (. . .) this has tended to reenforce a nonpositivist concept of law among jurists, one in which the legal system is intimately linked to morality. This is perhaps the single most important factor which distinguishes current understandings of constitutionalism [neoconstitutionalism] from traditional constitutionalism (. . .).[26]

24 Stone Sweet defines higher-law constitutionalism in the following way: "The precepts of this new constitutionalism ('higher-law constitutionalism') can be simply listed: (1) state institutions are established by, and derive their authority exclusively from, a written constitution; (2) this constitution assigns ultimate power to people by way of elections; (3) the use of public authority, including legislative authority, is lawful only insofar as it conforms with the constitutional law; (4) that law will include rights and a system of justice to defend those rights. As an overarching political ideology, or theory of the state, the new constitutionalism faces no serious rival today" (2000: 37).

25 "In Germany, Italy, and Spain, constitutional texts proclaim human rights before they establish state institutions and before they distribute governmental functions. In consequence of this fact, rights are considered by legal scholars and many judges to possess a juridical existence that is prior to and independent of the state. Doctrine has it that rights are invested with a kind of 'supraconstitutional' normativity that makes (at least some of) them immune to change through constitutional revision (. . .). This is inherently a natural law position, although natural law is rarely explicitly invoked" (Stone Sweet 2000: 95).

26 García Figueroa (2003: 164–5). Translation from Spanish by the author.

As this account of the basic features of neoconstitutionalism suggests, this theory implies a not too subtle return to natural law thinking[27] – at least in the domain of constitutional law – something apparent in the embrace of the notion that public law should be impregnated with morality. As noted earlier, such an understanding of the nature of constitutional law represents a revolutionary change in Latin America's legal scholarship, one that would have shocked the scores of jurists of the region who – throughout the twentieth century – adhered to the type of the legal positivism advocated by Hans Kelsen.[28]

However, the story does not end there. In addition to defending the idea that public law should be informed by strong moral values, neoconstitutionalism also asserts that the Constitution and, in particular, constitutional principles, ought to permeate the rest of the legal system, thus changing its content. Again in the words of García Figueroa:

> Due to their peculiar structure, constitutional principles have an enormous capacity to expand their area of influence. This is why Alexy speaks of the 'omnipresence of the Constitution' (Allgegenwart der Verfassung), which now influences the entire juridical system and its operation. Accordingly, the juridical order is now impregnated by constitutional principles. In the words of the German Constitutional Court there is an 'irradiation effect' (Ausstrahlungswirkung) of constitutional principles throughout the juridical order, whose interpretation should now be constrained by those said principles.[29]

The final, critical element of the neoconstitutionalist orthodoxy is the notion that judges should be endowed with powers to make sure the Constitution prevails over legislated law. This last aspect of the theory, its advocates recognize, has enormous political consequences, because it alters the subordinate position that the judiciary had in the political system in the traditional conception of constitutionalism:

> In political terms, neoconstitutionalism has important consequences for the correlation of forces between the different branches of government. The most important one is the displacement of protagonism from the legislature to the judiciary. Alexy thus speaks of the 'omnipotence of courts' in the (neo) constitutional state.[30]

[27] At this point a caveat is in order. When it is said that the new constitutional orthodoxy represents something like "natural law thinking," such representation is somewhat arbitrary, because not even those who espouse such ideas would necessarily recognize them to be natural law. Having said this, however, it seems clear that the constitutional theory just described has many traits in common with secular natural law, in that it appeals to moral principles that a judge should enforce, even against properly adopted legislation, thus rejecting the notion that law can have validity merely by the virtue of having been approved according to the formal requirements of the constitution.

[28] See Kelsen (1945).

[29] García Figueroa (2003: 165–6).

[30] García Figueroa (2003: 167).

As is apparent from some of the passages on the main features of the neoconstitutionalist paradigm transcribed earlier, the German constitutional theorist Robert Alexy is considered to be an authority on the matter. In fact, he has been (along with Luigi Ferrajoli, from Italy) one of the most influential scholars articulating the new constitutional orthodoxy for the civil law tradition. The case of Alexy is interesting, because he has served as an important "translator" of Anglo-American exponents of higher-law constitutionalism (in particular, Ronald Dworkin) into the Latin American constitutional world. The fact that Alexy is widely respected among constitutional scholars of the region in turn made the work of Dworkin widely known in Latin America, to the point that he has displaced Kelsen as the most influential author within constitutionalists.[31]

To sum up this point, a good indicator of the prevalence achieved in recent years by the new constitutional orthodoxy is the sudden popularity within Latin America's constitutional academic community of three important global exponents of higher-law constitutionalism: Ronald Dworkin (from the Anglo-American academic world), and Robert Alexy and Luigi Ferrajoli (from the Continental European one). The interesting aspect of the prominence of these authors among Latin American constitutional scholars is that it suggests that a kind of natural law perspective is permeating the region.

A final indicator of the rising influence of neoconstitutionalism in Latin America can be seen in the enormous interest that public-interest law has sparked in some of the most prestigious law schools of the region. These programs, which have received financial support from U.S.-based foundations, have built a powerful network that regularly publishes works that combine constitutional theory and human rights with different aspects of the public-interest law agenda in Latin America. The following excerpt from one such book, in its critique of a judicial practice considered to be

[31] In the case of Dworkin, his most influential work in Latin America is *Taking Rights Seriously*. Alexi's (1993) most influential work is *Teoría de los Derechos Fundamentales*. In a recent book on Chilean constitutional law, Pablo Ruiz-Tagle has this to say about the German scholar: "Alexy proposes a theory that, although based in German positive law, reaches the status of a general theory on fundamental rights which, in reference to the thesis of Ronald Dworkin and others, distinguishes between principles, values, rules, and constitutional norms. He also distinguishes between freedom rights, equality rights, and rights that demand a positive action by the state. Finally, he deals insightfully with the argumentation on fundamental rights, explaining the notion of vulnerability and balancing of fundamental rights, which we can adapt to the analysis of Chilean constitutional law. All of these can be of great significance for the development of a general theory ("*dogmática*") of fundamental rights adequate to our constitutional context (. . .). The analysis of Chile's Constitution has to be compatible with a future with stable links with the civilized world." See Cristi and Ruiz-Tagle (2006: 275). Carlos Peña's works also shows the dominance of Ronald Dworkin's taught in Chile's new constitutional theory. He wrote: "The failure of the ideas (of H. L. A. Hart and Kelsen) to provide a foundation of an adequate control of the constitutionality of law which is coherent with the notion of 'constitutionalism' in the strong sense and with the idea of the supremacy of the constitution is apparent when one engages with Dworkin's thesis." See Peña (1996: 77).

resistant to modern constitutional theory, speaks loudly of the alignment of this discourse with "higher-law constitutionalism":

> The rulings by the Chilean courts on constitutional matters maintain the traditional Civil Law conception from the mid-nineteenth century. Consequently, constitutional principles are not applied directly by the judges to the cases at hand. The scarce development of constitutional principles in the decisions by the Chilean courts generates a series of deficiencies in the legal system.[32]

Given this bleak diagnosis, proponents of this approach to legal action and teaching are openly embracing the U.S. model of constitutional discourse and practice, which most of them experienced firsthand as Master of Laws LL.M. students.

At this point it is relevant to point out that the transformation of Latin America's constitutional scholarship has not been confined to public law. In fact, it has affected the general outlook of legal theory. One example of the effect of the growing acceptance of higher-law constitutionalism is the decline on the degree of formalism exhibited by the judges of the region. As Diego López Medina (2004) has noted, the notion that legal principles have supremacy over mere legal rules (something in which Dworkin, Alexy, and Ferrajoli coincide), as well as the defense of the direct application of fundamental rights by the courts, has led to the encouragement of judicial activism. Related to this, in the new constitutional orthodoxy the value of legal certainty has been substituted by that of substantive justice, developments that would have shocked any legal theorist in the region just two or three decades ago. López Medina summarizes the impact of the new constitutional orthodoxy on the general outlook of legal theory in Latin America:

> The constitution used to be regarded as an organic document concerned with the regulation of the functions and roles of the different branches of government, but not as a bill of rights recognizing to the citizens fundamental rights that they could claim before the courts (. . .). Statutory law was (in this perspective) the main source of law. Judicial law was all but forbidden (. . .). By the 1980s, the law-centered political theory was in trouble. Citizens were skeptical of the convenience and legitimacy of statutory law. They started to look at the judiciary as a potential source of recognition of social, economic, and cultural rights (. . .). Law is now full of principles that courts should apply when in clash with mere legal rules (. . .). Textualism and literalism has been replaced with a finalist understanding of interpretation especially in constitutional adjudication, where constitutional clauses tend to be more openly textured than in codified law.[33]

This all suggests that the great transformation experienced by Latin America's constitutional scholarship can be described as the path from a "formalist and anti-judicial review" position, to a "quasi-natural law and pro-judicial review" new orthodoxy.

[32] See González (2003: 148). Translation from Spanish by author.
[33] López (2004: 414–15). Translation from Spanish by author.

CONCLUSION

Over the last two decades, so-called processes of judicialization of politics have made their mark in Latin America. With instances of great success in some countries and some setbacks in others, courts have reconstituted themselves as relevant political actors in the region. Although most social scientists account for this remarkable development solely in terms of structural reforms, incentive-structures, strategic-interaction, and other material causes, in this chapter I have aimed to complement those explanations with a cultural one, namely the role of constitutional scholarship.

As we have seen throughout the chapter, the change in the constitutional discourse of Latin America has been radical, going from a strict adherence to a formalist legal positivism hostile to judge-created law and routine interference with the elected branches of government, to a kind of natural-law approach ("neoconstitutionalism"), based on the preeminence of human rights and constitutional principles over legislated law, as well as an activist conception of the role of courts in a democracy. This new constitutional orthodoxy, in which the human rights provisions of the Constitution – and even international human rights law – can be invoked to void legislation by judges empowered with the power of judicial review, represents a crucial cultural factor encouraging the judicialization of Latin American politics.

We are, of course, very much aware that even a revolutionary transformation of constitutional theory is not enough to explain the emergence of judicialization. Having said this, it is an important factor in the supply-side of the story, because it socializes key legal actors (judges, lawyers, and law students) into new understandings of the nature and status of the Constitution, the courts, and the role of the judiciary in a democratic regime. This change in the constitutional ideology of the legal elite can in turn be mobilized to respond to demands of individuals and groups attempting to use the courts to further their policy preferences.

References

Aldunate Eduardo. 2009. "*Neoconstitucionalismo: aproximación a una etiqueta y discusión de contenidos*". Unpublished manuscript on file with the author.

Alexi Robert. 1993. *Teoría de los Derechos Fundamentales*. Madrid: Centro de Estudios Constitucionales.

Bauer Carl. 1998. "Derecho y economía en la Constitución de 1980." *Perspectivas en Política, Economía y Gestión*, 1(2): 23–47.

Carrasco, Albano, Manuel. 1858. *Comentarios Sobre la Constitución Política de 1833*. Valparaíso: Imprenta y Librería del Mercurio.

Cappelletti, Mauro, John H. Merryman, and Joseph M. Perillo. 1967. *The Italian Legal System: An Introduction*. Stanford: Stanford University Press.

Cristi, Renato and Pablo Ruiz-Tagle. 2006. *La República en Chile: Teoría y Práctica del Constitucionalismo Republicano*. Santiago: LOM.

Couso, Javier. 2007. "The Seduction of Judicially Triggered Social Transformation: The Impact of the 'Warren Court' in Latin America." In *The Global Impact of the Warren Court*. Harry Sheiber, ed. Lanham: Lexington Books.

Cuneo, Andrés. 1980. "La Corte Suprema de Chile, sus percepciones acerca del Derecho, su rol en el sistema legal y la relación de éste con el sistema político" In *Universidad de Costa Rica, La administración de justicia en América Latina*. San José, Costa Rica: Universidad de Costa Rica. 71–83.

Dezaley, Ives and Bryant Garth. 2003. "Patterns of Foreign Legal Investment and State Transformation in Latin America." In *Legal Culture in the Age of Globalization*. Lawrence Friedman and Rogelio Pérez-Perdomo, eds. Stanford: Stanford University Press.

Domingo, Pilar. 2004. "Judicialization of Politics or Politization of the Judiciary: Recent Trends in Latin America." *Democratization*, 11(1): 104–26.

Dworkin, Ronald. 1977. *Taking Rights Seriously*. Cambridge, Mass.: Harvard University Press.

Edelman, Martin. 1994. "The Judicialization of Politics in Israel." *International Political Science Review*, 15: 177–86.

Epp, Charles. 1998. *The Rights Revolution: Lawyers, Activists, and Supreme Courts in Comparative Perspective*. Chicago: University of Chicago Press.

Friedman, Lawrence. 1975. *The Legal System: A Social Science Perspective*. New York: Russell Sage Foundation.

Friedman, Lawrence and Rogelio Pérez-Perdomo (ed.). 2002. *Legal Culture in the Age of Globalization*. Stanford, CA: Stanford University Press.

García Figueroa, Alfonso. 2003. "La Teoría del Derecho en Tiempos del Constitucionalismo," in *Neoconstitutcionalismo(s)*. Miguel Carbonell, ed. Mexico: UNAM and Editorial Trotta.

Gillman, Howard. 1993. *The Constitution Besieged: The Rise and Demise of Lochner Era Police Powers Jurisprudence*. Durham, NC: Duke University Press.

Ginsburg, Thomas. 1999. *Growing Constitutions: Judicial Review in the New Democracies (Korea, Taiwan, China, Mongolia)*, Ph.D. Dissertation. University of California at Berkeley.

Gloppen, Siri, Roberto Gargarella, and Elin Skaar, eds. 2004. *Democratization and the Judiciary: The Accountability Function of Courts in New Democracies*. London: Frank Cass Publishers.

González, Felipe. 2003. "Cultura Judicial y Enseñanza del Derecho en Chile," *Clínicas de Interés Público y Enseñanza del Derecho. Argentina, Chile, Colombia, México y Perú*. Cuadernos de Análisis Jurídico, Facultad de Derecho, Universidad Diego Portales. 145–85.

Helmke, Gretchen. 2005. *Courts Under Constraints: Judges, Generals, and Presidents in Argentina*. Cambridge and New York: Cambridge University Press.

Holland, Kenneth. 1991. *Judicial Activism in Comparative Perspective*. London: MacMillan.

Huneeus, Jorge. 1880. *La Constitución ante el Congreso*. Santiago: Imprenta de Los Tiempos.

Jaksic, Iván. 2001. *Andrés Bello: La pasión por el orden*. Chile: Editorial Universitaria.

Kapiszewski, Diana and Matthew Taylor. 2008. "Doing Courts Justice? Studying Judicial Politics in Latin America," *Perspectives on Politics*, 6: 741–67.

Kelsen, Hans. 1945. *General Theory of Law and State*. Cambridge: Harvard University Press.

Landau, David. 2005. "The Two Discourses in Colombian Constitutional Jurisprudence: A New Approach to Modeling Judicial Behavior in Latin America," *George Washington International Law Review*, 37: 687–744.

Lastarria, José, Victorino. 1865. *Elementos de Derecho Público Constitucional, teórico, positivo i político*. Berlin: Eng. Vanderhaeghum.

López Medina, Diego. 2004. *Teoría impura del Derecho: La transformación de la cultura jurídica latinoamericana*. Bogotá: Legis.

Nelson, William. 2000. *Marbury v. Madison. The Origins and Legacy of Judicial Review*. Kansas: University Press of Kansas.

Nino, Carlos. 1992. *Fundamentos de Derecho Constitucional. Análisis filosófico, jurídico y politológico de la práctica constitucional*. Buenos Aires: Editorial Astrea.

Peña, Carlos, 1999a. "Sobre la relevancia de la justicia constitucional," in *La Jurisdicción Constitucional Chilena ante la Reforma*, Gastón Gómez, ed., (Cuadernos de Análisis Jurídico, Escuela de Derecho, Universidad Diego Portales). 11–16.

Peña, Carlos. 1999b. *Practica Constitucional y Derechos Fundamentales*. Colección Estudios No, 5, Corporación Nacional de Reparación y Reconciliación: Santiago.

Pérez-Perdomo, Rogelio. 2004. *Los abogados en América Latina. Una introducción histórica*. Bogotá: Universidad Externado de Colombia.

Ríos-Figueroa, Julio and Matthew Taylor. 2006. "Institutional Determinants of the Judicialization of Policy in Brazil and Mexico," *Journal of Latin American Studies*, 38(4): 739–66.

Rodríguez Bravo, Joaquín. 1888. *Estudios Constitucionales*. Santiago: Imprenta Victoria.

Shapiro, Martin and Alec Stone Sweet. 2002. *On Law, Politics, and Judicialization*. Oxford: Oxford University Press.

Sieder, Rachel, Line Schjolden, and Alan Angell, eds. 2005. *The Judicialization of Politics in Latin America*. New York: Palgrave Macmillan.

Sikkink, Kathryn. 1996. "The Emergence, Evolution, and Effectiveness of the Latin American Human Rights Network." In *Constructing Democracy: Human Rights, Citizenship and Society in Latin America*, Jelin and Hershberg, eds. Boulder, Co. and Oxford: Westview Press. 59–84.

Silva Bascuñán, Alejandro. 1963. *Tratado de Derecho Constitucional. Tomo I. Principios*. Santiago: Editorial Jurídica de Chile.

Smith, Roger. 1990. *Liberalism and American Constitutional Law*. Cambridge, MA: Harvard University Press.

Smulovitz, Catalina. 2002. "The Discovery of the Law. Political Consequences in the Argentine Experience." In *Global Prescriptions. The Production, Exportation, and Importation of a New Legal Orthodoxy*, Bryant Garth and Yves Dezalay, eds., Ann Arbor, MI: University of Michigan Press. 249–74.

Stone, Alec. 1992. *The Birth of Judicial Politics in France: The Constitutional Council in Comparative Perspective*. Oxford: Oxford University Press.

Stone Sweet, Alec. 2000. *Governing with Judges: Constitutional Politics in Europe*. Oxford: Oxford University Press.

Tate, Neal and Torbjorn Vallinder. 1995. *The Global Expansion of Judicial Power*. New York: New York University Press.

Taylor, Matthew. 2006. "Courts, Policy Contestation, and the Legitimation of Economic Reform Under Cardoso." In *Statecrafting Monetary Authority: Democracy and Financial Order in Brazil*, Lourdes Sola and Lawrence Whitehead, eds., Oxford: Centre for Brazilian Studies. 205–36.

Whittington, Keith. 2007. *Political Foundations of Judicial Supremacy: The Presidency, the Supreme Court, and Constitutional Leadership in U.S. History*. Princeton: Princeton University Press.

7

Legal Cultures in the (Un)Rule of Law: Indigenous Rights and Juridification in Guatemala

Rachel Sieder

INTRODUCTION

Reflecting on recent patterns of judicialization in Latin America, Guillermo O'Donnell pointed to the relationship between judicialization and juridification, stating: "The *judicialization* of social relations (whereby social claims are pursued through the courts or court-like structures) is probably an expression of the increasing *juridification* of social relations: the mounting degree to which social relations, formerly left to autonomous and/or informal regulation, are being textured by formal legal rules" (O'Donnell 2005: 293). Tate and Vallinder, writing about judicialization – which they define as the global expansion of judicial power, make a similar although subtly different distinction between "the judicialization of politics" and a second, distinct phenomenon, namely, the "less dramatic instance of the expansion of judicial power, or judicialization, [that is] the domination of nonjudicial negotiating or decision-making arenas by quasi-judicial (legalistic) procedures" (Tate and Vallinder 1995: 5).

In this chapter I focus on this second, more diffuse aspect of judicialization, which I refer to here as juridification. Discussion of the phenomenon of juridification has traditionally focused on advanced capitalist economies and welfare states rather than on the developing economies and fragile democracies of Latin America. Broadly speaking, in Western Europe and the United States, juridification signals Weberian processes of bureaucratization and the expansion of law into more and more areas of social life, such as industrial relations, social welfare provision, and economic production. Juridification has been closely associated with Habermas' idea of the colonization of the lifeworld and has tended to be seen as something negative; for example, Teubner's critique of over-institutionalization and "legal pollution" (Teubner 1987).

Yet juridification in Latin America does not correspond to a similar expansion of legal-bureaucratic regulation. As has been observed frequently, rather than overinstitutionalization, most countries in the region are characterized by weak institutions and an often highly inadequate or dysfunctional rule of law (Mendez, O'Donnell, and Pinheiro 1999). Rather than the spread of regulation per se, I suggest here that in many parts of Latin America, juridification instead involves the strategic invocation of legal instruments and the adoption and appropriation of law-like discourses and practices by different social actors. In line with O'Donnell's observations, this is clearly a way in which "social relations . . . are textured by formal legal rules." As with the judicialization of political and socioeconomic claims before the courts, such juridification is a response to institutional weaknesses and the particularly perverse forms of modernization prevailing throughout Latin America, characterized by acute socioeconomic inequalities, racism, and social and economic exclusion of large sectors of the population. Just as political and socioeconomic claims are often made before the courts precisely because of the failure of individuals and groups to secure them through the political process (Sieder, Schjolden, and Angell 2005; Uprimny, Rodríguez, and García 2006),[1] so too the strategic invocation of legal and quasi-legal instruments and the adoption of para-legal discourses and procedures similarly responds to such democratic deficits and historic exclusions.

This volume considers the relationship between "legal culture(s)" – or changing understandings and practices of law, and processes of judicialization in the region.[2] By paying attention to changing attitudes, understandings, and practices related to law within society, it hopes to illuminate the circumstances in which people do or do not turn to the law, or to other legal, quasi or paralegal instances or fora. My principal focus in this chapter is not on the actions of plaintiffs, lawyers, or judges within the formal structures of the courts. Rather, I consider processes of juridification whereby indigenous people's social movements stake their claims to greater autonomy not simply or principally by resorting to the tribunals but by mimicking the state and constituting alternative "(para)-legalities."[3] More broadly, this chapter seeks to reflect on the relationship between dominant legal cultures and social movement engagements with legality within a broader context of legal pluralism.

As I discuss later, addressing the specific case of Guatemala, indigenous people in Latin America have contested the exploitation of natural resources in their territories by resorting to symbolic representations and alternative practices that invoke international legal principles and, specifically, their collective rights to prior

[1] Catalina Smulovitz (2005 and in this volume) has noted that judicialization occurs even when citizens hold out little hope of gaining a positive resolution in court.

[2] It goes without saying that "cultures" – legal or otherwise – are not static or fixed but rather dynamic, hybrid and fluid (Merry 2003). On the concept of legal culture, see Nelken (2004).

[3] For example, the multiethnic community police (*policía comunitaria*) in the state of Guerrero, Mexico, where mixtec, tlapanec and mestizo communities have consolidated a system of security, justice and community rehabilitation outside the state legal system (Sierra 2009), or the systematization of indigenous law amongst the Nasa people in the Cauca region of Colombia (Rappaport 2005; Brunnegger, forthcoming).

consultation. New forms of social protest and resistance combine local customs and communal authority structures (customary law) with global rights discourses, as well as international instruments and institutions. In addition to judicializing their rights claims before the courts, indigenous peoples' juridification of social protest signals the ways in which their contemporary forms of collective action draw on both local and transnational understandings of entitlements, obligations, and rights. In effect, a dominant legal and political environment that is hostile to expanding or protecting citizens' rights encourages certain categories of citizens to constitute alternative legalities and to attempt to secure their claims by "law-like" actions outside the courts.[4] These subaltern (para) legal cultures can be understood as a response to current patterns of economic and legal globalization, and to the law's failure to guarantee basic human rights to security and subsistence for the majority of the population. Yet by mimicking and appropriating formal legal instruments and institutions, these forms of claim-making both challenge and legitimate law with potentially far-reaching consequences for counterhegemonic organization.

INDIGENOUS PEOPLE, LEGAL PLURALISM, AND JURIDIFICATION

Legal pluralism is not new in Latin America: indigenous forms of law preceded the emergence of the modern nation-state and continue to coexist alongside state law. Today, the absence, inaccessibility, ineffectiveness, and discriminatory nature of state law in much of the region, particularly for the poorest sectors of the population, mean that many of the region's indigenous people continue to look to their community authorities, rather than to the national courts, to protect their interests and resolve disputes.[5] However, across Latin America, new "legal cultures" and forms of political engagement developed by indigenous people are increasingly common, often consciously linked to global rights discourses (Brunnegger, forthcoming; Rappaport 2005; Sawyer 2004; Rodríguez-Garavito and Arenas 2005). These symbolic representations of claims as legal issues appeal to a range of international instruments or institutions and can be understood as expressions of the highly globalized legal pluralism described by Boaventura de Sousa Santos (2002), where legal institutions, codes, norms, and discourses are constantly intermixed. As Santos and others have noted, processes of contention are generating *hybrid legal spaces* – sociolegal fields where struggles are played out over the content, legitimacy and exercise of law (Santos 2006; Randeria 2007). Such developments form part of a wider regional and

4 See for example Santos's (1977) classic study of alternative law in a squatter settlement in Rio de Janeiro.

5 This is, of course, not to say indigenous people do not also interact with the formal judicial apparatus. Justice systems within indigenous communities have never been entirely autonomous and indeed are shaped by and reflect changing state practices: as the literature on customary law and legal pluralism has long made clear; see Chenaut and Sierra (1995); Moore (1978); Starr and Collier (1989); Nader (1990).

global dynamic, whereby indigenous social movements stake their political claims by invoking international legal principles and, to a certain extent, mimicking the state, constituting alternative (para-) legalities in contraposition to current state practices, while at the same time attempting to influence official policies and actions.

This form of juridification responds to a number of different factors: first, the increasing recognition of indigenous peoples' collective rights during the 1990s and 2000s within Latin American state constitutions and international law, and the failure to enforce those rights in practice. A second contributory factor is the limited but important official sanctioning and promotion of community-based forms of justice that has occurred across the region. Part of the global trend toward decentralizing certain kinds of justice provision, this policy orientation legitimated the greater participation of laypeople in what was traditionally considered to be the business of lawyers. Third, current patterns of economic globalization, particularly surrounding the exploitation of natural resources, and associated patterns of legal globalization – including legal guarantees for investors' interests and reform of domestic legislation to favor transnational capital – have spurred indigenous communities and organizations to try to secure, control, and protect their historic territories. Fourth, the acute deficiencies of the rule of law across the region, the unresponsive and exclusive nature of many countries' dominant legal cultures and the acute asymmetries of power relations between indigenous people and national elites have also encouraged a phenomenon whereby social movements resort to law outside formal legal institutions. The following sections consider each of these factors before turning to analyze current processes of juridification in response to large-scale mining projects in Guatemala.

INDIGENOUS RIGHTS: MULTICULTURAL CONSTITUTIONALISM

Indigenous peoples' rights and claims became increasingly politicized in Latin America throughout the 1990s. Governments across the region responded to indigenous demands and their own legitimacy deficits by constitutionally recognizing the existence of indigenous peoples, a trend Donna Van Cott (2000) referred to a decade ago as "multicultural constitutionalism." New or reformed constitutions enumerated a series of recognitions and collective entitlements of indigenous peoples living within states' borders, such as rights to customary law, collective property and bilingual education.[6] A range of different policies were subsequently implemented to advance the new multicultural model. These reforms initially raised expectations that indigenous peoples' rights to political and legal autonomy would be respected

[6] A detailed comparison of these reforms is beyond the scope of this chapter. The nature and extent of the constitutional rights extended to indigenous peoples through the first round of multicultural reforms continues to be a matter of controversy across the region; a second wave of "pluri-national and multiethnic" constitutional reforms have subsequently occurred in Bolivia (2009) and Ecuador (2008).

and that measures would be implemented to ensure respect for cultural differences and improved conditions for indigenous people, who constitute the poorest and most marginalized of Latin America's citizens.

The degree to which indigenous rights were formally incorporated within the region's constitutions varied. For example, in Guatemala, a constitutional reform to strengthen indigenous rights provisions in the 1985 Constitution was promised as part of the peace settlement, concluded in December 1996. However, the constitutional reforms were ultimately rejected in a popular referendum held in 1999. Some mention is made of indigenous peoples in two articles in the 1985 Constitution, but their rights are not specifically enumerated in such a way as to make them easily actionable in the courts. This partly explains the relatively limited evidence of such judicialization to date in Guatemala.[7]

By the early 2000s, disillusionment and frustration with the limits of what was termed "neoliberal multiculturalism" were in evidence across Latin America (Hale 2002; Richards 2004). To many indigenous activists and their supporters, it seemed that the region's neoliberal states were able to legally recognize cultural differences at the same time as they continued to implement economic policies that were highly prejudicial to indigenous people's ways of life. The exploitation of natural resources, such as timber, oil, and minerals accelerated throughout the decade, particularly in response to ever-increasing demand from Asia. Such projects directly affected areas of indigenous settlement, often with acute social and environmental impacts (Sawyer 2004). In spite of the rhetorical commitment made to respecting indigenous rights implied by new constitutions and the ratification of international instruments (discussed below), in case after case indigenous people continued to be persecuted by the state when they attempted to exercise rights of autonomy or challenge hegemonic patterns of economic "development."[8] Disillusioned with official multiculturalism, indigenous peoples' movements in many parts of the continent turned away from their previous focus on securing legislative changes and instead worked to strengthen autonomy and communal and supracommunal forms of indigenous authority, often in a conscious effort to develop alternatives to the "neoliberal state."

INDIGENOUS RIGHTS IN INTERNATIONAL LAW

Indigenous activists often stake their claims to greater legal and political autonomy by making reference to instruments that codify the collective rights of indigenous peoples within the international system, including the UN Declaration on

7 I have written about this issue in more detail elsewhere (see Sieder 2007).

8 For example, indigenous authorities often face criminal charges for "exceeding their functions" when they attempt to apply customary law in Peru, Mexico, and Guatemala; Chile's response to indigenous protest against logging, hydroelectric projects, and mining has been to criminalize indigenous social movements using antiterrorist legislation.

the Rights of Indigenous Peoples[9] (approved by the UN's General Assembly in September 2007), and the 1989 International Labor Organization's (ILO) Convention 169 on the Rights of Indigenous and Tribal Peoples in Independent Countries (currently the only international instrument that is binding on signatory states). Although there is no specific regional instrument dealing with indigenous rights,[10] a number of rulings by the Inter-American Court of Human Rights regarding states' obligations toward their indigenous populations have established precedents within the regional jurisprudence that have become a touchstone for indigenous movements.[11]

ILO 169 has been ratified by more states in Latin America than in any other part of the world. States party to the Convention include Argentina, Bolivia, Brazil, Chile, Colombia, Costa Rica, Ecuador, Honduras, Guatemala, Mexico, Peru, Paraguay, and Venezuela (non-Latin American signatories include Fiji, the Netherlands, Denmark, Dominica, Spain, and Norway). Although the process of ratification has often been contentious within individual countries, this regional endorsement signals the relative acceptance of the concept of indigenous peoples in Latin America, compared to Africa and Asia where the term is much more problematic. It can also be explained as part of the "rights cascade" that followed the return to constitutional democracy throughout Latin America in the 1980s and 1990s, which involved the ratification of numerous human rights treaties by new democratically elected governments (Lutz and Sikkink 2001).

Rights guaranteed by ILO 169 include equality of opportunity and treatment, protections for indigenous peoples' religion and spiritual values and customs, rights to ownership and possession of traditionally occupied lands, and rights to appropriate forms of health and education provision.[12] One area that has proved highly contentious is that of *prior consultation* about development projects affecting indigenous peoples. The Convention specifies that indigenous peoples have a right to prior consultation on development proposals affecting their livelihoods:

> In applying the provisions of this Convention, governments shall: consult the peoples concerned, through appropriate procedures and in particular through their representative institutions, whenever consideration is being given to legislative or administrative measures which may affect them directly. (Article 6.1.a)

9 For the full text of the declaration, see http://www.un.org/esa/socdev/unpfii/en/declaration.html (December 11, 2009).

10 An American Declaration on the Rights of Indigenous Peoples has been under discussion within the Organization of American States since 1997 (OEA/Ser/L/V/.II.95 Doc. 6 (1997)).

11 The Inter-American Commission and Court uphold the instruments of the Inter-American system (the Declaration and the Convention), but also have a mandate to ensure respect for all human rights treaties ratified by member states – such as ILO 169. On emerging jurisprudence, see the principles established in the celebrated case of *Awas Tingni v. Nicaragua* (Nash Rojas 2004; Rodríguez-Piñero Royo 2004).

12 See http://www.ilo.org/ilolex/cgi-lex/convde.pl?C169 (December 11, 2009).

> The peoples concerned shall have the right to decide their own priorities for the process of development as it affects their lives, beliefs, institutions and spiritual wellbeing and the lands they occupy or otherwise use, and to exercise control, to the extent possible, over their own economic, social, and cultural development. In addition, they shall participate in the formulation, implementation, and evaluation of plans and programs for national and regional development which may affect them directly. (Article 7.1)
>
> In cases in which the State retains the ownership of mineral or sub-surface resources or rights to other resources pertaining to lands, governments shall establish or maintain procedures through which they shall consult these peoples, with a view to ascertaining whether and to what degree their interests would be prejudiced, before undertaking or permitting any programs for the exploration or exploitation of such resources pertaining to their lands. The peoples concerned shall wherever possible participate in the benefits of such activities, and shall receive fair compensation for any damages which they may sustain as a result of such activities. (Article 15.2)[13]

Over ten years since ILO Convention 169 was first approved, "prior consultation" remains an unsettled and vague legal concept. For this reason, it has destabilized existing understandings of law and generated both new forms of legal mobilization and judicialization, specifically processes of juridification. Pablo Rueda refers to two factors that foment contests over legal meanings: "First, when the semantic field of the legal concept is linguistically rich and provides enough strands of meanings for litigants to use, and second, when the courts are under sufficient pressure to expand its meaning" (see Rueda in this volume). Disputes over the extent of indigenous autonomy rights and what is understood by prior consultation have come to feature more prominently in the domestic courts in Latin America and at the supranational level at the Inter-American Commission and Court of Human Rights. This is partly because no state signatory to ILO 169 has defined prior consultation through national legislation. This effectively means that the region's states have made a commitment to a broad, internationally sanctioned set of principles, yet there is no agreement about how those principles should be upheld in practice.

A number of contentious cases related to indigenous land claims and issues of prior consultation have been taken to the Inter-American Commission by indigenous movements and their allies. For example, in 1997 the U'wa people, in alliance with a number of Colombian and U.S.-based nongovernmental organizations (NGOs), brought a case against the Colombian government to try and stop a mining concession in their territory granted to the Oxy and Shell oil companies, alleging lack of prior consultation (Rodríguez-Garavito and Arenas 2005). In 2001, in the celebrated case of *Awas Tingni v. Nicaragua*, the Inter-American Court of Human Rights confirmed that indigenous peoples have collective rights not just to the land they occupy

[13] In Latin America, states retain ownership of mineral and subsurface resource.

but also to its resources. The judges declared that the rights of the indigenous community in question to territory and to judicial protection had been violated by the Nicaraguan government when it granted concessions to a Korean lumber company to log on their traditional land, and recommended a series of remedies (Anaya and Crider 1996; Nash Rojas 2004; Rodriguez-Piñero Royo 2004). The implementation of the Court's recommendations in the *Awas Tingni* case has been highly contentious and complex. Nonetheless, this innovatory jurisprudence is a clear example of indigenous social movements' transnational engagement with law and of the ways in which globalized legal pluralism offers new options for marginalized indigenous people to judicialize their claims.

In addition, as I explore next, the unsettled and vague legal concept of "prior consultation" has generated new forms of juridification of social and political protest outside the courts.[14]

COMMUNITY JUSTICE REFORMS

An additional feature that has encouraged juridification is the tendency for judicial reforms across Latin America to endorse experiments in community-based justice. Following the first wave of multicultural constitutional reforms, the recognition of legal pluralism became part of the public policy agenda across the region (Faundez 2005). In practice, this tended to interact with broader international trends in reforming justice systems toward "de-judicializing" certain areas of social conflict. This involves a greater role for mediation, conciliation, and arbitration mechanisms as well as an increase in the role of nonprofessional civil society actors in the provision of justice.

Initiatives involving hybrid, quasicommunal/quasistate fora such as indigenous community courts, community conciliation services, and lay justices of the peace have been promoted in recent years. These function, in effect, as courts of first instance or alternative dispute resolution (ADR) mechanisms for petty crimes, misdemeanors, and familial or intracommunal conflicts. For example, in Peru the local election of nonlawyer justices of the peace, many of whom use conciliation and mediation mechanisms and often operate in Quechua, was promoted following the

[14] The UN Declaration on Indigenous Peoples, approved by the General Assembly in 2007, goes further than ILO 169 on the issues of autonomy and prior consultation, enshrining the principles of participation and prior and informed consent. "Indigenous peoples have the right to participate in decision-making in matters which would affect their rights, through representatives chosen by themselves in accordance with their own procedures, as well as to maintain and develop their own indigenous decision-making institutions" (Article 18); "States shall consult and cooperate in good faith with the indigenous peoples concerned through their own representative institutions to obtain their free, prior, and informed consent before adopting and implementing legislative or administrative measures that may affect them" (Article 19). At the time of writing, Bolivia was the only country in Latin America to have ratified the Declaration. The general principles it sets out remained untested before the courts.

1993 Constitution. After new legislation was approved in 2001, these justices of the peace started to receive a salary from the state (Lovatón 2003; Faundez 2005). Also in Peru, conciliation centers, modeled on U.S. and British experiments in neighborhood dispute mediation, were set up with a mandate to apply customary law and community-based dispute resolution in urban and rural settings (Poole 2004). Conciliation and mediation centers staffed by trained paralegals were similarly promoted in Guatemala, their offices often located next to local courts. At the same time, indigenous community courts (*juzgados de paz indígena*) employing lay judges selected by their peers were set up in a number of sites of high indigenous residence throughout the country (Rasch 2008). In Colombia, lay-staffed "justice houses" (*casas de justicia*) in low-income urban settlements received considerable governmental support as a means to increase access to justice for the poor (Faundez 2005). These different measures were justified by policy-makers as a means to improve linguistic, physical, and cultural access to justice for marginalized populations, reduce costs, and alleviate pressure on the courts. They were often enthusiastically supported and funded by international development agencies, including the World Bank and USAID.

Such tendencies, in effect, endorsed greater lay participation in the business of law – previously perceived as a highly technical and specialized domain. In some instances, indigenous organizations have worked with the new officially promoted multicultural justice mechanisms, reappropriating and resignifying them (Sierra 2004). In others, indigenous organizations have denounced initiatives such as *juzgados de paz indígena* as a means to supplant indigenous law and curtail the autonomy of traditional authorities. Certainly efforts by indigenous peoples' social movements to secure greater political and legal autonomy have been opposed bitterly by governments and the private sector, particularly when the territories in question contain valuable natural resources.

NATURAL RESOURCES: ECONOMIC AND LEGAL GLOBALIZATION

Disputes involving indigenous people and natural resources – and associated processes of judicialization and juridification – are closely related to prevailing tendencies in economic and legal globalization. New laws relating to foreign investment are promoted by the U.S. government through bilateral trade agreements with Latin American countries, by international financial institutions and through the World Trade Organization (WTO) process. These include legislation regarding activities such as the exploitation of minerals and oil or intellectual property rights. Such legal changes directly affect indigenous peoples, as mineral resource exploitation and bioprospecting have encroached on traditional areas of indigenous settlement (Szablowski 2007).

Many analysts have pointed to new regulatory regimes, or "transnational legal fields," attaching to processes of free trade-driven economic integration, noting that free trade agreements have implied profound changes to national legal systems and state sovereignty (Dezaley and Garth 2002a, 2002b). For example, free trade agreements give private companies the right to sue national governments in international arbitration if they break contracts or change regulatory policy in such a way as to affect company profits. This effectively allows transnational companies to sidestep national courts and take their claims directly to the much less transparent arena of international arbitration (Dezaley and Garth 1998; Van Harten 2007).[15] The increasingly complex and transnationalized nature of legal pluralism means that different elements of state law may be in direct conflict with each other. When they approve constitutional reforms, ratify international legal instruments such as ILO 169, or receive loans from multilateral organizations, states acquire commitments to safeguard greater indigenous rights to autonomy and consult indigenous peoples over development initiatives. Yet these legal commitments can and do clash with new transnational norms and regulations protecting the rights of international capital and investors. This contributes, in turn, to incoherence in state policy, legal unpredictability, and greater social conflict. Civil society actors increasingly look to the law to protect their interests, perhaps judicializing their rights claims. Nevertheless, they invariably find these efforts frustrated or trumped by alternative legal instruments and norms.

In 1997, the Guatemalan Congress approved a new Mining Code (Decree No. 48-97) (Solano 2005). This legislation increased tax breaks and investment opportunities for transnational capital and reduced the royalties payable to the Guatemalan state from 6 to 1 percent. The reform constitutes part of a global trend of legal adjustment concerning natural resource exploitation that is part and parcel of the neoliberal development model: some campaigners estimate that more than seventy countries have "modernized" their mining legislation in recent years in line with World Bank recommendations (Cuffe 2005:9). After the new law was passed, a significant number of licenses for mineral, hydroelectric, and oil prospecting and exploitation were extended to domestic and foreign companies; at the time of writing over fifty mining licenses had been granted to foreign and domestic companies by the Ministry of Energy and Mines (Central America Report, May 23, 2008). As a consequence of these new policies toward transnational capital, mining operations began in different sites throughout Guatemala, many of them in areas of high indigenous residence and extreme poverty. Indigenous peoples in Guatemala have no legal rights to territorial autonomy and – in common with the rest of Latin America – the state retains the rights to subsoil resources. However, ILO Convention 169, which was ratified by the Guatemalan Congress in 1996, together with the "soft law" of the World Bank, Inter-American Development Bank and other donors who often lend financial support to

[15] Effectively, foreign investors now have the right to file suit against laws or regulations at the national, state, or local levels, even if they are enacted for public interest objectives, such as environmental protection or public health.

mining developments, clearly points to a requirement for adequate prior consultation about development projects that will affect indigenous people's ways of life.[16] Despite this, no consultation took place over the new mining legislation prior to its approval or regarding the granting of mining licenses to companies wishing to prospect in areas of indigenous residence (Central America Report, August 4, 2006).[17] This lack of consultation, commonplace in Guatemalan politics, has increasingly clashed with indigenous people's expectations about law, and particularly about the implications of ILO Convention 169. This is in part because of a new rights consciousness. In the decade following the signing of the peace accords, domestic and international NGOs and UN agencies working in Guatemala sought to systematize and promote indigenous people's awareness of their own rights and the commitments made by the government to guarantee them. ILO 169 in particular has now become a common point of reference for indigenous people and their supporters. Indeed, pocketbook copies of the Convention circulate widely and it is frequently discussed and invoked in indigenous organizations' workshops and meetings.[18] Although no definition of adequate prior consultation exists in law, indigenous communities and social movements are increasingly demanding this in practice.

GUATEMALA – THE (UN)RULE OF LAW

The ways in which indigenous people interact with and mobilize around legal norms and spaces ultimately depend on the nature of the states and social movements in question, and on the legal and political opportunity structures specific to each context. In Guatemala, the possibilities for judicializing rights claims are acutely limited within Latin America the country constitutes an extreme case of judicial dysfunctionality and lack of accountability. Although Guatemala has been a constitutional democracy since 1985, civil rights continue to be routinely violated, and judicial redress for even the most serious crimes is virtually nonexistent. For much of its recent history, Guatemala was characterized by restricted, semiauthoritarian forms of government (and outright military dictatorship between 1978 and 1984),

[16] See World Bank Article 4.20 (Davis 2002); Inter-American Development Bank, Indigenous Peoples and Community Development Unit, *Operational Policy on Indigenous Peoples* (GN-2296), approved by the Policy and Evaluation Committee of the Board of Directors of the Inter-American Development Bank on March 11, 2004.

[17] Article 59 of the 1997 Mining Law allows a period of just five days for objections to licenses to be lodged, hardly long enough for indigenous communities to find out that licenses have been approved, let alone organize a legal appeal. Indigenous communities in Guatemala have repeatedly protested that they are only informed by the government that licenses have been granted *after* the five-day period has expired.

[18] Interestingly, this echoes the pocketbook copies of the 1986 Constitution, popularized in the late 1980s by the office of the human rights ombudsman. The practice of "constitutional catechism" was used by popular organizations to resist forced paramilitary patrols imposed by the army in the context of the counterinsurgency war.

and extremely high levels of systematic state violence used against the civilian population. The armed conflict that ended in 1996 resulted in the death of more than 200,000 people, at least 50,000 of whom were disappeared (the vast majority of them murdered by the army, police, paramilitary civil patrols and clandestine death squads operated by military intelligence) (Comisión de Esclarecimiento Histórico 2000). The UN declared the Guatemalan state had perpetrated acts of genocide during the counterinsurgency war, which is the only recorded case of genocide in Latin America in the twentieth century. In its 2000 report, the UN-backed truth commission stated:

> The failure of the administration of justice to protect human rights during the internal armed confrontation has been clearly and fully established, by the thousands of violations . . . that were not investigated, tried, or punished by the Guatemalan State. . . . In general, the Judiciary neglected to address basic procedural remedies to control the authorities, in view of the grave abuses against personal liberty and security. . . . Moreover, on numerous occasions the courts of justice were directly subordinated to the Executive branch. . . . This whole situation made the population totally defenseless in the face of the abuses of the authorities, and has led the Judiciary to be seen as an instrument for defending and protecting the powerful, that has repressed or refused to protect fundamental rights, especially of those who have been victims of grave human rights violations.[19]

The postconflict state is weak with respect to both international capital and more powerful states in the international system. It is also highly elitist and marked by authoritarian enclaves, very high levels of violence and the "(un)rule of law" (Mendez, O'Donnell, and Pinheiro 1999). Since the end of the armed conflict, organized crime and violence has reached epidemic proportions. The country has one of the highest homicide rates in the Western Hemisphere and an acute problem of gang violence and public security. According to official police statistics, 5,885 murders were reported in 2006 – the highest murder toll in a decade, an increase of 547, or 9.3 percent, compared to 2005 (Central America Report, June 29, 2007). The legacy of the war and the failure of the justice system to guarantee redress have also contributed to a rise in extrajudicial executions, including mob killings or lynchings. The numbers average about two attempted lynchings a week and show few signs of declining (Snodgrass-Godoy 2006).

Beyond the right to vote, the vast majority of Guatemalans enjoy few of the benefits of formal citizenship. Levels of social and economic exclusion are among the worst in the region. In 2000 approximately 56 percent of Guatemala's population lived in poverty (about 6.4 million people), with some 16 percent living in extreme poverty (World Bank 2003).[20] Economic differences between different regions of the country and ethnic groups are stark. While Guatemala's twenty-three indigenous groups,

[19] Chapter II, Volume 3, "Denegación de justicia," paras. 285–6, (CEH 2000).

[20] Guatemala ranks worst in Latin America and the Caribbean (and among the worst in the world) for malnutrition. The Gini indices for consumption and income for Guatemala are 48 and 57, respectively,

by a conservative estimate, represented some 43 percent of the population, they accounted for 58 percent of the poor and 72 percent of the extreme poor in 2000. Almost three-quarters of indigenous people live in poverty, as compared with 41 percent for nonindigenous.[21] Levels of mistrust in the law – and in the institutions of state more generally – are thus related to economic and ethnic inequalities, histories and continuing practices of violence, and a dominant legal culture that continues to guarantee impunity.

Additionally, the organized indigenous movement in Guatemala is weak and fragmented – in part a consequence of the extraordinary violence visited on indigenous communities during the counterinsurgency war. While indigenous organizations have received significant support from international development cooperation agencies since the signing of the peace agreement in 1996, they conspicuously lack domestic political allies within congress. There is no strong tradition of legal mobilization and few effective legal support structures compared to other Latin American countries.[22] Domestic NGOs and human rights organizations are increasingly mounting public interest litigation; however, they often lack sufficient resources and judicial expertise to do so effectively. This, combined with the general unresponsiveness of the judicial branch, means that the prospects for effective strategic litigation and legal mobilization remain limited. Faced with such a panorama, indigenous communities in different parts of the country have increasingly resorted to paralegal forms of organization and protest outside the judicial system to press their claims.

Consultas Populares: *The Juridification of Social Protest*

In 2004 and 2005, indigenous community activists in the western Guatemalan department of San Marcos mobilized to call on the government to annul a concession for open cast gold and silver mining and processing, known as the Marlin project (Fulmer et al.).[23] The license for exploration was granted in 1996 to Montana Exploradora S.A., a subsidiary of Canadian mining company Glamis Gold, but the company only began operations in San Marcos in 2004. Although the license was approved after the national congress had ratified ILO Convention 169, the indigenous Maya Mam and Sipakapense communities of the directly affected municipalities of San Miguel Ixtahuacán and Sipakapa were not consulted about the proposed mining development.

The project received approximately $35 million in loans and $10 million in equity investment from the International Financial Corporation (IFC), the branch

making it one of the most unequal countries in Latin America, which also has the highest rates of wealth and income inequality in the world.

[21] Ibid.

[22] On the idea of legal support structures for legal mobilization, see Epp (1998). For a comparative analysis of the role of legal support structures in advancing human rights claims in Chile and El Salvador, see Collins (2010).

[23] Fulmer et al. (2008) provide a suggestive analysis of the multiple legal and regulatory regimes and ambiguity surrounding the Marlin mine project and subsequent challenges to its operation.

of the World Bank that lends to private companies. World Bank internal directive 4.20 specifies that indigenous people should be adequately consulted prior to the initiation of projects supported by the bank that affect them (Davis 2002). When Glamis sought loans from the IFC, one of the loan requirements was that the company should organize consultations with the affected populations. According to Glamis, it carried out consultations with approximately three thousand people in San Marcos. However, many of those supposedly consulted subsequently questioned these claims, saying company representatives had presented the mining operations as a done deal and that they were given no chance to make any decisions about the project and were not given information about the health and environmental impacts the project might have – for example, from possible cyanide contamination of the water table.

The Marlin project was denounced as an antidemocratic imposition and demands grew for development priorities for the municipality and surrounding areas to be decided by local people. Once Marlin's prospecting operations began, protests gained pace and drew support from environmentalists, the Catholic Church and indigenous and popular organizations in other parts of the country. These culminated in violent confrontations with the police in January 2005, as protestors attempted to block the transport of heavy machinery to San Marcos. One protestor died and sixteen were injured.

The municipal authorities of Sipakapa then announced that they would hold a public consultation on the mining operations. This was to be effected via open community assemblies in different villages according to "indigenous customary law." Although community activists defended such communal assemblies as part of their traditional forms of indigenous law and governance, Montana Exploradora immediately tried to impede the vote, submitting a legal injunction in an attempt to force the municipal authorities to suspend proceedings. In the end, pressure from the company forced the municipal mayor to back down. However, the local community development council, a relatively new body set up as part of the ongoing process of municipal decentralization, was the institutional space through which the community consultation was finally held on June 18, 2005. In all, eleven out of thirteen villages voted against the mining development, one in favor and the other abstained. Approximately 2,564 people voted in total, 95 percent of whom rejected the mining development (Central America Report, July 1, 2005). The Ministry of Energy and Mines submitted an injunction to the Constitutional Court, claiming that the popular vote was unconstitutional. Nevertheless, the court upheld the villagers' right to vote, citing ILO Convention 169 and Article 65 of the 2002 municipal code, which states that when an issue particularly affects the rights and interests of indigenous communities, municipal councils will carry out consultations at the request of the indigenous communities or authorities. The court's specific mention of the municipal councils was interpreted by some as an attempt to limit the sphere of consultation to existing official administrative structures and legal frameworks. However, indigenous social movements argue that while the Municipal Code passed in 2002 provides for consultations on matters of local concern via municipal plebiscites, it does not represent a comprehensive measure to ensure the guarantee of indigenous peoples' collective rights as defined in international law. While the villagers of Sipakapa turned to the municipal development council as a vehicle for carrying out the consultation, they were in fact staking a much broader claim than that recognized in national law: specifically the right of prior consultation of indigenous peoples as established in ILO 169, and of free, prior, and informed consent as stipulated in the UN Declaration on the Rights of Indigenous Peoples.[24]

The Sipakapa *consulta popular* (community plebiscite) provides a clear example of juridification in response to the failure of the government and the national legal system to guarantee internationally recognized indigenous rights. In addition, a series of judicial and administrative actions against the Merlin mining concession were filed outside the country by Guatemalan popular organizations and NGOs. A trade union confederation filed a complaint with the ILO itself, alleging that the government had failed to meet its obligations to ensure due consultation. Madre Selva, a local environmental NGO, together with community representatives from Sipakapa, filed a complaint with the Compliance Advisory Ombudsman, the body that investigates complaints funded by the World Bank's International Financial Corporation. The Compliance Advisory Ombudsman's office subsequently issued a report stating that the bank had failed to adequately consult the local community or properly evaluate the environmental and humanitarian impact of the mine (Office of the Compliance Advisor/Ombudsman International Finance Corporation 2005). The emanicipatory potential of these developments is questionable. Construction of the mine and plant for cyanide processing of the ore continued at Sipakapa, and villagers denounce violence and intimidation by company employees, along with environmental pollution and negative health effects due to the mining operations. Aggressive tactics and failure to consult with local communities have characterized mining developments elsewhere in the country. For example, a proposed nickel mining operation in El Estor, Izabal province, prompted a complaint by a Guatemalan trade union confederation before the International Labor Organization in protest at the Guatemalan government's failure to ensure consultation, as stipulated by ILO Convention 169 (Central America Report, March 31, 2006).[25] The proposed mine led to violent disputes over land, with indigenous Maya Q'eqchi' forcefully evicted by police and military forces operating to protect the interests of the Guatemalan Nickel Company, a subsidiary of Canadian company Skye Resources, which is seeking a license to extract nickel. Members of the former administration of Oscar Berger were accused of having vested interests in the proposed project and permitting a series of irregularities in the licensing process (Central America Report, January 26, 2006).

24 For the full text of the declaration, see http://www.un.org/esa/socdev/unpfii/en/declaration.html (December 11, 2009).

25 In March 2006, the ILO upheld the complaint, finding against Guatemala.

Subsequent to the Sipakapa community plebiscite other indigenous communities throughout Guatemala organized similar consultation processes in opposition to proposed projects to exploit natural resources, encouraged by growing social opposition to mining. Between 2005 and October 2009, in total thirty popular consultations or plebiscites concerning exploitation of natural resources were carried out in indigenous communities, involving more than half a million people. Two-thirds of these plebiscites related to mining concessions; the rest focused on proposed hydroelectric projects (Central America Report, October 2, 2009). In the majority of cases the consultations were organized through local indigenous municipal authorities (including community development councils); in others however, villagers organized their deliberations in communal assemblies in the face of widespread opposition from the local municipal authorities (Central America Report, 23 May, 2008; 22 June, 2007). Together, these consultas signalled the increasing juridification of indigenous claims to prior consent, irrespective of whether or not the procedures and outcomes were legally recognized by the national or local authorities. Between July 25 and 27, 2006, the five municipalities of Colotenango, Todos Santos Cuchumatán, Santiago Chimaltenango, Concepción Huista, and San Juan Atitán, all in the regional department of Huehuetenango, rejected open cast mining operations in popular plebiscites held in communal assemblies (Central America Report, October 13, 2006). Earlier in the year the government had granted a license to the Tenango Mining Company to allow the extraction of gold, silver, nickel, copper, lead, zinc and other minerals in the region. According to the local press, 99 percent of the 27,292 voters who took part in the Huehuetenango consulta rejected open pit mining; the turnout was higher than it had been for the 2003 general elections (Central America Report, August 4, 2006; October 13, 2006). On April 20, 2007, residents of 13 villages in Playa Grande Ixcán, Quiché province, held a consulta in which 93 percent of those who took part voted against government plans to allow oil extraction and the construction of hydroelectric dams in their communities. A proposed $350 million dam construction project will affect more than 2,300 people in eighteen different communities in the region (Central America Report, May 4, 2007).

In April 2007, a popular consultation was carried out in San Juan Sacatepequez without the support of the municipal authorities, and on May 13, thousands of *campesinos* (peasants) converged on the town hall to demand that the mayor back their opposition to mining (Central America Report, June 22, 2007). On June 13, 2007, more than seven thousand people, almost all indigenous Maya Mam campesinos, gathered in the highland community of Ixchiguán, San Marcos province, and voted to reject four exploration licenses granted by the government to Montana Exploradora without the community's prior consent (Central America Report, June 22, 2007).

These "soft law" and paralegal engagements by indigenous social movements and their allies represent a watershed in indigenous people's fight to defend their natural resources and territories. Juridification involving community plebiscites is part of a wider process whereby indigenous law is being strengthened, revitalized, and reinvented in Mayan communities across the country (Rasch 2008; Sieder forthcoming). Through the community plebiscites, indigenous people are effectively transforming local processes of participation, appealing to indigenous custom – such as deliberation in community assemblies and the importance of reaching a collective consensus- and invoking internationally enshrined collective rights to autonomy and consultation to challenge the prevailing economic model and the government's failure to take their views into account. At the same time, the battle over the rights of indigenous peoples and the rights of mining companies continues in the courts. Guatemalan NGOs achieved a major victory in April 2007 when the Constitutional Court upheld an appeal against the 1997 Mining Law lodged by the Center for Legal, Environmental, and Social Action (CALAS). The Constitutional Court declared that seven articles of the Mining Law were unconstitutional, primarily on the grounds that it did not require sufficient consideration of the environmental consequences of mining prior to the granting of a licence (Central America Report, June 27, 2008).[26] The court's ruling effectively signalled the need for new legislation and prevented the government from issuing new mining licenses (Central America Report, March 27, 2009; February 27, 2009).[27] However, on the question of indigenous peoples' rights to prior consultation judicial outcomes were less favorable. On May 8, 2007, the Guatemalan Constitutional Court ruled in favor of an appeal put forward by Montana Exploradora, claiming that the Sipakapa plebiscite was unconstitutional. The court's view was that popular consultations are not legally binding and have no basis in law. Magistrates argued that, according to Guatemalan law, only the Ministry of Energy and Mining was able to decide the government's energy policy (Central America Report, June 1, 2007). They therefore ruled that the Sipakapa municipal authorities had no right to forbid Montana from operating in the area. Within Guatemala, the court's decision was widely perceived as a measure favoring transnational mining corporations and as a direct rejection of the principle of prior

[26] The court found seven articles of the Mining Law to be unconstitutional. Although Articles 19 and 20 of the Mining Law state that environmental impact studies must be carried out before a mining project begins, if the studies are not approved by the Ministry of the Environment and Natural Resources (MARN) within thirty days, a corporation is permitted to go ahead with the project. The appeal launched by CALAS in 2007 argued that this violated Articles 64 and 97 of the Constitution, which state that the government must do everything within its power to "guarantee" environmental protection. This argument was accepted by the court. Article 75, section D, of the Mining Law also allowed mining companies to dump waste in streams and rivers, "taking appropriate measures to limit environmental damage." CALAS argued that this violated Article 128 of the Constitution, which states that water resources belong to the community and cannot be used "to benefit private interests." The Constitutional Court accepted this argument and in its ruling also forbade mining companies from polluting the environment.

[27] By mid-2009, new legislation governing mining operations had yet to be approved. A draft bill proposed by the government of Alvaro Colóm was challenged by environmental and civil society activists, who alleged it favored the mining companies. In August 2009 the Ministry of Energy and Mines issued a new mining concession, effectively ignoring the 2007 ruling of the Constitutional Court.

consultation contained in ILO 169.[28] In a subsequent ruling in December 2009 the court explicitly recognized indigenous peoples' collective rights to prior consultation, citing existing international law. However, the same ruling also stated that certain economic activities were of "national interest," and refused to endorse the right of prior consent specified in the UN Declaration on the Rights of Indigenous Peoples. In 2008 and 2009, indigenous organizations attempted to promote legislation to regulate prior consultation; their efforts have to date been unsuccessful.

CONCLUSIONS

The recognition of indigenous peoples' collective rights by states and within international law, combined with the failure of states to uphold those rights in practice, has led social movements to promote processes of judicialization and juridification in favor of indigenous claims across Latin America. This is, in part, a consequence of an increasingly complex and globalized legal pluralism whereby people, territories, and commodities are subject to multiple overlapping legal regimes, and poor peoples' livelihoods are increasingly threatened by patterns of economic globalization. Under prevailing global conditions, law continues to be one of the principal tools of neo colonial power, even as the kind of judicialization and juridification processes described here signal the counterhegemonic uses of law.

In Guatemala, juridification has occurred in the absence of a significant or strong process of judicialization. Social movements do resort to actions before the courts to defend rights, but very often with little hope that their petitions will find a hearing, much less that successful challenges before the courts will translate into effective policies to guarantee their rights. I have argued here that this is partly because of the weak constitutionalization of indigenous rights and the weakness of support structures for counter-hegemonic legal mobilization, and partly because of the highly dysfunctional nature of the rule of law, and the elitist, authoritarian, and violent character of government. The relationship between processes of judicialization before the courts and the juridification of social protest in contexts of strong legal pluralism is undoubtedly an area for further comparative inquiry.

In this chapter I have indicated how the combination of a new awareness of indigenous rights, as enshrined in ILO 169 and promised by the peace accords, and the lack of due process and adequate consultation of indigenous people over mining and hydroelectric projects has produced innovative processes of juridification and paralegal engagements around the consultas populares. In Tate and Vallinder's words, "nonjudicial negotiating or decision-making arenas" have come to be dominated by "quasi-judicial (legalistic) procedures" (1995:5). Through new kinds of informal, highly transnationalized justice practices involving cultural appropriation and reappropriation, Mayan activists and communities challenge the state's traditional monopoly on the production of law and publicly state their claim to being sources of

[28] For discussion of the court's ruling of December 21, 2009, see Clavero (2010).

legal norms and practice. Ultimately, juridification can be understood as a symbolic means by which indigenous social movements seek to stake a claim for sovereignty and for alternatives to dominant conceptions of development and democracy.

Yet powerful interests are stacked up against recognition of greater legal autonomy for local communities. Other areas of law, such as those related to foreign investment and intellectual property rights are effectively extraterritorialized or denationalized via free trade agreements and the legal processes associated with global economic integration, often with minimum or zero transparency. Within such a context of legal fragmentation, poor and marginalized indigenous people have framed a powerful critique of hegemonic forms of development and globalization by juxtaposing internationally sanctioned collective human rights of indigenous peoples with the failure of governments to deliver on those rights in practice. However, the emancipatory potential of such developments –and of legal mobilization more broadly-remains open to question.

References

Anaya, S. James and Todd Crider. 1996. "Indigenous Peoples, the Environment, and Commercial Forestry in Developing Countries: The Case of Awas Tingni, Nicaragua," *Human Rights Quarterly*, 18: 345–67.

Brunnegger, Sandra. Forthcoming. "Justice and Culture in Colombia: Negotiating Indigenous Law," *PoLAR: The Political and Legal Anthropology Review*. Central America Report, biweekly news bulletin. Inforpress Centroamericana. http://www.inforpressca.com/CAR/ (December 11, 2009).

Chenaut, Victoria, and María Teresa Sierra (eds). 1995. *Pueblos indígenas ante el derecho*, Mexico: Centro de Investigaciónes y Estudios Superiores en Antropología Social (CIESAS) and Centro Francés de Estudios Mexicanos y Centroamericanos (CEMCA).

Clavero, Bartolomé. 2010. "Guatemala: Importante Jurisprudencia Constitucional." http://elmercuriodigital.es/content/view/24586/392/ (January 29, 2010).

Collins, Cath. 2010. *Post-Transitional Justice: Human Rights Trials in Chile and El Salvador*. University Park: Penn State University Press.

Comisión de Esclarecimiento Histórico. 2000. *Guatemala. Memoria del Silencio*. Guatemala City: CEH.

Cuffe, Sandra. 2005. "A *Backwards, Upside-Down Kind of Development*": *Global Actors, Mining, and Community-Based Resistance in Honduras and Guatemala*. Rights Action, http://www.rightsaction.org/Reports/Cuffe%20mining%20report%202005-03.htm (July 29, 2009).

Davis, Shelton H. 2002. "Indigenous Peoples, Poverty, and Participatory Development: The Experience of the World Bank in Latin America." In *Multiculturalism in Latin America: Indigenous Rights, Diversity and Democracy*, Rachel Sieder (ed.), Basingstoke and London: Palgrave. 227–51.

Dezaley, Yves, and Bryant G. Garth. 1998. *Dealing in Virtue: International Commercial Arbitration and the Construction of a Transnational Legal Order*. Chicago: University of Chicago Press.

Dezaley, Yves, and Bryant G. Garth. 2002a. *The Internationalization of Palace Wars: Lawyers, Economists, and the Contest to Transform Latin American States*. Chicago: University of Chicago Press.

Dezaley, Yves, and Bryant G. Garth, eds. 2002b. *Global Prescriptions: The Production, Exportation, and Importation of a New Legal Orthodoxy*. University of Michigan Press.

Epp, Charles. 1998. *The Rights Revolution*. Chicago and London: University of Chicago Press.

Faundez, Julio. 2005. "Community Justice Institutions and Judicialization: Lessons from Rural Peru." In *The Judicialization of Politics in Latin America*, Rachel Sieder, Line Schjolden and Alan Angell, eds. New York: Palgrave McMillan. 187–210.

Amanda M. Fulmer, Angelina Snodgrass Godoy, and Philip Neff. 2008. "Indigenous Rights, Resistance, and the Law: Lessons from a Guatemalan Mine." *Latin American Politics and Society*, 50(4): 91–121.

Hale, Charles R. 2002. "Does Multiculturalism Menace? Governance, Cultural Rights, and the Politics of Identity in Guatemala." *Journal of Latin American Studies*, 34: 485–524.

Lovatón, David. 2003. "Nuevas tendencias y tareas pendientes para la justicia de paz." In *Justicia y violencia en las zonas rurales: La experiencia de la Región Andina*, Instituto de Defensa Legal Lima: Instituto de Defensa Legal. 115–119.

Lutz, Ellen, and Kathryn Sikkink. 2001. "The Justice Cascade: The Evolution and Impact of Human Rights Trials in Latin America." *Chicago Journal of International Law*, 2(1): 1–33.

Méndez, Juan, Guillermo O'Donnell, and Sergio Pinheiro, eds. 1999. *The (Un)Rule of Law in Latin America*. South Bend, IN: University of Notre Dame Press.

Merry, Sally Engle. 2003. "Human Rights Law and the Demonization of Culture (And Anthropology Along the Way)." *PoLAR: Political and Legal Anthropology Review*, 26(1): 55–77.

Moore, Sally Falk. 1978. *Law as Process: An Anthropological Approach*. London, Henley, and Boston: Routledge and Kegan Paul.

Nader, Laura. 1990. *Harmony Ideology: Justice and Control in a Zapotec Mountain Village*. Stanford: Stanford University Press.

Nash Rojas, Claudio. 2004. "Los derechos humanos de los indígenas en la jurisprudencia de la Corte Interamericana de Derechos Humanos." In *Derechos humanos y pueblos indígenas: tendencias internacionales y contexto chileno*, José Aylwin O., ed. Temuco: Instituto de Estudios Indígenas/Universidad de la Frontera. 29–43.

Nelken, David. 2004. "Using the Concept of Legal Culture," http://repositories.cdlib.org/csls/lss/20/ (July 31, 2009).

O'Donnell, Guillermo. 2005. "Afterword." In *The Judicialization of Politics in Latin America*, Rachel Sieder, Line Schjolden, and Alan Angell, eds. New York: Palgrave McMillan. 293–8.

Office of the Compliance Advisor/Ombudsman International Finance Corporation. 2005 *Assessment of complaint submitted to CAO in relation to the Marlin Mining Project in Guatemala, September 7, 2005*. http://www.caoombudsman.org/cases/document-links/documents/CAO-Marlin-assessment-English7Sep05.pdf (December 11, 2009).

Poole, Deborah. 2004. "Between Threat and Guarantee: Justice and Community in the Margins of the Peruvian State." In *Anthropology in the Margins of the State*, Veena Das and Deborah Poole, eds. Santa Fe and Oxford: School of American Research Press. 35–65.

Randeria, Shalini. 2007. "The State of Globalization: Legal Plurality, Overlapping Sovereignties, and Ambiguous Alliances between Civil Society and the Cunning State in India." *Theory and Culture and Society*, 34(1): 1–33.

Rappaport, Joanne. 2005. *Intercultural Utopias. Public Intellectuals, Cultural Experimentation, and Etnic Pluralism in Colombia*. Durham: Duke University Press.

Rasch, Elisabet. 2008. *Representing Mayas: Indigenous and the Local Politics of Identity in Guatemala*, Ph.D. Thesis, Department of Anthropology, University of Utrecht.

Richards, Patricia. 2004. *Pobladores, Indígenas, and the State*. Piscataway: Rutgers University Press.

Rodríguez-Garavito, César and Luis Carlos Arenas. 2005. "Indigenous Rights, Transnational Activism, and Legal Mobilization: The Struggle of the U'wa People in Colombia." In *Law and Globalization From Below: Towards a Cosmopolitan Legality*, Boaventura de Sousa Santos and César A. Rodríguez-Garavito, eds. Cambridge: Cambridge University Press. 241–66.

Rodríguez-Piñero Royo, Luis. 2004. "El caso Awas Tingni y el régimen de derechos territoriales indígenas en la Costa Atlántica de Nicaragua." In *Derechos humanos y pueblos indígenas: tendencias internacionales y contexto chileno*, José Aylwin O., ed. Temuco: Instituto de Estudios Indígenas/Universidad de la Frontera. 218–33.

Santos, Boaventura de Sousa. 1977. "The Law of the Oppressed: The Construction and Reproduction of Legality in Pasargada." *Law and Society Review*, 12:5–125.

Santos, Boaventura de Sousa. 2002. *Towards a New Legal Common Sense*. London: Butterworth/Lexis-Nexis.

Santos, Boaventura de Sousa. 2006. "The Heterogenous State and Legal Pluralism in Mozambique." *Law and Society Review*, 40(1): 39–76.

Sawyer, Susanne. 2004. *Crude Chronicles: Indigenous Politics, Multinational Oil, and Neoliberalism in Ecuador*. Durham: Duke University Press.

Sieder, Rachel, Line Schjolden, and Alan Angell, eds. 2005. *The Judicialization of Politics in Latin America*, New York: Palgrave McMillan.

Sieder, Rachel. 2007. "The Judiciary and Indigenous Rights in Guatemala." *International Journal of Constitutional Law*, 5(2): 211–41.

Sieder, Rachel. Forthcoming. "Constructing Mayan Authority: The 'Recuperation' of Indigenous Law in Postwar Guatemala." *Studies in Law, Politics and Society*.

Sierra, María Teresa (ed.). 2004. *Haciendo Justicia: Interlegalidad, derecho y género en regiones indígenas*. Mexico: CIESAS.

Sierra, María Teresa. 2009. "Entre la legitimidad y la ilegalidad: las apuestas de la policía comunitaria de Guerrero." Paper presented at the 53 Congress of Americanistas, Mexico City, 2009.

Smulovitz, Catalina. 2005. "Petitioning and Creating Rights: Judicialization in Argentina." In *The Judicialization of Politics in Latin America*, Rachel Sieder, Line Schjolden, and Alan Angell, eds. New York: Palgrave McMillan. 161–86.

Snodgrass-Godoy, Angelina. 2006. *A Popular Injustice: Violence, Community, and Law in Latin America*. Stanford: Stanford University Press.

Solano, Luis. 2005. *Guatemala petróleo y minería: en las entrañas del poder*. Guatemala: Inforpress Centroamericana.

Starr, June, and Jane Collier. 1989. *History and Power in the Study of Law: New Directions in Legal Anthropology*. Ithaca and London: Cornell University Press.

Szablowski, David. 2007. *Transnational Law and Local Struggles: Mining, Communities, and the World Bank*. Oxford and Portland: Hart Publishing.

Tate, C. Neal, and Torbjörn Vallinder. *The Global Expansion of Judicial Power*. New York and London: New York University Press.

Teubner, Gunther. 1987. *Juridification of Social Spheres: A Comparative Analysis in the Areas of Labor, Corporate, Antitrust, and Social Welfare Law*. Berlin and New York: De Gruyter.

Uprimny, Rodrigo, César Rodríguez, and Mauricio García, eds. 2006. *¿Justicia para todos? Sistema judicial, derechos sociales y democracia en Colombia*, Bogotá: Editorial Norma.

Van Cott, Donna Lee. 2000. *The Friendly Liquidation of the Past: The Politics of Diversity in Latin America*. Pittsburgh: Pittsburgh University Press.

Van Harten, Gus. 2007. *Investment Treaty Arbitration and Public Law*. New York and Oxford: Oxford University Press.

World Bank. (2003). *Guapa: Guatemala Poverty Assessment*. Washington: World Bank Publications.

8

Political Activism and the Practice of Law in Venezuela

Manuel A. Gomez

INTRODUCTION

In spite of the traditional involvement of Venezuelan lawyers in the country's social, political and economic life (Perez-Perdomo 1981, 1990, 2006) and their historic role as nation builders, social entrepreneurs and power brokers (Gomez 2008, 2009), the practice of law in Venezuela was largely traditional until the early 1990s. Venezuelan lawyers generally used their legal expertise, tools and resources without commitments to an ideological or social cause (Sarat and Scheingold 2001), and did not rely on litigation as a form of "moral activism" (Sarat and Scheingold 1998).

Cause lawyering emerged during the postdictatorship transition in other Latin American countries (Meili 2001: 307); in Venezuela, cause lawyering began to develop during a period of political and social instability and gained even more salience during a decade of radical change in Venezuela's social, political, and economic institutions. Specific events in Venezuela during the last twenty years define three different stages in the emergence and transformation of cause lawyering and human rights activism and in the growing involvement of lawyers in the country's political debate. Each of these three stages corresponds to important changes in the conception lawyers have about their role. Each stage also corresponds to changes in the image that other actors have about members of the legal profession and their role in society.

The first stage took place between 1958 and 1989, and coincided with the strengthening of democratic institutions after a period of military dictatorships and political instability. This is the era of the "pacted democracy," (*democracia pactada*), when the political scenario was dominated by two strong political parties that controlled the operation of all public institutions, including the courts, through very powerful social networks that often involved the participation of lawyers. During this period, legal professionals perceived themselves as power brokers, and did not have incentives to engage in any form of activism or cause lawyering. Their participation in the political process thus took place behind closed doors.

The second stage is defined by two specific instances of human rights violations that occurred between 1988 and 1989. At that time, the traditional political establishment was already entering into a deep crisis, and the country was in the midst of a social and economic upheaval. This period signals the rise of the first generation of cause lawyers, represented by a small contingent of nonelite legal professionals who became human rights activists. During this stage, members of the country's elite legal community, although sympathetic to the causes led by the activists, were still unresponsive to cause lawyering. Traditional lawyers continued to view themselves as power brokers despite the progressive deterioration of the once-powerful social networks that enabled them to negotiate virtually everything with the government.

The third stage began in 1999 with the radical transformation of the country's political, social, and economic spheres through the Bolivarian Revolution, led by President Hugo Chavez. The transition was further galvanized by an outbreak of political violence in April 2002 and its subsequent chain of events, which contributed to the polarization of the Venezuelan society. During this period, a second generation of cause lawyers arose. Unlike the first wave of cause lawyers that emerged in 1989, the new group was comprised of a handful of young and successful elite lawyers from traditional private practice who morphed into active participants in the struggle for political change. From the initial five or six lawyers who led this movement in 2002, the group has grown to more than twenty legal professionals in the last seven years, and it appears to continue growing as the number of victims of human rights abuses expands. These lawyers have shifted their legal practices to play an active role as advocates in a number of political, social, and ideological causes that go beyond their traditional professional roles. Their new role has exposed these new cause lawyers to a series of important risks, both personal and professional, that range from becoming targets of political persecution to receiving threats to their own safety and sacrificing their valuable portfolio of clients. Notwithstanding, they seem to remain strongly committed to their cause.

The new generation of Venezuelan cause lawyers has relied on litigation and other lawyerly strategies not only to defend their clients or to ensure the legal protection of collective interests, but, more importantly, as a vehicle for their political agenda. Thus, Venezuelan cause lawyers have helped infuse national politics with a legalistic discourse, placing law at the center of the political dialogue in a way that distinguishes them from other members of the local bar.

In this chapter we focus on cause lawyering as a form of political activism, examining it through the lens of Venezuelan legal practitioners. We give special attention to the unique relationship between the evolving perceptions and images that Venezuelan lawyers have about the law and legal institutions and their preference for using legal processes and courts as instruments to promote political and social change. Our research draws on previous work on the role of lawyers in the transformation of the state (Gomez 2009) and is also based on numerous interviews conducted between 2007 and 2009 with Venezuelan cause lawyers, nongovernmental organizations (NGOs) representatives, political actors, legal scholars, and both domestic and international activists. This research also relies on a number of secondary sources, including recent literature on cause lawyering (Sarat and Scheingold 1998, 2001), their involvement in human rights causes (Dezalay and Garth 2001; Dotan 2001; Hajjar 2001) and the infusion of politics into the judicial activity (Dor and Hofnung 2006; Halliday 1999; Lu 2008; Sieder, Angell, and Schjolden 2005; Smulovitz 2002).

In the second section, and as a way to explain why cause lawyering was traditionally absent from the Venezuelan context until the final decades of the twentieth century, we offer a brief account of the role of Venezuelan lawyers during the period known as the pacted democracy (1958–88) and the influence of the country's political and social developments on the practice of law. In the third section, we describe the conditions that led to the emergence of the first generation of Venezuelan cause lawyers, with special attention paid to the characteristics of these practitioners and to the rationale behind their increased participation in political activism. The fourth section explores the country's transition from the pacted democracy to the Bolivarian Revolution and the conditions that led to the rise of the current generation of Venezuelan cause lawyers. I conclude by briefly discussing the obstacles currently posed to Venezuelan cause lawyers, with special attention to their reasons for engaging in this particular form of activism.

LEGAL PRACTICE AND SOCIAL NETWORKS DURING THE PACTED DEMOCRACY

Traditionally, Venezuelan lawyers were among the most important players in the country's social, political and economic history (Perez-Perdomo 2006). A large number of Venezuelan presidents, ministers and other government officials graduated from law school (Perez-Perdomo 1981), as did an equally significant number of executives and key members of the country's private sector (Gomez 2003, 2008). Lawyers became particularly important during the second half of the twentieth century, as the country's public and private sectors grew exponentially, and with them the amount of increasingly complex and sophisticated regulations, processes and institutions that required the involvement of legal professionals to operate (Perez-Perdomo 2001).

In addition to their much-needed technical expertise, lawyers were also valued for their ability to act as social entrepreneurs and power brokers (Gomez 2009). As such, they were uniquely positioned to perform the role of go-between across the different layers of the Venezuelan society, and, more importantly, between the social, economic, and political elite that formed the private and public sectors. As a result, Venezuelan lawyers were able to achieve more influence and power than perhaps any other professional group during the same period (Gomez 2008; Perez-Perdomo 2005). Naturally, not all these social brokers practiced law, but those who did benefited immensely from their valuable portfolio of political and social contacts (Gomez 2008). Clients, in turn, treasured these lawyers not only because of their professional expertise in a particular field, but, more importantly, because of the social connections that enhanced their ability to navigate the system and achieve favorable results in a swift manner (Gomez 2003, Naím 1989).

The importance of these social networks was evident in the case of elite lawyers and their wealthy or otherwise powerful clients, whose frequent involvement in high-stake matters often required the assistance of well-connected professionals with easy access to high-level politicians and government officials (Coronil 1997). However, social networks were also important to those lawyers who operated at other levels, as the most trivial legal matter, such as obtaining a business license or a permit, was always easier if one knew the "right" people (Gomez 2003, 2009).

Although their social capital was progressively enhanced throughout their professional lives, lawyers started forming their networks in their law school years (Lomnitz and Salazar 2002). To many, the main value of going to law school was not the acquisition of a sophisticated technical expertise or the intellectually stimulating experience associated with the study of law as a discipline but rather the possibility of creating and strengthening the social connections that would help them navigate through society and its institutions (Dezalay and Garth 2002).

The late twentieth century was a period of relative political stability in Venezuela (Coronil 1997; Levine 1973). For over thirty years, between 1958 and 1989, the country was often portrayed as the role model of democracy, economic prosperity and upward social mobility in Latin America (Levine 1973). This image was enhanced by the fact that during that same period several other countries in the region were experiencing devastating economic crises, political instability and harsh military dictatorships (Karl 1997).

The Venezuelan democracy was, however, *sui generis*, as its operation depended more on a series of pacts and negotiations between political leaders than on the people's will manifested through the general elections (Rey 1988; Coronil 1997; Karl 1997). From the presidency down to the distribution of congressional seats and appointments to the judiciary, every key aspect in the operation of the country's public institutions resulted from a political deal known as the "Punto Fijo Pact" (*Pacto de Punto Fijo*) brokered by members of the two parties that dominated the political landscape (Karl 1997). This informal system of checks and balances was obviously enmeshed with the social networks that were just described, thus adding a series of extra layers to an already complicated political scenario (Gomez 2009; Coronil 1997).

The widespread prominence of social and political connections as important sources of power had a significant impact on how lawyers were perceived by ordinary citizens, and how they viewed themselves in relation to their clients and to society in general. In other words, it had an influence on both the internal and external legal cultures and affected how lawyers practiced their profession. Regarding the latter, as

I have argued elsewhere (Gomez 2008), their position within a specific network, and the social distance between those involved in a particular matter, determined the ways in which lawyers and their clients relied on the courts and other institutions to channel their cases. Social connections and networks of influence were, after all, what lubricated the squeaky wheels of justice (Gomez 2009).

It was an environment in which social capital was paramount; most conflicts – including a significant number of legal disputes – were channeled through social networks, and virtually any outcome could be achieved by pulling the appropriate strings or having the right connections (Gomez 2003; Naím 1989). Lawyers thus had little or no incentive to pursue "activist" agendas or to become outspoken supporters of a particular ideological or political cause. Solutions for alleged government abuses or collective harms, for instance, were quickly negotiated behind closed doors between political and private actors and either kept from the general public or tactfully treated by the media as unimportant events. If lawyers were involved in these matters they were discreet about it, and their strategies were never confrontational, at least in public. In spite of the occasional protest or demonstration, the public perception was one of general peace as well as of social and political stability.

Although most public institutions, including the courts, were under constant political influence and subject to the operation of social networks, litigation was not perceived as a tool for moral activism or social struggle. Nobody seemed to use the courts to vent political battles or to advance a particular political agenda. Moreover, the general perception seemed to be that legal institutions and legal actors were highly regarded (Perez-Perdomo 2009), that formal law held a prominent place in society, and that the preservation of judicial independence was important. At least on the surface, the legal system seemed insulated from outside pressure (because whatever manipulation took place occurred in a shrouded manner), contributing to the appearance of judges and lawyers as autonomous. Underneath this cloak, there was indeed a system of checks and balances but of an informal and political nature (Coronil 1997).

Lawyers, in turn, viewed their main role as bridging differences and helping others navigate institutional or political obstacles. They did not feel the need to use the legal system to challenge the establishment or to advance a particular political or ideological project. In order to operate effectively, lawyers needed to remain unfettered by political struggles. They needed to be seen as "neutral" agents or as hired-guns, and therefore were very careful to distance themselves from their clients' causes, so activism was obviously out of the question. Political neutrality was one of their most highly prized assets.

For their part, government officials and political actors viewed themselves as guarantors of the status quo (Coronil 1997). This implied a heavy reliance on social networks while preserving an appearance of institutional independence and respect for the rule of law. Despite the pervasive politicization of the judiciary, formal processes were generally followed, and the production of legislation emerged – as in any functioning democracy – from genuine debates in Congress and was subject to the controls of the bicameral legislative system. Law retained, after all, its intrinsic value in society and was generally upheld as a fairly stable concept.

At the time, only a handful of Venezuelan law schools had community-oriented clinical programs, such as VTEP (*Voluntariado de Trabajo en Establecimientos Penitenciarios*, Volunteer Work in Prison Establishments) at Andrés Bello Catholic University, and the Legal Clinic (*Clínica Jurídica*) at Central University of Venezuela.[1] Moreover, no law firms had pro bono practices, and the few existing NGOs did very little or no legal work.[2] As for individual practitioners, even though a small number of lawyers did "charity" legal work, none of them devoted more than an occasional weekend or few hours to it.[3]

The country had signed and ratified the majority of human rights treaties and conventions, and domestic legislation was somewhat sensitive to the protection of collective rights and public interest cases, but the language of human rights and cause lawyering was absent from the political discourse, the media and, most importantly, the legal profession.

Toward the end of the 1980s, things began to change as an economic crisis, followed by a series of corruption scandals, contributed to the rapid deterioration of the political system (Perez-Perdomo and Capriles 1991). The parties that had dominated the political scene for more than thirty years became severely fragmented and lost their traditional influence, thus undermining the strength of the once-powerful social networks that had manipulated the country's institutions (Gomez 2009) and the "efficient" system for dealing with social and political problems. Finding themselves unable to navigate the system without stumbling on significant obstacles, even the most politically powerful and best-connected lawyers and their allies were forced to adapt to a new environment that offered them little or no certainty.[4]

THE EMERGENCE OF CAUSE LAWYERING IN VENEZUELA: THE FIRST GENERATION

On October 29, 1988, a group of fourteen Venezuelan and Colombian citizens were killed by members of the CEJAP (*Comando Específico José Antonio Paez*, Specific Command Jose Antonio Paez), a special military-police unit, near El Amparo, a rural town located on the Venezuelan-Colombian border (Rohde et al. 1993). According to official reports, the killings occurred in the course of an exchange of

[1] Interview with clinical law professor (#13), April 2007; interview with Venezuelan political activist (#5), July 2008.

[2] Interview with corporate lawyer (#4), July 2007; interview with NGO representatives (#2, #6), March 2009.

[3] Id.

[4] Interview with corporate lawyer (#12), March 2009.

fire with members of Colombian armed guerrilla groups during a military operation launched to stop smuggling, drug trafficking and other criminal activities in the Venezuela-Colombia border area (Rohde et al. 1993).

Soon after the official story broke, another version, based on the testimony of two survivors and a CEJAP informant, revealed that the victims were not guerrilla soldiers but innocent peasants who had been massacred for no apparent reason while on a fishing trip (Marquez and Carias 1992). The government tried to contain the story, and political actors moved quickly to keep the case under wraps under the guise of national security. Their attempts, however, proved to be futile as an emerging group of activists moved even faster to organize a campaign that would mark the beginning of cause lawyering and human rights' activism in Venezuela.

With the help of several members of Congress, a few lawyers and representatives of the Catholic Church, the two survivors and some of the victims' relatives embarked on a determined struggle with the government until a congressional task force was appointed to investigate the killings (Marquez and Carias 1992). A public campaign followed, including demonstrations and rallies throughout the country, and an intensive court battle began. The task force's report would conclude, years later, that it had indeed been a massacre, and those in charge of CEJAP were eventually tried and convicted.[5]

With little or no experience in litigating cases against the state, and no previous exposure to human rights activism, the few lawyers who took on the representation of the victims and their relatives faced countless adversities (Marquez and Carias 1992). As their effort to obtain redress through traditional means in the local courts proved difficult, they turned to the media in order to raise public awareness about their cases and to expose the numerous official attempts to silence them (Marquez and Carias 1992).

As their clients were poor people from rural areas with no money or social connections and the adversary was a resourceful government apparatus, it became apparent that to succeed they would have to employ skills that were beyond traditional lawyering. As a result, aside from having to devise and deploy a complicated legal strategy, they also had to raise external support – both material and ideological – in ways deemed unconventional at the time. Since their local channels were blocked, these cause lawyers were also forced to mobilize in search of allies outside the country.

Aside from being one of the first events that ignited cause lawyering and human rights' activism in Venezuela, the *Massacre of El Amparo* or *La Colorada* – as this case became later known – revealed the failure of the traditional power brokers to reach a negotiated solution that would help to preserve the government's image and to prevent a string of abusive practices against Venezuelan citizens from becoming

5 *El Amparo* Case, Reparations (art. 63(1) American Convention on Human Rights), Judgment of September 14, 1996, Inter-Am. Ct. H.R. (Ser. C) No. 28 (1996).

public. The political parties were now in crisis, and a series of corruption scandals and internal struggles had weakened their leverage. More importantly, this case introduced Venezuelan lawyers to the influential transnational networks of human rights' activists that included the CEJIL (*Centro por la Justicia y el Derecho Internacional*, Center for Justice and International Law), Amnesty International and Human Rights Watch, among others; while simultaneously motivating them to create and develop a local platform for public interest advocacy. Several NGOs, such as PROVEA (*Programa Venezolano de Educación-Acción en Derechos Humanos*, Venezuelan Program on Education-Action in Human Rights) and the Support Network for Justice and Peace (*Red de Apoyo Para la Justicia y La Paz*) emerged or expanded their presence as a result of this movement.[6]

In the aftermath of *El Amparo*, two other high-profile cases known as *El Caracazo* and *La Peste* helped further galvanize the organization of human rights' activism in Venezuela. *El Caracazo* was a popular uprising followed by widespread riots and looting that took place in Caracas and other major Venezuelan cities during the week of February 27, 1989, over the announcement of an unpopular set of economic measures by the government (Lopez Maya 2003).

The social unrest that ensued spiraled out of control and prompted the government to deploy the armed forces. The result was an unprecedented toll of 398 dead civilians, as well as several other hundreds of victims of police abuse, torture and illegal incarceration.[7] The public's reaction to the disproportionate force with which the police and military responded to the riots helped a small but quite vocal group of socially minded lawyers to mobilize. In addition to representing the victims, they took a public stand against the government's actions, thus attracting widespread public sympathy and support.

The second case, *La Peste*, named after the location where government officials illegally disposed and buried more than sixty-eight bodies of *El Caracazo*'s victims, encouraged the embryonic group of human rights' activists to join forces with some of the victims' relatives to form COFAVIC (Comité de Familiares de las Víctimas de los sucesos ocurridos entre el 27 de febrero y los primeros días de marzo de 1989, *Committee of Relatives of the Victims of February and March of* 1989). Over time, COFAVIC would become the flagship of human rights' activism in Venezuela and a fierce advocate on behalf of a growing number of victims of different abuses and violations attributed to government authorities.[8] In years to come, COFAVIC and the few other NGOs that emerged in Venezuela would focus primarily on a defensive strategy that involved the increased use of lawyerly tools, including the filing of cases in domestic courts and international tribunals.[9]

6 http://www.derechos.org.ve/recursos/alegal/mamparo/indexamparo.htm (July 29, 2009).

7 *El Caracazo* Case, Judgment of November 11, 1999, Inter-Am. Ct. H.R. (Ser. C) No. 58 (1999).

8 http://www.cofavic.org.ve/index.php?id=8&idcaso=6 (July 29, 2009).

9 *El Caracazo* Case, Judgment of November 11, 1999, Inter-Am. Ct. H.R. (Ser. C) No. 58 (1999).

These organizations were headed by lawyers who were sensitized to their clients' causes, and who relied on the media to voice their views. They frequently organized public demonstrations, and with the assistance of a transnational network of human rights activists, reached out to other audiences and obtained support beyond national borders.[10]

Despite that most of their advocacy was directed at government officials and that their initial support came from a number of legislators, cause lawyers from COFAVIC and similar organizations never viewed themselves as political actors.[11] All along, cause lawyers made clear their disinterest in supporting any political party or participating in electoral campaigns. Their only goals, they said, were to raise awareness of human rights, to help ordinary citizens obtain redress for abuses and violations committed by government agents, and to inform the public about the reprehensible acts that lay underneath.[12]

The use of public demonstrations and media appearances by cause lawyers was an accessory to their litigation strategy. They mainly viewed it as a way to expose the government's undue influence on the courts and to place the conduct of the judges and lawyers involved in the cases under public scrutiny. In so doing, they were also moving away from the client-driven approach of traditional lawyering while becoming advocates of a cause benefiting what they viewed as the collective interest.

In their constant struggle to remain independent and to appear to be politically neutral before their clients and the media, cause lawyers encountered many difficulties in raising funds to support their causes.[13] However, at least during the early stages, several international human rights organizations helped them obtain the support needed to do their job.[14]

Members of the local bar were generally sympathetic toward the small group of cause lawyers involved in human rights cases but very few of them felt persuaded to join, support or even volunteer for any of their causes.[15] Most Venezuelan lawyers preferred to keep a distance from any form of activism that could hinder their ability to navigate the country's social and political environment.

Political Crisis

The 1990s was a particularly turbulent decade in the political life of Venezuela. On May 21, 1993, Carlos Andrés Perez was impeached on corruption charges while serving as president for a second period (Perez-Liñan 2007). During his first presidency

[10] Interview with NGO representative #6, March 2009.
[11] Interview with NGO representative #2, March 2009.
[12] Interview with activist #1, April 2009; interview with NGO representative #6, March 2009.
[13] Id.
[14] Interview with NGO representative #6, March 2009.
[15] Interview with corporate lawyer #11, August 2008; interview with corporate lawyer #4, July 2007.

(1974–9), Perez had led the country through a period of unprecedented economic boom resulting from soaring oil prices, which helped put Venezuela on the world map as an important player (Karl 1997). When elected for a second term, Perez faced a very different country. Venezuela was suffering from an unmanageable debt, an increasingly dangerous level of social inequality and a deep political crisis (Ellner and Hellinger 2003). During his campaign, Perez vowed to transform the government in order to make it more efficient and to bring Venezuela back to its old glory. His strategic plan was called "the great turnaround" (*El Gran Viraje*) as a signal of Perez's departure from traditional party politics (Kornblith 1998). The key economic posts within the government were assigned to independent technocrats instead of the president's allies, thereby creating deep resentment among members of the traditional political establishment (Perez-Liñan 2007; Corrales 2002). Merely three weeks after Perez's inauguration, as he announced the first package of economic measures, the country entered into an uncontrollable spiral of social unrest that began with the *El Caracazo* events. It marked the beginning of a tragic end to Perez's lifelong political career. In 1992, Perez was the victim of two frustrated coup d'états (Perez-Liñan 2007), the first of which was led by Lt. Col. Hugo Chavez.

The impeachment of Carlos Andres Perez was a clear sign of the deep crisis that affected the traditional political establishment and of his inability to compromise with members of his own party (Perez-Liñan 2007). This case was also one of the first and most significant instances in which the Venezuelan courts were used as a forum to settle political quarrels. Despite its enormous impact, the Perez impeachment case did not attract the attention of any lawyers aside from those directly involved in it. It was clearly a political vendetta disguised as a legal case in order to give it some degree of legitimacy.

In the aftermath of Perez's impeachment, the country's political crisis deepened. Within one year Congress appointed two interim presidents in succession, Octavio Lepage and Ramón J. Velazquez. The next presidential election, which took place in December 1993, brought Rafael Caldera, a prominent lawyer and politician who had served as president between 1969 and 1974, to a second term in office (Kornblith 1998).

Even though Caldera's election brought a slight sense of relief to the country's difficult political environment, during his presidency Venezuela faced the worst financial crisis of its modern history. The financial sector collapsed and the government took a series of drastic measures to intervene in the economy and regain control of the banking system. The bankruptcies that followed were so complex and numerous that the government was prompted to create a special banking jurisdiction to handle the financial cases (Crisp 1997).

This new wave of judicial activity gave many lawyers and their political contacts another opportunity to rebuild the once-powerful social networks that had permeated the country for more than three decades. Even though during his presidential campaign Caldera adopted an antiestablishment discourse and made public his formal rupture with the traditional party system that he had once helped to create, many members of the local elite considered his administration to be "business as usual."[16]

By the mid-1990s, Venezuelan cause lawyers were still a small but very visible group whose agenda was limited to human rights cases. Gradually, they were able to expand their activities beyond their original defensive strategy and began participating in the organization of educational and other outreach programs. During this time, several universities became involved with human rights initiatives, and some important members of the transnational human rights community strengthened their presence in Venezuela. Even though the struggle was usually against the state, cause lawyering was still apolitical.

While most members of the local bar were still indifferent to cause lawyering, a group of law students from Andrés Bello Catholic University founded Justice First (*Primero Justicia*), an NGO aimed at promoting judicial reform at a grassroots level, through the implementation of a justice of the peace system. Justice First's main goal was to lead policy changes and legislative initiatives rather than to intervene in individual cases. Over the years, Justice First would gain notoriety for its continued efforts to promote judicial reform and for its support of alternative dispute resolution mechanisms at the community level. Although its initial discourse was antiestablishment, in 1999 Justice First morphed into a political party as it became involved in the reform process initiated by the then-recently elected president Chavez to change the constitution. In congressional elections a year later, the newly formed party obtained five seats in the National Assembly (as the former Congress became known under Chavez). It continued growing at such a fast pace that in 2006 it became the main opposition party.

CAUSE LAWYERING IN THE TIME OF THE BOLIVARIAN REVOLUTION

The rise to power of Lt. Col. Hugo Chavez in the December 1998 presidential elections formally marked the end of the pacted democracy and traditional party politics in Venezuela. The deep economic and social instability, as well as the series of corruption scandals that rocked the political establishment during most of the 1990s (Hellinger 2004), bolstered Chavez's antiparty, antiestablishment platform. With a promise to fight corruption and rethink government institutions in a way that empowered the disenfranchised and contributed to social justice and economic prosperity, President Chavez began his presidential term with broad support from all sectors of Venezuelan society, including some members of the country's traditional social and economic elites. The new administration also vowed to finally provide

[16] Interview with corporate lawyer (#4), July 2007; interview with corporate lawyer (#12), March 2009.

justice for the victims of past atrocities, which resonated with the small but vocal community of human rights activists and cause lawyers.[17]

A constituent assembly was elected and a sweeping constitutional reform was approved by national referendum in December 1999. The new constitution included a series of broad socially oriented provisions; it renamed the country the Bolivarian Republic of Venezuela and created two new branches, the electoral (*Poder Electoral*) and the popular (*Poder Ciudadano*). The text also gave importance to a number of third-generation rights and established as an express policy the promotion of mechanisms to facilitate access to justice.

By portraying the new constitution as the backbone of the government's political project, and energetically condemning the corrupt political practices of the past, members of the new government brought law to the center stage and helped generate a perception that the new administration was truly committed to upholding the supremacy of the legal system. From the beginning, it was clear to many that the new constitution was a platform for a particular ideological project rather than a basis for a long-lasting institutional framework insulated from the interests of competing political factions. By focusing on the constitutional reform as one of its prime objectives, the new government transformed political speech into a speech of "rights." During his numerous televised appearances, for example, the president often appeared brandishing a pocket-sized version of the Constitution as a symbolic weapon with which to quash his political opponents. He commonly referred to the constitutional text as *la bicha*[18] (the snake), as if it was some sort of animal or beast with extraordinary powers that would help the government destroy its enemies and solve most national problems.

The legal system became very important to the new government, but mainly as an instrument for eliminating ideological adversaries and retaining political power (Perez-Perdomo 2009). Based on the idea that the new government represented some sort of political revolution – a "Bolivarian" Revolution – the autonomy of law was denied and all legal principles were subject to an elastic interpretation that depended on the ever-changing needs of the political establishment (Delgado Ocando 1979). Unlike the moderate instrumentalism and the covert manipulation of legal institutions that took place during the times of the pacted democracy, the Chavez administration made no secret of its perception of law as a political weapon.

The approval of the new constitution was an important step in ensuring the complete subordination of the remaining parts of the legal system to the executive branch. The law-making process was streamlined by transforming the legislature into

[17] Interview with activist #1, April 2009; interview with NGO representative #6, March 2009.

[18] In Venezuela, *bicho* or *bicha* is a colloquial term used to denote a kind of animal – generally an insect – that is dangerous and malicious. It is also used to refer to a bad or mean person. In the context of Venezuelan politics, President Chavez's reference to the constitution as a *bicha* has been construed as a symbol of a "powerful animal that will devour the president's political enemies" (Perez-Perdomo, Rogelio 2003a, 2003b).

a unicameral body (the National Assembly) and also by empowering the president to legislate extensively via special decrees in areas otherwise limited to congressional power. Another important move toward executive domination of all government branches was the subordination of the courts to the political establishment. One of the first strategies employed by the government to achieve total political control of the courts was an aggressive campaign that included the summary dismissal of more than 90 percent of judges between 1999 and early 2000, and the appointment of a special commission to handle the "judicial emergency" and the overhaul of the courts (Gomez 2008). In no time, the judiciary became highly politicized in favor of the new administration and new social networks took control of the legal system in a fashion similar to their predecessors during the pacted democracy (Gomez 2008).

On April 11, 2002, more than 200,000 Venezuelan citizens took to the streets of Caracas to protest against these increasingly radical government policies and most notably against the executive's attempt to take over the national oil company (PDVSA) in order to bring its revenues under direct control of the president. As the protesters approached the presidential palace, at least twenty people were killed and more than one hundred were wounded during an ambush in the streets of downtown Caracas. The private television stations began to broadcast the disturbing images of unarmed civilians being shot at in the streets when the government took control of their signals, accusing them of manipulating public opinion. In the hours that followed, several top military commanders allegedly rebelled against the president's orders to launch an attack on the crowds of unarmed civilians heading towards the palace. After persuading Chavez to resign they took him prisoner.

The following two days were of chaos and confusion as the government's top officials went into hiding and a group headed by Pedro Carmona, the then-president of FEDECAMARAS (*Federación de Cámaras y Asociaciones de Comercio y Producción de Venezuela*, Venezuelan Federation of Chambers and Associations of Commerce and Manufacture), drafted a decree dissolving the Supreme Court and the National Assembly and suspending the leading public officials from their posts. Carmona was installed as interim-president. More than 350 individuals, notably members of the country's political and social elites, signed Carmona's decree,[19] a move that brought extremely negative consequences to many of them after Chavez returned to power. Meanwhile, at least twenty more people died, and hundreds were wounded, tortured or illegally detained in various violent episodes in different cities. Following a very puzzling chain of events, Chavez was released from prison and returned to Caracas to be reinstated in the presidency. Carmona and his followers were immediately accused of staging a coup d'état.

Once back, President Chavez first vowed to lead a national campaign of reconciliation, but quickly turned his offensive against members of the political opposition or anyone who criticized or failed to openly support the government's ideology.

[19] http://www.analitica.com/bitblio/carmona_estanga/decreto1.asp#firmantes (December 14, 2009).

Society became increasingly polarized between pro- and anti-Chavez followers, and the use of the justice system as a weapon to squash any attempt to dissent from the establishment became more profound and widespread.

The government intensified its legal offensive against anyone who had taken part in the numerous marches and demonstrations held in Caracas and other major cities between November 2001 and April 2002, as well as in the strikes organized in support of the hundreds of oil industry employees who had been fired for political reasons during that same period or to oppose the state's intervention in private education. Indictments were filed in criminal courts across the country, and a handful of "loyal" prosecutors were selected by the government to lead the cases against the most powerful members of the opposition.[20] The government set in motion proceedings by other agencies, including the tax administration, against selected individuals.

As a result of these measures, many people left the country and went into exile, while others stood trial and were imprisoned on charges of conspiracy to overthrow the government, provoke social unrest or promote general civil disobedience, among other crimes. In cases where criminal charges were difficult to prove, other forms of retaliation were used, including threats of expropriations, confiscations, or the imposition of hefty fines and the revocation of licenses to operate in the case of several media groups linked to the opposition.

The broad overhaul of the judiciary that had taken place since 1999 and the appointment of politically loyal judges throughout the country facilitated the government's campaign against its opponents. In the years that followed, politics openly penetrated the courts. Judges were not shy about publicly affirming their allegiance to the ideology of the Bolivarian Revolution. In their view, the main role of the legal system was to ensure the success of the president's political project, even if it ran afoul the traditional notion of justice (Carrasquero 2008).

Supreme Court Justices frequently voiced this line of thinking in speeches (Carrasquero 2008) and important judicial opinions. The president also did so during his weekly televised appearances, which he often used to give judges direct orders on how to decide particular cases that he deemed to be of national importance. One of the first and most striking examples of this practice was when the president threatened the Supreme Court Justices who were about to decide a case against several military officers accused of conspiring in the April 2002 coup attempt. The president warned the justices thought to be unsympathetic to his policies that they would face harsh consequences should they vote "against the government" (Chavez 2002). In the aftermath of a vote dismissing the case against the military officers, Justice Franklin Arrieche was dismissed. Other justices opted for early retirement.

Judges who have not given in to the numerous government threats have faced summary dismissals or some other form of retaliation. One case serves to illustrate this pattern. In 2003, three judges who had served on the First Contentious

[20] Interview with former judge Monica Fernandez, June 2009.

Administrative Court (*Corte Primera de lo Contencioso Administrativo*), were dismissed after being accused of incurring in an "inexcusable error" for having decided politically sensitive cases against the government (Perez-Perdomo 2009). After a long battle at the IACtHR (Inter-American Court of Human Rights), in August 2008 the Court ruled that the judges' rights had been violated and ordered the Venezuelan government to reinstate them. On December 18, 2009, Venezuela's highest court, the TSJ (*Tribunal Supremo de Justicia*, Supreme Justice Tribunal), ruled that the Court's decision was unenforceable, thus formally reaffirming the government's position of not abiding by unfavorable decisions rendered by an international court.

Lines between the judicial and the political terrains, indeed, have become so blurred that judges may be publicly reprimanded for not following the party line, or praised and rewarded when their decisions favor the government (Perez-Perdomo 2009). In addition, legal proceedings have increasingly been used to settle political quarrels that would not otherwise have fallen within the purview of the courts. The difference between the political manipulation that took place during the pacted democracy and the Bolivarian Revolution is that now public institutions have fallen under the open and direct control of a single leader, who is unwilling to negotiate his personal political project or share power with any other group.

Between the Corner Office and the Street Corner: The New Generation of Venezuelan Cause Lawyers

The numerous human rights abuses committed against ordinary citizens on and after April 11, 2002, gave a new boost to cause lawyering and human rights activism in Venezuela. Several organizations, including PROVEA, Foro por la Vida (Forum for Life) and COFAVIC, took an active role in advocating the prosecution and conviction of those responsible for the murders, torture, and illegal detention of hundreds of civilians. The fact that these events had taken place during anti-Chavez demonstrations was enough for the government to treat these cases as political and to consider the victims and their lawyers as adversaries. As a result, and despite COFAVIC's and PROVEA's longstanding reputation as nonpartisan, apolitical organizations, their representatives were dragged into the political battleground and accused of favoring the antigovernment cause. COFAVIC's president Liliana Ortega received several death threats and obtained a protective measure from the IACtHR ordering the Venezuelan government to guarantee her safety.[21]

Unlike the Caracazo and the Amparo massacre victims, many of the April 11 victims were middle-class demonstrators, which brought a different group of lawyers center stage. Pedro Carmona's rise as leader of the short-lived de facto government that seized power after President Chavez's alleged resignation in April 2002, gave the government a pretext to initiate a witch hunt against members of the leading

[21] *Liliana Ortega et al.* Case, Order of the Court of February 21, 2003, Inter-Am. Ct. H.R. (Ser. E) (2003).

opposition parties as well as against key members of the private sector. The number of indictments against businesspeople and political leaders grew and the preferential treatment that some of them had enjoyed in the past disappeared. Those who were not able to show unconditional loyalty to the president's political project were often demonized as "oligarchs" and treated as enemies of the state (Amsterdam, Rosich, and Himiob 2009).

Unlike during the years of the pacted democracy, political channels to negotiate a solution were now largely unavailable to members of the country's private sector and traditional political elite. The once powerful and influential social networks that had shaped the operation of the state apparatus during the previous administrations, and to which many members of the traditional business and political elites had easy access, disappeared from the map. The new networks that emerged within the Chavez government were inaccessible to those identified with the opposition (Gomez 2009). Many lawyers were also singled out and labelled as pro- or anti-Chavez, and thus deprived of the political elasticity that had been one of their most precious assets. To many, it became clear that the Bolivarian Revolution did not allow neutrality.

The overwhelming official campaign geared to treating those not openly sympathetic to the government as political enemies had a chilling effect on the work of the traditional human rights activists. Furthermore, their role was overshadowed by the presence of a new generation of activist lawyers representing a growing list of high profile victims, ranging from members of the traditional business and political elites to former military commanders and government officials.

When faced by an aggressive campaign initiated by government prosecutors against them, most of these high profile victims began mobilizing to secure an adequate legal strategy. Instead of reaching out to the traditional cause lawyers and human rights organizations, they instead contacted a group of relatively young and successful private practitioners from boutique law firms, largely specialized in white collar crime and commercial litigation, but with little or no experience in handling human rights or political cases.[22]

From their clients' standpoint, however, these lawyers had several advantages over the traditional human rights activists. First, their firms offered a stable organizational platform insulated from external pressure: its operation did not depend on the larger and sometimes conflicting agendas of traditional advocacy NGOs.[23] Second, these lawyers still had contacts with the private-sector networks, guaranteeing them steady financial and logistical support, and facilitating their access to foreign aid and media exposure.[24]

[22] Interview with cause lawyer #7, June 2009; interview with cause lawyer #8, June 2009; interview with NGO representative, March 2009.

[23] Interview with cause lawyer #8, June 2009; interview with Robert Amsterdam, July 2009.

[24] Interview with cause lawyer #7, June 2009; interview with cause lawyer #8, June 2009.

Finally, and perhaps most importantly, because of their proximity to the country's traditional business and political elites and resulting in part from the polarization created by the government, these elite lawyers were openly identified with the opposition. Many of them had been trying to ride out the political storm by keeping a low profile or by quietly seeking ways to rebuild their portfolio of contacts and to reach out to the social networks that had risen to the top during the first two years of the Bolivarian Revolution. However, their strategy of neutrality in the ideological struggle became increasingly unviable as virtually everybody was forced to take sides in the political debate. The fact that these elite lawyers were personally affected by the situation made them more likely to display solidarity with their clients' causes, which was perceived as a gain.

The growing polarization of Venezuelan society between pro- and antigovernment blocs and the penetration of politics into every major aspect of social life caused rapid changes in the country's legal culture. Ordinary citizens on both sides of the political spectrum adopted a language of rights in their everyday speech and quickly became familiar with the use of the legal system as an instrument to achieve political ends. Even in the most casual conversations, those in favor of the government justified its actions in legal terms, often reciting specific constitutional provisions that had been referred to by the president during one of his almost daily speeches. As part of a mass media campaign, the government printed millions of pocket-sized Bolivarian Constitutions to be distributed among the people, so that even the residents of the most remote villages often carried around the little book and were ready to brandish it during any casual conversation.[25] Those identified with the opposition also grew accustomed to using the legal system as a tool in their resistance to the ideological project initiated in 1999 and in their effort to restore democracy.[26]

The way judges and lawyers perceived their own role within the legal system also changed. Notably, the elite lawyers who took on the representation of political victims understood that their new function was not simply to help their clients navigate institutional or political obstacles, or to serve as hired guns completely detached from any political ideology. In the new scenario, there was no more room for neutrality. Furthermore, the Bolivarian Revolution had replaced the traditional social networks with new ones that blocked them from preferential access to circles of power, so the social capital of the legal professionals identified with the private sector was significantly altered (Gomez 2009).

Who Are the New Cause Lawyers?

As lawyers were forced to take sides in the political debate and were boxed into one of the two possible ideological categories, they felt naturally inclined to embrace their

[25] Interview with political leader #14, May 2008.

[26] Interview with cause lawyer #7, June 2009; interview with cause lawyer #8, June 2009; interview with NGO representative, March 2009.

clients' causes, which in a way had become their own cause. Many of them acted as if they had been charged with a special responsibility to restore democracy and became active participants in different movements and political causes in the aftermath of the April 11, 2002, events.[27] A group called *Fuerza Integradora* (Uniting Force) was one of these early initiatives led by at least three of the new activist lawyers.[28] As members of these causes, lawyers were expected to offer their expertise and represent some of the victims on a pro bono basis, which they generally did.[29] Most of their high-profile clients, however, retained them on a remunerated basis, which enabled these lawyers to hold on to their lucrative professional practices while remaining engaged in political activism. The prospect of involvement in this type of case was not unattractive to the lawyers from a business standpoint, even though the probability of achieving success or any form of favorable outcome was slim at best.

The fact that these new cause lawyers had a longstanding relationship with members of the country's traditional private sector facilitated their access to most privately owned local and international media outlets, which became one of their most valuable tools in gaining support for their clients. Their portfolio of business contacts also helped these lawyers mobilize different stakeholders in order to raise the necessary financial support that allowed them to continue taking cases on behalf of victims who were unable to pay.[30] These contributions often came from other firm clients who agreed to pay a differential above their bills toward a special litigation fund,[31] or from members of the business community who offered in-kind donations to help finance the often complex and costly legal strategies.

As the number of political victims grew rapidly, the five or six boutique lawyers who initially led the upcoming generation of legal activists[32] were later joined by a handful of former judges under the direction of Monica Fernandez and the members of the FPV (*Foro Penal Venezolano*,Venezuelan Penal Forum). Other groups led by victims' relatives appeared later.[33] The FPV gained enormous visibility for its involvement in a request submitted in January 2004 to the pretrial chamber of the International Criminal Court seeking to indict the leaders of the Venezuelan government for allegedly violating the human rights of more than seventy citizens.

27 Interview with cause lawyer #7, June 2009.

28 Interview with cause lawyer #7, June 2009; interview with cause lawyer #8, June 2009.

29 Id.

30 Interview with cause lawyer #7, June 2009; interview with cause lawyer #8, June 2009; interview with NGO representative #9, July 2009.

31 Interview with cause lawyer #8, June 2009; interview with NGO representative #9, July 2009.

32 Most of these lawyers came from the firms of Echeverria & Asociados and Rosich, Himiob, Romero & Asociados.

33 Namely, *Presos Politicos de Venezuela* (Political Prisoners of Venezuela) and the *Fundacion por el Debido Proceso* (Due Process Foundation) promoted by Jackeline Sandoval de Guevara; *Damas de Blanco* (Women in White), led by Tamara Sujú, and VIVE (*Victimas Venezolanas de la Violencia Política*, Venezuelan Victims of Political Violence), led by Mohamed Merhi.

TABLE 8.1. *Cause lawyering and human rights activists in Venezuela (2002–2009)*

Name of organization	Type	Representative clients (type of cases)
Echeverria & Asociados	Local law firm	– NGO in charge of organizing recall referendum – Former PDVSA employees dismissed during 2002 oil strike (Gente del Petroleo) – RCTV (local TV station and important media group)
Rosich, Himiob, Romero, & Asociados	Local law firm	– Eligio Cedeño (banker accused of helping opposition) – Gen. Francisco Uson (former Chavez Minister of Finance) – Mohamad Merhi, Maria Concepcion Capote and others (relatives of April 11 victims)
Presos Politicos de Venezuela	Local NGO	Otoniel Guevara, Rolando Guevara and Juan Guevara (citizens indicted for the assassination of a prosecutor)
Fundación para el Debido Proceso[34]	Local NGO	Otto Gebauer, Lazaro Forero, Ivan Simonovis, and others (Police chiefs accused of April 11 killings)
Damas de Blanco	Local NGO	Manuel Rosales (former opposition governor and presidential candidate)
Victimas de la Violencia Política (VIVE)	Local NGO	Mohamed Merhi and others (relatives of April 11 victims)

Source: Amsterdam, Rosich, and Himiob 2009; interview with cause lawyer #7, June 2009; interview with cause lawyer #8, June 2009; interview with NGO representative, March 2009.

Table 8.1 contains the names of the different cause lawyers and human rights activists who have emerged in Venezuela since 2002.

Largely absent from the group of cause lawyers and human rights activists are the several international law firms that operate in Venezuela. Although some of their lawyers have offered occasional support to different groups of activists, these firms have insisted in staying away from the frontal political battle. They are concerned with protecting their own portfolio of clients, which often includes multinational corporations and other foreign-based clients whose presence in Venezuela had become somewhat precarious with the rise of an antiforeign sentiment.

Litigating against the government in a heavily politicized judiciary turned out to be much more challenging than most activist lawyers had anticipated.[35] Complaints from private lawyers about not having access to court files or the evidence presented against their clients became part of their everyday war stories. Defense lawyers

34 http://www.funderpro.com.ve (July 29, 2009).

35 Interview with cause lawyer #7, June 2009; interview with cause lawyer #8, June 2009.

also denounced the fact that appeals were often decided summarily without proper notice and that procedural rules were not being followed. Some defendants were allegedly detained during long periods of time without being notified of the charges against them, or they complained of having been subject to interrogation without due-process formalities (Amsterdam, Rosich, and Himiob 2009).

The new political and social reality essentially deprived most elite legal practitioners of the privileged access that they once had to high government officials, influential lobbyists and prominent judges. They even lost all influence over the law clerks, bailiffs and other court bureaucrats who used to help them circumvent even the most trivial hurdles associated with litigating in the Venezuelan courts (Gomez 2008). Unable to deploy their traditional skills and reluctant to leave their clients' fate solely in the hands of the local progovernment judges, defense lawyers were forced to develop a different form of advocacy. In a similar fashion to the human rights activists of the early 1990s, defense lawyers found a powerful ally in the media, which helped them communicate to the public the injustices suffered by their clients. It became common for lawyers to offer press conferences on a daily basis, usually on the steps of the court buildings, to protest against a particular ruling or to accuse a judge for lack of impartiality.[36] Defense lawyers also began spending significant amounts of time as guests of radio and television programs, which were also frequented by political figures. Before they realized it, most of their days would be spent between their corner offices where they deployed their traditional lawyerly skills and the street corners where they relied on media outlets to communicate with the public. Government officials led by the president himself usually fired back by accusing some of these lawyers as agents of the "antidemocratic opposition" or disqualifying them in some other way.

In such a polarized political environment, the frequent exchanges between private lawyers and government supporters turned into some form of "trial by media,"[37] whereby the parties constantly voiced their different positions before the cameras. The official rulings thus became irrelevant in the eyes of the general public, because it had already created its own perception of a fair outcome. The increased public exposure of private lawyers and their fierce advocacy on behalf of victims of the political regime made them de facto political activists as they increasingly incorporated political language into their legal arguments.

During frequent interviews and public appearances, lawyers rarely limited themselves to discussing the implications of specific legal rules or relevant facts to the case. Their speech was commonly infused with political opinions and they increasingly portrayed themselves as "charged with a duty to defend the Venezuelan democracy beyond their clients' own private interest."[38] When criticizing specific judicial

[36] Interview with cause lawyer #7, June 2009; interview with cause lawyer #8, June 2009; interview with NGO representative, March 2009.

[37] Interview with Robert Amsterdam, July 2009.

[38] Interview with cause lawyer #7, June 2009.

behavior that affected their cases, these lawyers also made frequent references to the antidemocratic practices of the government and were never shy about declaring the need for "a change in the country's political leadership for one that really respects the constitution."[39] This form of trial by media was by no means unique to Venezuelan cause lawyers. Many activists around the world have traditionally relied on public media campaigns to advance their causes and attain popular support. However, it was indeed a novel tactic for these corporate lawyers who, during their previous life as private practitioners, had avoided public exposure at all costs, and whose past success was largely measured by their neutrality and discretion.

This radical shift of strategy was necessary. Some even perceived their new constant public exposure as a form of insurance, because all their actions were recorded and continuously broadcast to audiences all over the country, making it harder for their political enemies to endanger their personal safety.[40] As part of their communications strategy, cause lawyers traveled widely to speak at numerous conferences about their multiple challenges, and disseminated their views through frequent op-ed columns in local and foreign newspapers, as well as through independent reports, books and articles published in academic journals and other venues.[41]

Another prong of the strategy deployed by the new group of cause lawyers was the development of a transnational platform involving key players with experience in handling difficult political cases in other countries. Perhaps the most visible lawyer of this kind is Robert Amsterdam, a London-based Canadian attorney who rose to international fame as the lead defense counsel for Russian oil tycoon Mikhail Khodorkovsky in a multibillion dollar case known as the Yukos affair.[42] Amsterdam has also been involved in other politically controversial cases, including a dispute between members of a prominent business conglomerate and the Guatemalan government.[43] A few years ago, Amsterdam became a member of the legal team representing Eligio Cedeño, a Venezuelan banker indicted in retaliation for his support of the Venezuelan political opposition and held in pretrial detention for more than two years.[44] Since then, he has worked in close coordination with several Venezuelan cause lawyers.[45]

Considered by his colleagues to be a "super-litigator,"[46] Amsterdam has developed an unusual model of human rights advocacy that includes the formation of interdisciplinary teams of lawyers, political activists and media relations experts tailored to each specific case.[47] Amsterdam does not consider himself to be a standard human

39 Interview with cause lawyer #8, June 2009.

40 Interview with cause lawyer #7, June 2009; interview with cause lawyer #8, June 2009.

41 Interview with Robert Amsterdam, July 2009.

42 http://www.khodorkovskycenter.com/ (July 29, 2009).

43 http://www.casogutierrez.com/ (July 29, 2009).

44 http://www.eligiocedeno.com/ (July 29, 2009).

45 Interview with Robert Amsterdam, July 2009.

46 Interview with cause lawyer #7, June 2009; interview with cause lawyer #8, June 2009.

47 http://www.amsterdamandperoff.com/strategy.html (July 29, 2009).

rights lawyer but rather as an international lawyer representing clients whose cases are not attractive to traditional NGOs, despite having become victims of deinstitutionalized states or governments that have turned into predatory instruments of totalitarian rulers.[48]

Despite the apparent commonality of goals between the new private cause lawyers and the traditional Venezuelan NGOs such as COFAVIC, Foro por la Vida, and PROVEA, these groups seem to operate at different levels.[49] Most of the victims who are represented by the new cause lawyers have been deemed to be too political and risky by representatives of the traditional human rights NGOs, who prefer to limit themselves to act on behalf of a limited group of ordinary citizens and tend to avoid high-profile clients.[50]

By taking on a number of politically charged cases, Venezuelan cause lawyers have exposed themselves to some important challenges at both the personal and professional levels. Although at the time of this writing no activist lawyer has been detained or imprisoned for political reasons, some have been threatened with charges on crimes allegedly committed in the course of their advocacy[51] or have become target of personal attacks.[52] In addition, by accepting high-profile and politically controversial clients, some cause lawyers have sacrificed their portfolio of other clients, some of whom have preferred to avoid controversy and so migrated to other firms. It is true, however, that most of these human rights cases are taken on a remunerated basis, thus allowing cause lawyers to maintain the profitability of their professional practice. It is also true that their chances of obtaining a favorable result for their clients are remote.

Despite these challenges, Venezuelan cause lawyers have remained committed not only to assisting their clients and providing them with the best possible legal representation but also to actively participating in the country's political strife. As most of them indicated during the interviews conducted for this research,[53] they view litigation as a way to have their voices heard or to leave proof of the violations that their clients have been subject to. Litigation in this instance is not about obtaining a favorable judgment; it is simply as a form of protest or political activism.

None of these cause lawyers have indicated a desire to begin a full-time political career or to run for office in the short term, but their comments reveals an aspiration for political change and a willingness to lead a movement that could help reach

48 Interview with Robert Amsterdam, July 2009.

49 Interview with cause lawyer #7, June 2009; interview with cause lawyer #8, June 2009.

50 Interview with former judge Monica Fernandez, June 2009; interview with Gonzalo Himiob, June 2009; Interview with Antonio Rosich, June 2009.

51 Interview with cause lawyer #8, June 2009.

52 Interview with former judge Monica Fernandez, June 2009.

53 Interview with cause lawyer #7, June 2009; interview with cause lawyer #8, June 2009; interview with corporate lawyer #4 June 2009; interview with NGO representatives #2, #6, March 2009; April 2007; interview with Venezuelan political activist #5, July 2008.

that goal. Although their views may be aligned with those of certain political parties, cause lawyers are not backed by any formal organization and do not aspire to create an infrastructure similar to any of them. The extreme politicization of legal actors and of the legal system as a whole has contributed to erase the boundaries that once existed between law and politics in Venezuela. Law seems to have permeated every single facet of political life and politics seem to have permeated every single facet of the law, and lawyers have been instrumental in these transitions.

References

Amsterdam, Robert, Rosich, Antonio, and Himiob, Gonzalo. 2009. *The Bolivarian Rule of Lawlessness*. http://www.robertamsterdam.com/venezuela/Bolivarian%20Rule%20of%20Lawlessness.pdf (July 29, 2009).

Carrasquero, Francisco. 2008. "Poder Judicial debe garantizar continuidad transformadora del proyecto revolucionario." Discurso de inauguración del año judicial, January 28. Agencia Bolivariana de Noticias. www.abn.info.ve (July 29, 2009).

Chavez, Hugo. 2002. Aló Presidente No. 115. Venezolana de Television. August 18.

Coronil, Fernando. 1997. *The Magical State: Nature, Money, and Modernity in Venezuela*. Chicago: University of Chicago Press.

Corrales, Javier. 2002. *Presidents Without Parties*. University Park: Pennsylvania State University.

Crisp, Brian P. 1997. "Presidential Behavior in a System with Strong Parties: Venezuela, 1958–1995." In *Presidentialism and Democracy in Latin America*, Scott Mainwaring and Matthew Soberg Shugart, eds. Cambridge: Cambridge University Press. 160–98.

Delgado Ocando, José M. 1979. "Revolución y Derecho." In *Estudios sobre la Constitución. Libro Homenaje a Rafael Caldera*. Caracas: Universidad Central de Venezuela. 2595–600.

Dezalay, Yves, and Bryant Garth. 2001. "Constructing Law Out of Power." In *Cause Lawyering and the State in a Global Era*, Austin Sarat and Stuart Scheingold, eds.New York: Oxford University Press. 354–81.

Dor, Galand Menachem Hofnung. 2006. "Litigation as Political Participation." *Israel Studies*, 11:131–57.

Dotan, Yoav. 2001. "The Global Language of Human Rights." In *Cause Lawyers and the State in a Global Era*, Austin Sarat and Stuart Scheingold, eds. New York: Oxford University Press. 244–63.

Ellner, Steve, and Daniel Hellinger, eds. 2003. *Venezuelan Politics in the Chávez Era: Class, Polarization, and Conflict*. Boulder: Lynne Rienner Publishers.

Gomez, Manuel. 2003. "Los Abogados de Negocios en Venezuela." *Revista de la Facultad de Ciencias Juridicas y Politicas de la UCV*, 125:23–51.

Gomez, Manuel. 2008. "All In The Family: The Influence of Social Networks in Dispute Processing (A Case Study of a Developing Economy)." *Georgia Journal of International and Comparative Law*, 36:291–354.

Gomez, Manuel. Forthcoming. "Greasing the Squeaky Wheel of Justice: Networks of Venezuelan Lawyers from the Pacted Democracy to the Bolivarian Revolution." In *Lawyers and the Rule of Law in an Era of Globalization*, Yves Dezalay and Bryant Garth, eds. New York: Routledge.

Hajjar, Lisa. 2001. "From the Fight for Legal Rights to the Promotion of Human Rights." In *Cause Lawyering and the State in a Global Era*, Austin Sarat and Stuart Scheingold, eds. New York: Oxford University Press. 68–95.

Halliday, Terence C. 1999. "The Politics of Lawyers: An Emerging Agenda." *Law and Social Inquiry*, 24:1007–11.

Hellinger, Daniel. 2004. "Political Overview: The breakdown of Puntofijismo and the Rise of Chavismo." In *Venezuelan Politics in the Chavez era: Class, Polarization, and Conflict*, Steve Ellner and Daniel Hellinger, eds. Boulder: Lynne Rienner Publishers. 27–54.

Karl, Terry. 1997. *The Paradox of Plenty*. Los Angeles: University of California Press.

Kornblith, Miriam. 1998. *Venezuela en los noventa: Las crisis de la Democracia*. Caracas: Ediciones IESA.

Levine, Daniel. 1973. *Conflict and Political Change in Venezuela*. Princeton: Princeton University Press.

Lomnitz, Clarissa, and Salazar, Rodrigo. 2002. "Cultural Elements in the Practice of Law in Mexico: Informal Networks in a Formal System." In *Global Prescriptions: The Production, Exportation, and Importation of a New Legal Orthodoxy*, Yves Dezalay and Bryant Garth, eds. Ann Arbor: The University of Michigan Press. 209–48.

Lopez Maya, Margarita. 2003. "The Venezuelan Caracazo of 1989: Popular Protest and Institutional Weakness." *Journal of Latin American Studies*, 35:117–37.

Lu, Yiyi. 2008. *Public Interest Litigation and Political Activism in China*. Montreal: International Center for Human Rights and Democratic Development.

Marquez, Walter, and Carias, German. 1992. *Comandos del Crimen: La Masacre del Amparo*. Caracas: Fuentes Editores.

Meili, Stephen. 2001. "Latin American Cause-Lawyering Networks." In *Cause Lawyering and the State in a Global Era*, Austin Sarat and Stuart Scheingold, eds. New York: Oxford University Press. 307–33.

Naím, Moisés. 1989. *Las Empresas Venezolanas: Su Gerencia*. Caracas: IESA.

Perez-Liñan, Anibal. 2007. *Presidential Impeachment and the New Political Instability in Latin America*. Cambridge: Cambridge University Press.

Perez-Perdomo, Rogelio. 1981. *Los Abogados en Venezuela*. Caracas: Monte Avila Editores.

Perez-Perdomo, Rogelio. 1990. "La Organización del Estado en el siglo XIX (1830–1899)." *Politeia*, 14:349–404.

Perez-Perdomo, Rogelio. 2001. "Oil Lawyers and the Globalization of the Venezuelan Oil Industry." In *The Legal Culture of Global Business Transactions*, R. Appelbaum, W. Felstiner and V. Gessner, eds. Oxford: Hart. 301–24.

Perez-Perdomo, Rogelio. 2003a. "Venezuela 2002: Crisis Política y Derecho." *Revista de Derecho Político*, 57:307–24.

Perez-Perdomo, Rogelio. 2003b. "La Dimension Constitucional de la Crisis Politica." In *En Esta Venezuela: Realidades, y Nuevos Caminos*, Patricia Marquez and Ramon Piñango, eds. Caracas: IESA. Insert chapter page range.

Perez-Perdomo, Rogelio. 2005. "Judicialization and Regime Change: The Venezuelan Supreme Court." In *The Judicialization of Politics in Latin America*, Rachel Sieder, Alan Angell and Line Schjolden, eds. London: Palgrave McMillan. 131–60.

Perez-Perdomo, Rogelio. 2006. *Latin American Lawyers: A Historical Introduction*. Stanford: Stanford University Press.

Perez-Perdomo, Rogelio. 2009. *Derecho y Cultura en Venezuela en Tiempos de Revolucion (1999–2009)*. Caracas: Fundacion Garcia Pelayo.

Perez-Perdomo, Rogelio, and Capriles, Ruth. 1991. "Corrupcion y Ambiente de Negocios en Venezuela." In *Corrupcion y Control: Una perspectiva comparada*. Caracas: IESA. 1–28.

Rey, Juan Carlos. 1988. *El Futuro de la Democracia en Venezuela*. Caracas: Universidad Central de Venezuela.

Rohde, Clifford C., Jamie Fellner, and Cynthia G. Brown. 1993. *Human Rights in Venezuela*. Human Rights Watch (Organization), Americas Watch Committee (U.S.). Human Rights Watch.

Sarat, Austin, and Scheingold, Stuart. 1998. *Cause Lawyering: Political Commitments and Professional Responsibilities*. Oxford: Oxford University Press.

Sarat Austin, and Scheingold, Stuart. 2001. *Cause Lawyering and the State in a Global Era*. New York: Oxford University Press.

Sieder, Rachel, Alan Angell, and Line Schjolden. 2005. *The Judicialization of Politics in Latin America*. New York: Palgrave McMillan.

Smulovitz, Catalina. 2002. "The Discovery of Law: Political Consequences in the Argentine Case." In *Global Prescriptions: The Production, Exportation, and Importation of a New Legal Orthodoxy*, Yves Dezalay and Bryant Garth, eds. Ann Arbor: University of Michigan Press. 249–75.

9

The Mapuche People's Battle for Indigenous Land: Litigation as a Strategy to Defend Indigenous Land Rights

Anne Skjævestad

INTRODUCTION

Land constitutes the basis for the livelihoods and cultures of indigenous peoples. They rely on access to their traditional lands and natural resources for their economic sustenance, as well as for the continued survival of their cultural and spiritual identity. The deprivation of their land has consequences for the economic well-being and the living conditions of the indigenous peoples (Stavenhagen 2002). Indigenous communities are often among the poorest and most marginalized groups of society. Studies on indigenous peoples and poverty in Latin America conclude that "poverty among Latin America's indigenous population is pervasive and severe [and] the living conditions of the indigenous people are generally abysmal, especially when compared to those of the non-indigenous population" (Stavenhagen 2002: 13, par. 35).

Rights to land and natural resources are thus fundamental to indigenous peoples, and protecting these rights remains one of the central issues for their organizations. Courts may constitute an arena for mobilizing around indigenous land rights and may play a role in improving respect for them. Thus, indigenous peoples of Latin America increasingly turn to the legal system for the defense of their rights (Sieder 2005: 1). The prospect of achieving significant results by means of litigation depends on the accessibility of the judicial system, but there are numerous obstacles that may prevent poor and marginalized people from accessing justice, and in Latin America, access to justice is in many cases restricted for these groups.[1] This chapter deals with the issue of indigenous peoples' land rights and the possibilities for advancing these rights through the legal system. This will be done by examining the case of the Mapuche people in Chile.

The Mapuche constitute the largest indigenous population in the country and are grouped into five large territorial identities: Huenteche, Nagche, Lafkenche,

[1] See Méndez et al. (1999).

Huilliche, and Pehuenche.[2] They are among the poorest and most marginalized groups in Chile, and the rural Mapuche population lives in extreme poverty. Among the Mapuche population, 38.4 percent live below the poverty line, and the incidence of poverty is highest in the Bío Bío region, where 52.3 percent are considered poor (UDP 2003–5: 2). The human development index of the Mapuche population is one point lower than that of the non-indigenous population (0.6 versus 0.7),[3] while the average Mapuche income is less than half of that of non-indigenous persons.

One can establish a direct relationship between the incidence of poverty among the Mapuche and the gradual loss of their lands and resources. First, the Mapuche were impoverished as a consequence of the reduction of their lands at the end of the nineteenth and the beginning of the twentieth century.[4] Second, globalization and liberal market economies caused prices to drop on agricultural products traditionally produced by the Mapuche. This severely undermined their traditional agriculture, thereby eroding their means of sustenance. Finally, the Mapuche were affected by the expansion of the forestry industry in Southern Chile, which had grave implications for the environment in these areas, such as the drying up of water sources, permanent droughts, and difficult conditions for agriculture (FIDH 2006: 5–6). The substitution of native forest with exotic species such as pine and eucalyptus has led to the decline or loss of woodland fauna and flora. Rivers and streams are contaminated because of the use of herbicides and pesticides, which also affect the health of community members. Access to the woods – and consequentially, access to the means of sustenance – is reduced due to vast forest plantations that are fenced off (Stavenhagen 2004: 10). The Mapuche are also increasingly affected by forest logging and infrastructure projects such as road constructions and dam constructions. Refuse heaps and wastewater treatment plants located in their territory cause severe environmental damage and constitute a threat to nearby Mapuche residents (Tricot 2006: 11).

This chapter examines a case involving the construction of a hydroelectric power dam in Ralco, in Southern Chile, an incident that caused the forced resettlement of five hundred members of Mapuche-Pehuenche communities and the

[2] The Mapuche population is 604,349 people, equivalent to 87.3% of the entire indigenous population (FIDH 2006: 5).

[3] The index comprises three dimensions: health, education and income (UNDP 2003: 14). There is also a significant difference between urban and rural Mapuche; the human development index among the urban Mapuche population is 0.5, compared to 0.4 among the rural population (UNDP 2003: 21).

[4] In the period after the creation of the Chilean state in 1818, the Mapuche's lands, resources and sovereignty were gradually lost. The Mapuche were confined to reservations that all together covered about 6 percent of their original territory (UFRO 2002: 2). The remaining lands were seized by the Chilean state and distributed to national and European colonies. During the following decades, much of what was left of Mapuche lands was divided and transferred to nonindigenous people. This process culminated during the military government of Augusto Pinochet, when most of the communities and reservations were divided into individual plots (UFRO 2002: 2).

subsequent flooding of their ancestral territory.[5] The process that led to the approval of Ralco was full of irregularities. The environmental impact study (EIS) required to authorize Ralco was initially rejected by the National Environment Commission, (CONAMA) (COIT 2005: 13–14). The National Corporation for Indigenous Development (CONADI), was also critical of the project, claiming that it would risk the Pehuenche culture and their survival as a people. The government responded to this criticism by firing the two directors of CONADI, as well as two advisors working for CONADI (COIT 2005: 14). The project was initiated without the consent of all the Pehuenche landowners, and some of those who agreed on resettlement were manipulated or pressured into doing so.[6]

In analyzing this case, the chapter deals with the relationship among legal consciousness, legal mobilization, and legal culture. These are concepts that are relevant for explaining the process of judicialization of rights claims. The aim is to examine the strategy of litigation for the advancement of indigenous peoples' land rights by analyzing two aspects: (1) *voice*; the ability of indigenous groups to articulate their concerns and effectively voice their claims in court; and (2) *responsiveness*; the willingness of courts to respond to such claims.[7] While voice refers to the ability of the indigenous to legally mobilize around their rights, responsiveness refers to how courts respond to their efforts to judicialize these demands. I use the term *judicialization* here to refer to the process of indigenous peoples gaining influence on public policies by means of rights litigation. This conceptualization is based on two definitions articulated by Guillermo O'Donnell: (1) the judicialization of social relations, "whereby social claims are pursued through the courts or court-like institutions"; and (2) the judicialization of politics, "the process by which the judiciary gains prominence within the political system of which it is part" (O'Donnell 2005: 292).

The specific aim here is to determine the role of Chilean courts in the defense of the Mapuche rights by analyzing the Mapuche people's ability to voice their land rights claims through the judicial system, and the courts' responsiveness toward such claims. Voice and responsiveness constitute the first stages of a litigation process, and each of them depends on several factors. For indigenous people to be able to effectively voice their claims and legally mobilize, they must first of all be aware of their rights and the possibilities for redress through the legal system. Factors such as

5 The Ralco dam was the second in a series of six dams planned to be constructed on the Bío Bío River to meet the electricity demands in the southern part of Chile. The first dam, Pangue, was completed in 1996, despite the opposition from Mapuche organizations and environmentalists.

6 Interviews with the Pehuenche who would be affected by the project revealed that many of the Pehuenche who had signed contracts for land exchange had found themselves in a situation of forced consent and felt that they had no other option than to leave. Some did not fully understand the contents of the contracts (Lillo 2002).

7 These are based on the analytical framework for courts and social transformation presented in Gloppen (2004).

legal literacy and rights awareness programs, as well as the existence of organizations mobilizing around indigenous rights issues, may increase their legal consciousness. Human rights education and a general focus on the rights of indigenous people in the media may also contribute to knowledge and awareness.

To be able to judicialize their claims, indigenous groups must overcome a number of barriers. Some of these are practical, such as the economic costs of taking a case to court, geographical distance, language, and lack of information. Indigenous people are often not fluent in the national language and in addition the legal language is complex, sometimes incomprehensible. Other barriers to seeking justice are motivational. Social and cultural distance between the victims and the judges causes fear and mistrust of the justice system. Victims of a rights violation may abstain from pursuing legal action out of fear of humiliation or prejudice, or fear of judges' ruling on class position (Gargarella 2002: 4). Indeed, many disadvantaged people consider the legal system a tool for the rich and powerful to use against them (Anderson 2003: 18). Negative prior experience with the judicial system or negative perceptions of corruption, bias, or delays may also prevent poor people from claiming their rights in court. Access to the justice system further depends on the nature of the legal system. The legal bases for litigating indigenous land rights claims, and in particular whether international norms on indigenous rights have a status as justiciable rights, are of particular importance. The degree of bureaucracy and formalism influences the ability to voice one's rights claims in court (Gloppen 2004: 12). A slow judicial system and detailed formal procedures create a disincentive to pursue a legal strategy.

Access to various resources may help indigenous groups overcome the multiple barriers facing them and enable them to effectively articulate their claims. Associative capacity is important in this respect; by forming associations that can create a common identity and solidarity, and generate expertise and financial resources, indigenous groups are better prepared to voice their claims through the judiciary. The availability and quality of legal aid is a particularly relevant factor. The extent to which poor people can receive free or affordable legal assistance, either through public legal aid schemes or from legal organizations, is critical (Gloppen 2004: 13).

Even with the presence of all the previously mentioned factors, successful litigation on indigenous rights requires the willingness and ability of courts to respond to the claims that are voiced. The responsiveness of the judicial system depends, first of all, on the manner in which claims are voiced. The nature of the legal system, in particular the formal position of indigenous rights in the legal framework (including the status of international conventions) is also important. Furthermore, courts' responsiveness depends on the legal culture: the norms of appropriateness and judges' perceptions of their own role in enforcing human rights influence the manner in which courts respond to the claims voiced (Gloppen 2004: 15). Judges are likely to be more responsive to indigenous people's land rights claims when they are generally committed to human rights and consider it part of their mandate to advance them. The ability to innovate and move away from conservative, formalistic and rigid concepts has a positive impact on courts' responsiveness to the claims of indigenous peoples.

Variations in courts' responsiveness can be explained by judges' sensitivity to human rights issues. Judges' sensitivity relates to their social and ideological background as well as their legal education and experience, and thus depends on the composition of the bench – which is a function of appointment procedures and criteria (Gloppen 2004: 15). Lack of diversity on the bench often creates distance between the judges and the people making it harder for judges to relate to the concerns of various groups of society (Gargarella 2002: 8). Sensitivity training, or training toward human rights, could help the judges become more responsive to the concerns of marginalized groups.

Litigation has an impact when judgments are complied with by the authorities and their implementation creates a basis for policy change on indigenous issues. However, apart from the direct effects, litigation may also have an indirect impact on policies.[8] Litigation may raise awareness of indigenous peoples' land rights issues, draw media attention to these issues, and stimulate social mobilization. Hence, litigation may have important impacts on indigenous policies, regardless of the outcome of a case. The potential of litigation must be assessed in terms of the broader impact it may have on policies by creating awareness, inducing social mobilization and influencing public discourse.

I maintain that the judicialization of their demands has an effect on the legal consciousness of the litigants regardless of the judicial outcome. Thus, even though the litigants do not attain the desired outcome through the courts, they may still acquire a legal discourse for defining and advancing their cause by participating in processes of litigation. On the issue, I refer to McCann's (1994) study on legal consciousness and the politics of legal mobilization, where he argued that, even though the courts failed to respond adequately to feminist activists' claims for equal pay, the process of judicialization of their demands still provided reformers with the legal discourse for defining and advancing their cause. McCann suggested that processes of judicialization made activists more aware of, and more active users, of legal concepts and ideas. In other words, it changed their legal consciousness.

VOICING LAND RIGHTS CLAIMS

Although this chapter focuses on the possibilities for litigating land rights, litigation is seen as merely one of several possible strategies that can be used alone or in combination with other strategies. The choice of legal mobilization as a strategy to advance indigenous land rights depends on the costs of this compared to other options, such as political mobilization. If other strategies – such as demonstrations,

[8] On the broader impact of litigation, see Gloppen (2005: 13–18).

media campaigns, or pressuring political bodies – are considered more effective or advantageous, this may affect the motivation for pursuing legal action (Gloppen 2004: 12). However, litigation may also be part of a broader mobilization strategy comprising legal mobilization and political mobilization. Political strategies – both legal and illegal – may also complement litigation and strengthen the voice of the Mapuche.

The Mapuche people's possibilities for voicing their land rights claims, and the factors relevant to explaining "voice" – awareness, resources, barriers to access, the law, and the legal system – are analyzed next.

Awareness

The articulation and effective voicing of claims in court requires that the victims of a rights violation are aware of their rights and the possibilities for redress through the courts. The media may strongly influence the level of rights awareness, so it is therefore important that the media have a focus on human rights in general, and indigenous' rights in particular. According to UN Special Rapporteur Stavenhagen, the Chilean media pay little attention to indigenous people's human rights. Stavenhagen maintains that it is the duty of the media to "put forward an objective and balanced view of such important issues as the struggle for the human rights of indigenous peoples" (4: 20). This duty has not been fulfilled by the Chilean media, which on the contrary have played a significant role in the stigmatization of the Mapuche. This is evident in the 2004 report of Human Rights Watch and Indigenous Peoples' Rights Watch, according to which the press has advanced a view of the Mapuche as inciters:

> In coverage of the land conflicts in leading newspapers and journals, writers continue to emphasize the "infiltration" of Mapuche communities, reinforcing a view of the Mapuche as subversives and terrorists. (HRW/IPRW 2004: 15)

The press does not hesitate to stress the violent character of the activities of Mapuche activists, and phrases like "rural terrorism," "racial conflict," and "spiral of violence" are frequently seen in the newspapers.

Rights awareness programs may enhance the Mapuche's awareness about their collective rights, including land rights. CONADI has established a Program of Promotion and Information on Indigenous Rights, PIDI, with the aim of promoting indigenous rights, extending information and aiding indigenous persons, families, communities, associations and organizations in effectively accessing the benefits of the public and private social network.[9]

9 See http://www.conadi.cl/pidi.htm (March 10, 2006).

It is important to underline the impact of nongovernmental organizations (NGOs) and institutes specializing in indigenous issues on the awareness-raising of indigenous rights. One such organization is Indigenous Peoples' Rights Watch (*Observatorio Ciudadano*), whose purpose is the promotion, documentation and defense of indigenous peoples' rights. One of the organization's main objectives is to increase the awareness within Chilean society and the state with respect to the situation of Chile's indigenous peoples and the need for recognition of and respect for the individual and collective rights of the indigenous. Indigenous Peoples' Rights Watch also aims at enhancing the knowledge and capacity of the indigenous and their organizations for them to claim their rights.[10] The Institute of Indigenous Studies at the University of the Frontier, Temuco, is an academic and interdisciplinary research unit that aims to promote indigenous people's rights through intercultural investigation. The institute's fundamental principles are to contribute to greater knowledge about the indigenous peoples of Chile within society and in students' education, as well as to search for ways to improve the living standard of indigenous people and strengthen their position in Chilean society.[11] Another aim is to serve as a training center for indigenous organizations (and also for state officials). A great deal of information about indigenous peoples' rights is provided by Mapuche organizations, of which many offer a large amount of documents, news and publications online, thereby contributing to a greater knowledge of the rights of the Mapuche people within society, as well as increased awareness among the Mapuche.

Resources

Access to important resources may enable the Mapuche to effectively articulate their land rights claims. In this respect, associative capacity – the ability to form associations with the capacity to mobilize around indigenous land rights issues – is an important factor. The Mapuche may benefit from their common identity and community solidarity to mobilize and sustain collective action. Associative capacity also refers to what strategies are chosen to mobilize and to the ability to gain international support in mobilization efforts.

Over the last few years, there has been an increase in Mapuche mobilization, which may be seen in relation to the recent resurgence of Mapuche culture and identity. In fact, more and more Mapuche are becoming aware of their tribal identity, and it is becoming increasingly popular among the Mapuche to learn their native language, Mapudungun.[12] Furthermore, the ability to communicate and spread information using modern means of communication, such as the Internet, as well as

[10] See http://www.observatorioderechosindigenas.cl/ (March 10, 2006).

[11] See http://www.estudiosindigenas.cl/ (March 10, 2006).

[12] *Los Angeles Times* 2003.

the increase in international attention and support, has contributed to the Mapuches' capacity to join forces and form associations that can make their voice heard.

Mapuche communities increasingly mobilize around land rights issues, actively opposing the large-scale investment projects that affect their situation. The communities carry out different kinds of protest actions such as demonstrations, hunger strikes and road blockings, and have also brought legal actions. During the planning of the Ralco dam, for example, Mapuche–Pehuenche leaders and members of other communities joined together to manifest their objection toward the project, and through their mobilization they managed to slow down the construction of the dam. The Ralco project met strong resistance from *Mapu Domuche Newen* (Women with the Force of the Earth), a group of Pehuenche women resisting relocation from their lands in the Upper Bío Bío in negotiations with the owner of the project, the private energy company *Empresa Nacional de Electricidad* (ENDESA). This organization played a significant role in fighting for the Pehuenche families who refused relocation (Aylwin et al. 2001: 5). Some of the members of the organization brought several actions against ENDESA and the authority responsible for approving it, CONAMA.

The Action Group for Bío Bío (*Grupo de Acción por el Bío Bío*, hereafter GABB) played a crucial role in opposing the Ralco project and contributed significantly to drawing attention to the negative implications of the dam. One of the tasks undertaken by GABB was to provide, through their journal *Bío Bío Update* (*Bío Bío al Día*), detailed information about the process, the implications of the project, and the latest developments. GABB also participated in protest actions and led meetings with other organizations to coordinate support for the Pehuenche.[13] The coordination of support in the Ralco case was impressive. The organizations managed to join forces in the resistance against the project, and the Pehuenche received support not only from Mapuche leaders and communities from other areas but also from other indigenous peoples, such as the Aymará.[14]

Increased international attention and support from organizations such as Amnesty International, Human Rights Watch, and the United Nations has strengthened the Mapuches' motivation and hopes about the possibilities for protecting their ancestral territories. Over the Internet, Mapuche activists are able to communicate with other groups or individuals that share an interest in their situation, and form allies in other countries. Some of the most important organizations to spread news and information about the Mapuche people are based in Europe, and are aimed at developing contacts between Mapuche organizations and European organizations. These organizations offer information in several languages, which makes information about the Mapuche people easily available. Building networks abroad and cooperating with other organizations with similar aims helps generate international support, which is extremely important to the Mapuche in their struggle for justice.

[13] See, for instance, GABB (2000).

[14] GABB (2000).

One of the most important resources for disadvantaged people who wish to access justice is legal aid. Legal aid for indigenous individuals and communities involved in land conflicts in Chile is provided by CONADI's Legal Defense Program (*Programa Nacional de Defensa Jurídica*, hereafter PDJ). Law 19.253 on the Promotion, Support, and Development of the Indigenous, otherwise referred to as the Indigenous Law, establishes as one of the functions of CONADI the legal defense of the indigenous and their communities in conflicts concerning land and waters, in addition to the functions of arbitration and conciliation (Article 39, section d).

There are several legal advice centers in the southern regions inhabited by the Mapuche; Bío Bío, Araucanía and Los Lagos.[15] The PDJ provides assistance in cases such as the fixing of boundaries, petitions, transference, illegal occupations, usurpation of land, the restoration of terrain and writs of protection (Aylwin 2000: 48).

Despite the efforts of CONADI, it has been difficult to satisfy the legal needs of the Mapuche, at least in the first few years of the legal program's functioning (Aylwin 2000: 49). The reason for this is that the demand for legal aid has generally surpassed the capacity of the staff to respond adequately to the people who seek their assistance. The program has simply not had enough personnel and financial resources. Because of the latter, not all Mapuches have had a legal assistance office for territorial conflicts in their neighboring areas, and some of those in need of legal assistance have had to travel a long distance to obtain it. This is costly for people with limited resources and may create a disincentive to seeking assistance. Geographical distance was a barrier to legal assistance for the Mapuche-Pehuenche in Upper Bío Bío in their territorial conflicts. Until 1997, CONADI only had one lawyer for the whole Bío Bío-region, with the office situated about three hundred kilometers away from Ralco (Aylwin 2000: 51). The problems related to CONADI's legal assistance at the time are documented in a 1998 report on the dam projects on the Bío Bío River:

> CONADI lacks the institutional capacity to defend the interests of the Pehuenche communities. Its single lawyer does not have a staff and receives a gasoline allowance of only 150 dollars for the entire fiscal year; his regional office is 300 km from Pehuenche territory. The Pehuenche do not have travel funds to meet with him. CONADI has been ineffective in dealing with small conflicts and is already overwhelmed by the negotiations with ENDESA over the issue of land exchange in Ralco-Lepoy, which is only one part of the overall resettlement planning problem. (Johnston and Turner 1998: 28, note 3)

However, the situation changed in 1997, when CONADI decided to add a lawyer to the Upper Bío Bío region to attend to the defense of its communities (Aylwin 2000: 51).

[15] See www.conadi.cl/djuridica.htm (February 25, 2006).

Legal assistance has also been offered by university clinics and institutes. At the Catholic University of Temuco (UCT), students at the Law School participate in a litigation program, attending to legal consults and taking on cases at the Lonko Quilapán legal clinic, oriented toward assisting people of Mapuche descent.[16] During the Ralco conflict, additional programs were initiated to offer legal assistance to the Pehuenche communities. From 1997 onwards, CONADI financed a legal aid program that was managed by the Arcis University of Santiago. The same year, a legal assistance program was established at the Indigenous Institute Foundation in Temuco. During 1998, the public-interest litigation program at the Temuco Catholic University law school offered legal counseling to Pehuenche who opposed the construction of the Ralco hydroelectric plant (Lillo 2002: 11).

Barriers to Access

A number of barriers may prevent the Mapuche from pursuing a legal strategy. Some of these are practical, and primarily relate to the costs of litigation and language. Most Mapuche cannot afford to pay for the services of a lawyer, and are thus dependent on free legal assistance to obtain access to justice. Concerning language, the whole operation of the legal system is in Spanish, something that could constitute a barrier for many indigenous people who seek legal aid (Davinson 2000: 185). Spanish is not the native language of the Mapuche, and in addition, there are also problems of illiteracy (Opsvik 1998: 3). Adding the specifics of the legal language, which is complicated for the common citizen, one can easily understand that the legal process may be confusing and incomprehensible for the indigenous.

Other barriers to access are motivational, such as fear and distrust because of social and cultural distance between the Mapuche and judges. Lack of legitimacy and perceptions of discrimination also have a negative impact on the Mapuche's motivation to defend their land rights through the legal system. In studies carried out in the beginning of the 1990s in Chile's poor urban sectors, the results showed that the majority of the respondents were under the impression that the legal system was discriminatory and corrupt and that justice depended on one's wealth. Slightly more than 88 percent shared the opinion that in Chile there is one kind of justice for the rich and another for the poor. More than 77 percent meant that lawyers were corrupt (Correa Sutil 1999: 2). This gives evidence of a profound distrust toward the Chilean judiciary in some poor groups of society.

In the case of the Mapuche, the most decisive factors limiting their motivation for pursuing legal strategies are fear and distrust toward the Chilean judicial apparatus because of their past experience with it. A very important reason for the distrust is the rough manner in which the judiciary has responded to the Mapuche's social protest.

[16] See http://www.derecho.uct.cl/2clinicas.htm (February 23, 2006).

Protest actions for the defense of indigenous land rights have included peaceful demonstrations but also illegal actions such as the occupation of land or setting fire to property or forestry machinery and vehicles. The judiciary has been brutal in its response to the illegal actions that are carried out by the Mapuche in the struggle for protection of their lands. The legal remedies the courts have employed have been grounded in antiterrorist laws that were passed during the Pinochet era. The employment of antiterrorist legislation permits the courts to measure out unusually severe sentences. For instance, in the *Poluco-Pidenco* case, five Mapuche individuals were sentenced to ten years of prison for arson committed against two estates owned by a forestry company (FIDH 2006: 41). On the sentence, Human Rights Watch said that "it is a tremendously exaggerated response to the agitation in Southern Chile" and that "by using the most possible rigid legal rule against the Mapuches, the Chilean government is unjustly comparing them to people responsible for cruel crimes such as homicide" (UDP 2005: 305).

Amendments were introduced to the law in 1991, during the Aylwin government, in order to bring the public security legislation, inherited from the dictatorship, in line with human rights standards. Paradoxically, it was these amendments that changed the law into what prosecutors have considered an appropriate instrument to apply to the kind of offenses committed in land conflicts. The consequence of the reforms was the conception of terrorism not as a political or ideological offense but simply as an extremely violent crime against the person (HRW/IPRW 2004: 21). Among the crimes listed as potential crimes of terrorism is arson, the crime most frequently applied to the Mapuche (HRW/IPRW 2004: 22).

Mapuches charged with illicit terrorist action are in part denied the guarantees available to criminal defendants in the new criminal justice system.[17] The employment of the antiterrorism law entails a much stricter criminal prosecution, in which the rights of the defendants are limited (UDP 2005: 303). Under the antiterrorism law, criminal investigations are conducted in secret for long periods of time (up to six months), the names of many of the accusers are kept secret from the defendants and prosecutors may to a greater extent than in ordinary criminal proceedings intercept the defendants' correspondence and tap their phones. There are limitations with regard to visits and release pending trial is usually denied for months (UDP 2005: 303; HRW/IPRW: 2004: 20).

The application of antiterrorist legislation in the context of Mapuche social protest is discriminatory, and constitutes a violation of the principle of equality before the law, to which Chile is committed through the Covenant on Civil and Political

[17] Chile's new criminal justice system, in force since December 2000, offers several rights to criminal defendants. Under the new system, hearings are oral and public, the fairness of the criminal investigation is supervised by a *juez de garantía* (a judge responsible for the pre-trial hearings) and the defendant is provided with professional legal counsel by the Public Defender's Office. Defendants may have their pre-trial detention periodically reviewed (HRW/IPRW 2004: 20).

Rights. The UN Special Rapporteur on indigenous rights expressed concern about the criminalization of the Mapuche's social protest:

> Under no circumstances should legitimate protest activities or social demands by indigenous organizations and communities be outlawed or penalized. . . . [c]harges for offences in other contexts ("terrorist threat," "criminal association") should not be applied to acts related to the social struggle for land and legitimate indigenous complaints. (Stavenhagen 2004: 22)

The government has recently presented a plan for the modification of the antiterrorist law but the process so far has made little progress. The government states that it is analyzing the law and that a revision is needed (Anaya 2009: 24, para 47). Aside from discriminatory, the application of antiterrorist legislation in the prosecution of the Mapuche – and the implications this has for the legal process and the type of sentences rendered – has caused a profound distrust toward the judiciary. Indeed, the Mapuche have little faith in the judicial system, which they conceive as discriminatory and racist. The Chilean legal system's discrimination of the indigenous is confirmed by the UN Special Rapporteur, who maintains that the indigenous in Chile are discriminated and disproportionately represented in the criminal justice system.[18] As pointed out by Jaime Madariaga, a lawyer and defender of many Mapuche, it is reasonable that the Mapuche lack confidence in a justice system that in the past has stolen their lands, and that currently prosecutes them as terrorists.[19]

The Law and the Legal System

Access to justice for the Mapuche also depends on the nature of the law and the legal system. There must be a clear legal basis for indigenous rights to lands, territories, and resources in Chile's constitutional or legal framework. The degree of formalism and bureaucracy influences the ability to voice land rights claims, because legal formalities and complex procedures discourage litigation.

In Chile, a formalist legal culture and formalist processes, combined with a hierarchical structure, constitute obstacles to the citizens' possibilities for claiming their rights in court (UDP 2004b: 14). The judicial process generally involves numerous formalities that slow down the process and obstruct the possibilities for achieving results. Practically all claims before jurisdictional entities require the services of a lawyer. Hence, there is a significant gap with regard to access to justice between those who are in possession of the resources to hire a lawyer and those who are not (UDP 2004b: 16).

[18] UN News Centre, April 8, 2004 (http://www.un.org/News/, May 10, 2006).

[19] Interview with Madariaga by Cor Doeswijk, Radio Nederland Werelomroep, June 2004, Amsterdam. See http://www.rnw.nl/distrib/realaudio/.

The constitutional actions established for the protection of fundamental rights are designed and implemented by the judicial apparatus in a manner that impedes an effective protection. The main mechanism that protects basic human rights in Chile is the *recurso de protección* (writ of protection). It is a procedure for the protection of constitutional rights, or a mechanism to initiate legal actions for the defense of one's rights (UDP 2004b: 25–26). The writ of protection "allows individuals to seek relief from a court of appeals when their constitutional rights are violated or put in danger" (Couso 2004: 73). However, it is a judicial tool that is increasingly used for lawsuits that are not related to constitutional litigation (Couso 2004: 74). Despite its apparent advantages, there are a number of problems related to its employment. In accordance with the writ of protection, persons affected by a violation must present their claims before the courts within fifteen days from the act of violation or from the point of time when they become aware of the violation (UDP 2004b: 31). In many situations, the time frame of fifteen days is insufficient for a person to seek legal protection of his or her rights. The victim of a violation may not be aware that what has occurred is actually a violation of a constitutional right, and it may take some time before the person realizes or is made aware of this. By the time the person consults a lawyer, who has only limited time to prepare the case, it might be too late. The situation is even more problematic if the litigant is a person with scarce resources and little knowledge of the legal mechanisms (UDP 2004b: 30).

Another obstacle is the possibility that the lawsuit be declared inadmissible. The "examination of admissibility" was supposedly introduced by the Supreme Court as a response to the high increase in writs of protection presented during the last decade, with the aim of rejecting actions presented outside of the time limit as well as those that have "an obvious lack of foundation."[20] According to a study on the subject, the number of lawsuits declared inadmissible amounts to 40 to 45 percent of the total number of actions that reach the appellate courts (UDP 2004b: 33). One of the advantages related to the writ of protection is that it does not require the defense of a lawyer, which means that the citizens can personally call on a judge to intervene in a particular matter concerning a possible violation of a fundamental right. A person pursuing legal action may file a form at the office of a court of appeals, from which his or her case may evolve. However, this solution offers only limited possibilities for success, as demonstrated by the study described earlier:

> [A]lmost 10% [of the lawsuits that reach the Court of Appeals of Santiago] are presented by means of letters and the like [not specified] through forms prepared by officials at the court. . . . all of the lawsuits that were presented in this manner were declared inadmissible. (UDP 2004b: 35)

20 Without specifying what exactly constitutes a lawsuit with an "obvious lack of foundation" (UDP 2004b: 33).

Another crucial matter is the legal basis for litigating on indigenous land rights, and the status of international conventions on indigenous rights. In the existing international instruments, one can distinguish between two concepts that are different and at the same time complementary: indigenous *land* and *territory*. While the notion of *land* refers to the classic idea of the possession of land and property guarantees, *territory* is a broader concept that also covers natural resources. In addition, the concept covers a jurisdictional space, in other words, an area in which the indigenous exercise their influence or their self-determination. The concept of territory incorporates "all the elements that constitute the *indigenous habitat*; soil, subsoil, water, forest, animals, etc." (Lillo 2002: 29). The ILO (International Labour Organization) Convention concerning Indigenous and Tribal Peoples in Independent Countries (otherwise known as ILO Convention No. 169) is among the international instruments containing provisions for the protection of the land rights of indigenous peoples. In ILO Convention No. 169, the term *lands* includes the concept of territory, which covers "the total environment of the areas which the peoples concerned occupy or otherwise use" (Art.13.2). Chile ratified the convention in September 2008 and is now bound to ensure its implementation through public policies (Anaya 2009: 8, para 6). This should entail some major changes, since the rights established in Convention 169 will have constitutional status and should guide the actions of the state.

Over the last three decades, the majority of Latin American states have reformed their constitutions and recognized indigenous peoples' individual and collective rights. The reforms have included not only land rights but also norms concerning cultural rights, indigenous customs and customary law and recognition of the state's multiethnic character. Indigenous peoples' rights to land, territories and resources have been given special attention and are incorporated into the constitutions of, among others, Argentina, Brazil, Colombia, Mexico, Guatemala, Paraguay and Peru (Aylwin 2002: 30). Apart from the constitutional reforms, most Latin American states have developed legislation for the regulation of such rights.

The Chilean legislation that protects the rights of the indigenous is Law 19.253 on the Protection, Support, and Development of the Indigenous, otherwise known as the aforementioned Indigenous Law. The Indigenous Law contains norms concerning the protection of indigenous lands, the development of indigenous people and communities and the respect for and protection of the indigenous cultures and languages. Law 19.253 promotes the participation of indigenous peoples in policy-making and declares it a duty of the State and territorial organizations to hear and consider the opinion of the indigenous organizations recognized by the law in matters that affect them. It established CONADI, which coordinates and executes the state's indigenous policies and establishes a special legal procedure in cases involving issues related to land.

Concerning lands, Law 19.253 recognizes the lands traditionally owned or occupied by the indigenous peoples and contains norms aimed at preventing these lands from being conveyed to non-indigenous persons, as well as norms intended to forestall any further division of those lands. The law grants CONADI the following responsibilities: the protection of indigenous lands through the mechanisms established by the law; the promotion of greater access to and expansion of indigenous lands and waters; the promotion of adequate exploitation of indigenous lands; and the legal defense of the indigenous and their communities in conflicts related to lands and waters (Art. 39).

Although Law 19.253 represents an important advance, it also presents some limitations to prevailing international norms with respect to the concepts of territories and natural resources. Law 19.253 is the first in Chile to guarantee the protection of indigenous lands in terms of prohibiting the transference of these lands to persons who do not belong to the same ethnicity. It also contains provisions that protect the lands from seizure, taxation, and leasing. In this sense, the new law establishes a vigorous right to property for indigenous peoples. However, the legal protection of indigenous lands has been inefficient in the context of some of the economic development projects carried out over the last few years. It did not prevent indigenous communities from being deprived of their lands for the construction of the Ralco dam.

Most importantly, Law 19.253 leaves out the term *peoples* – a term that is internationally recognized for denominating the indigenous entities of the world. The law only recognizes the existence of various *ethnicities*. The recognition of the indigenous as a people is crucial to secure collective rights, such as the right to self-determination; hence, the non-recognition of indigenous peoples in the Chilean Constitution has a number of consequences for the Mapuche and for the other indigenous peoples.[21] The right to self-determination guarantees the indigenous sovereign management of their territories and natural resources. The fact that Chile still has not recognized the country's indigenous peoples in its legal framework sets Chile apart from the other Latin American countries, most of which recognize cultural diversity in their constitutions. During the last three decades, the majority of the states in the region have constitutionally recognized the multicultural or multiethnic character of their nations (including Guatemala in 1985; Brazil in 1988; Colombia in 1991; Mexico and Paraguay in 1992; Peru in 1993; Argentina, Bolivia and Panama in 1994; Nicaragua in 1995; and Ecuador in 1998).[22]

However, the recent ratification of ILO Convention 169 should generate the establishment of a new legal and institutional setting in the area of indigenous peoples. In April 2009, the senate approved a proposition to carry through a legal reform within indigenous matters (Anaya 2009: 9, para 14). Another important governmental initiative is the "Re-Conocer" plan, a plan concerning diversity that mentions as one of

[21] Article 1.1 of the International Covenant on Civil and Political Rights establishes that: "All *peoples* have the right to *self-determination*" (emphasis added).

[22] See http://www.prodiversitas.bioetica.org/doc7.htm (March 15, 2006).

the current challenges the recognition of new legal provisions concerning natural resources on indigenous land. Furthermore, the government has outlined a code of conduct applicable to the investments in indigenous lands (Anaya 2009: 18, para 34).

In sum, the Mapuches' prospects for voicing land rights claims have been relatively good in some aspects. Chilean NGOs and institutes focusing on indigenous rights, as well as the rights awareness program, PIDI, may raise the Mapuches' awareness of their rights. The Mapuche movement has a strong associative capacity and has had the ability to form associations and collectively mobilize around issues relating to their land rights. The numerous Mapuche organizations constitute a significant resource. Having said this, Mapuche individuals or communities seeking redress through the judicial system still face numerous obstacles, particularly in terms of motivational barriers. The Mapuche conceive the justice system as discriminatory and racist because of the stigmatization of the Mapuche and the use of the antiterrorism law in the context of their social protest. Distrust seems to be one of the main factors affecting the Mapuches' motivation to defend their rights through the judiciary. The costs of litigation and language also constitute barriers. The legal system is bureaucratic, and a number of formalist and complex procedures impede a speedy and efficient process. Finally, the legal framework for the protection of indigenous peoples' land rights has so far been insufficient in relation to international standards. While Law 19.253 represents a step forward in the recognition and protection of indigenous lands, it leaves out important elements that are present in the international legal instruments on indigenous peoples and land rights, such as the concepts of territories and natural resources.

However, the recent ratification of ILO Convention 169 and the government's signalled legal reforms should bring about important changes to the legal framework.

COURTS' RESPONSIVENESS TOWARD MAPUCHE CLAIMS

In the case concerning the Ralco power plant in the Mapuche-Pehuenche communities' ancestral territory in Upper Bío Bío, several actions were brought against the authorities and the private energy company ENDESA. In what follows, three cases will be discussed: one that was won by the Pehuenche litigants, and two that were lost. The two cases that were lost are important because they drew attention to the Mapuche people's situation from the media, as well as from national and international indigenous rights organizations, and because they shed light on some of the factors that may determine courts' responsiveness to Mapuche claims.

Three members of the organization Mapu Domuche Newen filed a lawsuit to the Sixth Civil Court in Santiago in 1997, demanding the annulment of the Environmental Impact Study (EIS) that had led to the approval of the Ralco project.[23] The

[23] The litigants contended that the EIS was invalid because the procedure applied to the evaluation did not legally exist on the date of its initiation. (For text of the legal action presented, see http://www.xs4all.nl/~rehue/ralco/ral028b.html, May 8, 2006).

suit was brought against ENDESA and CONAMA for violating the indigenous law and the environmental law. In an unexpected decision on September 8, 1999, the court accepted a legal motion filed by the Pehuenche litigants to suspend works on Ralco while the case was being resolved, and ordered an indefinite halt to the construction (GABB 1999a). When the ruling was appealed by CONAMA and ENDESA a few days later, the court upheld its previous decision and rejected the appeal, thereby further postponing construction on Ralco (Mapuche Nation 1999). However, the decision was ultimately reversed following an injunction ruled by the Court of Appeals of Santiago, and the works in Upper Bío Bío were allowed to continue (GABB 1999b).

In March 2000, Pehuenche families brought two writs of protection before the Court of Appeals in Santiago (*El Sur* 2000). Both lawsuits were aimed at reversing the final electricity license authorizing the Ralco project. The first of these actions was filed against the Minister of Economy for violations of the Waters Code, on the grounds that ENDESA did not have the sufficient water rights to construct the dam (*El Sur* 2000). The second writ of protection was brought against the president of the Republic and the Minister of Economy for violating the indigenous law by granting ENDESA the electricity license without having acquired all the necessary land exchange contracts from Pehuenche residents (*El Sur* 2000). The indigenous law establishes that indigenous lands can be traded for land of a similar value only with the free consent of the owners. The authorities, on the other hand, claimed that the electricity law of 1981 permitted expropriation of private property to provide energy for the public good.

Both cases were ultimately rejected in a decision that established the effectiveness of the license based on the electricity law (*El Mercurio* 2001a). The court recognized that ENDESA had fulfilled its obligations with respect to the environmental authorizations, such as the relocation plan for the Pehuenche affected by Ralco. The ruling also established that ENDESA did have the sufficient water rights to carry through the construction (*El Mercurio* 2001b). The decision was confirmed by the Supreme Court in January of 2002 (*El Mercurio* 2002).

In May 2003, the Sixth Civil Court in Santiago finally accepted the legal action brought in 1997, and nullified the EIS and the decision that had given approval for Ralco (*El Mercurio* 2003). The court ruling was based mainly on the fact that the process of the environmental impact evaluation was based on an agreement between CONAMA and ENDESA that lacked legal foundation, because at the time the agreement was signed, the legal norms regulating the system of environmental impact evaluation (Law 19.300 of 1994) had not yet come into existence (Aylwin 2003a: 1). Thus, the construction of the dam on the Bío Bío River was in fact illegal (*Mapuexpress* 2003). However, although the court nullified the authorization for Ralco, it did not order a suspension of the works on the dam. Therefore, construction (of which 82 percent was already completed), was allowed to continue. CONAMA immediately expressed their intention to appeal the court's decision. However, the parties entered into negotiations not long after the Inter-American Commission on Human Rights had accepted a legal action filed by the Pehuenche against the Chilean state (*Mapuexpress* 2003). In September 2003, an agreement was reached among the government, ENDESA, and the remaining four Pehuenche landowners refusing to exchange their lands in Upper Bío Bío (Aylwin 2003b: 1). The agreement put an end to the conflict and the Pehuenche renounced the legal actions they had filed. The agreement involved economic compensation for the Pehuenche women, terrain in exchange for the Pehuenche lands and economic contributions to indigenous development programs.

In sum, the Santiago Sixth Civil Court showed a notable willingness to acknowledge the land rights of the Pehuenche, more specifically their right not to have their lands traded. The court ordered the suspension of the construction of Ralco, and upheld its decision when CONAMA and ENDESA appealed. It was not until it reached the Court of Appeals in Santiago that the decision was reversed. The civil court further annulled the environmental authorization for Ralco, thereby declaring the illegality of the project. In the other two cases, the Santiago Court of Appeals and the Supreme Court demonstrated a reluctance to give effect to the Pehuenche's land rights claims, allowing the electricity law to take precedence over the indigenous law.

What are the reasons for the courts' reluctance to accept the land rights claims of the Pehuenche in the Ralco case and of the Mapuche people in general? Is there something specific about indigenous rights claims that provokes this lack of responsiveness on the part of the courts, or does this reflect a more general lack of responsiveness of the Chilean courts to citizens' social, economic and cultural claims? The judiciary's record with regard to some civil and political rights provides evidence that the latter might be the case. For instance, in the domain of free speech and equal protection, the response of the judiciary has been unsatisfactory, as explained by Couso:

> Even after the end of authoritarian rule, the Chilean judiciary has been remarkably passive about – if not actively contributing to – violations of those fundamental rights. Such denial of judicial redress is also apparent in what the courts have not done against statutes in blatant violation of the constitution. (Couso 2005: 121)

Couso illustrates the courts' neglect in this area with an issue treated in the previous sections of this chapter: the employment of antiterrorist legislation in the criminalization of Mapuche protest.

> Indeed, to this day the Mapuche movement – made up of members of the country's most important indigenous population – is repressed by the government with the help of antiterrorist legislation that should have been declared unconstitutional a long time ago, both because it is applied to social protest which does not amount to terrorism, and because it allows the government to violate due process guarantees. The judiciary has so far been silent on this issue." (Couso 2005: 121)

The following section of the chapter seeks to identify some of the reasons for the courts' lack of responsiveness to the Mapuches' land rights claims, as well as the reasons for why some courts are more responsive than others. According to this chapter's framework, courts' response to indigenous land rights claims is partly a function of the voicing of such claims (the first stage of the litigation process), the manner in which their concerns are articulated and the choice of legal strategy. Courts' responsiveness further depends on factors relating to the legal framework governing indigenous land rights, the legal culture, and judges' sensitivity toward human rights issues.

The Legal Framework

The insufficiencies of the legal framework for the protection of indigenous land rights, and the low status of international standards on indigenous rights, are factors that affect the voicing of indigenous land rights, but they also have an impact on courts' response to such claims. Whether a court accepts claims related to the Mapuche's land rights depends on the legal basis for their claims, including the protection of land rights in the legal framework and the status of international indigenous rights standards. In addition to the insufficiencies of the indigenous law, one must add the problems related to the application of sectoral laws in conflicts over indigenous land. In many conflicts, various concession laws are given precedence over the indigenous law, thereby restraining the effect of the latter (UDP 2003: 10).

In the Ralco case, the indigenous law turned out to be ineffective in terms of protecting the indigenous lands that were threatened by the construction of the dam. The government forced the expropriation of the Pehuenche's lands by applying the electricity law of 1981, which imposed obligations on the indigenous, without considering the regulations of the indigenous law. In the cases regarding the final electricity license for Ralco, the electricity law took precedence over the indigenous law. The electricity license severely affected the property rights of the Pehuenche litigants because it was based on the electricity law, which allowed expropriation of their lands as long as it served the purpose of providing energy for the public good (UDP 2003: 17). The case illustrates how the legal framework for the protection of indigenous rights is rendered ineffective when sectoral laws are ranked higher in the legislative hierarchy.

Sectoral laws have also taken precedence over the indigenous law in other cases related to land conflict. For the Mapuche-Lafkenche communities living on Southern Chile's coast, access to coastal resources and fisheries was restricted when vast coastal areas were registered in the name of non-indigenous persons, in conformity with the provisions of the Fisheries Act (Stavenhagen 2004: 12). Other indigenous peoples have also been affected by sectoral regulations. For instance, access to waters has become restricted for the Aymara, Quechua and Atacameño peoples because of the application of the Water Code, which takes precedence over the indigenous law and facilitates the registration of private property rights over their traditional resources (Stavenhagen 2004: 12).

However, there have been positive developments in this area. The government has recently signalled a reform in the sectoral laws that affect the interests of the indigenous peoples, in light of the ratification of ILO Convention 169 (Anaya 2009: 17, para 33). In practice, the ratification entails the obligation of Chile to reform domestic laws that are inconsistent with its provisions, in particular sectoral legislation relating to matters such as natural resources, waters and mining, among others.

Judicial Culture

Judicial culture has an impact on courts' response to efforts to judicialize Mapuche demands. The manner in which judges interpret the law is important for explaining how courts respond to legal claims, and the interpretation of law is influenced by the legal culture. Courts also interpret laws differently, which may explain why some courts are responsive to Mapuche claims while others are not. The legal culture influences judges' understanding of what is the appropriate manner to handle human rights issues, and has an impact on judges' perceptions of the justiciability of human rights norms. The willingness to apply international legal standards to judicial decisions has a positive impact on judges' responsiveness. I argue that courts are more likely to acknowledge indigenous rights and be responsive to claims related to such rights if they are generally committed to human rights. A conservative and formalistic legal culture may have a negative impact on judges' response to claims related to indigenous peoples' land rights.

The Chilean legal system has been described as a conservative system with a bias toward conservative values and interests, particularly in the area of human rights (Hilbink 2003: 87). Various studies of the Chilean legal system have documented its corporatist and formalist character.[24] The judicial system is characterized as extremely bureaucratic and hierarchically organized, a structure that contributes to preserving the traditional legal culture. Judges usually commence their career in the judicial system immediately after graduating from law school, and are slowly socialized as professionals as they work their way up the hierarchy of the court system. As the years pass, they are increasingly influenced by superior judges (Couso 2005: 122).

According to Couso, the socialization process noted here, together with the judges' isolation from other social forces, has resulted in a strong corporate identity within the judiciary (Couso 2005: 122). The superior courts' deferential attitude toward the political branches is imitated by the lower courts, so the majority of judges share the idea that the judiciary should not be involved in political debates. Morales (2003) explains how the Chilean judiciary has demonstrated an unwillingness to check the constitutionality of law. Crucial decisions have traditionally been left to political

[24] See, for instance, Vargas and Duce (2000); Morales (2003); UDP (2004).

actors, and judges have avoided adopting decisions that challenge these actors. This cautiousness has resulted in a rather scarce jurisprudence with regard to declarations of unconstitutionality.

The formalist perspective prevalent in the judicial system has been expressed by a lack of attention toward the principles of the juridical system and, particularly, fundamental rights (Morales 2003: 4). Human rights make up the core of constitutional principles, and the connection between fundamental rights and such principles is discernible in democratic regimes. However, the prevailing view in the Chilean judicial system accentuates the role of legal norms and disregards the importance of principles. Judges' decisions are exclusively based on the application of legal norms, or on the "mechanic" application of the law. Principles, on the other hand, are regarded as vague and supplementary, resorted to only in the absence of clearly applicable norms. Hence, constitutional principles have to a very limited extent been applied to the courts' decisions (Morales 2003: 4–5).

The insufficient development of constitutional principles in courts' decisions affects the courts' function to deliver information about their practices, as well as the contents of citizens' rights and how these are realized. Moreover, the lack of a significant jurisprudence negatively affects the motivation to carry out case-based research in the country's law schools (Morales 2003: 5). Morales describes the situation as a vicious circle: the lack of innovative national jurisprudence reduces the integration of new concepts and perspectives into the education in law schools, lawyers base their argumentations in court on rigid and formalist concepts taught to them in law schools, and the lack of progressive arguments by lawyers is one of the factors explaining the insufficient development of constitutional principles in courts' decisions.

The application of international human rights instruments in the Chilean justice system is another factor that might make constitutional guarantees more effective. The application of international standards on human rights introduces new elements to national law and might therefore contribute to reduce the degree of formalism. Chilean courts, however, have generally been reluctant to apply the standards contained in international instruments on human rights (Vargas and Duce 2000: 23).

Sensitization to Human Rights

How judges interpret the law depends on their sensitivity to human right issues. In this context, judges' sensitivity to the concerns of the Mapuche is crucial to how they respond to their claims. Judges' sensitivity is influenced by education and training, as well as their social and ideological background.

Ongoing training, in particular, may educate and sensitize judges toward human rights in general and indigenous rights. The Judicial Academy was established in 1995 for the purpose of creating an institution dedicated to the training of the members of the judicial branch and concerned with "the achievement and broadening of knowledge, abilities, skills, and basic criteria for the adequate exercise of the judicial function."[25] The Academy's training program (*Programa de Formación*) is directed at lawyers wishing to commence a judicial career. Candidates are trained in topics such as judicial ethics, evaluation of evidence, judicial reasoning and interpretation of the law. The Judicial Academy aims at reflecting a broad range of perspectives in its training program and has therefore incorporated a diverse group of people into its organization – judicial branch officials, academics, private-sector attorneys and professionals from other fields (Morales 2003: 11). Graduates of the academy express positive opinions about the program and consider its activities to shape legal standards and to provide them with the critical reasoning required for a judicial position (Morales 2003: 12). The academy also offers continuous training to those who are already members of the judiciary. In this it is unique in Latin America and has had a favorable response within the judiciary (Morales 2003: 13).

Judges' sensitivity to human rights is also influenced by their social background and their experience, and a court's response to indigenous rights claims thus depends on the composition of the bench. Pluralism in the legal system is critical to the ability to relate to the concerns of a broad range of various social groups. It is important that the judiciary include representatives from disadvantaged groups, such as the poor, women, and ethnic minorities, because this increases the chances of ruling fairly with regard to those groups. There is a general lack of social diversity in Latin American courts today. The representation of indigenous groups in the Chilean judicial system is practically nonexistent. In 1998, only 1 out of 188 officials at the superior levels, and 4 out of 643 officials at the lower levels, had a Mapuche surname (Correa Sutil 1999: 3). The Chilean justice system has traditionally been profoundly marked by a class bias; in fact, its judiciary has according to Gargarella been "more class biased than those of most other countries in the region" (Gargarella 2002: 11, note 11). This is relevant here because a system that is highly class biased may have implications for the responsiveness of courts to the Mapuche, who constitute one of the poorest and most marginalized groups in Chile.

The composition of the bench depends on the process and the criteria for appointing judges. The Minister of Justice is responsible for the appointment of Supreme Court justices, and selects one of the candidates off a list nominated by the Supreme Court itself. The appointment must be confirmed by a two-thirds majority in the Senate (USAID 2002: 107). Because the Supreme Court itself is responsible for generating the short list, it is in a position to select candidates with profiles similar or, for that matter, identical to that of the existing court (Vargas and Duce 2000: 9). This may contribute to strengthening conservatism because it prevents the introduction of new perspectives and values to the legal system. Lower court judges are recruited through the Judicial Academy by a process of evaluations, tests and interviews, followed by the training program described earlier, the *Programa de Formación*.

[25] See http://www.academiajudicial.cl/quienes_somos.php (May 2, 2006).

Candidates are suggested by the immediate superior tribunal in the judicial hierarchy, and the Ministry of Justice is responsible for appointing the judges (USAID 2002: 110).

In sum, the legal basis for litigating on indigenous land rights has been an important variable in explaining courts' response to Mapuche claims. In some cases sectoral laws, such as the electricity law and the water code, take precedence over the indigenous law, rendering the latter ineffective. The Santiago appeals court decision illustrates this. In addition to the nature of the law and the legal system, the legal culture is formalist and conservative. I consider this to have an impact on courts' responsiveness toward Mapuche claims, because the legal culture influences judges' perceptions of norms of appropriateness on how to handle human rights issues, and conservatism may make them less committed to human rights. Judges rarely apply international human rights standards to their decisions, and I maintain that this has a negative impact on courts' response to indigenous rights claims.

The Chilean judiciary is generally characterized by lack of diversity on the bench, in particular with respect to the representation of indigenous peoples. The system is also class biased. These factors combine to make judges less sensitive to indigenous rights issues, which in turn make courts less responsive to Mapuche claims. The selection mechanisms for lower court judges are transparent and are considered to strengthen judicial independence. The appointment procedures for Supreme Court justices, on the other hand, entail a system that allows the court to nominate candidates who have the most affinity to the existing court. This system favors conservatism, and may to some extent explain why the higher courts seem less responsive to indigenous land rights claims than the lower courts.

CONCLUDING REMARKS

The findings of this chapter lead to the conclusion that Chilean courts have not assumed an active role in defending the land rights of the Mapuche people. There are a number of reasons for this. Some of them have to do with the basis for voicing indigenous land rights claims, and others relate to the manner in which courts respond to Mapuche claims. Regarding the ability to voice one's claims, at first glance, it seems the Mapuche have a good starting point, considering some aspects – mainly related to rights awareness and associative capacity. However, the Mapuche face a number of obstacles that impede access to justice. Despite the barriers affecting the voice of the Mapuche, they have been able to bring legal actions related to their land rights. The courts responded quite differently to the Pehuenche's claims in the lawsuits brought against the Ralco project. The Santiago Sixth Civil Court acknowledged the Pehuenche's land rights, first by ordering the suspension of the construction on the dam, then by nullifying the environmental authorization for Ralco. The Court of Appeals of Santiago, on the other hand, reversed the decision to nullify the environmental authorization, and rejected both cases filed by the Pehuenche in 2000, allowing the electricity law to take precedence over the indigenous law.

Litigation has been an unsuccessful strategy in the narrow sense, because it has not been sufficient to protect the Mapuche against violations of their land rights. However, I maintain that litigation has had a positive impact as part of a broader mobilization strategy. Litigation has had the effect of stimulating social mobilization, creating awareness and legal consciousness among the Mapuche, drawing attention to the Mapuche cause from the media and human rights organizations and influencing public discourse on indigenous land rights. Thus, litigation may have an impact on policies on indigenous land rights, regardless of the outcome of a case in court. I maintain that the efforts to judicialize land rights claims have had an impact on Mapuche legal consciousness. Even though litigants may have failed to attain the desired outcome through the judicial system, the Mapuche movement has acquired a legal discourse for advancing their cause. The strengthened legal consciousness achieved through processes of litigation may in turn be a motivation for future legal actions. Hopefully, Chilean courts will be more responsive to Mapuche claims in the future, and will develop significant and progressive jurisprudence with regard to indigenous peoples' rights to lands, territories, and resources.

References

Anaya, James. 2009: "Report of the Special Rapporteur on the situation of human rights and fundamental freedoms of indigenous people. Addendum: the situation of indigenous peoples in Chile: follow-up to the recommendations made by the previous Special Rapporteur." UN Human Rights Council. http://www.unhcr.org/refworld/publisher,UNHRC, 4ae5b9f02,0.html (November 2 2009).

Anderson, Michael R. 2003. "Access to Justice and Legal Process: Making Legal Institutions Responsive to Poor People in LDCs." *IDS Working Paper*, 178. Sussex: Institute of Development Studies.

Aylwin, José. 2000. *Materializaciones y Conflictos. Aplicación de la Ley Indígena en el Territorio Mapuche*. Temuco: Institute of Indigenous Studies, University of the Frontier.

Aylwin, José. 2002. "Tierra y Territorio Mapuche: Un Anánisis desde una Perspectiva Histórico Jurídica." Paper published for the project Mapu Territorialidad. Temuco: Institute of Indigenous Studies, University of the Frontier.

Aylwin, José. 2003a. "Fallo de Sexto Juzgado Civil de Santiago confirma irregularidades en las abrobaciones de Ralco." Institute of Indigenous Studies, University of the Frontier. http://www.mapuche-nation.org/espanol/html/noticias/ntcs-63.htm (July 29, 2009).

Aylwin, José. 2003b. "Ralco: Un conflicto mal resuelto y sus lecciones." September 24. http://www.business-humanrights.org/Categories/Individualcompanies/E/Endesa?&batch_start=61 (August 3 2009).

Aylwin, José, Christian Opaso, and Elias Paillán. 2001. "Las lecciones de las represas del Alto Bío Bío para el manejo alternativo de conflictos etnoambientales." Temuco: Institute of Indigenous Studies, University of the Frontier.

COIT (Coordinación de Identidades Territoriales). 2005. *Informe: Situación de los Derechos Humanos del Pueblo Mapuche en Chile*. Report on the Human Rights Situation of the

Mapuche Community, March. http://www.mapuche.info//mapuint/coridmap050302.html (December 6 2005).

Couso, Javier. 2004. "The Politics of Judicial Review in Chile in the Era of Democratic Transition, 1990–2002." In *Democratization and the Judicary*, Siri Gloppen, Roberto Gargarella, and Elin Skaar, eds. London: Frank Cass. Chapter 5, pages 70–91.

Couso, Javier. 2005. "The Judicialization of Chilean Politics: The Rights Revolution That Never Was." In *The Judicialization of Politics in Latin America*, Rachel Sieder, Line Schjolden, and Alan Angell, eds. New York: Palgrave-Macmillan. 105–129.

Correa Sutil, Jorge. 1999. "Acceso a la Justicia y Reformas Judiciales en América Latina: Alguna Esperanza de Mayor Igualdad?" Paper presented at the Latin American seminar on constitutional and political theory (SELA, Seminario Latinoamericano de Teoría Constitucional y Política), La Serena, Chile, June 7–20. http://islandia.law.yale.edu/sela/jcorrs.pdf (May 7 2006).

Davinson, Guillermo. 2000. "La gratuidad en la atención a la población indígena: Un elemento a discutir desde la práctica." In *Derecho consuetudinario y pluralismo legal*, Milka Castro, ed. Arica: University of Chile Pages 180–190. http://www2.estudiosindigenas.cl/images/_publ/Art%20_ximena%20zedan_%201.pdf (March 11 2006).

El Mercurio. 2001a. "Fallo acepta Central Ralco." November 22, *El Mercurio*, http://mapuche.info.scorpionshops.com/fakta/merc011122.html (July 30, 2009).

El Murcurio. 2001b. "Fallo sobre Ralco." *El Mercurio*, December 17.

El Mercurio. 2002. "La Corte Suprema confirma el rechazo a los recursos interpuestos en contra de la construcción de Ralco." *El Mercurio*, January 29, http://www.derechos.org/nizkor/espana/doc/endesa/corterechaza.html (July 30, 2009).

El Mercurio. 2003. "Fallo anula permiso para construir Ralco." *El Mercurio*, May 16.

El Sur. 2000. "Endesa reanuda construcción de la Central Ralco." April 1, *El Sur*, http://www.mapuche.info/news01/dsur000401.html (July 30, 2009).

FIDH (Federación Internacional de Derechos Humanos. 2006. *La otra transición chilena: Derechos del pueblo Mapuche, política penal y protesta social en un estado democrático.* FIDH report no. 445/3, April 2006. Paris: FIDH.

GABB (Grupo de Acción por el Bío Bío). 1999a. Bío Bío al Día, no. 16, http://www.xs4all.nl/~rehue/ralco/ral054.html (July 30 2009).

GABB (Grupo de Acción por el Bío Bío). 1999b. Bio Bio al Dia, no.17, http://www.xs4all.nl/~rehue/ralco/ral055.html (July 30 2009).

GABB (Grupo de Acción por el Bío Bío). 2000. Bio Bio al Dia, no. 19, http://www.xs4all.nl/~rehue/ralco/ral059.html (July 30 2009).

Gargarella, Roberto. 2002. "'Too Far Removed from the People.' Access to Justice for the Poor: The Case of Latin America." Paper presented at the "Accountability and Responsiveness-workshop", Chr. Michelsen Institute, Bergen, Norway, November 18–19.

Gloppen, Siri. 2004. "Courts and Social Transformation: an Analytical Framework." Paper presented at "Courts and Social Transformation in New Democracies. An Institutional Voice for the Poor," Torquado de Tella University, Buenos Aires, December 2–3.

Gloppen, Siri. 2005. "Public Interest Litigation, Social Rights, and Social Policy." Paper presented to the conference on "New Frontiers of Social Policy," Arusha, Tanzania, December 12–15.

Hilbink, Lisa. 2003. "An Exception to Chilean Exceptionalism? The Historical Role of Chile's Judiciary." In *What Justice? Whose Justice? Fighting for Fairness in Latin America*, Susan Eckstein, ed. Ewing: University of California Press. 64–97.

HRW (Human Rights Watch) and IPRW (Indigenous Peoples' Rights Watch/*Observatorio de Derechos Indígenas*). 2004. *Undue Process: Terrorism Trials, Military Courts, and the Mapuche in Southern Chile*. New York/Temuco: HRW/IPRW.

Johnston, Barbara, and Terence Turner. 1998. "The Pehuenche, the World Bank Group, and ENDESA S.A.," Report of the Committee for Human Rights. Arlington: American Anthropological Association.

Lillo Vera, Rodrigo. 2002. "Conflictos Ambientales en Territorios Indígenas," http://www2.estudiosindigenas.cl/trabajados/lillo.pdf (July 30 2006).

Los Angeles Times. 2003. "Where forests are foes," March 14, *LA Times*, http://www.mapuche-nation.org/english/html/news/n-56.htm (July 30, 2009).

Mapuche Nation. 1999. "Work at Ralco suspended indefinitely," September 23, http://www.mapuche-nation.org/english/html/news/n-45.htm (July 30, 2009).

Mapuexpress. 2003. "Fallo a favor de Recurso de Nulidad contra aprobación ambiental de Ralco en 1997 (Construcciones de obras de Endesa serían ilegales)," *Mapuexpress*, May 16, http://www.mapuche.info/mapu/wallma030516.html (July 30, 2009).

McCann, Michael W. 1994. *Rights at Work: Pay Equity Reform and the Politics of Legal Mobilization*. Chicago: University of Chicago Press.

Méndez, Juan E., Guillermo O'Donnell, and Paulo S. Pinheiro. 1999. *The (Un)Rule of Law and the Underprivileged in Latin America*. Notre Dame: University of Notre Dame Press.

Morales, Felipe G. 2003. "Cultura judicial y enseñanza del derecho en Chile." Expanded version of the study "Cultura judicial y enseñanza del derecho en Chile: una aproximación," Informe de Investigación No 14, June 2003, Centre for Legal Investigations (CIJ), Diego Portales University Law School. http://www.udp.cl/derecho/derechoshumanos/publicaciones/15/laensenanzadelderecho.pdf (July 30 2009).

O'Donnell, Guillermo. 2005. "Afterword" in *The Judicialization of Politics in Latin America*, Rachel Sieder, Line Schjolden, and Alan Angell, eds. *The Judicialization of Politics in Latin America* New York: Palgrave Macmillan. Chapter 11, pages ?.

Opsvik, Tor. 1998. "Vannkraft og vanskjøtsel i Chile," *FIVASskraft*, 3:1–4.

Sieder, Rachel. 2005. "The Judiciary and Indigenous Rights in Guatemala." Paper presentedat the workshop *Courts and the Marginalized: Comparative Experiences*, 1–2 December, Diego Portales University, Santiago.

Stavenhagen, Rodolfo. 2002. "Report of the Special Rapporteur on the Situation of Human Rights and Fundamental Freedoms of Indigenous People." UN Economic and Social Council, Commission on Human Rights. http://daccess-dds-ny.un.org/doc/UNDOC/GEN/G02/106/29/PDF/G0210629.pdf?OpenElement (May 21 2009).

Stavenhagen, Rodolfo. 2004. "Report of the Special Rapporteur on the situation of human rights and fundamental freedoms of indigenous people. Addendum: mission to Chile." UN Economic and Social Council, Commission on Human Rights. http://daccess-dds-ny.un.org/doc/UNDOC/GEN/G03/170/91/PDF/G0317091.pdf?OpenElement (May 21 2009).

Tricot, Tito. 2006. "Democracia formal y derechos indígenas," *Periódico Mapuche Azkintuwe*, March 7.

UDP (Diego Portales University). 2003–5. *Derechos Humanos de los Pueblos Indígenas, Informe Anual sobre Derechos Humanos en Chile*. Annual Report on the Human Rights Situation of the Indigenous Peoples of Chile, Program of Actions of Public Interest and Human Rights at the Universidad Diego Portales, Santiago. Reports from 2003, 2004, and 2005. http://www.udp.cl/derecho/derechoshumanos/informesddhh.htm (July 30, 2009).

UDP (Diego Portales University). 2004b. *Sistema Judicial y Protección de Derechos, Informe Anual sobre Derechos Humanos en Chile.* Report on the Judicial System and the Protection of Human Rights, Program of Actions of Public Interest and Human Rights at the Universidad Diego Portales, Santiago. http://www.udp.cl/derecho/derechoshumanos/informesddhh/informe04.htm (July 30 2009).

UFRO (University of the Frontier). 2002. *Informe sobre la Situación de los Derechos del Pueblo Mapuche.* Report on the Rights Situation of the Mapuche Community. Temuco: Chile.

UNDP Chile (United Nations Development Program Chile) / UFRO (University of the Frontier. 2003. *Índice de desarrollo humano en la población Mapuche de la Araucanía.* http://www.desarrollohumano.cl/otraspub/Pub08/pub08.pdf (July 30 2009).

USAID (U.S. Agency for International Development). 2002. *Guidance for Promoting Judicial Independence and Impartiality (revised edition).* Washington: USAID Office for Democracy and Governance.

Vargas, Enrique and Mauricio Duce. 2000. "Los Obstáculos Principales a la Independencia Judicial," Report on Judicial Independence in Chile, Fundacíon para el Debido Proceso Legal (Foundation for due legal process). http://dplf.org (July 30 2009).

Others

Ley no. 19.253 sobre protección, fomento y desarrollo de los indígenas. (Law 19.253 on the protection and development of the indigenous, the Indigenous Law).

ILO (International Labour Organization): Convention (No. 169) concerning Indigenous and Tribal Peoples in Independent Countries (1989).

UN Office of the High Commissioner on Human Rights: International Covenant on Civil and Political Rights (1976).

10

Judicialization in Argentina: Legal Culture or Opportunities and Support Structures?

Catalina Smulovitz

Since 1983, Argentina has experienced a process of judicialization of conflicts and of juridification of social interactions. Why and when did people turn to the law? Are these processes associated with changes in legal culture? Are they related to modifications of the opportunity structure for rights claiming? Alternatively, are they explained by the existence of support structures for legal mobilization? This chapter will argue that judicialization in Argentina is not related to ex ante changes in legal culture, but rather to the combined effects of changes in opportunity structures for claim making and the earlier emergence of a support structure for legal mobilization consisting of labor lawyers and a new rights advocacy network of nongovernmental organizations (NGO). These two developments resulted in an increase in the judicialization of claims insofar as they transformed legal demands into a strategic political tool.

INTRODUCTION

In many parts of the world, courts and the law are playing an increasingly important political role. Courts are redefining public policies decided by representative authorities, and citizens are using the law and rights-framed discourses as political tools to address private and social demands, as well as to govern everyday social interactions previously regulated by cooperation, trust, or kinship. This increased use of legal procedures and rights-framed discourses is taking place in various forms and places and has given birth to a growing literature on the judicialization of politics.[1] Argentina is not exempt from this process. Elsewhere I have analyzed the different types of judicialization that are occurring in Argentina and the political and social consequences of this phenomenon (Smulovitz 2005). The goal of this chapter

[1] See for example McCann (1994); Tate and Vallinder (1995); Garapon (1997); Guarneri and Pederzoli (1999); Shapiro and Stone Sweet (2002).

is to analyze the causes that explain this phenomenon. However, a few preliminary comments about the different types of judicialization that take place in Argentina are in order.

As noted previously, one of the forms in which judicialization can take place involves the growing participation of bodies able to make constitutional reviews of political decisions, such as Constitutional Courts, or in other cases where there is a diffuse control of constitutionality (as in Argentina), in the greater activism of courts that questions the constitutional legitimacy of certain rules. Data regarding the evolution of judicial review by the Argentine Supreme Court show that between 1935 and 1995, the exercise of constitutional control was significant but that its frequency has decreased in the past few years. The comparison between the 1935–83 and 1984–95 periods indicates that the annual average of constitutionality reviews and norms declared unconstitutional declined in the last years of the century (Molinelli 1999; Bercholc 2004). Thus, while in comparison with other countries this particular form of judicialization remains significant in Argentina, data (see Table 10.1) show that the country does not follow the upward trend that Tate and Vallinder described for other latitudes (Tate and Vallinder 1995).

TABLE 10.1. *Constitutionality and unconstitutionality decisions 1935–1995*

Years	Total constitutional reviews	Constitutionality sentences		Unconstitutionality sentences		Annual average of unconstitutionality sentences	Annual average of constitutionality reviews
1936/1983	1,428	887	62.1%	541	37.84%	11.5	30.3
1984/1995	233	148	63.52%	85	36.48%	7.72	21.1

Source: Molinelli (1999) and Bercholc (2004).

A second type of judicialization involves the use of ordinary procedures and rights-framed discourses as political tools to address private and social demands. This type of judicialization implies that actors choose to use institutionalized procedures to "solve" not only legal disputes over established positive rights but also as a strategic tool to advance political and social goals. This type of judicialization also serves to redress certain policy outcomes and can result in political and additional legal benefits as far as it helps to legitimize and give public recognition to social and political claims. Legally framed political disputes allow claimants to incorporate other actors into conflicts and to alter the resources involved in the decision-making process. They situate judges and tribunals as legitimate parties in a given conflict and introduce legal precedents and preestablished rules as mechanisms to address political disputes. As Southworth (2000) and others have noted, courts are not the only arena in which the strategic use of legally framed political and social claims takes place. However, in this chapter I will only consider those cases that arise in this particular scenario.

The evolution of the number of cases and litigation rates are some of the indicators usually considered to evaluate this type of judicialization. Over the past few years, Argentina has witnessed an increase in the number of proceedings filed at different levels of the judiciary (see Table 10.2). Between 1993 and 2005, the total number of claims presented within the National Judiciary increased by 28 percent, the number of cases at the National Supreme Court increased by 48 percent, and the number of federal cases presented in state jurisdictions by 71 percent. Another indicator that shows the existence of this type of judicialization and that confirms the use of legal claims as a strategic political tool is the percentage of abandoned cases. The existence of a high proportion of cases abandoned before they reach sentencing can be understood as a sign that case initiation is being used to put pressure on political negotiations and to achieve extrajudicial resolutions (Hammergren 2002). This reveals that legal claims are being used to achieve results that cannot be obtained through other means. Although information regarding abandoned cases is far from exhaustive, the existing data reconfirm that, although with less intensity than in other Latin American cases, this alternative use of the courts can also be found in Argentina.

TABLE 10.2. *Case files submitted to the Supreme Court of Justice, federal courts, and state jurisdictions 1991–2005 (number of case files)*

Year	Total national judiciary	Supreme Court	Federal courts	State jurisdictions
1993	780,089	24,507	590,081	165,501
1994	1,017,941	36,657	691,155	290,129
1995	1,103,004	16,880	736,835	349,289
1996	913,395	23,519	661,172	228,704
1997	1,103,945	9,639	753,483	340,823
1998	1,004,777	7,888	719,908	276,981
1999	1,089,798	13,595	760,909	315,294
2000	1,003,781	17,290	766,685	219,806
2001	956,104	14,262	714,375	227,467
2002	1,343,275	41,860	894,490	406,925
2003	1,053,179	31,290	726,806	295,083
2004	993,889	37,559	674,492	281,838
2005	1,000,317	36,202	681,147	282,968

Source: Poder Judicial de la Nación. Corte Suprema de Justicia. *Estadísticas* 1999–2005.

Why and when did people turn to the law in Argentina? As mentioned earlier, explanatory hypotheses include cultural motivations, changes in political and legal opportunity structures, as well as the presence of a dense support structure enabling legal mobilization. The cultural explanation holds that changes in the country's legal culture that occurred after the transition to democracy in 1983 resulted in an increased use of the legal system. This hypothesis implies that the transition to democracy produced changes in citizens' perceptions about the role of the law, which in turn led to an increased use of the law. To demonstrate the cultural hypothesis, we need to establish not only that the legal culture changed, but also to demonstrate that these changes gave rise to different behaviors with regard to the law and the judicial system. Even if it is possible to indicate changes in legal culture, establishing this causal relationship between legal culture and legal behaviors is more problematic. As the literature has shown, the main challenge to the cultural argument is not so much the identification of something that can be labeled as "legal culture" or the identification of changes in the legal culture, but rather proving how those changes bring about specific behaviors.

An alternative explanation is that the judicialization process results not from changes in legal culture, but rather from changes in the opportunity structure for legal claiming. This argument assumes that certain social behavior, such as an increase in the use of the legal procedures, is related to the differential costs the institutional opportunity structure imposes on the actors' strategic choices. These opportunities can facilitate or hinder certain behaviors (Tarrow 1994).[2] Evaluations of the institutional opportunity structures affecting judicialization must consider variables such as the constitutional guarantee for individual rights (bill of rights), judicial independence, rules governing the selection and tenure of judges, and procedural rules regulating access to the courts. These variables affect the confidence litigants have in the ability of the judiciary to address their claims, the extent to which they see the legal process as a strategic resource for the achievement of goals, and the strength and height of the access thresholds to the judicial system. It is expected that highly complex procedural mechanisms, low judicial independence, and nontransparent designation and destitution procedures will be related to lower levels of judicial activity. Recent judicial reforms in Latin America concentrated on the transformation of these variables. They introduced changes to ensure less politicized mechanisms for the selection, for the promotion, and demotion of judges, they lowered access barriers and modified the legal standing of those able to initiate claims, and attempted to increase transparency by enlarging the number of actors involved in the selection of judges.

A third argument states that the increased use of legal procedures is related to the existence of support structures that democratize access to the courts (Epp 1998). Support structures are important because they allow plaintiffs to make and persist with their claims and because they provide them with specialized resources to enable access the courts. Support structures include organizations dedicated to

[2] Tarrow defines the political opportunity structure as the "consistent – but not necessarily formal, permanent, or national – signals to social or political actors which either encourage or discourage them to use their internal resources to form social movements" (1994: 54). Although in Tarrow's writing the characteristics of the political opportunity structure are intended to explain the emergence of a particular social movement, other authors have also related its features to the success or failures of their actions (see, for example, Kitschelt 1986).

litigating rights issues, willing and competent lawyers, and financial resources for legal claiming. In a classic article, Galanter (1974) argued that the "haves" enjoy more litigating resources because their repeated interventions provide them with more sophisticated knowledge of the legal processes, access to specialists, and allows them to build a "bargaining reputation." Support organizations provide individual weak legal actors with the benefits usually enjoyed by "repeat players"; that is, they provide them with specialists, a refined knowledge of the law and legal processes, and the possibility of persisting in their claims. Support structures therefore enlarge access to the courts and result in the expansion of the process of judicialization. This is related to specific political and institutional conditions, but also to the existence of specific structures that increase actors' abilities to take advantage of those conditions. Indeed, favorable settings and low institutional thresholds for legal claiming are irrelevant if potential legal actors face an unfriendly opportunity structure or if there are no agents able to take advantage of favorable opportunity structures: in such circumstances judicialization of claims will likely not occur.

JUDICIALIZATION AND LEGAL CULTURE IN ARGENTINA

As signaled in the previous section, the cultural explanation assumes that modifications in perceptions or beliefs about the intrinsic value of the law bring about changes in behavior regarding its use. Specifically, this implies that increases in positive perceptions about the performance of the judiciary will increase the use of legal procedures and lead, in turn, to an intensification of the judicialization process. This chapter does not discuss what can be identified as legal culture or whether or not a causal relationship between legal culture and legal behavior exists. It will show instead that even assuming that there is something that can be identified as legal culture and even assuming a causal relationship between culture and behavior, the Argentine case does not provide evidence of a positive relationship between perceptions and judicialization. Indeed, data for the Argentine case show that although in the last twenty years normative perceptions about the law and evaluations about performance of the judiciary have worsened, the use of legal procedures and the process of judicialization has intensified (See Table 10.3 and 10.4).

To evaluate this relationship, I draw on public opinion surveys that have assessed perceptions about the performance and credibility of the judiciary since 1983. Given the lack of systematic and historical statistics to cover the entire period under study, data are drawn from a range of different sources. In spite of the methodological problems this may involve, it should be noted that there is no other information available and that the trends shown by these pieces of information are consistent. "Confidence in the judiciary" or "prestige of the judicial institution" are the only dimensions that have been evaluated in a systematic way since 1983. For the first part of the period (1984–2001), data come from a survey conducted by "Portal de la Justicia Argentina" (Table 10.3); data for the second part (1995–2004) come from the Latinobarómetro (Table 10.4).

TABLE 10.3. *Public opinion survey about institutional prestige*

	1984	1991	1995	1999	2000	2001
Church	46%	46%	47%	60%	58%	50%
Educational institutions	54%	38%	34%	33%	50%	–
Press	45%	27%	34%	38%	42%	36%
Armed forces	19%	28%	23%	27%	34%	28%
Police	24%	26%	23%	24%	24%	17%
Congress	72%	16%	17%	11%	20%	8%
Big corporations	35%	25%	29%	26%	20%	19%
Justice	57%	26%	26%	21%	18%	12%
Public servants	49%	8%	8%	7%	14%	5%
Trade unions	30%	8%	10%	12%	11%	7%
Political parties	–	12%	9%	7%	10%	7%

Source: http://www.justiciaargentina.gov.ar/estadisticas/imag_jus.htm.

TABLE 10.4. *Confidence in the judicial system, Argentina*

	1995	1996	1997	1998	2000	2001	2002	2003	2004
High and medium confidence	33.6	23.1	20.5	19.9	27.0	20.5	8.7	16.2	26.2
None and low confidence	62.1	72.4	75.1	78.4	67.6	77.0	90.3	81.2	72.4
NS/NC	4.4	4.5	4.2	1.9	5.6	2.5	1.0	2.6	1.4

Source: Latinobarómetro.

Both data series show that "confidence in the performance of the judiciary" and "perceptions about its prestige" have declined since the return to democracy. In addition, although the Latinobarómetro shows that confidence increased a little in 2002 and 2003, levels of distrust are still extremely high. Although throughout the world, opinion polls show that confidence levels in the judiciary tend to be low, the results for Argentina are extreme.[3] Table 10.3 also indicates that confidence was relatively high at the outset of the transition process and that it nosedived at the peak of the economic and political crisis in 2002. In spite of all caveats regarding these polls, the trend is consistent and indicates that in Argentina increased resort to the courts is not related to positive changes in perceptions about the judiciary.

Table 10.5 shows that negative evaluations about performance do not match perceptions about the usefulness of legal procedures for right claiming. In 2002,

[3] Toharia, cited in Hammergren, notes that "... figures for Europe are not much better, although there is often a difference between system approval and faith in judicial integrity, with the former lower than the latter" (2002: 2).

TABLE 10.5. *Which of the following assertions is closer to your point of view? (2002)*

Assertions	Percentage
NS/NC	2.3%
It is useless to make a claim	18.8%
You have to be careful when making a claim	14.2%
Although it is useful, making claims is very expensive	25.9%
Claiming solves problems	38.8%

Source: Latinobarómetro.

64.7 percent of the population understood that legal claims could be useful, even though 25.9 percent also thought they could be expensive.

The preceding picture is disconcerting. It shows a population that distrusts the judiciary but at the same time asserts its willingness to use it. Which of these contradictory pieces of information reveal the characteristics of legal culture in Argentina? Those that systematically illustrate distrust in the judiciary? Alternatively, those that indicate that when confronted with a conflict, the population is willing to initiate a legal claim?[4] Perhaps willingness to use the judiciary, or opinions regarding its usefulness, are more adequate indicators of legal culture. However, even if that is the case, we still need to explain why opinions regarding its usefulness are apparently independent from distrust in the judicial institutions. The preceding information shows that negative perceptions about the judicial system do not explain why citizens and social actors end up using judicial procedures. In the following sections, some alternative explanations regarding the causes of judicialization in the Argentine case are considered.

OPPORTUNITY STRUCTURES AND JUDICIALIZATION IN ARGENTINA

The emergence of judicialization has also been linked to changes in the opportunity structure for legal claiming. Institutional and political opportunity structures impose differential costs on actors' strategic choices, and this in turn facilitates or hinders certain behaviors such as legal claiming. The specific institutional conditions that affect the opportunity structure include: the existence of constitutional rights guarantees, the extent of judicial independence, the degree of competitiveness of the political

4 International statistics show that polls measuring trust in judicial institutions tend to overvalue dissatisfaction with its performance. However, consistency of the negative trends, the fact that results vary throughout the period, and that polls using the same methodology show different outcomes in other countries of the region indicate that in Argentina distrust and dissatisfaction is a "hard core" perception.

system, and the barriers for access (such as mandatory legal assistance requirements, legal standing of collective associations to initiate legal actions, or to claim on diffuse interest cases).

The following paragraphs describe some of the institutional conditions present in Argentina and the changes that occurred after 1983. Although the constitution was originally promulgated in 1853, prior to 1983 the political system was characterized by constant instability. Repeated changes between authoritarian and democratic governments distinguished the first eight decades of the twentieth century, weakening not only the guarantee of the constitution itself, but also negatively affecting judicial independence. The 1983 transition inaugurated the longest and most stable democratic regime Argentina has enjoyed since independence. In 1994, a constitutional reform expanded individual and collective rights and introduced reforms in the nominations procedures for judges with the aim of increasing judicial independence. Individual and collective rights guarantees have been in place since 1983, no gross politically motivated human rights violations have occurred,[5] electoral competition has been free, and no major restrictions on free speech have been reported.

The 1994 constitutional reform established several important changes usually associated with an increase in judicialization.[6] Although the judiciary was created as a bureaucratically differentiated system in 1853, in the 1990s a number of its functions were allocated to specific institutions such as the Office of the Public Prosecutor, the Public Defender's Office, the National Ombudsman, the Magistrates Council, and the Judicial School. The 1994 reforms also gave constitutional rank to several human rights conventions[7] and incorporated collective rights such as environmental, consumer, and indigenous rights as well as protections against discrimination. The new constitution also increased the number of actors entitled to advance injunctions and authorized the ombudsman and civic associations to defend diffuse rights.[8] To promote judicial independence, the new constitution also modified the mechanisms to appoint judges and the bodies in charge of judicial review.

5 For a review of human rights violations that have taken place in democracy, see the different annual reports elaborated by the Centro de Estudios Legales y Sociales (www.cels.org.ar).

6 On the 1994 constitutional reform, see Smulovitz (1995); Negretto (1999); Sabsay (2000); Gelli (2005).

7 The 1994 constitution established in Section 75, article 22 that the following international treaties are "part of this Constitution and are to be understood as complementing the rights and guarantees recognized herein": the American Declaration of the Rights and Duties of Man; the Universal Declaration of Human Rights; the American Convention on Human Rights; the International Pact on Economic, Social, and Cultural Rights; the International Pact on Civil and Political Rights and its empowering Protocol; the Convention on the Prevention and Punishment of Genocide; the International Convention on the Elimination of all Forms of Racial Discrimination; the Convention on the Elimination of all Forms of Discrimination against Women; the Convention against Torture and other Cruel, Inhumane, or Degrading Treatments or Punishments; the Convention on the Rights of the Child. It should be also noted that, for example, the United Nations International Agreement on Economic, Social, and Cultural Rights assumes that rights might be violated by the absence of public policies.

8 See Article 43, Argentine Constitution (1995) and Saba and Bohmer (2000).

These changes modified the opportunity structure in ways that promote judicialization as far as they expanded constitutional guarantees, enlarged the number of actors entitled to advance cases, and reinforced mechanisms for strengthening judicial independence. However, legal changes by themselves did not ensure the enforcement of the new measures; indeed, since 1994, constant political battles have occurred to try and secure the guarantees set out in the reforms. For example, measures to increase judicial independence such as the creation of the National Judicial Council (Consejo Nacional de la Magistratura) took a long time to be approved and were subsequently reformed in ways that led to heated debates about new forms of political interference.[9] Indeed, one of the main issues in posttransitional political debates in Argentina has been the extent of the judiciary's independence. Judicial independence is difficult to measure and studies have been few[10]; however, surveys consistently show that the public and experts complain about the lack of external independence of the Argentine judiciary. Although as Helmke notes, opinions do not necessarily reflect the actual independence of the judiciary (2005), when actors assess whether the new opportunity structures have become a reality, the impact of this general perception cannot be underestimated. In addition, following the transition, Argentina experienced one episode of Court packing in 1990[11] and after 2003 the impeachment of two Supreme Court judges.[12] In 2003, concerns about the politicized and dependent character of judges of the Supreme Court led to the approval of presidential decree 222, which limited the president's discretion to select judges to fill Supreme Court vacancies. These self-imposed limitations included a public commitment to maintain a gender, technical, and legal expertise balance on the Court and procedural changes that included a thirty-day period for public commentary prior to the submission of the nominations.[13]

The right to advance *amparos* (injunctions)[14] is also related to the openness of the institutional opportunity structure. *Amparos* are actions that can be initiated

[9] The 1994 Constitutional Reform created the Judicial Council. The Council did not start meeting until 1999, when the legislature finally agreed on its composition. In 2006, a new law modified its initial composition.

[10] Recent studies have evaluated judicial independence by considering the number of judicial decisions against the government in the Supreme Court (Helmke 2005), using expert surveys (Kapiszewski 2006), or considering a set of variables such as the composition and stability of the Court (the appointment process, judicial tenure protection, and presidential use of court-packing) and justice voting against the executive and justice salary protection (Chavez 2004a).

[11] In 1990, Menem almost doubled the size of the Court when he expanded it from five to nine judges; see Chavez (2004b).

[12] Although the political cloud and threats from the government led to the resignation of three judges (Nazareno, Lopez, and Vazquez), when the impeachments of Judges Boggiano and Moliné O'Connor took place, they followed constitutional procedures in a legislature controlled by the governmental party.

[13] Since Decree 222 was promulgated, four vacancies were filled in the Supreme Court according to the newly established procedures. Although there are still no studies regarding the independence of the new judges, controversy about their technical merits has disappeared.

[14] See Smulovitz (1997); Sabsay (1996).

against acts or omissions by public agents that potentially or actually hurt, restrict, or threaten rights recognized by the constitution or national laws. In Argentina, *amparos* were first introduced through two Supreme Court decisions, and they were later included in two laws and in the 1994 constitution.[15] In May of 2006, the House of Representatives approved a project that intended to reform the regulation of *amparo*. The project approved by the House of Representatives established that individuals, ombudsman's offices, public prosecutors, and civil associations dedicated to the protection of human, environmental, or consumer rights were entitled to present *amparos*. Debates pitted sectors that feared an explosion of cases against others that emphasized the need to facilitate the protection of individual and collective rights and access to the judiciary. In the end, the senate did not approve the law and the project lost its parliamentary standing in August of 2008.[16] However, the extended resort to *amparos* during the crisis of 2001 and 2002 converted them into a central and accessible tool of the judicialization process (Smulovitz 2006).

In sum, since 1983 Argentina has experienced important legal modifications that have transformed the institutional opportunity structure in ways that are likely to favor judicialization. Those transformations include certainty over constitutional stability and due process, changes in procedures to increase judicial independence, and important expansions of the Bill of Rights (such as incorporation of International Conventions to the constitution and a broadening of rules of standing to claim for collective rights, habeas data, and habeas corpus). At the same time, during this period, Argentina experienced continuous political struggle to enforce those changes and persistent suspicions about the independence of judicial decisions. Disputes over enforcement of these legal transformations have had several consequences. On the one hand, they informed actors about the uncertain scope and resilience of the new opportunity structure. On the other, they "forced" actors to participate constantly in battles to ensure the enforcement of these new opportunities. Thus, uncertainty over the consolidation of the transformed opportunity structure ended up being an invitation for its judicialization. Some actors advanced claims to try to ensure the effectiveness of the new opportunities and rights, while others intervened to curtail their expansion. The new institutional opportunities have become not only a set of rules that may promote judicialization but also, in many cases, the object of judicialization. Claims regarding the constitutionality of the reforms modifying the composition of the National Judicial Council (Consejo Nacional de la Magistratura), or regarding the legitimate standing of NGOs to present claims for diffuse interests, illustrate some of the unintended consequences of this process. In spite of these caveats, at the end of the day there is no doubt that the new institutional and political opportunity structure is more permeable than the one that was in place before the

15 *Siri Case*. Fallo 239:459; *Kott Case*. Fallo 241:291; Laws 16.986 and 17.454 and Constitution 1994, article 43.

16 See http://votaciones.senado.gov.ar/web/proyectos/verExpe.php?origen=CD&tipo=PL&numexp=24/06&nro_comision=%tConsulta=2 (July 31, 2009).

transition to democracy. Yet this increased permeability does not necessarily translate into effective enforcement.

SUPPORT STRUCTURES AND JUDICIALIZATION IN ARGENTINA

Support structures encompass rights advocacy organizations and lawyers, as well as availability of financing sources or free legal services. According to Charles Epp (1998: 18–19), support structures are important insofar as they enable widespread and sustained litigation by weak or powerless actors and because they provide these actors with resources such as technical capacities, time for rights claiming, bargaining reputation, and experience. To evaluate their impact in the case of Argentina, this section considers the nature of the support structure prior to 1983, and the ways in which changes in the support structure since 1983 relate to increased use of the courts.

My argument regarding the construction of the support structure in Argentina is as follows: the expansion in the number of lawyers[17] at the outset of the twentieth century and the changes in labor legislation in the 1940s and 1950s created a supply of legal professionals willing to address nontraditional conflicts, increased the demand of lawyers specialized in labor disputes, and put a new public in contact with them. When political conditions deteriorated in the 1960s and 1970s, the novel legal needs of their previous clients favored the adjustment of the skills of some of these lawyers. History forced their transformation into civil liberties lawyers and changes in macropolitical circumstances (dictatorship and transition) led lawyers and plaintiffs to explore new uses of the law. If law was previously viewed as a defensive tool for protection against unfavorable circumstances, after the transition, law became a tool for advancing social and political demands. In turn, rights advocacy lawyers and victims created not only rights advocacy organizations but also sought financial resources to sustain and expand their actions.

At the outset of the twentieth century, most of the legal profession performed traditional roles.[18] In the 1930s, the increase in the number of lawyers led to changes in the social background of the members of the legal profession and adverse political conditions gave way to their involvement in the defense of political and social prisoners and to the organization of different support associations. The expansion of university enrollment resulted in the emergence of a significant segment of middle-class lawyers that was not part of the traditional social networks of the profession. Their political and professional exclusion led them to search for alternative arenas and ways to exercise their professional skills.[19] These alternative spaces and

[17] See Leiva (2005: 287–9); Verchioli (2006: 68).

[18] The section draws on Verchioli (2006), Schjolden (2005), Saldivia (2002), Carnovale (2009), Chama (2003) and Meili (1998).

[19] In 1917, for example, these new lawyers together with law students created a free legal service in the University (Consultorio Jurídico Gratuito). Verchioli (2006: 78).

activities included the legal defense of political and social prisoners, participation as legal representatives of trade unions, and the creation of several civil associations, such as Liga Argentina por los Derechos del Hombre (LADH), Comité de Ayuda Antifascista, and Comité Pro-Amnistía por los Exiliados y Presos Políticos de América. These activities allowed "outsiders" to exercise the profession and to bypass the obstacles imposed by their lack of social links with the more traditional sectors of the profession.[20] These activities created new venues for professional insertion and the development of specialized legal skills. At the same time, intervention in these arenas put lawyers in contact with trade unions and with a new public.[21] Their activities involved denunciation of public liberties violations, claims for damages related to the transformation of labor conditions, participation in the design of new labor laws, legal representation of workers and trade unions, and the creation of specialized university courses and journals. Insofar as involvement in the world of labor invariably included attending to the repression of political and social activists, lawyers ended up being gradually introduced into other fields of the practice of law. Thus, the exercise of the legal profession unexpectedly transformed them into early advocates of "the rights of man."

In the 1940s, with the triumph of Peronism, trade union membership expanded and the regulation of employment conditions enlarged the supply of lawyers specialized in labor matters and the demand for their skills by workers and trade unions. The creation of a mass of lawyers with expertise in labor issues also enabled the establishment of a privileged relationship between sectors of the legal profession and a public of social activists and potential plaintiffs. When in the 1950s and again in the 1970s political conditions changed and adversely affected workers, trade unionists, political activists, and common citizens, those victimized resorted to the legal professionals they knew. Whereas in the past they had requested their expertise to remedy damages related to labor disputes, they now demanded their skills to confront challenges associated with forced disappearance and illegal imprisonment. Plaintiffs appealed to the lawyers they had met in their previous encounters with the law and lawyers specialized in labor matters adjusted their skills to the new demands of their clients. "La Forza del Destino" facilitated the encounter and transformed them into civil liberties lawyers. Once this transformation took place, other related changes came about.

[20] Juan Atilio Bramuglia was an honorary member of the Argentine Labor Confederation (Confederación Obrera Argentina), of the General Confederation of Labor (CGT), and legal representative of the Telecommunication Workers' Union (Unión Telefónica), of the Transportation Union (Unión Tranviarios) and of the Railroad Union (Unión Ferroviaria). Another lawyer, Nicolás Solito, was a member of the central committee of the Railroad Union and of the Social Pension Institute (Cámara Gremial del Instituto Nacional de Previsión Social) (Verchioli 2006: 83).

[21] As Line Schjolden has shown, at the outset of the twentieth century, workers started to use the courts in an attempt to redress grievances with their employers on an individual level. Schjolden also notes that "throughout the first forty years of the twentieth century, judges. . . . occupied a central position as professionals in the resolution of the social question" (2005: 273).

In the late 1960s, lawyers defending social and political prisoners created a series of professional associations, including the Asociación Gremial de Abogados de Buenos Aires, the Asociación Gremial de Abogados de Mar del Plata, the Asociación Gremial de Abogados de Bahía Blanca,[22] and the Comisión de Familiares de Presos Políticos y Gremiales (CoFaDe). Virginia Verchioli has shown that lawyers' involvement in these associations was in many cases the result of their previous activities as labor lawyers. Her study shows that not all of them became human rights lawyers because of ex ante ideological commitments and that it was their previous participation as labor lawyers that brought about their gradual involvement in the political defense of some of their former clients who had become political prisoners. Verchioli (2006); Carnevale (2009), Saldivia (2002), and Chama (2003) all confirm that a significant number of these lawyers had previous experience as legal representatives of trade unions. Some had been members of the legal staff of the Argentine General Workers' Confederation (CGT, a militant and opposition workers union created in 1968). Others such as Rodolfo Ortega Peña and Eduardo Luis Duhalde had been lawyers of the powerful Union of Metal Workers. Analysis of their trajectories shows that it was their role as defenders of trade unionists under dictatorship that transformed them into civil and human rights lawyers.[23]

Participation in the "Gremial de Abogados" was an important learning experience for the future establishment of a professional support structure. Junior lawyers learnt from senior ones with whom they collaborated, created associations, established free legal clinics in slums and working-class neighborhoods, and developed publications to advise on and promote the use of the law by poor populations. In some cases, the relationship between lawyers and their defendants led to the lawyer's involvement with the political goals of their clients. In others, lawyers were careful to differentiate their ideological stance from their professional activities. The human rights rhetoric that started to frame their interventions became a strategic tool to preserve their role as defenders of constitutional rights and to question the repressive activities of the state.

In the late 1970s, new human rights organizations were created because of massive forced disappearances.[24] Some of them were formed by relatives of victims and

[22] Data regarding the number of lawyers that participated in the Gremial vary according to source: in Saldivia's study, one of the lawyers that participated in the Gremial mentions the figure of 130 (Saldivia 2002: 14), but in her dissertation Verchioli mentions that in 1972, 250 lawyers came to the first national Congress organized by the Gremial (2006: 196).

[23] When these lawyers started to file habeas corpus on behalf of their clients, they were also incarcerated. At a certain point, forty of these trade union lawyers were detained in the same prison. This episode is usually mentioned as a turning point in the organization of their association (Verchioli 2006: 150).

[24] Some of the human rights organizations created in this period include: Madres de Plaza de Mayo (1979), Familiares de Detenidos y Desaparecidos por Razones Políticas (1977), Abuelas de Plaza de Mayo (1977), Servicio de Paz y Justicia (1974), Movimiento Ecuménico de Derechos Humanos (1976), and Centro de Estudios Legales y Sociales (1979). The Liga Argentina por los Derechos del Hombre was created in 1937.

by lawyers with previous social involvement, including the Comisión Argentina de Derechos Humanos (CADHU), the Asamblea Permanente por los Derechos Humanos (APDH), and the Centro de Estudios Legales y Sociales (CELS).[25] The "de facto" specialization of lawyers in human rights issues that had taken place in previous periods started to become more systematic, and these lawyers began to be recognized as professional "human rights experts." The strategies they developed during those formative years indicate that their public role was redefined: they became both legal experts and legal militants. Lawyers participating in these associations understood they had to use the loopholes of existing laws to achieve advantages in their claims against the dictatorial government. Whereas lawyers belonging to APDH favored filing collective claims, lawyers associated with CELS preferred to present paradigmatic cases that could have jurisprudential consequences and potentially multiplying legal effects. One by-product of their activities was the intensification of international connections with other lawyers and transnational organizations, and the creation of a new and ideologically diversified cohort of young professional lawyers that became "human rights" experts.

Thus, when the transition to democracy took place in 1983, a new cohort of lawyers and associations were in place. Their previous professional practice had showed them that they could use the law to achieve political and social transformation. In the new political circumstances, they started to use their acquired professional and expert skills to strengthen the democratic institutions, expand the rights agenda, and promote the enforcement of rights. Signal events such as the trial of the Junta Commanders in 1985[26] not only revealed a judiciary that could discipline the powerful and defend the rights of the weak but also showed that the law could become an institutional mechanism for the resolution of other types of disputes. After the 1994 constitutional reform modified the resources available for the promotion of rights,

[25] The Comisión Argentina de Derechos Humanos (CADHU) (1973–83) was mainly integrated by lawyers who had been part of the Peronist Lawyer Association and by members of the Asociación Gremial de Abogados de Buenos Aires. The Asamblea Permanente por los Derechos Humanos (APDH), created in 1975, was formed by leaders of political parties and lawyers. Many of its lawyers had participated in the Liga por los Derechos del Hombre as defenders of political prisoners. Relatives of victims subsequently joined the organization. The Centro de Estudios Legales y Sociales (CELS), created in 1978, was formed by relatives of the disappeared. Most of its members were also lawyers. Its activities included documentation of state terrorism and provision of legal counseling and assistance to the victims' relatives, especially in the case of the disappeared. Since the democratic transition, CELS' activities have expanded to include other areas for legal intervention, such as social, women, and environmental rights.

[26] In 1985, members of the four military Juntas that ruled Argentina between 1976 and 1983 were tried for gross violations of human rights. As a consequence of this trial, former military President Jorge Videla and ex-Commander in Chief of the Navy Admiral E. Massera were given life sentences, ex-President E. Viola was given seventeen years in prison, and the Junta members for the Navy and Air Force, Admirals Lambruschini and Brigadier Agosti, were given eight years and three years and nine months, respectively. Members of the fourth Junta were acquitted because the Court considered that evidence against them was insufficient and inconclusive. See Acuña and Smulovitz (1997).

human rights lawyers started a process of conversion to becoming public interest lawyers. Although most of them did not abandon their previous engagement with human rights issues, many of them – and most of the existing advocacy associations – expanded the range of topics addressed and started to include other matters, such as minority, social, and environmental rights.

This brief historical reconstruction signals the process that led to the emergence of a supply of advocacy lawyers and organizations. Although the information to trace the evolution and magnitude of their universe is still unsystematic, this reconstruction indicates that by 1983 a supply of specialized cause lawyers had been in the making for some time. They had experience in adjusting their trade to different social and political challenges and they had already met some of their potential clients in their previous interactions with labor law.

Other more recent and scattered pieces of information reconfirm the trends outlined here. A recent study about rights advocacy NGOs in Argentina[27] shows that 15 percent of them were created before the transition to democracy, 40 percent between 1983 and 2000, and the rest after the political and economic crisis of 2001.[28] Information regarding the number of users of free legal services is also incomplete; however, these are now provided by an increasing number of public agencies, lawyers' councils, and universities.[29] In addition, several universities have

[27] See Smulovitz and Urribarri (2006).

[28] The survey identified the following rights advocacy organizations: ADC; ACIJ; CEDHA; CEJIL; CELS; INECIP; AAPS; ARGENJUS; Biosfera; CIPPEC; Conciencia; Ejercicio Ciudadano; FORES; Fundación Ambiente y Recursos Naturales; Fundación Atlas; Fundación Cambio Democrático; Fundación Contemporánea; Fundación El Otro; Fundación Nueva Generación Argentina; Fundación Vida Silvestre; Greenpeace; Habitat y Desarrollo; Ideas; IIED-AL; Instituto Social y Político de la Mujer; OIKOS; Poder ciudadano; Proteger. Some of these, such as COFAVI, have branches in more than one city in Argentina.

[29] The following agencies and universities provide free legal services: Defensoría de Pobres y Ausentes en lo Civil y Comercial, Defensoría General de la Nación; Defensoría Contencioso Administrativa de la Ciudad Autónoma de Buenos Aires; Centro de Formación Profesional de la Facultad de Derecho y Ciencias Sociales de la UBA; Colegio Público de Abogados de la Capital Federal; Programa Asistir del Ministerio de Trabajo; División Jurídica Asistencial de la Procuración General de la Ciudad de Buenos Aires; Consejo de los Derechos de Niñas, Niños y Adolescentes del Gobierno de la Ciudad de Buenos Aires; Dirección General de la Mujer del Gobierno de la Ciudad de Buenos Aires; Asociación de Abogados de Buenos Aires; Centro de Formación Profesional de la Facultad de Derecho de la Universidad de Belgrano; Fundación Ambiente y Recursos Naturales – Programa Control Ciudadano del Medio Ambiente; Fundación Poder Ciudadano; Fundación Sur Argentina; Red Argentina de Asistencia Legal y Social; Oficina de Asistencia Integral a la Víctima de la Procuración General de la Nación; Centros del Plan Social de Asistencia Jurídica a la Comunidad del Ministerio de Justicia; Dirección General de Atención y Asistencia a la Víctima Subsecretaría de Derechos Humanos; COPINE – Gobierno de la Ciudad de Buenos Aires; Consejo Nacional de Niñez, Adolescencia y Familia; centro de Información Social, Asesoría Legal Popular (C.I.S.A.L.P.); Defensoría del Pueblo de la Ciudad de Buenos Aires; Ministerio de Trabajo Asesoramiento Gratuito; Subsecretaría de Derechos Humanos del Gobierno de la Ciudad de Buenos Aires; INADI – Instituto Nacional contra la Discriminación; Defensor del Pueblo de la Nación – Lic. Eduardo Mondino.

established free legal clinics.[30] For example, a recent study of free legal services in the city of Buenos Aires showed that the number of claims dealt with by the Women's Municipal Office grew from 10,984 in 1995 to 39,874 in 1999.[31]

After the transition, financial resources for advocacy NGOs and for the promotion of access to justice policies have been supported by private and public international donors such as the USAID, the Ford Foundation, the Open Society, the National Endowment for Democracy, and the British Council. In 1983, the Ford Foundation defined two major priorities for its grants in the South American region: promotion of civil and political liberties and access to social justice and legal services. Their goal was to strengthen the ability of local, nonpartisan human rights organizations to investigate, document, and publicize human rights abuses and to promote rights awareness among disenfranchised groups. Frühling signals that the Foundation's human rights program had two additional aspects. First, it awarded grants "to research centers, universities, and bar associations not previously involved with these issues" and, second, it promoted the inclusion of research and actions on topics related to institutional violence, administration of justice, and with a new range of nonpolitically motivated rights violations (Frühling 2000: 67). Different sources agree that financial support to the associations that promoted the use of public interest litigation was critical for the development of legal strategies as a political tool.[32] Since then, advocacy lawyers and organizations have participated in the legal reform of institutions, such as the nomination process of Supreme Court, and have advanced public interest claims that include poverty discrimination cases against public bureaucracies, environmental claims against private and public enterprises, and claims arising from violations in the provision of health services.[33]

Although the creation of rights advocacy organizations and lawyers intensified after 1983, as indicated here advocacy lawyers and organizations have been in the making in Argentina since the beginning of the twentieth century. Thus, the growth in the numbers of advocacy organizations and lawyers cannot be seen simply as the result of the transplantation of legal agendas and procedures in the posttransition. A preexisting number of organizations and a dense network of lawyers with expertise and experience in dealing with political and social claims were critical for the development and success of the advocacy organizations created in the wake of

30 Free legal clinics have been established at Universidad de Buenos Aires (UBA), Universidad de Palermo (UP), Universidad Torcuato Di Tella, Universidad Nacional de Tucumán, Universidad Nacional del Comahue, Universidad Nacional de Córdoba, and Universidad Nacional de La Plata. The UBA and UP clinics work jointly with CELS and ADC.

31 Defensoría del Pueblo de la Ciudad de Buenos Aires. *Servicios de Patrocinio y Asesoramiento Jurídico Gratuito en la Ciudad de Buenos Aires*.(n/d). For information regarding the free legal clinic at Universidad de Buenos Aires, see Scioscioli (2005).

32 See Sikkink (1996: 67) and Sikkink and Keck (1998: 97–102).

33 For an illustration of the claims filed by these different advocacy organizations, see www.adc.org.ar; www.acij.org.ar; and www.cels.org.ar.

the dictatorship. New organizations expanded the legal agenda and tactics and took advantage of the expertise, experience, and international exposure that had been achieved by a preexisting network of lawyers. While innovation allowed them to adjust their agenda to the challenges of the new democratic scenario, a preexisting network of advocacy and labor lawyers gave them access to two invaluable social resources: expertise and experience. In addition, although it is unlikely that they could have survived without international funding, it is also true that international donors achieved the expected results because a supply of actors with skills and abilities were already in place. The previous existence of a supply of labor lawyers had another consequence for the construction of a network of right advocacy organizations and lawyers: it allowed claimants to get in touch and become acquainted with the workings of the law and lawyers. In those previous encounters, claimants were introduced to the instrumental capabilities of the law and exposed to the crafts of lawyers. Thus, when the transition took place and the institutional opportunity structure became friendlier, social actors and individual citizens already knew that these lawyers could behave as legal entrepreneurs for their causes.

In conclusion, the confluence of these variables – favorable institutional opportunities, supply of cause lawyers, and experience in the instrumental abilities of the law – rather than ex ante changes in perceptions about the normative value of the law, encouraged contemporary processes of judicialization. Regardless of the perceptions actors had about the normative value of the law, these variables allowed them to use legal tools as an instrument to intervene in a diverse and ever-wider spectrum of political and social struggles.

CONCLUSION

This chapter has argued that, at least in the Argentine case, changes in legal culture do not explain the emergence of judicialization. Although opinion polls show that perceptions about the performance of the judiciary and judges are negative, the number of claims and topics brought before the courts has continued to increase. To explain the incongruence between perceptions about performance of the judiciary and behavior regarding the courts, this chapter has explored the impact of two other variables: institutional opportunity structures for legal claiming and the existence of a legal support structure.

With regard to the institutional opportunity structure, it has shown that since 1983, Argentina has experienced important legal modifications usually associated with the promotion of judicialization. These transformations include greater constitutional stability and due process, changes in the procedures to ensure greater judicial independence and important expansions of the bill of rights (including the incorporation of International Conventions to the constitution and widening of rules of standing for collective rights, habeas data, and habeas corpus). However, the political battles fought to achieve these changes, combined with continuing uncertainties about the consolidation of these new institutional opportunity structures, became an unexpected invitation for judicialization. The new institutional opportunities became, in effect, a set of rules that promoted judicialization and in many cases they also became the object of judicialization.

This chapter has also pointed to the historical and sociological dimensions of the formation of a legal support structure in Argentina. I have argued that the early expansion in the number of lawyers and in the regulation of labor relationships created a supply of available professionals, a demand for lawyers specialized in labor disputes, and also familiarized a new public with the workings and potentialities of the law. Subsequently under military dictatorship, victims resorted to the legal professionals they knew, and lawyers adjusted their skills to the new legal needs of their clients. Political circumstances transformed some of them into civil liberties lawyers and in the process, claimants and lawyers created associations for protecting and petitioning rights. By 1983, a supply of specialized cause lawyers, advocacy organizations, and an audience with experience with the law were in place. Lawyers again adjusted their trade to new social and political challenges, and their clients were already familiar with the instrumental capabilities of the law. In the posttransition period, lawyers used their acquired skills to expand the rights agenda and promote the enforcement of rights. Their previous professional practice encouraged them to use the law to advance political and social transformation. Clients and new advocacy organizations used the newly discovered strategic tool of the law to make political and social demands, resist the enforcement of certain policies, and extend the domain of law into social practices still governed by informal mechanisms. Social actors and individual citizens could count on an established supply of specialized lawyers with experience to behave as legal entrepreneurs for their causes. The confluence of these variables – institutional opportunities, a supply of cause lawyers, and experience in the instrumental abilities of the law – explains the contemporary process of judicialization in Argentina.

References

Acuña, Carlos and Smulovitz, Catalina. 1997. "Guarding the Guardians in Argentina: Some Lessons about the Risks and Benefits of Empowering the Courts." In *Transitional Justice and the Rule of Law in New Democracies*. James McAdams (ed.). Notre Dame: University of Notre Dame Press, pp. 93–122.

Argentine Constitution. 1995. Accessed at http://www1.hcdn.gov.ar/dependencias/dip/congreso/Constitucion%20sola.pdf.

Bercholc, Jorge. 2004. *La independencia de la Corte suprema a través del control de Constitucionalidad. Respecto de los otros poderes políticos del Estado (1935–1998)*. Buenos Aires, Ediar.

Carnovale, Vera. 2009. Memoria Abierta, Colección *Abogados, Derecho y Política*. Buenos Aires: MIMEO: unpublished working paper.

Chama, Mauricio. 2003. "Movilización y politización: los abogados de Buenos Aires, 1968–1973." Accessed at http://historiapolitica.com/datos/biblioteca/Chama.pdf.

Chavez, Rebecca Bill. 2004a. *The Rule of Law in Nascent Democracies*. Stanford: Stanford University Press.
Chavez, Rebecca Bill. 2004b. "The Evolution of Judicial Autonomy in Argentina: Establishing the Rule of Law in an Ultrapresidential System." *Journal of Latin American Studies* 36: 451–478.
Epp, Charles. 1998. *The Rights Revolution*. Chicago: The University of Chicago Press.
Frühling, Hugo. 2000. "From Dictatorship to Democracy: Law and Social Change in the Andean Region and the Southern Cone of South America." In *Many Roads to Justice: The Law-Related Work of Ford Foundation Grantees Around the World*. McClymont, Mary and Stephen Golub (eds.). New York: Ford Foundation, pp. 55–88.
Galanter, Marc. 1974. "Why the 'Haves' Come Out Ahead: Speculations on the Limits of Legal Change." 9 *Law & Soc'y Rev*. 95: 108–11.
Garapon, Antoine. 1997. *Juez y Democracia*. Madrid: Flor del Viento Ediciones.
Gelli, María Angélica. 2005. *Constitución de la Nación Argentina Comentada y Concordada*. Buenos Aires: Editorial La Ley.
Guarneri, Carlo and Patrizia Pederzoli. 1999. *Los Jueces y la Política. Poder Judicial y Democracia*, Madrid: Taurus.
Hammergren, Lynn. 2002. "Uses Of Empirical Research in Refocusing Judicial Reforms: Lessons from Five Countries." Washington DC: World Bank. Available at http://www.argenjus.org.ar/argenjus/articulos/leen.pdf.
Helmke, Gretchen. 2005. *Courts Under Constraints: Judges, Generals, and Presidents in Argentina*. New York: Cambridge University Press.
Kapiszewski, Diana. 2006. "La Corte Suprema y la Política Constitucional en la Argentina Post-Menem." *Revista Jurídica de la Universidad de Palermo*, Año 7, Número 1 Julio: 5–46.
Kitschelt, Herbert. January 1986. "Political Opportunity Structures and Political Protest: Anti-Nuclear Movements in Four Democracies." *British Journal of Political Science*, 16(1): 57–85.
Leiva, Alberto. 2005. *Historia del Foro de Buenos Aires. La Tarea de Pedir Justicia durante los Siglos XVIII a XX*. Buenos Aires: Ad-Hoc.
McCann, Michael. 1994. *Rights at Work: Pay Equity Reform and the Politics of Legal Mobilization*. Chicago: The University of Chicago Press.
Meili, Stephen. 1998. "Cause Lawyers and Social Movements: A Comparative Perspective on Democratic Change in Argentina and Brazil." In *Cause Lawyering: Political Commitments and Professional Responsabilities*, Sarat Austin and Sturart Scheingold eds. New York: Oxford University Press, pp. 487–522.
Molinelli, Guillermo. 1999. "La Corte Suprema de Justicia de la Nación frente a los poderes políticos a través del control de Constitucionalidad, 1983–98." MIMEO: unpublished working paper.
Negretto, Gabriel. 1999. "Constitution-Making and Institutional Design: The Transformations of Presidentialism in Argentina." *Archives Européennes de Sociologie*, Vol. XL, No 2, Fall 1999, pp. 193–233.
Saba, Roberto and Bohmer, Martín. 2000. "*Participación Ciudadana en Argentina: Estrategias para el efectivo ejercicio de los derechos*," accessed at http://www.abogadosvoluntarios.net/contenido.asp?idcontenido/225.
Sabsay, Daniel. 1996. "El amparo como garantía para la defensa de los derechos fundamentales," *Revista Jurídica del Centro de Estudiantes de la Facultad de Derecho y Ciencias Sociales de la Universidad de Buenos Aires*. 6: 28–34.
Sabsay, Daniel. 2000. *La Constitución de los Argentinos*. Buenos Aires: ERREPAR.

Saldivia, Laura. 2002. "Derechos Humanos y Derecho de Interés Público en Argentina: ¿Quiebre o Continuidad?" Buenos Aires: Documento de Trabajo. Programa de Derecho de Interés Público. Law Faculty, Universidad de Palermo.

Schjolden, Line. 2005. *Suing for Justice: Labor and the Courts in Argentina, 1900–1943*. Ph.D. Dissertation, University of California, Berkeley.

Scioscioli, Sebastián. 2005. *"Acceso a la Justicia para Todos." Encrucijadas*, 39: 64–6. Buenos Aires: Universidad de Buenos Aires.

Shapiro, Martin and Alec Stone Sweet. 2002. *On Law, Politics, and Judicialization*. Oxford: Oxford University Press.

Sikkink Kathryn. 1996. "The Emergence, Evolution, and Effectiveness of the Latin American Human Rights Network." In *Constructing Democracy: Human Rights, Citizenship, and Society in Latin America*. E. Jelin and Eric Hershberg (ed.). Boulder, CO: Westview Press, pp. 59–84.

Sikkink, Kathryn and Margaret Keck. 1998. *Activist Beyond Borders*. Ithaca, NY: Cornell University Press.

Smulovitz, Catalina. 1995. "Constitución y Poder Judicial en la Nueva Democracia Argentina. La Experiencia de las Instituciones." In *La Nueva Matriz Política Argentina*, Carlos Acuña (comp.). Buenos Aires: Nueva Visión, p. 71–114.

Smulovitz, Catalina. 1997. "Ciudadanos, Derechos y Política." In *Las Acciones de Interés Público. Argentina, Chile, Colombia y Perú*. Gonzalez Morales, Felipe (ed.), Santiago de Chile: Escuela de Derecho. Universidad Diego Portales. Serie Publicaciones Especiales No. 7: 407–38.

Smulovitz, Catalina. 2005. "Petitioning and Creating Rights: Judicialization in Argentina." In *The Judicialization of Politics in Latin America*, Sieder, Rachel, Alan Angell, and Line Schjolden (eds.). New York: Palgrave Macmillan, pp. 161–81.

Smulovitz, Catalina. 2006. "Judicialization of Protest in Argentina. The case of 'corralito'" In *Enforcing the Rule of Law: Citizens and the Media in Latin America*. Peruzzotti, Enrique and Catalina Smulovitz (eds.). Pittsburgh: Pittsburgh University Press, pp. 55–74.

Smulovitz, Catalina and Urribarri Daniela. 2006. *"Organizaciones Sociales e Incidencia en Políticas Públicas: Actores y Contexto en el Caso Argentino."* Accessed at http://new.lasociedadcivil.org/docs/ciberteca/incidencia_argentina.pdf.

Southworth, Anne. 2000. "The Rights Revolution and Support Structures for Rights Advocacy." *Law and Society Review*, 34(4): 1203–19.

Tarrow, Sydney. 1994. *Power in Movement: Collective Action, Social Movements, and Politics*. New York: Cambridge University Press.

Tate, Neal and Torbjorn Vallinder (eds.). 1995. *The Global Expansion of Judicial Power*. New York: New York University Press.

Toharia, Jose Juan. 2003. "Assessing a Judiciary's Performance Through Public Opinion." In *Beyond Common Knowledge: Empirical Approaches to the Rule of Law*, Erik Jensen and Thomas Heller, eds. Stanford, California: Stanford University Press.

Verchioli, Virginia. 2006. "A Luta Pelo Direito," Engajamento Miliante E Profissionalizacao Dos Advogados Na Causa Pelos Direitos Humanos Na Argentina. Doctoral Thesis. Universidade Federal do Rio de Janeiro.

11

Novel Appropriations of the Law in the Pursuit of Political and Social Change in Latin America

Pilar Domingo

INTRODUCTION

The purpose in this chapter is to develop a framework of analysis to advance our understanding of the processes that have led to the adoption of novel legal strategies by a variety of social and political actors in recent Latin American politics, as well as to examine the changing political narratives around rights and the rule of law that have accompanied these new strategies. The emphasis is on tracking what appear to be new forms of judicial activism, legal mobilization and what have been called "rights revolutions" in the region, and doing so from the broader perspective of legal culture and beyond the confines of the formal legal institutions or the courtroom.

Bearing in mind the diversity of experiences in Latin America, the emphasis of the chapter is on societies that share some of the following characteristics: where regime transition is relatively recent and brings with it a variety of political experiences connected to the struggle to redress human rights abuses of the past (with varying levels of effectiveness); where the notions of rule of law and rights-based democracy remain weak projects in reality, but have acquired greater discursive projection than at any other time of constitutional and state-building endeavors in the region; and (in some cases) where legal pluralism has acquired to varying degrees a prominent political face.[1] These are processes that to all appearances coincide with and are causally connected to new forms and greater levels of judicial activism, or judicialization of political and social conflict.[2]

[1] I will also refer to cases that fall outside these limits in order to illustrate the points made throughout the chapter. Although the emphasis in the main is on countries that share the features mentioned, there are some interesting "judicializing" experiences taking place in some countries that do not. An example is Costa Rica, which has had no recent transition, is relatively culturally homogenous, and is free of transitional justice dilemmas.

[2] Scholarship on judicial politics and judicialization in Latin America has blossomed in the last fifteen years. See, among others, Sieder et al. (2005); Gloppen et al. (2004); Pasara (2004); Prillaman (2000); Taylor (2008); Chavez (2004); Hilbink (2007); Helmke (2005); Rios-Figueroa and Taylor (2006);

The analytical perspective of legal culture, as outlined by Couso, Huneeus, and Sieder in this volume, allows us to address the complex interface between legal institutions and broader attitudes and beliefs about the law, legality, and law-like discourses (such as rights discourses).The chapter looks at the intersection between: legal culture and judicialization processes through the prism of changing narratives around rights; citizenship and rule of law; new forms of legal mobilization; and recent institutional developments that are affecting how judiciaries respond to, promote (say, through judicial activism) or resist legal action based on rights claims. It is the complex interaction between these processes that this volume endeavors to capture in the different chapters. Added to this, as Couso, Huneeus, and Sieder (Chapter 1) indicate, Santos's (2002) analysis of multiple or plural socio-legal spheres coexisting within the same space (reflecting personal, local or community, national, and global systems of rules) with different degrees of compatibility or tension, but that are deeply interconnected, is an especially useful perspective for understanding the political role of law and shifting attitudes toward the law in contemporary Latin America. It allows for a more nuanced understanding of the layers of rules and norms that shape the political and social fabric of societies characterized by social, cultural, and/or ethnic differences (although this is quite variable), as well as by political histories of poorly embedded state formation. Moreover, it allows for a better reading of the connection of these rules and norms to different constellations of power structures.

It is the relational and changing dynamics of the different layers of legal culture, loci of norm production and judicial developments that are important in advancing our understanding of processes of judicialization of politics and the implications for redefining (or sedimenting) structures of political and social power. Changes in legal culture and attitudes toward the law and legality are processes that are historically, culturally and politically situated. By identifying the processes behind shifts in legal culture we can advance our understanding of how norms and value systems are renegotiated and redefined over time. The concern of this chapter is to reflect on what these legal transformations look like in Latin America and the political implications that they have. Specifically, it maps out changing political narratives and symbolic representations about citizenship, rights and rule of law in connection to new trends in judicial activism and legal mobilization. Essentially, the social and political dynamics analyzed here speak of multiple layers of legal understandings and norm production that surface outside the state and state law. Recent trends in Latin America concerning the politicization of legal pluralism around community justice systems and indigenous rights in connection to transformative narratives of

Domingo (2004); Gargarella et al. (2006); Gauri and Brinks (2008); Brinks (2008). On the bottom-up processes of mobilization around rights and accountability, see, for instance, essays in Tulchin and Ruthenberg (2006); Peruzzoti and Smulovitz (2006); Molyneux and Lazar (1999); Santos and Rodriguez-Garavito (2005).

citizenship and state society relations are an example of this. Rights revolutions are examples of such processes of change. Rights battles are essentially about struggles over the distribution of power and social transformation. They mirror normative (and changing) aspirations of what society should look like. They are historically situated and are constantly open to redefinition and renegotiation. Rights battles reflect the shifting balance of political and social forces, and they can be more or less violent, or more or less channeled through state institutions, such as courts (Epp 1998). However, transformations of legal forms and legal languages, and the prominence of these, also take place at other levels and in different spaces. The discursive and symbolic dimension, say, of rights revolutions, while indeed connected to what is happening in the formal legal sphere, speaks to other levels of shifting values and beliefs regarding social, political, and economic power relations.

Over the last few decades in Latin America, more visibly so than at any other time in the region's political development, allusions to the concepts of "rights," "rule of law" and "citizenship" have become relatively prominent features of the legitimation currency across a broad range of social and political actors. What is interesting is that these terms constitute political narratives that are being appropriated by very diverse actors in not dissimilar ways, but in fact are likely to have very different meanings within the same national context. Thus, they remain inevitably deeply contested concepts, and often they reflect opposing political aspirations in what are, to varying degrees, heterogeneous and culturally diverse societies.The recent discursive prominence of these concepts coincides with, and is causally linked to parallel processes of state-building and institutional reform – including widespread judicial reform in the context of the global agenda of *good governance* (and variations on the theme). Thus, changing social perceptions about rights, legal forms, and the usefulness of legal mobilization strategies from below are interacting at the same time with top-down processes of institutional change.

What follows is less about engaging with the theoretical issues outlined here and more about mapping the social, political, and institutional processes that might amount to novel appropriations of the language of law and legality by different actors in politically instrumental ways in Latin America. So what constitutes judicialization from this broader perspective of changes in legal culture? The following features, none of which are either necessary or exhaustive components of judicialization, serve by way of a preliminary description of the phenomenon under observation, and may in different ways be causally connected (here the specific national experiences vary enormously).

First, legal representations may acquire greater symbolic prominence at the level of ideas and at the level of practice of political and social engagement. Second, this reflects changes in legal culture and attitudes about law and legality, and the usefulness of legal forms, which may prompt instrumental forms of legal mobilization to advance particular interests. Third, constitutional changes, such as the revision of bills of rights, may prompt this kind of subjective alterations in attitudes toward legal forms. Fourth, institutional change, such as judicial reform, may create new opportunity structures for new forms of legal mobilization from below. New forms of judicial activism within the courts (whatever the cause of this – judicial reform from above, or legal mobilization from below) may contribute to generating a greater public prominence of legal forms. Finally, we may see new legitimation discourses (both from above and within grassroots movements) framed in legally rooted language – such as that of rights, promoting a culture of rule of law and legal accountability. These kinds of alterations may be nationally located (but may respond also to global processes of legal globalization in a variety of ways) and promoted by very diverse actors.

It is important to stress that in the endeavor to observe the changing role of law and legal discourses in political and social life in Latin America by no means do I suggest that the law, legality, and legal forms have necessarily become the main form of political and social exchange either strategically or symbolically. It is not the case that the law is everywhere, nor that political and social mobilization in the region is even predominantly structured around this. The premise is much more modest, but I think true: legal representations have become more frequently resorted to in instrumental ways by a wide range of actors who in the past either were not prominent in the political and social landscape (judges and litigating lawyers), or tended to use other strategies and languages that were not framed in terms of rights or rule of law (social movements and subaltern actors) to advance particular social and political causes.

To the extent that the chapter addresses whether this contributes to processes of social transformation, or the emancipatory potential of rights and legal mobilization overall, it takes as given that this is a piecemeal process at best. Nonetheless, important changes have taken place that have shifted some important normative premises and symbolic representations regarding law and legality, citizenship and rights, which may have a lasting effect on power structures – and their redefinition. Indeed, in some cases – for instance, recently in Bolivia, albeit still with very uncertain consequences – the political enthusiasm around foundational experiences of constitution writing in any event reflects a deep confidence in the empowering, and even revolutionary, potential of legal change led by grassroots movements.

In the following section I identify three clusters of processes that constitute the judicialization of social and political life that we are witnessing in the region– notwithstanding the enormous variations between (and within) countries in terms of how these are playing out. First, I consider the impact of the power of ideas, which in the current wave of democratization includes as never before emerging narratives around rights, due process, accountable government and rule of law, and how these ideas connect to discourses of legitimation and empowerment. Second, I stress the multiactor dimension of these processes that both drives and, in turn, is driven by the process of juridification. Third, I distinguish the institutional processes of change that are afoot and the institutional spaces within which judicialization processes are playing out. Here, in some cases judicial and related reforms have created opportunity structures that facilitate new forms of legal voice and new spaces for rights claims to be articulated.

JUDICIALIZATION, RULE OF LAW AND THE DEVELOPMENT OF *RIGHTS REVOLUTIONS* IN LATIN AMERICA

So what does the process of judicialization look like to the extent that it is taking place in Latin America? The three clusters of processes developed below can help us work out the different pieces of the puzzle. Crucially, it is the interaction between the three that lies behind the changes in legal culture and judicial politics.

The Power of Ideas

Locating the process of judicialization within the realm of ideas allows us to think about how normative shifts are articulated in connection to our perceptions about legality and law. The power of ideas can, under certain conditions, be a force of change. However, this is historically situated. Moreover, the process by which different social groups or political actors appropriate discourse and ideas in itself inevitably involves transforming and adapting their meaning and representation to reflect specific power struggles and aspirations of social transformation.

With regard to contemporary political development in Latin America, three interconnected sets of ideas have achieved prominence in the language and design of political projects and social aspirations and stand out as dominant and recurrent themes in the phenomenon of judicialization: rights, rule of law, and legal accountability. These are, in turn, inextricably tied to how current political projects in Latin America, whether they be top-down or subaltern manifestations of political struggle, either (a) legitimate their strategies; (b) define, voice, and publicly defend their interests and demands; (c) articulate their claims through law and legal forms; or (d) seek to limit and check holders of public office in their exercise of power.

If we look first at the question of rights, it is no coincidence that their growing visibility is taking place at the pinnacle of the era of human rights, namely, the end of the Cold War period and the third wave of global democratization. Human rights and universal rights-based conceptions of democracy have come to the fore in the legitimation discourse of modern states in the last sixty years, but more explicitly so in the last wave of democratization.

This is particularly the case in Latin America where already earlier cycles of political liberalization, in terms of constitutional development, reflected a classical (and at times especially precocious) incorporation and expansion of modern notions of citizenship rights following the traditional "Marshallian" sequence of civil, political, social and economic rights and, more recently, community rights.[3] Mexican constitutional history is an example of liberal modernity on paper, for instance in the 1857 constitutional Bill of Rights, and social modernity in the revolutionary constitution of 1917, which represents the first truly social constitution of the twentieth century with the incorporation of social and economic entitlements – well ahead of European social democracies. Significantly, revolutionary forces reshaped the rules of the game to bring the oligarchic order to an end. However, the reality on the ground of the social contract in Mexico has been far removed from the citizenship rights promises of both texts.

Thus, on paper and in the intellectual history of the region, the language of rights is built on a rooted tradition of modern constitution writing. However, constitutional projects were generally interspersed with cycles of authoritarian rule that undermined any possibility of the spirit of limited government taking root. Moreover, rule of law, rights, and law-bound government had gained little substantive prominence in terms of the texture of citizenship and of state and society relations for the majority of the population. Rather, state-building projects since independence and the terms of political engagement tended to revolve around other issues of political legitimation that had to do first with order (nineteenth century especially), and later on, with distributive battles fought in the language of social distributive populism (early twentieth century).[4]

The evolution of the constitutional contents of rights has generally not accurately reflected either the real quality of citizenship or the dominant normative aspirations of previous cycles of state-building. The old oligarchic structures – even when they engaged in modernizing forms of liberal nineteenth-century constitutionalism – overall sought to sidestep the expansion of rights and political participation. As economic liberalism unraveled in the first decades of last century, the reformist (populist) political projects of the 1930s–50s were captured overall by corporatist structures of authority, albeit containing socially progressive agendas of more inclusive nation- and state-building and expanded notions of citizenship rights. However, the political order save in a few cases (for instance, Chile and Uruguay) was not settled generally around the establishment of democratic forms of rights-based citizenship. Political and civil rights remained precarious well into the 1980s – civil rights are still precarious – and social and economic rights were the domain of top-down corporatist structures of patronage and clientelism to varying degrees. Significantly, it was not until the 1990s that cultural and legal pluralism featured in any of the debates on constitutional rights. In addition, rule of law, as a principle of accountability and

3 See Adelman and Centeno (2002); O'Donnell (2004); chapters in Tulchin and Ruthenberg (2006); Whitehead (1994); and Wright-Carozza (2003) for discussions on the quality of citizenship and the normative features of the history state-building projects in the region.

4 See Sabato (2001) for a discussion on historiographical trends regarding bottom-up uses of discourses of citizenship in the nineteenth century.

government bound by law, remained fundamentally underdeveloped in the logic of the exercise of political power.

Thus, the evolution of constitutional projects of nation-building (which were mostly top-down processes) bore little relation to the real nature of social and political power structures in postcolonial Latin America. (It is important to stress the different national experiences in this regard.) It was perhaps only with the third wave of democratization that the language of rights and rule of law began to acquire a more pervasive presence not only in the political legitimation discourse from above, but in the imaginings of entitlements from below as rights-based democratic citizenship began to acquire an unprecedented symbolic presence in contemporary public debate.

Before looking more closely at how this has been playing out, there are two points to be made about the strength of the idea of rights as an important normative and symbolic factor that influences how attitudes about law and legality (and legitimacy) are shaped in society. First is the formidable (and in the twentieth and twenty-first centuries it seems unparalleled) moral force of the human rights discourse as a source of legitimation for political projects and social struggles, at the global, national, and community level that has especially become present in the post-Cold War era. That this observation is not new does not diminish its important. This force gives rights discourses tremendous political value as a legitimating discourse behind which political struggles of social transformation may be appealingly articulated. Second, the logic of rights discourses inherently carries with it the empowering and emancipatory potential of the idea of rights, however these are defined. Rights are about entitlements to lead a life of dignity. They also represent the possibility of self-realization for the citizens who become active rights bearers and champions of rights battles – which are empowering processes in themselves.

The relationship between human rights discourses and the development of specific national democratic citizenship rights (on paper and at the level of "imagined communities") is complex but inextricably tight; both are constantly shifting in terms of the ascendancy – or decline – of different types of rights and meanings of rights, in relation to how political and social power battles evolve, and how state society relations unfold. The different national narratives of rights in Latin America in recent decades have played out against a shifting and complex relationship between the global discourses of human rights, the specific trajectories of democratization and the emergence of aspirations to rights-based notions of citizenship from below at the domestic level. But what rights are we talking about? And what are the projects of citizenship that are emerging? Let us briefly unpack some of these narratives of rights, to see how they have evolved and how they are being redefined and appropriated by a very diverse range of social and political actors.

First, the question of human rights made its first public appearance in a meaningful way in the context of the dilemmas around transitional justice. In most cases, the transition moment included, to begin with, an assumption that impunity in exchange for a peaceful process of democratization was necessary or inevitable. In Uruguay this was legitimated through a referendum vote in which just over half the population voted for not prosecuting human rights violations. In other cases of top-down controlled political liberalization, as in Chile, impunity was effectively imposed from above – at least for a while. In Argentina, the activism of an organized movement from below, led by the Madres de la Plaza de Mayo and supported by a web of human rights organizations, achieved a first round of indictments of military officers in the first years of civilian rule in the 1980s.[5] Although these officers would be pardoned under the Menem presidency in the 1990s, the Argentine breakthough left a legacy of bottom-up legal mobilization that has had region-wide consequences in terms of later rounds of posttransitional justice. By the end of the 1990s, new cases were being taken to the courts. Overall, the experience of transitional justice has varied enormously throughout the region. Nonetheless, it has proved to be an ongoing and recurrent feature of political life, even in countries where it had been thought that the criminals would get away with it (as in Chile), and has left an indelible mark on the rights discourse. The ethical dimension of the issues at stake in the question of transitional justice not only has not gone away but has seemingly acquired an enduring and, indeed growing, moral presence in subsequent political debate. Moreover, the local, national and international dimensions throughout the region have undergone seismic shifts in terms of jurisprudence and the political and symbolic gains in the name of righting the wrongs of human rights violations of the past – despite the shortcomings and the ongoing sense of impunity in many cases. Pinochet's arrest in London in 1998, the resulting developments in international jurisprudence on the principle of universal jurisdiction for certain types of crimes and the subsequent unfolding (and, indeed, almost routinization) of criminal investigations and indictments in Chile of hundreds of individuals responsible for gross human rights during the dictatorship is a particularly telling example of transitional justice on the move (Collins 2008). More recently, the televised trial of Fujimori in Peru had a tremendously cathartic and pedagogic impact on Peruvian society that – whatever else happens in the Peruvian political landscape – represented a landmark event that is likely to affect public imaginaries about accountability and the rule of law (Burt and Youngers 2008).

In some respects, the issue of transitional justice is now more visible on the political agenda in ways that were not obvious fifteen years ago. This has an impact on the nature of political narratives around rights, rule of law and the definition of citizenship, whether these come from the political elites or are generated at the grassroots level. Transitional justice battles, even when they have not been won, have engendered new perceptions about notions of entitlement with regard to state – society relations. Moreover, they have produced specific learning processes among

[5] See Barahona de Brito et al. (2001); Roniger and Snjazder (1999); and Roht-Arriaza and Mariezcurrena (2006), among others.

the advocacy and human rights NGO community regarding how to engage in legal battles on rights issues at the local, domestic and international levels. In addition, these struggles have not been only about judicial victories but also about establishing symbolic gains and winning on the ethical front (Smulovitz 2005). The importance of the experience of transitional justice cannot be underestimated in terms of its contribution to reshaping attitudes toward the rule of law and the possible benefits of legal mobilization (Smulovitz 2002).

Second, the symbolic and normative link between democracy and rights-based citizenship seems to be more visible. This varies enormously in the region. It is truer for Argentina than Mexico, and extremely precarious in Guatemala. This is somewhat linked to the activation of the *garantiste* aspects of constitutionalism in Latin America, at least at a discursive level – and it is also connected to the rights narratives being pushed by the transitional justice processes. In the early stages of the transitions to democracy, a prevalent concern was about securing political rights and cleaning up the process of electoral competition. The advances in this respect have been formidable – the United States would have much to learn from many Latin American countries about electoral probity and clean competition. Over time, concerns with other dimensions of citizenship rights have become more vocal, in part under the leadership of a growing community of human rights NGOs, and, in some cases, because of the expansion of rights through constitutional reform processes (Brazil in 1988 and Colombia in 1991 are ready examples). Increasingly, more *garantiste* aspects of constitutional democracy have come to the foreground of rights narratives. Questions about civil liberties, freedom of the press, and due process in criminal justice are more visible in the public debate. This in part has driven the wave of criminal justice reforms aimed at replacing investigative systems with accusatorial systems that are more propitious for due process and for securing the rights of the accused (Duce and Perez-Perdomo 2003). At the same time, as Brinks's (2008) telling study of Argentina, Brazil and Uruguay shows, the change on the ground remains extremely patchy and uneven. Especially as far as criminal justice and policing are concerned, impunity, corruption and the "unrule" of law continue to prevail, and systemic disregard for civil liberties correlates strongly with high levels of inequality.

Nonetheless, what has gained normative strength is the notion of empowerment through rights.[6] Over time, what has emerged is the discovery of the citizen as the moral centerpiece of any political (and indeed developmental) project, at least in discursive terms both among the political science community of transitions scholars

6 The transitions literature was initially loathe to engage with the messy notion of more substantive questions about rights. More recently, the studies on the quality of democracy, (notably spurred on by O'Donnell 1993 and 2004), have acknowledged the defects of more minimalist understandings of democracy as an analytical tool by which to observe the features of political development in the region.

(with greater or lesser enthusiasm) and the community of practitioners who have not been successful in consolidating their political projects on the strength of electoral reform alone (important as this has been).

Moreover, the top-down incorporation of notions of rights-based citizenship into political discourses has also been facilitated by emerging patterns of social and legal mobilization from below, pressing for rights claims to be part of the political agenda, or for concrete rights conflicts to be resolved. These include such disparate examples as the U'wa community's legal and transnationalized battle with the petroleum company Oxy over territorial rights in Colombia (Rodriguez-Garavito and Arenas 2005); the rights claims by savers in Argentina around the *corralito* (restrictions on withdrawals of bank deposits) government decision following the financial crisis in 2001 (Smulovitz 2005); and in Bolivia the social mobilization in Cochabamba in 2000 around the right to water, where the main battlefield was the street rather than the courtroom, but the discourse was around entitlements. This enthusiasm with rights discourses must be seen against the backdrop of very diverse – and potentially conflicting – understandings and symbolic meanings about what they entail. Moreover, mobilizational strategies from below are not limited to the courtroom but to varying degrees combine with other forms of protest politics.

A third area of rights narrative that is also contributing to shaping contemporary imaginings about citizenship, legality and state–society relations is connected to the political struggles around notions of cultural difference, indigenous rights and legal pluralism in some countries in the region. An important normative shift in the language and public debate around rights was the acceptance of the principle of difference as the product of two global but also locally specific struggles: gender politics and indigenous rights movements. While these have become powerful normative claims, the debate regarding universalism versus the principle of difference is still playing out in the complex quest to reconcile what are two potentially conflicting perspectives. For instance, the politics of indigenous rights is taking different forms throughout the region. Important changes have already been assimilated through widespread (but differentiated) constitutional reform in the 1990s in recognition of indigenous rights and legal pluralism.[7] Regardless of how these issues evolve and are politically resolved in the end, since the 1990s there has been a region-wide movement toward engaging with claims for the recognition and formalization of legal pluralism. This is proving to be important in terms of how different legal spaces and understandings of law and norm production are being negotiated in the wake of political victories by subaltern projects, such as that of the socialist and indigenous movement *Movimiento al Socialismo* (MAS) in Bolivia led by the indigenous and *cocalero* (coca-leaf producer) leader Evo Morales, who won the presidential elections in 2005 and in 2009. Here the constituent process of 2006 included an attempt

[7] The politicization of indigenous claims and legal pluralism are discussed in the essays in Sieder (2002a); Yashar (2005); Assies et al. (1999); and Van Cott (2000).

at redefining the relationship between different juridical orders: the formal and the customary.

At the judicial level, the Colombian constitutional tribunal has been especially innovative in rulings regarding the relationship between customary law and other jurisdictional authorities, giving primacy to the former as in the Whip case in 1997 (Cepeda Espinosa 2005). I do not wish to linger on the complexities of how constitutionalized legal pluralism is unfolding but merely want to point out the novel political and public visibility of this struggle and the normative shifts that have been obtained, discursively, symbolically, politically, and institutionally by what are still in the main marginalized sectors of society.

An important factor in enhancing the legal and political voice of indigenous movements has been the interaction between local and global processes of mobilization around indigenous rights (Sieder 2002b). Convention 169 of the International Labour Organization (ILO) was crucial in opening up political space for the discussion about multiculturalism, indigenous rights and nonstate legal systems. This combined with the cycle of democratization to interact with local processes of indigenous mobilization with varying degrees of political impact regarding how legal pluralism could be politically negotiated as part of a reconceptualization of state–society relations, legal space and legal authority.

The experience of the Bolivian constituent assembly (2006–8), as a political space within which legal pluralism could be negotiated and emerge as a truly innovative basis for state–society relations in a culturally diverse context, is an especially interesting example of the appropriation and redefinition of a rights narrative to achieve radical social change. It remains to be seen what the long-term political outcome of the new constitutional text passed in 2009 will be in Bolivia, given the high levels of conflict that enveloped the constituent process and the ongoing rejection by the opposition forces of the MAS constitutional project for a "plurinational" state. The new constitution recognizes the multicultural, or "plurinational," nature of Bolivian society. The novelty, in contrast to the milder multicultural constitutionalism of the 1990s, lies in that it establishes equal rank between state and nonstate law (community justice systems), while both remain subordinate to the rights and principles of the new constitution. The interface between different legal spheres, in principle, will be negotiated through ongoing intercultural dialogue. These are early days and there is as yet little clarity about what this will look like in reality (Domingo 2009).

A fourth set of ideas about rights has emerged from within the community of development economists and practitioners through the notion of human development and related concepts of agency through rights. Human development is enabled through citizens who have the capability for self-realization and agency, and this in turn relies on the possibility of active rights-based citizenship. The intellectual leadership of Amartya Sen has been important in linking development to rights.[8] In addition,

[8] Sen (2000); Molyneux and Lazar (1999); O'Donnell (2004).

rights-based citizenship is taken to encompass a broad array of rights, including social and economic rights, as essential requirements and entitlements for basic human dignity and for taking control of one's life. Rights, then, are imagined not only as aspirational ends but also as necessary means to achieve human development through the enhancement of agency. In this regard, social and economic rights have acquired a new discursive presence, which is in varying degrees also translating into new patterns of legal mobilization from below.[9]

Thus, the idea of rights has gained strength within the legal culture of much of the region. At the same time, though, this convergent and recurrent appeal to the language of rights by no means suggests the emergence of consensual and shared understandings of what citizenship should entail. There does indeed appear to be a novel normative enthusiasm with the notion of rights-based citizenship as a democratizing and emancipatory concept shared by a variety of social actors, but this should not obscure the fact that understandings and symbolic meanings of rights and citizenship are diverse in what are not only societies of extreme social and economic inequalities but also of plural cultures.

Alongside the idea of rights, but which has developed separately and more closely linked to the international agenda of good governance that emerged in the 1990s, was the preoccupation with the idea of the rule of law. Related to this was the concern with improving mechanisms of "accountability" regarding the exercise of public office. Rule of law and accountability became popular buzzwords in the language of state reform in its different dimensions and incarnations.

The ideas driving the rule of law agenda were in part related to notions of rights, but in the earlier days were more about legal security, law-bound government and improving the administration of justice in a formal sense. They sometimes addressed issues of access to justice, also often in connection with improving the conditions for foreign investment and the development of market economies.[10] Increasingly, the concern with accountability has permeated more visibly the rule of law agenda. Of note here is the way in which the idea and discourse of rule of law promotion has become a pervasive element in the legitimation discourse of political elites. Rarely do electoral campaigns fail to allude to a strong commitment to strengthening the rule of law – in all its variants.

Accountability alludes to different levels of state and society relations. It involves the principles of answerability (framed within legal and ethical measures of expected good conduct) and enforceability (effectiveness of decisions to do with checks and balance and capacity of oversight bodies to be heeded). Accountability is a term that has been appropriated, as in the case of rights, by different actors and different interests. Frequently categorized along the three dimensions of horizontal, vertical and social, it has become a cornerstone of good governance and the principle and

9 Gargarella, Domingo, and Roux (2006); Gauri and Brinks (2008); Langford (2009).

10 Carothers (2001); Faundez (1997, 2005); Dezalay and Garth (2002b), among others.

corresponding mechanisms by which government and public office can be held to account according to specific legally and constitutionally defined standards. The concern with accountability has been taken up by the community of rule of law promoters (academic and practitioners), and anticorruption champions. Overall, the emphasis has been to render more robust the mechanisms of institutional oversight and judicial review.[11]

In terms of the appropriation of legal strategies as a form of empowerment from below through the voicing of rights claims, or denouncing wrongdoing by public authorities and thus activating the appropriate judicial investigation, the scholarly contributions by Peruzzotti and Smulovitz (2006) on the study of social forms of accountability significantly advance our knowledge of how attitudes toward legal forms and the instrumental use of law have been redefined in some important respects at the level of society.[12] Here the emphasis, perhaps more than on enforceability, is on answerability and often more at the ethical, denunciatory and reputational level than at the level of concrete courtroom successes and actual convictions of wrongdoers. Nonetheless, the media airing of corruption scandals or rights conflicts, whether they are staged in a courtroom or not, may have a knock-on effect on how attitudes toward the law and legality are unfolding. However, to the extent that patterns of impunity persist over time,incipient faith in narratives of rule of law and accountability (if not in judicial institutions themselves that continue to be poorly viewed) are likely to weaken.

Thus, ideas about rights, rule of law and accountability have permeated the language of politics and legal mobilization, albeit in diverse and complex ways and with different meanings and symbolic representations about the law, legal forms and understandings of social justice. Tracing the genealogy of how ideas about law, legality and legally rooted discourses are shaped and used within state and society contributes to our mapping of processes of judicialization. Here we have visited some novel ways in which ideational discourses and perceptions about rights and rule of law are texturing attitudes toward the law and legality. We must also ask who is using this legalistic language and resorting to legal forms, to what purpose and what this tells us about judicialization. In connection to this, to what extent are these actors being driven by the ideational trends discussed earlier in their appropriation of legal forms? To what extent are they in fact generating new ideas about norms and legal truths (whether these are formally articulated or not)? And to what extent are they constrained by the structural, institutional and global context within which they are operating? These are important research questions that should be the subject of further inquiry.

The following section unpacks the different actors involved in new forms of judicialization.

11 See essays in Mainwaring and Welna (2004); Maravall and Przeworski (2003); Schedler et al. (1999).

12 Smulovitz and Peruzzotti (2003); Peruzzotti and Smulovitz (2006); Smulovitz (2002).

Multiactor Nature of Judicialization Processes

Identifying the multiactor nature of judicialization allows us to map the different levels at which changes in legal culture are taking place and with what consequences for the different social actors and legal spaces involved.

Here I identify four types of actors. At one level, judicialization processes in the region in the last twenty years have been the fruit of developments within the broad family of civil society, grassroots social movements and NGO activism, both locally and globally situated in relation to the instrumental use of law. Typically – but not exclusively – these processes have been led by human rights and victims' associations in the wake of transitional justice struggles. Second, I briefly review the development of legal strategies and changing attitudes toward the law at the level of political elites and top-down manifestations of state-building projects. One example is the way in which competing political parties (as in Mexico) are increasingly using the courts to exercise political oversight over each other, especially in connection to electoral disputes (Berruecos 2001). Third, there is the community of legal professionals, namely, judges and the formal legal community more broadly speaking, which now has greater political and public visibility than in the past. Finally, at the international level, the donor community's support for good governance and rule of law promotion, and the work of international human rights activists and organizations, has considerably contributed to the process of judicialization. The boundaries among these different communities and interests are by no means always clearly delineated, and there is considerable overlap between some of these actors.

The point here is that in different ways and at different levels we can observe novel forms of appropriation of legal strategies and legally rooted discourses to advance specific normative goals, and political and ideological agendas, some of which are at odds with one another in many respects, while others coalesce to a considerable extent. In some respects, it is perhaps even possible to speak of a historically unprecedented convergence of an unlikely coalition of interests between traditional political opponents in the history of many of these countries. The confluence from different political, ideological, and cultural perspectives toward a seemingly relatively common language of rights, rule of law and accountability and commensurate recourse to apparently similar forms of engagement with the rules of political and social interaction – and the law – is relatively unprecedented in much of the region (with some notable exceptions – Chile, pre-1973, or Costa Rica, for instance).

At the same time, though, this convergence of rights-based discourse and legal mobilization strategies should not obscure the different political agendas they represent and the diversity of aspirations regarding alternative views about the ordering of social, political and economic life that they stand for (albeit in complex, sometimes overlapping, sometimes contradictory ways). What is noteworthy, in this process of judicialization of social and political conflict, is that similar legal structures and narratives are being appropriated in not dissimilar ways to serve very different interests and agendas, and, in some cases, to attempt to redefine the rules of the game from different political and normative premises. For instance, the expansion of constitutional review in Chile in 2005 was intended as a progressive move. However, it opened up the possibility for the conservative sectors of Chilean society to mobilize legally to achieve a constitutional review ruling in 2008 against the "morning-after-pill." (Couso and Hilbink 2009).

On the one hand, a broad family of civil society associations, social movements and rights-related NGOs have deployed, over the last two decades, an array of legal mobilization strategies, which developed a range of legally rooted discourses around which to articulate and voice concrete claims of justice and social reform. The first wave of this activity occurred with regard to human rights and victims organizations, such as the Mothers (*Madres*) and Grandmothers (*Abuelas*) of the Plaza de Mayo in Argentina, deploying a range of legal and nonlegal strategies to secure some degree of transitional justice, either through the courts or through different exercises in truth-telling, historic memory and public denunciation in connection to human rights abuses committed under authoritarian rule. The experience in this field of rights advocacy led to an ongoing commitment by human rights activists, and a transfer of their accumulated legal expertise and knowledge to other forms of human rights abuses, now taking place under democratic rule. Human rights NGOs have developed, moreover, transnational advocacy networks that worked beyond national boundaries.[13] The *Centro de Estudios Legales y Sociales* (CELS, Centre for Legal and Social Studies) in Argentina is an especially telling example of an advocacy and human rights organization that has put its accumulated experience and legal expertise, originally focused on transitional justice issues, to the service of other rights claims and emerging legal debates around judicial politics and rights battles.

The neoliberal public policy orientation of the 1980s and 1990s paradoxically through a decentring of the state led to the discovery of civil society and the activation of civil society associative capacity in response to these policies. In some cases, this bred novel forms of legal mobilization and social accountability at the grassroots level driven by the language of rights, rule of law and social accountability. I have already made mention of the U'wa case in Colombia and the savers' claims in the *corralito* case in Argentina. To this we can add the Barzon debtors' movement in Mexico, which in a similar spirit mobilized legally against what were seen to be illegal hikes in interest payments following the 1994 financial crisis (Domingo 2005). The adoption of legal mobilization strategies or rights languages as a mobilizing instrument has taken many forms in recent decades throughout the region among traditionally subaltern actors. Legal strategies may be neither a prominent feature of their mobilization arsenal nor especially successful in the courts, but political and social struggles from below now, more so than at any other time, seem to be framed explicitly in the language of rights.

13 Keck and Sikkink (1998); Sikkink (2002 and 2005).

Now civil society is made up of highly disparate forms of associative social actors (NGOs, various types of associative organizations, community-based social movements, etc.). It is a contested and disperse concept in terms of the range of interests it covers, the types of voice it includes and the strategies it deploys. Moreover, civil society (in its different guises) by no means necessarily reproduces practices of social conduct conducive to representative, deliberative, participative – or even law-abiding – modes of democratic conduct. The point here is about how novel forms of engagement with the law and legal instruments are emerging from different social spaces to contest particular areas of power relations.

The novelty lies first in the recourse to legal mobilization strategies to pursue goals of social transformation or in defense of particular interests. Here the instrumental value of resorting to the law is not always about obtaining judicial victories in the court, but rather about channeling specific demands into the public sphere through acts of legal mobilization to render them visible, thereby activating public debate on previously ignored issues (Smulovitz 2005). Second, framing claims that voice aspirations of social transformation in the language of rights has the possible advantage of bestowing the legitimate power of legal voice upon the political struggle at hand (in contrast to other, perhaps more radical, strategies that may not have proved successful in the past). Finally, there is a sense that the very process of appropriation of the language of rights in itself constitutes an act of empowerment and political participation.

To the degree that the community of human rights NGOs and the transnational network of advocacy activists have become established, it is possible to observe a degree of normalization and routinization of the recourse to legal mobilization from below.[14] Overall, though, it is important not to overstate the scale of change in terms of rights revolutions and legal mobilization strategies from below that this represents. These phenomena are now visible perhaps in ways that are unprecedented in the history of subaltern political struggles in the region. Even so, judicialization has neither fundamentally altered the rules of political and social engagement, nor necessarily delivered the goods effectively in terms of the substantive aspirations of social transformation behind these struggles. Nonetheless, even piecemeal victories can make a difference to the interested parties.

New forms of engagement with the discourse of rule of law and legality have also taken place within the political elites and related top-down projects of state reform. To some extent, this reflects a conjunctural engagement with the remit of the good governance agenda by governing coalitions of political forces. However, it also reflects recourse to a legitimation strategy in the face of regionwide deficits in the political credibility of more traditional forms of political representation (political parties and parliaments) in liberal democratic structures that were weakly embedded

[14] This is true for instance of Argentina through the work of such organizations as CELS, which has successfully orchestrated a wide range of legal mobilization strategies to secure a number of legal battles before the courts from below and also at the level of the Inter-American Court of Justice.

in society. Top-down and elite recourse to the language of legality, and even to attempts at rule of law reform, may well have originated in systemic crises of regime legitimacy. The juridification consequences of these processes can be found in the repetitive allusion in public debate to the need to strengthen rule of law, limited government and democratic rights. Of note is that this narrative occurs very similarly across the ideological spectrum. For instance, forty years ago the political left and grassroots movements in Latin America were in the main not interested in the law or training in law. Rather, what abounded in the left were sociologists and development economists. Now there is a new drive for activists of the left to train in law in order to be well equipped for contemporary political engagement in which constitutional reform features strongly, and the political impact of judicial activism is more prominent (Couso 2005a). On the right, the discourse of economic liberalism has included allusions to the merits of legal security and predictability, the rule of law in the market and the imperative of protecting property rights.

Changes in the community of legal professionals (judges and lawyers) have also contributed to processes of judicialization of politics. Judicial activism is more visible now than at any other time in the region's political history, and this reflects how judges and the legal community have adapted to a changing environment of the new rule of law discourse. In some countries judges are also rethinking their role in society as a result of the combined processes of democratization, rule of law reform (discussed next), changing societal expectations about judicial processes and the ideational shifts described earlier. This, in turn, may be manifested through increased judicial activism.

There is a need for further research on these changes in the legal culture of the justice community, and we also need to develop a clearer understanding of the kind of dialogue that seems to be emerging between the world of jurists (traditionally a closed and inaccessible community, linguistically and almost deliberately obtuse and exclusionary; the aim was to exclude the layperson from the world of laws and legal forms) and the world of social movements now more engaged in rights narratives and legal mobilization strategies (Pasara 2004). Much of this dialogue until recently has been mediated by human rights organizations. Increasingly though, a new generation of lawyers and advocacy activists is emerging from the very ranks of the social movements and communities themselves that are mobilizing legally.[15]

Finally, at the global level, human rights activists and organizations have played an important role in mobilizing regionally and internationally and in providing a network of support and shared knowledge for local and grassroots efforts at legal mobilization around rights issues (Sikkink 2002). In addition, the growing international and regional networks of law-related professionals, such as organizations and

[15] This is the case among the rank-and-file members of Evo Morales's MAS movement in Bolivia. This has been evident in connection to the experience of "constitution-writing," where legal expertise has become especially valuable.

associations of judges and public prosecutors who meet regularly, create epistemological communities that increasingly share ideas and discourses about law, rules and legality, which then has an impact on developments in legal culture at the national level (Slaughter 2002). Legal globalization then shapes global and, in some ways, converging discourses across a range of actors that affect how struggles around rights and mobilization strategies at the local level develop.

It is the interface between these different communities of social and political actors that contributes to reshaping the plurality of legal cultures and attitudes that coexist within the same national boundaries and at the global level. In some ways, this may create a greater impression of shared understandings and consensus around ideas of rights and rule of law. At the same time there is the sense that, in fact, what we see is the coexistence of parallel but disconnected or opposing normative aspirations that are behind the different understandings about rights and citizenship.

Institutional Change and Judicialization Processes

In addition to the previous two clusters of factors behind the phenomenon of judicialization, a dimension of institutional change and state reform has been part of the process of democratization. The scale of institutional renovation in the last thirty years is formidable, and it is to be expected that it will have affected legal culture and societal expectations about the world of law and legality. In addition, it has advanced new opportunity structures within which the different manifestations of the judicialization of political and social life have been able to develop.

First, late twentieth century democratization itself brought with it the discourse of rights-based citizenship, rule of law and limited government. In the absence of other discourses of legitimation, and given the hegemonic model of neoliberal market rule and the depleted discursive arsenal of the political left, alternative political projects were limited – at least until the late 1990s. Somewhat under the guidance of the good governance agenda, an array of state reform efforts were implemented that, in those areas to do with rule of law reform, have tended not to be challenged by any political current in any fundamental way. Critiques have emerged among scholars and practitioners, but more in connection with how reforms have been carried out than necessarily with the aim of rule of law construction in itself (Dezalay and Garth 2002b; Faundez 2005). Of importance, though, is the broad variety of reforms that have not only had an impact on legal culture but also on how different social and political actors perceive the usefulness of legal and judicial institutions.

First, at different stages of the democratization experience some countries in Latin America engaged in constitutional reform that altered or redefined the standing of rights. In the main, where constitutional reform entailed rewriting Bills of Rights, this has generally involved the expansion of rights (for instance, Brazil in 1988, Colombia in 1991). The degree of political controversy or acceptance has varied in accordance with the degree of political consensus around the constitution-writing exercise or the particular political conditions of the foundational moment. The expansion of the Bill of Rights attempted by the MAS government in the Constituent Assembly of 2006–8 was met with virulent and violent opposition by the political right. Overall, though, the tendency in the region has been toward an expansion of rights, in accordance with the evolution of the UN treaties and global struggles around specific rights. For instance, national commitments to support gender rights and children's rights are very much part of the evolution of constitutional law in accordance with international norms of good state conduct. During the 1990s, the constitutional formalization of indigenous rights and recognition of legal pluralism had been relatively widespread following the ILO Convention 169, while at the same time being increasingly politically controversial.

Second, almost every country in the region undertook comprehensive judicial reforms with far-reaching, overall effects, although it did not necessarily significantly improve the credibility or quality of rule of law. Judicial reforms addressed the explicit political standing of the courts through changing the review powers of high court judges, the judicial appointment systems to reduce political control, and in some cases included the establishment of constitutional courts. Other reforms were aimed at enhancing the quality of justice administration, improving access to justice, efficiency and increasing transparency.

With regard to the former, there is little doubt that these changes affected the political standing of high court judges, although with varying political and social impact and with different responses in terms of judicial activism. In Costa Rica (Wilson 2005, 2006) and Colombia (Cepeda Espinosa 2005; Uprimny 2006), the creation of new constitutional tribunals has led to new forms of social pressure on the state to meet commitments in their respective Bills of Rights through the development of socially progressive and innovative constitutional jurisprudence. This has been particularly so regarding social and economic rights and, in Colombia, indigenous rights. In both cases, this has affected public policy decisions in connection to the distribution of public resources. Not all new constitutional courts have engaged in the same type of judicial activism. In Chile, for instance, the constitutional court has opted for maintaining rigorous control of the legality of the acts of government but has shied away from judicial activism overall (Couso 2005b). Other courts have been active but more erratic in terms of the political line they have displayed – such as the Argentine Supreme Court. The rules of appointment and the degree of politicization of the high courts have been relevant factors in this respect. In the new constitution of Bolivia, a plurinational constitutional tribunal is provided for, the appointment mechanism of which includes an element of election by popular vote. Overall, the change in rules of review and standing of courts on constitutional matters has an impact in shifting public perceptions regarding the role of judges in matters of public importance (for better or for worse) and, in some cases, in creating new opportunity structures that have encouraged new forms of legal mobilization from different social and political quarters.

Other reforms have aimed at improving the administration of justice. These have ranged from reforms aimed at improving questions of efficiency and quality in the nature of judicial procedures, addressing issues of access to justice (by earmarking resources to increase the number of courts, improving legal aid, providing translation into indigenous languages, and facilitating alternative dispute resolution) and, with regard to criminal justice, addressing problems of due process. The impact and effectiveness of these reforms has varied considerably. Often they were seen as misguided and poorly planned foreign imports that bore little relation to the specific local needs of justice administration. In any event, there is by now sufficient academic consensus regarding the impact these reforms have had on advancing (for better or for worse) a greater political and public protagonism of court life and judicial decisions.[16] Reforms also included the establishment of other levels of quasi-legal oversight mechanisms. These include, for instance, the creation of the human rights ombudsman position, with varying levels of influence in terms of effect on encouraging rights awareness and denunciation of rights violations (Uggla 2004).

There is no doubt that the scale and breadth of these reforms has had much effect on ways in which judicialization processes have come about. In some cases, new opportunity structures were created that facilitated the possibility of legal mobilization from below. Nowhere is this more illustrative than the introduction of the *tutela* suit in Colombia with the constitutional reform of 1991, which has led to creative and novel forms of judicial activism (until recently, with a bias toward socially progressive outcomes) at the hands of the constitutional tribunal, which was also a 1991 creation (Uprimny 2006). The *tutela* (writ for the protection of constitutional rights) suit is a form of immediate judicial review by which any individual can demand judicial action in protection of his or her constitutional rights. In Colombia, this has led to an unprecedented judicialization of political conflict.

Finally, it is important to mention the regional and international dimensions of institutional change, by which international and regional human rights instruments not only have been strengthened, but to which Latin American states have become keen signatories (probably less out of conviction than through the contagion effect of wanting to convince the international community of their democratic credentials, it would seem). The "justice cascade" (Lutz and Sikkink 2001) refers to the process by which there has been a thickening of international and regional norms and rights mechanisms. This has had a bearing both on bottom-up legal mobilization strategies, which resort to, for instance, the Inter-American system of rights, and on how judges decide on cases, increasingly deferring to an emerging body of Inter-American Court jurisprudence and recommendations.

[16] See essays in Domingo and Sieder (2001); Pásara (2004), Prillaman (2000); Faundez (2005); and Ciurlizza (2000), among others, for critical analyses of the rule of law agenda and its development.

CONCLUSION

This chapter has developed a preliminary mapping of the different component pieces that constitute the process of judicialization that has emerged in Latin America over the last two to three decades, taking into account the different forms that this has taken in country-specific experiences, but which nonetheless reveal recurrent themes.

Three clusters of processes were identified that contribute to the process of judicialization, albeit in complex, uneven and contradictory ways. First, at the level of ideas, it would seem that more so than in the past the language of political and social conflict is framed in a convergent use of legally rooted discourses around rights, rule of law and accountability. Second, the multiactor nature of this process of judicialization was identified. The appropriation of the language of rights and law is taking place across a broad spectrum of political and social actors who are using this language and with associated forms of legal mobilization in the pursuit of particular political projects and agendas of change (or protection of the status quo, in the case of established political elites). Third, the chapter described the backdrop of far-reaching institutional and constitutional reform against which these processes have taken place. These reforms have provided new opportunity structures for processes of judicialization of politics to take place, either through new forms of judicial activism reflection, a new form of engagement with political context by judicial actors (judges), or through greater activity in litigation strategies, which are taking up the opportunities afforded by some of these reforms.

It is at the intersection among these three clusters of processes of change in relation to social perceptions about law, legality and judicial processes where we can observe the process of judicialization of social and political conflict in Latin America. Of note is the complexity of rights discourses and the plurality of legal meanings attached to these in the context of rapidly changing institutional environment. There are parallel processes developing in interconnected ways – and possibly in some cases, contributing to what amounts to a rights revolution of sorts, bearing in mind the very modest achievements. This is evident through greater representational and symbolic manifestations of uses of the law, legal instrument and legal discourses. This is occurring not only at the level of ideas but also at the level of practices. In turn, these processes are connected to novel ways in which political power is being disputed and transformation discourses are being legitimated. Bolivia's constituent process is especially telling, as competing social groups are essentially fighting to stake their claim over the official legal and constitutional narrative.

It is worth ending on a cautionary note. The skeptics of the transformative or emancipatory potential of judicial politics or legalization of political discourses around rights will rightly point out that on the ground poor quality citizenship and deficient rule of law characterize the reality of a vast proportion of the population in Latin America. The recent years of the war on drugs and terror and the escalation of the problem of citizen security in much of the region is affecting narratives around rights and civil liberties. In addition, we have yet to see what the full impact of the financial crisis will be on levels of inequality and social decomposition. The consequences for citizenship and rights narratives do not augur well in the current climate.

References

Adelman, Jeremy, and Miguel Angel Centeno. 2002. "Between Liberalism Neoliberalism: Law's Dilemmas in Latin America." In *Global Prescriptions: The Production, Exportation, and Importation of a New Legal Orthodoxy*, Yves Dezalay and Bryant Garth, eds. Ann Arbor: Michigan University Press. 139–62.

Assies, Willem, Gemma Van DerHaar, and André Hoekema, eds. 1999. *The Challenge of Diversity: Indigenous Peoples and Reform of the State in Latin America*. Amsterdam: Thela Thesis.

Barahona de Brito, Alexandra, Carmen González, and Paloma Aguilar, eds. 2001. *The Politics of Memory: Transitional Justice in Democratizing Societies*. Oxford: Oxford University Press.

Berruecos, Susana. 2003. "Electoral Justice in Mexico: The Role of the Electoral Tribunal under new Federalism." *Journal of Latin American Studies*, 35(3): 801–25.

Brinks, Daniel. 2008. *The Judicial Response to Police Killings in Latin America: Inequality and the Rule of Law*. Cambridge: Cambridge University Press.

Burt, Jo Marie, and Coleta Youngers. 2008. "Informe de Conferencia a internacional, Tribunales de derechos humanos en America Latina: El juicio a Fujimori en perspectiva comparada," http://cgs.gmu.edu/publications/hjd/OSI2009RappReportSpan.pdf (August 5, 2009).

Carothers, Thomas. 2001. "The Many Agendas of Rule of Law Reform in Latin America." In *Rule of Law in Latin America: The International Promotion of Judicial Reform*, Pilar Domingo and Rachel Sieder, eds. London: ILAS. 4–16.

Cepeda Espinoza, and Manuel José. 2005. "The Judicialization of Politics in Colombia: The Old and the New." In *The Judicialization of Politics in Latin America*, Rachel Sieder, Line Schjolden, and Alan Angell, eds. Houndsmill: Palgrave McMillan. 67–131.

Chavez, Rebecca Bill. 2004. *The Rule of Law in Nascent Democracies: Judicial Politics in Argentina*. Stanford: Stanford University Press.

Ciurlizza, Javier. 2000. "Judicial Reform and International Legal Technical Assistance in Latin America." *Democratization*, 7(2): 211–30.

Collins, Cath. 2008. "State Terror and the Law: The Rejudicialization of Human Rights Accountability in Chile and El Salvador," *Latin American Perspectives*, 35(5): 20–37.

Couso, Javier. 2005a. "The Changing Role of Law and Courts in Latin America: From an Obstacle to Social Change to a Tool of Social Equity." In *Courts and Social Transformation: An Institutional Voice for the Poor?* Roberto Gargarella, Pilar Domingo, and Theunis Roux, eds. London: Ashgate. 61–82.

Couso, Javier. 2005b. "The Judicialization of Chilean Politics: The Rights Revolution that Never Was." In *The Judicialization of Politics in Latin America*, Rachel Sieder, Line Schjolden, and Alan Angell, eds. Houndsmill: Palgrave McMillan. 105–31.

Couso, Javier, and Lisa Hilbink. 2009. "From Quietism to Incipient Activism: The Institutional and Ideational Roots of Rights Adjudication in Chile," paper presented the conference, "Judicial Politics in Latin America," at Centro de Investigacion y Docencia Economicas, Mexico DF.

Dezalay, Yves, and Bryant Garth, eds. 2002a. *Global Prescriptions: The Production, Exportation, and Importation of a New Legal Orthodoxy*. Ann Arbor: Michigan University Press.
Dezalay, Yves, and Bryant Garth, eds. 2002b. "Legitimating the New Legal Orthodoxy." In *Global Prescriptions: The Production, Exportation, and Importation of a New Legal Orthodoxy*. Ann Arbor: Michigan University Press. 306–34.
Domingo, Pilar. 2004. "Judicialization of Politics or Politicization of the Judiciary? Recent Trends in Latin America." *Democratization*, 11(1): 104–26.
Domingo, Pilar. 2005. "Judicialisation of Politics: The Changing Political Role of the Judiciary in Mexico." In *The Judicialization of Politics in Latin America*, Rachel Sieder, Line Schjolden, and Alan Angell, eds. Houndsmill: Palgrave McMillan. 20–44.
Domingo, Pilar. 2009. "Governance after Neo-liberalism: The Case of Bolivia." In *Governance after Neo-liberalism*, Jean Grugel and Pia Riggirozzi, eds. New York: Palgrave-Macmillan. 113–48.
Domingo, Pilar, and Rachel Sieder, eds. 2001. *Rule of Law in Latin America: The International Promotion of Judicial Reform*. London: Institute of Latin American Studies.
Duce, Mauricio, and Rogelio Pérez Perdomo. 2003. "Citizen Security and Reform of the Criminal Justice System in Latin America." In *Crime and Violence in Latin America: Citizen Security, Democracy, and the State*, Hugo Frühling, Joseph S. Tulchin, and Heather A. Golding, eds, Baltimore and Washington, D.C.: The Johns Hopkins University Press and Woodrow Wilson Center Press. 69–91.
Epp, Charles. 1998. *The Rights Revolution: Lawyers, Activists, and Supreme Courts in Comparative Perspective*. Chicago: University of Chicago Press.
Faundez, Julio, ed. 1997. *Good Government and Law, Legal and Institutional Reform in Developing Countries*. London: Macmillan.
Faundez, Julio. 2005. "Democratization Thorugh Law: Perspectives from Latin America," *Democratization*, 12(5): 749–65.
Gargarella, Roberto, Pilar Domingo, and Theunis Roux, eds. 2006. *Courts and Social Transformation: An Institutional Voice for the Poor?* London: Ashgate.
Gauri, Varun, and Daniel Brinks, eds. 2008. *Courting Social Justice: Judicial Enforcement of Social and Economic Rights in the Developing World*. Cambridge: Cambridge University Press.
Gloppen, Siri, Robert Gargarella, and Elin Skaar, eds. 2004. *Democratization and the Judiciary: The Accountability Function of Courts in New Democracies*. London: Frank Cass.
Helmke, Gretchen. 2005. *Courts Under Constraints: Judges, Generals, and Presidents in Argentina*. Cambridge: Cambridge University Press.
Hilbink, Lisa. 2007. *Judges beyond Politics in Democracy and Dictatorship: Lessons from Chile*. Cambridge: Cambridge University Press.
Keck, Margaret, and Kathryn Sikkink. 1998. *Activists beyond Borders: Advocacy Networks in International Politics*. Ithaca: Cornell University Press.
Langford, Malcolm, ed. 2009. *Social Rights Jurisprudence: Emerging Trends in Comparative and International Law*. Cambridge: Cambridge University Press.
Lutz, Ellen, and Kathryn Sikkink. 2001. "The Justice Cascade: The Evolution and Impact of Human Rights Trials in Latin America." *Chicago Journal of International Law*, 2(1): 1–33.
Mainwaring, Scott, and Christopher Welna, eds. *Democratic Accountability in Latin America*. Oxford: Oxford University Press.
Maravall, Jose Maria, and Adam Przeworski, eds. 2003. *Democracy and the Rule of Law*. Cambridge: Cambridge University Press.
Molyneux, Maxine, and Sian Lazar. 1999. *Doing the Rights Thing: Rights-Based Development and Latin American NGOs*. London: ITDG Publishing.

O'Donnell, Guillermo. 1993. "On the State, Democratization, and Some Conceptual Problems: A Latin American View with Glances at Some Post-Communist Countries." *World Development* (Special Issue), 21(8): 1355–70.

O'Donnell, Guillermo. 2004. "Notas sobre la democracia en América Latina." In *El Debate Conceptual sobre la Democracia*. New York: PNUD.

Pásara, Luis. 2004. "Lecciones ¿aprendidas o por aprender?" In *En busca de una justicia diferente*, Pásara, Luis, ed. Lima: Consorcio Justicia Viva. 515–69.

Peruzzotti, Enrique, and Smulovitz, Catalina, eds. 2006. *Enforcing the Rule of Law: Social Accountability in the New Latin American Democracies*. Pittsburgh: University of Pittsburgh Press.

Prillaman, William C. 2000. *The Judiciary and Democratic Decay in Latin America: Declining Confidence in the Rule of Law*. Westport: Praeger.

Ríos Figueroa, Julio, and Matthew M. Taylor. 2006. "Institutional Determinants of the Judicialization of Policy in Brazil and Mexico." *Journal of Latin American Studies*, 38(4): 739–766.

Rodriguez-Garavito, Cesar, and Luis Carlos Arenas. 2005. "Indigenous Rights, Transnational Activism, and Legal Mobilization: The Struggle of the U'wa People in Colombia." In *Law and Globalizatino from Below: Towards a Cosmopolitan Legality*, Boaventura de Sousa Santos and Cesar Rodriguez-Garavit, eds. Cambridge: Cambridge University Press. 241–67.

Roht-Arriaza, Naomi, and Javier Mariezcurrena, eds. 2006. *Transitional Justice in the Twenty-First Century: Beyond Truth versus Justice*. Cambridge: Cambridge University Press.

Roniger, Luis, and Mario Sznajder. 1999. *The Legacy of Human Rights Violations in the Southern Cone: Argentina, Chile, and Uruguay*. New York: Oxford University Press.

Sabato, Hilda. 2001. "On political citizenship in Nineteenth Century Latin America." *American Historical Review*, 104(4): 1290–315.

Santos, Boaventura de Sousa. 2002. *Toward a New Legal Common Sense*. London: Butterworth LexisNexis Group.

Santos, Boaventura de Sousa, and César Rodríguez-Garavito, eds. 2005. *Law and Globalization from Below: Towards a Cosmopolitan Legality*. New York and Cambridge: Cambridge University Press.

Schedler, Andreas, Larry Diamond, and Marc F. Plattner, eds. 1999. *The Self-Restraining State: Power and Accountability in New Democracies*. Boulder: Lynne Reinner.

Sen, Amartya. 2000. *Development as Freedom*. New York: Anchor Books.

Sieder, Rachel, ed. 2002a. *Multiculturalism in Latin America: Indigenous Rights, Diversity, and Democracy*. New York: Palgrave Macmillan.

Sieder, Rachel, ed. 2002b. "Multiculturalism in Latin America: Indigenous Rights, Diversity, and Democracy." Introduction in *Multiculturalism in Latin America: Indigenous Rights, Diversity, and Democracy*. London: Palgrave Press. 1–24.

Sieder, Rachel, Line Schjolden, and Alan Angell, eds. 2005. *The Judicialization of Politics in Latin America*. Houndsmill: Palgrave Macmillan.

Sikkink, Kathryn. 2002. "Transnational Advocacy Networks and the Social Construction of Legal Rules." In *Global Prescriptions: The Production, Exportation, and Importation of a New Legal Orthodoxy*, Yves Dezalay and Bryant Garth, eds. Ann Arbor: Michigan University Press. 37–64.

Sikkink, Kathryn. 2005. "The Transnational Dimension of the Judicialization of Politics in Latin America." In *The Judicialization of Politics in Latin America*, Rachel Sieder, Line Schjolden and Alan Angell, eds. London: Palgrave. 262–92.

Slaughter, Anne-Marie. 2002. "Breaking Out: the Proliferation of Actors in the International System." In *Global Prescriptions: The Production, Exportation, and Importation of a New Legal Orthodoxy*, Yves Dezalay and Bryant Garth, eds. Ann Arbor: Michigan University Press. 12–64.

Smulovitz, Catalina, and Enrique Peruzzotti. 2003. "Societal and Horizontal Control: Two Cases of a Fruitful Relationship." In *Democratic Accountability in Latin America*, Mainwaring, Scott and Christopher Welna, eds. Oxford: Oxford University Press. 309–32.

Smulovitz, Catalina. 2002. "The Discovery of Law: Political Consequences in the Argentine Case." In *Global Prescriptions: The Production, Exportation, and Importation of a New Legal Orthodoxy*, Yves Dezalay and Bryant Garth, eds. Ann Arbor: Michigan University Press. 249–75.

Smulovitz, Catalina. 2005. "Petitioning and Creating Rights: Judicialization in Argentina." In *The Judicialization of Politics in Latin America*, Rachel Sieder, Line Schjolden, and Alan Angell, eds. Houndsmill: Palgrave McMillan. 161–86.

Taylor, Matthew M. 2008. *Judging Policy: Courts and Policy Reform in Democratic Brazil*. Stanford: Stanford University Press.

Tulchin, Joseph and Meg Ruthenberg, eds. 2006. *Citizenship in Latin America*. Boulder: Lynne Reinner.

Uggla, Frederik. 2004. "The Ombudsman in Latin America." *Journal of Latin American Studies*, 36(3): 423–50.

Uprimny, Rodrigo. 2006. "The Enforcement of Social Rights by the Colombian Constitutional Court." In *Courts and Social Transformation: An Institutional Voice for the Poor?* Roberto Gargarella, Pilar Domingo, and Theunis Roux, eds. London: Ashgate. 127–152.

Van Cott, Donna 2000. *The Friendly Liquidation of the Past: The Politics of Diversity in Latin America*. Pittsburgh: University of Pittsburgh Press.

Whitehead, Lawrence. 1994. "A Note on Citizenship." In *Latin America: Politics and Society since 1930*, Leslie Bethell, ed. Cambridge: Cambridge University Press. 67–74.

Wilson, Bruce. 2005. "Changing Dynamics: The Political Impact of Costa Rica's Constitutional Court." In *The Judicialization of Politics in Latin America*, Rachel Sieder, Line Schjolden and Alan Angell, eds. Houndsmill: Palgrave Mcmillan. 47–66.

Wilson, Bruce. 2006. "Legal Opportunity Structures and Social Movements: The Effects of Institutional Change on Costa Rican Politics." *Comparative Political Studies*, 39(3): 325–51.

Wright-Carozza, Paolo. 2003. "From Conquest to Constitutions: Retrieving a Latin American Tradition of the Idea of Human Rights." *Human Rights Quarterly*, 25(2): 281–313.

Yashar, Deborah. 2005. *Contesting Citizenship in Latin America: The Rise of Indigenous Movements and the Postliberal Challenge*. Cambridge: Cambridge University Press.

Index

abstract review, 45, 46, 47, 57, 65, 66, 67
accountability, 259, 261, 265, 267, 274
Ackerman, Bruce, 152
Action Group for Bío Bío (GABB), 214
advocacy network, 234
Africa, 166
African Union, 114
Aldunate, Eduardo, 147
Alexy, Robert, 155, 156
Alfonsín, Raúl, 123
Allende, Salvador, 151
Almonacid, Arellano, 120, 121
Almond, Gabriel, 82
Alter, Karen, 112, 113, 115, 116, 131, 135
alternative dispute resolution, 192
alternative dispute resolution (ADR), 168
Alvez, Bueno, 124
American Convention of Human Rights, 85, 117, 120, 124, 128
American Declaration of the Rights and Duties of Man, 125, 126
Amnesty International, 129, 189, 214
amparos, 242
Amsterdam, Robert, 197, 201, 202
Anaya, James, 168, 218, 220, 221
Anderson, Michael R., 210
Andrés Bello Catholic University, 187, 192
Angell, Alan, 3, 11, 12, 21, 162, 184
Ansolabehere, Karina, 14, 15, 82, 83, 85, 99
Arantes, Rogélio Bastos, 56, 71
Araucanía, 215
Arcis University of Santiago, 216
Arenas, Luis Carlos, 163, 167, 263
Argentina, 10, 17, 42, 56, 60, 106–108, 113, 123, 147, 166, 220, 221, 234–251, 262
  Bill of Rights, 243
  Bueno Alvez v. Argentina, 125
  Bulacio vs. Argentina, 126
  Constitution, 130
  corralito, 123
  General Workers' Confederation (CGT), 246
  House of Representatives, 243
  Judicial School, 241
  Madres de la Plaza de Mayo, 261
  Magistrates Council, 241
  National Judicial Council, 242, 243
  National Ombudsman, 241
  Office of the Public Prosecutor, 241
  Public Defender's Office, 241
  Public Ministry, 125
  Supreme Court, 12, 13, 113, 114, 119, 123, 124, 125, 126, 130, 131, 134, 142, 235, 236, 242, 243, 249, 272
  Union of Metal Workers, 246
Arrieche, Franklin, 195
Asamblea General de la Organización de Estados Americanos, 85
Asamblea Permanente por los Derechos Humanos (APDH), 247
Asia, 166
Asociación Gremial de Abogados de Bahía Blanca, 246
Asociación Gremial de Abogados de Buenos Aires, 246
Asociación Gremial de Abogados de Mar del Plata, 246
Atacameño, 225
Atria, Fernando, 120
Aurélio, Marco, 64
Awas Tingni v. Nicaragua, 167
Aylwin, José, 214, 215
Aymará, 214, 225

Bachelet, Michelle, 120, 122
Ballard, Megan J., 55
Barbosa, Joaquím, 55
Barzon debtors' movement, 268
Bauer, Carl, 147
Becker, Arnulf, 135
Bello, Andrés, 149, 150
Benford, Robert, 82
Bercholc, Jorge, 235
Berger, Oscar, 175
Berger, Peter, 26
Berruecos, Susana, 267
Bickel, Alexander, 152
Bío Bío region, 208, 222
  Bío Bío River, 215
Bolivarian Alliance for the People of Our Americas (ALBA), 132
Bolivarian revolution, 14
Bolivarian Revolution, 113, 133, 183, 193, 195, 196, 197, 198
Bolivia, 132, 166, 221, 263, 264, 272
  constitution, 11
  National Assembly, 193
  Supreme Court, 142
Brazil, 10, 42, 166, 220, 221, 262, 271
  Article 5 of the Constitution, 10
  Attorney General, 56
  Constitution of 1988, 56
  judicial reform, 58, 74
  Supreme Court, 13, 15, 142
  Supreme Court of Sào Paulo, 55
  transition to democracy, 56, 69
Brewer, Stephanie Erin, 118
Brewers-Carías, Allan R., 113, 128
Brinks, Daniel, 54, 56, 262
British Council, 249
Brunnegger, Sandra, 163
Buenos Aires, 249
Burt, Jo Marie, 261

Caldera, Rafael, 191
Campbell, John L., 13, 19
Canada, 117
  Glamis Gold, 173
  Skye Resources, 175
Cappelletti, Mauro, 144
Caracas, 189, 194
Carbonell, Miguel, 113, 134
Cardoso, Fernando Henrique, 55
Carias, German, 188
Caribbean, 117
Carmona, Pedro, 194, 196
Carnevale, Vera, 246
Carrasquero, Francisco, 195
Catholic University of Temuco (UCT), 216
cause lawyers, 182–204, 248, 250, 251
Cavallaro, James L., 118
Cedeño, Eligio, 202
Center for Justice and International Law (CEJIL), 189
Center for Legal, Environmental and Social Action (CALAS), 177
Central University of Venezuela, 187
Centro de Estudios Legales y Sociales (CELS), 247, 268
Cepeda Espinosa, Manuel, 81
Chama, Mauricio, 246
Chavez, Hugo, 14, 17, 113, 126, 127, 129, 132, 183, 191, 192, 193, 194, 196
Chavez, Rebecca Bill, 4, 12, 19, 54
Chile, 9, 10, 17, 59, 80, 119, 120, 142, 147, 166, 216, 259, 261, 267, 268
  Caso Almonacid y otros v. Chile, 120, 121, 122, 123
  Amnesty Decree, 120, 121, 122, 123
  Caso Claude Reyes y otros v. Chile, 120
  Christian Democrats, 122
  Civil Code, 149
  Congress, 121, 122
  Constitution, 119
  Court of Appeals of Santiago, 223, 229
  Judicial Academy, 227, 228
  judiciary, 13
  National Commission for Scientific and Technological Research (CONICYT), 148
  Supreme Court, 113, 119, 120, 121, 122, 123, 130, 142, 223
  The Santiago Sixth Civil Court, 229
  Water Code, 225
citizenship, 259, 273–275
civil associations, 243, 245
civil law, 142, 144, 150
civil liberties lawyers, 244, 245, 251
Claro Solar, Luis, 150
Cleary, Matthew, 82
cocalero, 263
Cochabamba, 263
Cold War, 258, 260
Coleman, Jules, 152
collective rights, 187, 212
Collins, Cath, 261
Colombia, 14, 15, 80, 81, 108, 147, 149, 166, 220, 221, 262, 263, 271, 272
  central bank, 46
  Congress, 41, 46, 47
  connectivity doctrine, 33
  constitutional court, 10, 14, 15, 29, 33, 34, 44, 264

the doctrine of the "unconstitutional state of affairs", 45
economic crisis, 25, 41, 43
economic liberalization, 32, 42
Gross Domestic Product (GDP), 31, 32, 42
guerrilla, 32, 188
human dignity, 33, 35, 39
justice houses, 169
Los Andes University, 30
middle-class, 26, 41, 46
Office of the Public Prosecutor, 72
pensions, 43
privatization, 32
regional and municipal governments, 42
Supreme Court, 142
UPAC (Unit of Constant Purchasing Power) decisions, 31, 45
Colotenango, 176
Comaroff, Jean, 5, 8, 11, 19
Comaroff, John, 5
Comisión Argentina de Derechos Humanos (CADHU), 247
Comisión de Esclarecimiento Histórico, 172
Comisión de Familiares de Presos Políticos y Gremiales (CoFaDe), 246
Comité de Ayuda Antifascista, 245
Comité Pro-Amnistía por los Exiliados y Presos Políticos de América, 245
Committee of Relatives of the Victims of February and March of 1989 (COFAVIC), 189
community justice, 168
Concepción Huista, 176
conceptual history, 30
conciliation, 168
Conley, John M., 29, 49
consequencialista, 63, 64, 71, 72
constitutionalism
constitutional courts, 235
constitutional culture, 27
constitutional discourse, 141–158
constitutional reform, 240, 241
constitutional scholarship, 144, 146, 147, 148, 157
constitutional theory, 141, 145, 151, 152, 153, 155, 156
constitutionalization of law, 147
Constitutionalism
higher law constitutionalism, 154
multicultural constitutionalism, 164
new constitutionalism, 113
consulta popular, 175
Cordeiro, Jose Luis, 9
Coronil, Fernando, 185, 186
Corporation for Indigenous Development (CONADI), 212, 215, 220
Legal Defense Program, 215
Corrales, Javier, 191
corralito, 263, 268
Correa Sutil, Jorge, 216, 228
Costa Rica, 80, 147, 166, 267, 272
constitutional court, 10
recurso de amparo, 81
Supreme Court, 142
Cotterell, Roger, 6, 82
Couso, Javier A., 54, 59, 113, 119, 120, 149
International Covenant on Civil and Political Rights, 218
Crider, Todd, 168
Crisp, Brian P., 191
Spanish monarchy, 9
Cuba, 117
Cuffe, Sandra, 170
culture
judicial culture, 15
legal culture, 3, 4, 5, 6, 7, 8, 12, 14, 15, 16, 17, 18, 19, 114, 129
Cuneo, Andrés, 151

Dahl, Robert, 82, 152
Davinson, Guillermo, 216
Davis, Shelton H., 174
Delgado Ocando, José M., 193
democratization, 10, 11, 260
Denmark, 166
Dezalay, Yves, 170, 184, 185, 271
Domingo, Pilar, 3, 12, 17, 18, 19, 82, 87, 123, 124, 141, 268
Dominica, 166
Dor, Gal, 184
Duce, Mauricio, 227, 228, 262
Dugas, John C., 32
Duhalde, Eduardo Luis, 246
Dworkin, Ronald, 114, 152, 153, 156

Eckstein, Harry, 28, 49, 75
Ecuador, 132, 149, 166, 221
constitution, 11
Supreme Court, 142
Edelman, Martin, 143
El Salvador, 10, 149
Ellner, Steve, 191
empowerment, 257, 262, 266, 269
Empresa Nacional de Electricidad (ENDESA), 214
Environmental Impact Study (EIS), 209
Epp, Charles, 80, 81, 119, 142, 237, 244, 256
erga omnes, 57
estado social, 33, 35, 40

European Convention, 118
European Council, 115
European Court of Human Rights (ECHR), 114
European Court of Justice (ECJ), 112, 114, 115
European Union (EU), 112
Existenzminimum, 35

Faro de Castro, Marcus, 70
Faundez, Julio, 168, 169, 271
Fernández, Monica, 199
Ferrajoli, Luigi, 156
fetishization of the law, 5
Fiji, 166
Finkel, Jodi, 88
Fisheries Act, 225
Fix Fierro, Héctor, 81, 87
Ford Foundation, 249
forestry, 217
Forum for Life, 196, 203
France, 143, 154
  French Revolution, 149
free trade agreements, 170
freedom of association, 78, 79, 85, 89, 91, 96, 97, 98, 104, 105
freedom of expression, 78, 79, 85, 89, 91, 92, 93, 94, 95, 96, 104, 105
French, John, 9
Friedman, Lawrence, 6, 7, 8, 19, 82
Frühling, Hugo, 59, 249
Fujimori, 10, 261
Fundamentos de Derecho Constitucional. Análisis filosófico, jurídico y politológico de la práctica constitucional, 152

Galanter, Marc, 238
garantiste, 262
García Figueroa, Alfonso, 154
García, Mauricio, 162
Gargarella, Roberto, 210, 211, 228
Garth, Bryant, 170, 184, 185, 271
Geneva Conventions, 123
German Federal Administrative Tribunal, 35
Germany
  German Constitutional Court, 155
Gillman, Howard, 82, 109, 145
globalization, 6, 11
Gloppen, Siri, 141, 210, 211, 212
Glossators, 144
Gomez, Manuel, 182, 184, 185, 187, 194, 197, 198, 201
Gonzalez, Felipe, 118
good governance, 256, 265
Goodale, Mark, 9, 10, 14, 19
Grattet, Ryken, 26, 27, 50
Gremial de Abogados, 246
Guatemala, 16, 17, 162, 166, 220, 221, 262
  1985 Constitution, 165
  armed conflict, 172
  Congress, 170
  Marlin project, 173
  Mining Code, 170
  Ministry of Energy and Mines, 170
  peace accords, 171
Guatemalan Nickel Company, 175

Habermas, Jurgen, 161
Hajjar, Lisa, 184
Hale, Charles R., 165
Haley, John Owen, 6
Halliday, Terrence C., 184
Hammergren, Lynn, 236
Hart, H. L. A., 152
Hawkins, Darren, 114, 118
Hay, Colin, 13, 19
Helfer, Laurence, 115, 116, 135
Hellinger, Daniel, 191, 192
Helmke, Gretchen, 11, 12, 20, 51, 53, 60, 61, 67, 141, 242
Hertogh, Marc, 82
HI. See new institutionalism
Hilbink, Lisa, 6, 12, 13, 20, 51, 52, 59, 76, 80, 113, 120, 133, 226, 268
Himiob, Gonzalo, 197, 201
Hirschl, Ran, 26
Hofnung, Menachem, 184
Holland, Kenneth, 142
Honduras, 150, 166
Huehuetenango, 176
Huenteche, 207
Huilliche, 208
human rights
  transnational human rights discourse, 6
Human Rights Watch, 129, 189, 212, 214, 217

indigenous groups, 9, 11, 14, 16, 101, 162, 163, 164, 165, 173, 207, 209, 210
  indigenous community courts, 169
  indigenous law, 169, 174, 177
  Maya Mam, 173
  Sipakapense, 173
Indigenous Institute in Temuco, 216
Indigenous Law, 215, 220
Indigenous Peoples' Rights Watch, 212, 213
Ingram, Matthew, 51, 76
injunctions, 36, 37, 38, 39, 46, 47
Institute of Access to Public Information (IFAI), 95
Institute of Indigenous Studies, 213

institutionalization, 27
inter partes, 57
Inter-American Commission for Human Rights, 10, 98, 117, 120, 124, 167, 224
Inter-American Court for Human Rights, 16, 112–136, 166, 167, 196, 273
Inter-American Development Bank, 170
Inter-American human rights system, 16, 142
interlegality, 7
International Association of Constitutional Law (IACL), 149
International Court of Justice (ICJ), 112
International Criminal Court, 199
International Financial Corporation (IFC), 173
International Labour Organization Convention 169 (ILO), 10, 179, 264
International Labour Organization Convention No, 14, 220, 221, 226
isolated thesis, 89
Israel, 143
Italy, 144, 156
Ixchiguán, 176
Ixtahuacán, 173
Izabal, 175

Jacoby, Wade, 114, 118
Jobim, Nelson, 64
judicial activism, 149, 254, 255, 257, 270, 272
judicial independence, 186, 237, 242, 243
judicial reform, 168, 256, 257
judicial review, 10, 16, 32, 45, 52, 55, 57, 59, 60, 63, 64, 68, 70, 78, 141, 148, 152, 157, 235, 241, 266
judicialization of politics, 3–19, 31, 52, 141, 142, 146, 147, 158, 161, 209, 234
judicialization of rights, 209
Junta Commanders, 247
juridification, 161–179, 257, 270
Justice First, 192

Kapiszewski, Diana, 64
Karl, Terry, 185, 191
Karst, Kenneth L., 59
Keller, Helen, 115
Kelsen, Hans, 155
Khodorkovsky, Mikhail, 202
Knight, Alan, 82
Koerner, Andrei, 71
Korea
  lumber company, 168
Kornblith, Miriam, 191

La Colorada, 188
la doctrina.. *See* legal scholarship
La Forza del Destino, 245
La Peste, 189
labor unions, 28
Lafkenche, 207
Lagos, 120
Lakoff, George, 28
Landau, David, 134, 148
Larkins, Christopher, 124
Latinobarómetro, 238
Lauth, Han-Joachim, 67
Law and Society Movement
  Law and Society Association, 4, 5, 14
law firms
  boutique firm, 16
legal consciousness, 143, 209, 210, 211, 230
legal culture, 59, 63, 82, 141, 143, 144, 146, 162, 163, 198, 209, 210, 218, 225, 226, 229, 234, 236, 237, 238, 240, 250, 254, 255, 256, 258, 271
  external culture, 6, 143
  high court culture, 53
  internal culture, 6, 53, 54, 59, 61, 63, 67, 69, 71, 143, 185
  judicial culture, 53, 59, 226
legal framework, 222, 225
legal globalization, 164, 169
legal ideology, 143, 146
legal literacy, 210
legal mobilization, 167, 173, 178, 209, 211, 212, 234, 236, 273–275
legal pluralism, 5, 6, 7, 162, 163, 168, 254, 255, 263, 264
legal positivism, 152, 155, 158
legal profession, 245
legal values, 143
Lepage, Octavio, 191
Levine, Daniel, 185
Levit, Janet Koven, 124, 126
Levitsky, Stephen, 53, 67
Liga Argentina por los Derechos del Hombre (LADH), 245
Lillo Vera, Rodrigo, 216, 220
Lomnitz, Clarissa, 185
London, 121, 133, 261
Lonko Quilapán legal clinic, 216
López Ayllón, Sergio, 81
Lopez Maya, Margarita, 189
López Medina, Diego, 145, 157
Los Lagos, 215
Lovatón, David, 169
Loveman, Brian, 9
Lu, Yiyi, 184
Luckman, Thomas, 26
Lula, Luiz Inácio, 55, 56, 64, 71
Lutz, Ellen, 166, 273

Madariaga, Jaime, 218
Madre Selva, 175
Magaloni, Beatriz, 81, 87
Malagón Barceló, Javier, 9
Mallon, Florencia E., 9, 20
Mapuche people, 9, 17, 207, 208, 209, 212, 215, 216, 222
  Mapudungun, 214
  Women with the Force of the Earth, 214
Marquez, Walter, 188
Marshallian, 258
Massacre of El Amparo, 188
Master of Laws, 157
Maya Q'eqchi, 175
McCann, Michael W., 211
meaning settling, 26, 27
Medellín cartel, 32
media, 18, 120, 188, 195, 199, 201, 212
  trial by media, 202
Meili, Stephen, 182
Mello, Marco Aurelio, 70
Méndez, Juan, 5, 20, 162, 172
Menem, Carlos, 124, 261
Merino, Mauricio, 88
Merry, Sally, 6, 10, 19, 20
Merryman, John H., 6, 144
Mertz, Elizabeth, 26
Mexico, 42, 166, 220, 221, 262, 267
  amparo, 87
  appeals tribunals (*Tribunales Colegiados de Circuito*), 79, 87
  Cámara de Diputados, 85
  Constitution of 1857, 259
  Constitution of 1917, 259
  criterios, 79, 81, 82, 89, 97
  Electoral Tribunal of the Federal Judiciary, 79
  Federal Judicial Council (Consejo de la Judicatura Federal), 88
  jurisprudential doctrines (*criterios*), 81
  jurisprudential theses, 89, 97, 105
  Law of Transparency and Access to Public Information, 93
  Mexican Constitution of 1917, 105
  Mexican Federal Law of Transparency and Access, 88, 93, 95
  Mexican Supreme Court, 14, 15, 78, 79, 81, 85, 87, 89, 105
mínimo vital, 14, 15, 29–49
Mitchell, Timothy, 26
Molinelli, Guillermo, 235
Montana Exploradora, 173, 174, 177
Morales, Evo, 132, 263
Morales, Felipe G., 226, 227, 228
Movimiento al Socialismo (MAS), 263

Naddeo, Cecilia, 113, 125, 126, 131
Nagche, 207
Naím, Moisés, 185, 186
Nash Rojas, Claudio, 168
National Assembly. *See* Venezuela (Congress)
National Corporation for Indigenous Development (CONADI), 209
National Endowment for Democracy, 249
National Environment Commission, (CONAMA), 209
natural law, 150, 151, 154, 155, 156, 157
Nelken, David, 82
Nelson, William, 143
neoconstitutionalism, 141–158
neoliberal multiculturalism, 165
neoliberalism, 4, 11
Netherlands, 166
Neuman, Gerald L., 114
new institutionalism, 12, 13
  discourse institutionalism, 13
  historical institutionalism (HI), 12, 13
  Rational Choice Institutionalism (RI), 12
New Spain, 9
Nicaragua, 132, 149, 221
Nino, Carlos, 152, 154
non-governmental organizations (NGO), 11, 17, 120, 167, 175, 177, 184, 187, 192, 197, 213, 222, 234, 243, 248, 262, 268
North, Douglass C., 75
Northfleet, Ellen Gracie, 55
Norway, 166

O'Barr, William M., 29, 49
O'Donnell, Guillermo, 5, 20, 53, 162, 172, 209
Open Society, 249
Opsvik, Tor, 216
Oquendo, Ángel, 11, 20
Organization of American States (OAS), 116, 118
Ortega, Liliana, 196
Oxy, 167, 263

Panama, 221
Paraguay, 166, 220, 221
Partido Revolucionario Institucional (PRI), 79, 92
Pásara, Luis, 82, 270
Pastrana, Andrés, 47
Paulo, Vicente, 57, 73
Pehuenche, 208, 209, 214
Peña, Carlos, 153
Peña, Rodolfo Ortega, 246
Perez Perdomo, Rogelio, 113, 126
Perez, Carlos Andrés, 190
Perez-Liñan, Anibal, 190, 191

Pérez-Perdomo, Rogelio, 7, 182, 184, 186, 187, 193, 196, 262
Perillo, Joseph M., 144
Peronism, 245
Peru, 9, 10, 21, 56, 166, 168, 220, 221, 261
  Supreme Court, 131, 142
Peruzzotti, Enrique, 82, 266
Phillips, Scott, 26, 27, 50
Pinheiro, Paulo Sérgio, 5, 20, 162, 172
Pinochet, Augusto, 10, 21, 119, 120, 122, 133, 217, 261
Pisarello, Gerardo, 134
Playa Grande Ixcán, 176
political science, 262
Poluco-Pidenco, 217
Poole, Deborah, 169
Popper, Karl, 28
Portal de la Justicia Argentina, 238
Presidential Decrees, 222, 242
prior consultation, 166, 167, 168
Program of Promotion and Information on Indigenous Rights (PIDI), 212, 222
PROVEA, 203

Quechua, 168, 225

Ralco Dam, 208, 214, 215, 221
Randeria, Shalini, 163
Rappaport, Joanna, 9, 20, 163
Rasch, Elisabet, 177
Rawls, John, 152
RI. See new institutionalism
Richards, Patricia, 165
rights
  collective rights, 28, 164, 220, 241, 243
  constitutional rights, 246
  fundamental rights, 31, 32, 36, 39, 45, 120, 219, 224, 227
  rights talk, 14
  social rights, 25, 29, 30, 31, 32, 33, 36, 37, 38, 39, 40, 44, 45
  subsistence rights, 25, 26, 31, 37
rights revolution, 273–275
Ríos Figueroa, Julio, 11, 89, 141
Rocha, Zélio Maia da, 57, 73
Rodríguez-Garavito, César, 162, 163, 167, 263
Rodriguez-Piñero Royo, Luis, 168
Rohde, Clifford C., 188
Rosenn, Keith, 3, 56, 58, 59, 61, 76
Rosich, Antonio, 197, 201
rule of law, 265, 267, 271
rulings
  preliminary rulings, 58
  summary rulings, 58

Sadek, Mara Teresa, 56, 71
Salazar, Rodrigo, 185
Saldivia, Laura, 246
Samper, Ernesto, 42
San Juan Atitán, 176
San Marcos, 173, 174
San Miguel, 173
Santiso, Carlos, 56
Santos, Boaventura de Sousa, 7, 11, 20, 163
Sarat, Austin, 182, 184
Sawyer, Susanne, 163, 165
Scheingold, Stuart, 182, 184
Schjolden, Line, 9, 162, 184
Schmidt, Vivien A., 13, 21
Scott, Rebecca, 9
semantic field, 27, 29, 30, 33, 35, 39, 40
Sen, Amartya, 152, 264
Shapiro, Martin, 25, 28, 50, 142
Shell, 167
Sieder, Rachel, 82, 141
Siegel, Reva B., 28
Sierra, María Teresa, 169
Sikkink, Kathryn, 114, 142, 166, 270, 273
Silva Bascuñán, Alejandro, 150
Sipakapa, 173, 174, 175, 176, 177
Slaughter, Anne-Marie, 271
Smulovitz, Catalina, 113, 123, 124, 134, 141, 142, 184
Snodgrass-Godoy, Angelina, 14, 21, 172
Snow, David, 82
social movement, 16, 17, 257
socio-legal studies, 6
Solano, Luis, 170
Southworth, Anne, 235
Spain, 154, 166
Specific Command Jose Antonio Paez (CEJAP), 187
Stacey, Helen, 114
Staton, Jeffrey, 51
Stavenhagen, Rodolfo, 207, 212
Steinmetz, George, 7, 8, 21
Stern, Steven J., 9, 21
Stokes, Susan, 82
Stone Sweet, Alec, 8, 21, 28, 50, 75, 115, 142, 154
subsistence minimum. *See mínimo vital*
support structure for litigation, 244
Supreme Federal Tribunal of Brazil (STF), 51–68
  appeals, 55, 57, 70
  case load, 58
  collegiality, 62, 72
  consequencialistas, 63
  Constitutional Amendment No, 6, 58
  dean of Court, 62
  injunctions, 70

Supreme Federal Tribunal of Brazil (*cont.*)
judicial role perception, 63
jurisdiction, 57, 63
legalistas, 63
Regimento Interno, 62, 65
transparency, 62, 66
TV Justica, 66
Syrett, Keith, 28, 50
Szablowski, David, 10, 169

Tapia, Enrique, 130
Tarrow, Sydney, 237
Tate, Neal, 8, 51, 119, 142, 161, 178, 235
Taylor, Charles, 152
Taylor, Matthew M., 9, 52, 53, 55, 56, 58, 65, 71, 141, 145
Tenango Mining Company, 176
Teubner, Gunther, 161
Thatcherites, 28
Todos Santos Cuchumatán, 176
trade unions, 96, 97, 245
transitional justice, 254, 260, 261, 262, 267, 268
Tribunal of Justice of the Andean Community (ATJ), 114, 115
Tribunales Colegiados de Circuit (TCC). See appeals tribunals
Tribunales Colegiados de Circuito (TCC), 87
Tricot, Tito, 208
Tsai, Kellee S., 67
tutela, 32, 35, 36, 37, 44, 45, 46, 81, 273

U'wa, 167, 263, 268
UN Declaration on the Rights of Indigenous Peoples, 85, 166, 175
Union of South American Nations (Unasur), 132
United Kingdom, 28
United Nations (UN)
General Assembly, 85, 166
United Nations, 214
UN Declaration of the Rights and Duties of Man, 116
United States, 145, 149, 262
Bill of Rights, 143
Supreme Court, 112
United States Agency for International Development (USAID), 169
Uniting Force, 199
Universidad Diego Portales, 153
University of the Frontier, Temuco, 213
University of Wisconsin Law School, 4
Uprimny, Rodrigo, 162, 272, 273
Uribe, Álvaro, 47
Uruguay, 10, 259, 262

Valdez, Juan Gabriel, 4
Vallinder, Torbjorn, 8, 51, 119, 142, 161, 178, 235
Van Cott, Donna, 164
Van Harten, Gus, 170
Vargas, Enrique, 227, 228
Velazquez, Ramón, J., 191
Venezuela, 10, 17, 149, 166
Apitz v. Venezuela, 127, 128
Bolivarian Republic of Venezuela, 193
Comisión de Funcionamiento y Reestructuración del Sistema Judicial (CFRSJ), 127
Congress, 191
Constitution, 127, 193
El Amparo, 187, 189
El Caracazo, 189
El Gran Viraje, 191
First Contentious Administrative Court, 196
Judicial Emergency Commission, 126, 127
National Constituent Assembly, 126
pacted democracy, 182
Support Network for Justice and Peace, 189
Supreme Court, 113, 119, 127, 128, 129, 133
Supreme Justice Tribunal, 196
the electoral branch (*Poder Electoral*), 193
the popular branch (*Poder Ciudadano*), 193
Venezuelan Program on Education Action in Human Rights, 189
Venezuelan Federation of Chambers and Associations of Commerce and Manufacture (FEDECAMARAS), 194
Venezuelan Penal Forum (FPV), 199
Verba, Sidney, 82
Verchioli, Virginia, 246
Viotti da Costa, Emilia, 63
Volunteer Work in Prison Establishments (VTEP), 187

Wahlbeck, Paul J., 26
Walzer, Michael, 152
Warren Court, 149
Washington D.C., 117
Weber, Robert, 85
Weissbourd, Bernard, 26
Werneck Vianna, Luiz, 71
Whittington, Keith, 51, 145

Wilson, Bruce, 4, 10, 11, 53, 54, 55, 80, 81, 272
Women's Municipal Office, 249
World Bank, 169, 170, 172, 174
World Trade Organization (WTO), 169
World War II, 35, 116
writ of protection, 219

Yale Law School, 152
Youngers, Coleta, 261
Yukos affair, 202

Zapatista National Liberation Army, 99
Zedillo, Ernesto, 97

Books in the Series (continued from page iii)

Justice and Reconciliation in Post-Apartheid South Africa
Edited by François du Bois and Antje du Bois-Pedain

Judicial Review and Bureaucratic Impact: International and Interdisciplinary Perspectives
Edited by Marc Hertogh and Simon Halliday

Paths to International Justice: Social and Legal Perspectives
Edited by Marie-Bénédicte Dembour and Tobias Kelly

The Practice of Human Rights: Tracking Law Between the Global and the Local
Edited by Mark Goodale and Sally Engle Merry

Public Accountability: Designs, Dilemmas and Experiences
Edited by Michael W. Dowdle

Autonomy and Ethnicity: Negotiating Competing Claims in Multi-Ethnic States
Edited by Yash Ghai

The Ritual of Rights in Japan: Law, Society, and Health Policy
Eric A. Feldman

Constituting Democracy: Law, Globalism and South Africa's Political Reconstruction
Heinz Klug

Planted Flags: Trees, Land, and Law in Israel/Palestine
Irus Braverman

Social Citizenship and Workfare in the United States and Western Europe: The Paradox of Inclusion
Joel F. Handler

Darfur and the Crime of Genocide
John Hagan and Wenona Rymond-Richmond

The Invention of the Passport: Surveillance, Citizenship, and the State
John Torpey

Fictions of Justice: The International Criminal Court and the Challenge of Legal Pluralism in Sub-Sahara Africa
Kamari Maxine Clarke

Immigrants at the Margins: Law, Race, and Exclusion in Southern Europe
Kitty Calavita

Judges beyond Politics in Democracy and Dictatorship: Lessons from Chile
Lisa Hilbink

Diseases of the Will:
Alcohol and the Dilemmas of Freedom
Mariana Valverde

Law and Society in Vietnam:
The Transition from Socialism in Comparative Perspective
Mark Sidel

Militarization and Violence against Women in Conflict Zones in the Middle East:
A Palestinian Case Study
Nadera Shalhoub-Kevorkian

Lawyers and Regulation:
The Politics of the Administrative Process
Patrick Schmidt

Modernism and the Grounds of Law
Peter Fitzpatrick

The Politics of Truth and Reconciliation in South Africa:
Legitimizing the Post-Apartheid State
Richard A. Wilson

The Colonies of Law:
Colonialism, Zionism, and Law in Early Mandate Palestine
Ronen Shamir

Legal Reform and Administrative Detention Powers in China
Sarah Biddulph

After Abu Ghraib:
Exploring Human Rights in America and the Middle East
Shadi Mokhtari

Conducting Law and Society Research:
Reflections on Methods and Practices
Simon Halliday and Patrick Schmidt

Child Pornography and Sexual Grooming:
Legal and Societal Responses
Suzanne Ost

Culture under Cross-Examination:
International Justice and the Special Court for Sierra Leone
Tim Kelsall

Law, Violence, and Sovereignty Among West Bank Palestinians
Tobias Kelly

Unemployment and Government:
Genealogies of the Social
William Walters

Globalisation, Human Rights, and Labour Law in Pacific Asia
Anthony Woodiwiss

Courting Democracy in Bosnia and Herzegovina:
The Hague Tribunal's Impact in a Post-War State
Lara J. Nettelfield